# While China Faced West

Harvard East Asian Series 38

The East Asian Research Center at Harvard University administers research projects designed to further scholarly understanding of China, Korea, Japan, and adjacent areas.

# While China Faced West

American Reformers in
Nationalist China, 1928–1937

# James C. Thomson Jr.

Harvard University Press

Cambridge, Massachusetts, and London, England

Fourth printing, 1980

Preparation of this volume has been aided by a grant from
the Ford Foundation.

Library of Congress Catalog Card Number 76-82298
ISBN 0-674-95137-9
Printed in the United States of America

To my parents

# Contents

"We are flotsam in a whirlpool with which we have no connection."

—An American missionary, April 1927.

"Is the welfare of mankind best served by enlarging our investment in China? . . . Is there no other sector of the world where we can hope to obtain as large a return in human happiness and welfare as we can in China?"

—Committee on Appraisal and Plan, Rockefeller Foundation, December 1934.

"What would Borodin do with a chance like this? What will the Christian Church do with it? What should I do about it?"

—George W. Shepherd, March 1936.

"All of us have been the tools of American cultural aggression, perhaps without being wholly conscious of it."

—Y. T. Wu, July 1951.

# Preface

Thirty-five years ago I emigrated to China. I did so under duress. I was less than two years old, and my parents—having completed an extended furlough—were eager to get back to work. Both were educational missionaries, Presbyterians attached to the University of Nanking since 1917.

In moving to China I inadvertently became part of something bigger than my family and bigger than the mission movement. I became what the Chinese Communists now call a "cultural imperialist," albeit an infant member of the species. More important, I became a minor and very late participant in an ongoing process of collision between civilizations. After all, the civilization of "the West"—Mediterranean, European, Atlantic, or whatever—had been interacting with that of East Asia and specifically China for more than three centuries, since the arrival of the Portuguese. Interaction became collision in the first half of the nineteenth century. Characteristic of the collision were attempts by Westerners to force, cajole, or persuade Chinese to participate in the international order—to adjust to Western law, economics, habits, and religion. Also characteristic, of course, was resistance by the Chinese.

My arrival in China coincided with a special phase of the process: the years of the Nanking government. It was a brief period of excitement, hope, creativeness, and promise. But it gave way to tragedy and to more violent collision which continues today, with no end in sight.

The foregoing paragraphs may serve to explain my interest in both the Nanking decade and the problem of China's relations with the West. More narrowly, they should account for my special concern with the mystery of the Sino-American relationship.

In probing the Nanking years of this relationship I have chosen a relatively quiescent period of American governmental involvement. As in decades before, hundreds of Americans were at work in a formidable undertaking: the transformation of China. At their best, they were involved in the export of benevolence. They did so as private citizens, the disparate representatives of a pluralistic society. They did so with miniscule funds, at great personal sacrifice, sustained by little but faith and hope. Their failure was apparently total, at least for the time being. A transformed China did emerge; but it was one that rejected their offering, threw them out, and embraced a Western heresy with which to resist the West.

My probing, then, is of interest mainly as a brief chapter in the process of collision. And yet our present perspective provokes larger questions. The export of benevolence is an old American habit, preserved in both rhetoric and action from the days of our founding. Tides of mission and manifest destiny are recurrent in our history.

What more can be said, from the special vantage point of the sixties, about the efforts of Americans in the thirties—when China "faced West"? A first judgment might be that the private reformers of the earlier period were a microcosm of something to come: the American governmental effort, in the post-war era, to help "modernize" less developed societies throughout the world—from Point IV and foreign aid to "nation building" and the "struggle for the hearts and minds of men."

A second judgment might be that the mistakes and setbacks the private reformers experienced were ones that would recur time and again in situations of national revolution where men of a different color, culture, and language sought to guide their "less developed" brethren toward modernization through the slow paths of gradualism: mistakes that relate to ignorance, naivete, preoccupation with stability, abhorrence of violence, attraction toward elites, isolation from the oppressed, and rejection by nationalism.

A further judgment: the radical alternative of communism, which challenged and threatened the private reformers (and which often shaped their actions), is one that has regularly beset and often distorted the governmental effort in the postwar years. The dictates of the Cold War have transformed the best intentions.

There is, of course, a crucial difference between the efforts of the thirties and the efforts of the sixties. In the thirties Americans traveled to Asia as the private representatives of a multitude of institutions—as the variegated reflection of a pluralistic society. They lived hard lives of frugality and exile. Furthermore, most of them came as believers in the supremacy of a deity. As such they tended to accept the fallibility of men and institutions.

In the postwar era we have witnessed a fundamental change: not simply a massive increase in the export of benevolence, but also the secularization of that export. Today's reformers and modernizers are largely representatives of a state of vast wealth and power. With them go the flag and prestige of that state. Private reformers still abound, to be sure; but their efforts have been submerged by the programs of the state.

In this context, one might ask if the quantitative change has not produced a qualitative change—if the escalation of international reformism has not altered the character of the enterprise. Further, one might ask if the mistakes and setbacks of the thirties, recurring on such a grand scale and assaulting the state itself, do not throw grave doubts on the value of the undertaking.

Private citizens could afford to "fail"—to allow nationalism and even communism to run its course. And their faith could sustain them despite the failure. But states find failure unacceptable. And the states that find failure most unacceptable of all are those infused with concepts of mission and manifest destiny.

If there is a present relevance to the pages that follow it may well relate to the feasibility and appropriateness of the secularized export of benevolence by the United States government thirty years after the failure of the Nanking reformers.

Along with scores of other students of modern China, I owe a central and incalculable debt to John K. Fairbank. From the time I first read *The United States and China* as a wandering teenager in Szechwan in early 1949, I resolved—some day—to come and learn from him. This book is largely a product of his inscrutable but relentless encouragement once I moved under his tutelage.

Over the years many others have also contributed to my understanding of modern China and of America's relations with East Asia. A partial list would include Benjamin I. Schwartz, Dorothy Borg, Edwin O. Reischauer, Kwang-Ching Liu, Mary Clabaugh Wright, and Ernest R. May.

As for the present study, it could not have been undertaken at all without the assistance of the American Board of Commissioners for Foreign Missions (Congregational), which kindly permitted me access to its extensive archival materials in Harvard's Houghton Library. I am also grateful to the keepers of two important collections in New York City: the Missionary Research Library at Union Theological Seminary and the Historical Library of the YMCA National Council. Furthermore, inasmuch as the Rockefeller Foundation does not currently permit researchers to make use of its files, my examination of the Rockefeller contribution would have been impossible without the help of Raymond B. Fosdick and, most especially, of Mrs. Selskar M. Gunn in lending me her own copies of her late husband's reports. Finally, this study was completed despite an academic hiatus resulting from service in the federal bureaucracy; it would certainly not have been completed except for the instinctive understanding and support of my first Washington employer, Chester Bowles.

It is the researcher's good fortune that many of those who played a central role in pre-Communist China are still living, vigorous, and accessible. I myself have benefited greatly, as a result, from the comments, suggestions, and criticisms of Eugene E. Barnett, M. Searle Bates, Fu-liang Chang, Franklin L. Ho, Hugh W. Hubbard, and Harry B. Price, all of whom read the manuscript in its entirety. I have also benefited from conversations with two other major activists of the period, Frank W. Price and George W. Shepherd. Needless to say, none of these people should be held responsible for my conclusions about an era—and an enterprise—that remains a focus of controversy.

This study has been supported, in part, through grants from Harvard University's Committee on American–Far Eastern Policy Studies and Institute of Politics; I am grateful for this help, for additional aid from Harvard's East Asian Research Center and Department of History, and for careful research assistance from C. S. Liao. Finally, I have received invaluable editorial and secretarial support from Norma Farquhar and, more recently, Nancy Sullivan.

This book is dedicated to my parents, who took me to China. But it owes a great deal to my wife, Diana.

James C. Thomson Jr.

Truro, Massachusetts
July 1968

# While China Faced West

Throughout the text and the notes, all figures quoted in *dollars* are understood to be Chinese National currency unless otherwise indicated. During the decade under study the Chinese dollar fluctuated in value between US $0.25 and US $0.50.

# Chapter One

# Introduction: China under the Nanking Government

*Scope of the Study*

The study of intercultural "influence" is a notoriously risky enterprise, an invitation to generalization on the basis of tenuous evidence. The study of recent history, the newsprint barely yellowing, is equally risky business; the memoirs remain unwritten, the documents locked away, the shapes of events still two-dimensional, lacking in perspective.

The present undertaking runs both risks. It seeks to probe American involvement in the affairs of an alien culture; and it does so for a period that all too recently was the exclusive domain of the journalist, revivalist, and pamphleteer.

A few words of caution are required. This is a study only of what *some* Americans tried to do in conjunction with *some* Chinese to alter aspects of Chinese society during the ten years of nominal unification under the Nanking government. Most of these Americans were Protestant missionaries or foundation representatives, and most of their Chinese colleagues were Christians, academics, officials, or often some combination of the three. The chief problems to which they devoted their efforts were the reconstruction of village China and the reform of Chinese thought and character.

As a result, this cannot pretend to be a study of what all or even most Americans and their Chinese colleagues tried to do in this period of time. Nor is it claimed that rural reconstruction and ideological reform were the only, or even necessarily the most important, areas of American concern under the Nanking government. In no sense, then, is the aim here to construct a complete picture of United States policies toward Kuomintang China, or of the missionary enterprise between 1928 and 1937, or of the Nanking government itself.

What is attempted, however, is an exploration of certain lines of emphasis that characterized the activities of leading American institutions and articulate American citizens in the prewar decade of the Nationalist regime. Inevitably, these lines of emphasis relate to problems deeply rooted in revolutionary China. As a result, they relate as well to the political development of modern China in the last years of Western dominance, because the problems that consumed the attention of Americans and their Chinese colleagues were problems that profoundly affected the fortunes of the chief contenders for leadership of the Chinese revolution.

The Americans who sought to influence the course of Chinese civilization in these years did so near the end of China's first century of response to the modern West. From the vantage point of the present, their efforts came very late indeed. From the present view, as well, their efforts were a failure. To the extent that a liberal, democratic, and evolutionary alternative—a gradualist alternative —existed for the development of post-imperial China, these Americans and their Chinese allies were among the chief proponents of that alternative. With their expulsion and the triumph of communism, the gradualist alternative disappeared from the Chinese mainland.

In the context of this outcome, a study of American reform efforts under the Nanking government has several possible values. It can illuminate the nature and significance of these efforts. It can explore the factors that limited the effectiveness of the reformers. It can offer a tentative appraisal of America's capacity to influence the course of recent Chinese history. And it can suggest, as well, some more general lessons of relevance to effective American action in other situations of national revolution and cultural collision.

*The Westerner as a Reformer in Modern China*

The foreigner residing in a totally alien culture faces two ultimate alternatives: he can attempt to sensitize himself to the mores, traditions, and speech of his environment so as to pass over and become no longer a foreigner; or he can live his life as a sojourner in what must remain the exotic isolation of the zoo.[1] To the Westerner introduced into the Chinese scene, the alternative of assimilation was generally precluded by barriers of race and language. This is not to say that he could remain altogether immune to the subtle "sinicizing" processes that so affected the outlook of alien visitors from the Polos and Ricci to the "old China hands" and lady novelists of more recent decades. But by his almost ineradicable foreignness, the Westerner in China could not but be, initially and perhaps only passively, a cultural agent: the bearer of a profoundly alien culture.

Such a simple truth was compounded, from the early days of China's relations with the post-Renaissance West, by the fact that the Europeans—and later Americans—who came to Asia were almost universally propelled by an unusual zeal. Until very recent times, the physical and geographic obstacles to such travel were so formidable as to exclude all but those with a sense of mission. Historians have long recognized the two primary inducements that generated such a sense: commerce and religion—the lure of profits for one's self and souls for one's God. The traders usually came first; but close behind them, and sometimes on the same boat, came the missionaries. Recall only the image of Dr. Gutzlaff with his stock of Bibles, plying the China coast on an opium smuggler.[2]

The zeal that drove energetic Westerners to China in the modern era made them far more than passive cultural agents. Not only did they look, wear, and speak their foreignness; their whole purpose was to sell it as well, to win Chinese customers and converts. The role of the missionary fits such a description far better, of course, than that of the trader prior to the high tide of the industrial revolution in Britain. The first men of commerce came in pursuit of Chinese silks and tea, and only later did they begin to dream in terms of 400 million customers decked out in Manchester cotton shirts.

Nonetheless, the Westerner came to China in order to *do* something to China, in order to leave his mark on the Chinese. To this extent, he was inevitably more than a passive cultural intermediary: he was a conscious agent of change, of transformation. Begin as he might with a desire to alter the consumption and worship habits of the individual Chinese, he could not but move on to a conscious or unconscious desire to remake Chinese society itself.[3] Given the individualism of nineteenth-century Anglo-American society—and given the pluralistic nature of its involvement with China—the degree of consciousness may have been small indeed. But in the context of late Ch'ing China, the impact of the foreigner was infinitely greater than that of a tribute-bearing emissary. It was that of a chemical catalyst—and, potentially, that of a revolutionary. Once the zeal of trader and missionary was reinforced by gunboats and consuls, the chemical reaction passed beyond control, and the revolution was under way.

The role of the Westerner in Chinese society, then, was inherently destructive once he broke free of the constricting if beneficent institutions long employed to deal with barbarians. When the dynasty moved in to check such a deviation from traditional procedures—as it did in the late 1830's and the late 1850's—the Westerners were quick to impose their own institutions through the unequal treaties. The legal provisions of extraterritoriality gave the agents of alien culture a cocoon of inviolability.[4] They also gave foreigners a class status most of them had never known at home. After 1860 the Westerner in China was the automatic recipient of most of the perquisites of officialdom. And in the collapse of imperial institutions after 1911, the rapid decline of the gentry-scholar-official class heightened the uniqueness of foreigners as a protected elite.[5]

Legal immunities and upper-class status gave to energetic Western missionaries a specially wide field for action in the post-1840 years of China's response to the West. It is not surprising that they moved in on this field, that they brought with them not only their religion but other aspects of their civilization as well: medicine, science, technology, and education. There is a firm line of continuity leading from Peter Parker's eye hospital at Canton in 1834 to Asia's foremost teaching hospital in 1948, Peking Union Medical College. It is a continuity of extra-religious endeavor that includes the activities of W. A. P. Martin at the *T'ung-wen Kuan* (Interpreters' School), of John Fryer at the Shanghai Arsenal, and of Young J. Allen at the *Wan-kuo kung-pao* (The Globe Magazine).[6] In a variety of realms individual American missionaries became conscious agents for the reshaping of Chinese institutions and, ultimately, of Chinese civilization. Meanwhile, other missionaries exerted their influence on the course of Chinese development by doubling as American diplomatic representatives in the area; both Peter Parker and S. Wells Williams served in the legation. Once again, such activities had their later parallel in America's last ambassador to pre-Communist China, the missionary educator John Leighton Stuart.

It must not be concluded, of course, that the few missionaries who gave their inherently reformist role overt political trappings through service either with the Chinese or American governments were typical of the breed. The overwhelming majority of the missionaries pursued their evangelical enterprise with little direct involvement in officialdom. This was to be the case in later years as well. The dominant theme of Christian missions in China between 1800 and 1949 was "China for Christ," and the chief instrument to be used for this objective was the conversion, one by one, of the individual Chinese.

Yet even evangelism had its political effects. From the 1860's onward, recurrent anti-Christian movements testified to the destructive impact of purely evangelical missionaries on the old social and political order.[7] The vital point to be grasped is the privileged and inevitably catalytic role of all Westerners who chose to reside in China during the pre-Communist era. Their activities must be viewed and understood in the primary context of their de facto status as a disruptive elite.

For a study of American influence during the decade of the Nanking government, there are other contexts as well. It is to these subjects that we must now turn our attention.

## The Nanking Decade

American involvement in China during the nineteen thirties had as its Chinese political setting a twofold development. Its negative phase was the deepening disintegration of China's traditional imperial-bureaucratic institutions and ideology in the wake of the 1911 Revolution. Its positive phase was the rapid rise of what might be termed "Leninized nationalism" in the aftermath of 1919. Together these two continuing processes envelop, infuse, and affect all aspects of China between the two world wars.

This setting's primary qualities were instability and portentousness. And they left their mark on the foreigners present in China. Western book titles in the interwar period betray a state of mind: *China Awakened* (1922), *The Awakening of China* (1926), *What's Wrong With China* (1926), *Whither China* (1927), *Explaining China* (1928), *What and Why in China* (1928), *China at the Crossroads* (1928), *China: A Nation in Evolution* (1928), *China: The Collapse of a Civilization* (1930), *Tortured China* (1930), *China in Revolution* (1931), *The Great Wall Crumbles* (1935), *Chaos in China* (1939), and *Deadlock in China* (1940). For all the volumes of interpretation and explanation, the foreign observer's predicament remained that of the American missionary woman in 1927 whose pro-Nationalist husband had just been slain by Nationalist troops in the vanguard of the Northern Expedition. "We are flotsam," she wrote, "in a whirlpool with which we have no connection." [8] Yet despite such staggering instability, American activities also had a narrower and more clearly defined context by the end of the nineteen twenties. In 1928 China had been nominally reunified for the first time since the collapse of the Ch'ing. From 1927 to 1937 a national government extended its authority with considerable and increasing success, despite recurrent internal and external challenges to its existence.

The decade preceding the Japanese attack at Marco Polo Bridge in 1937 is the decade of the Kuomintang government at Nanking. It is this regime that provides the immediate setting for Sino-American relations in the nineteen thirties. A brief examination of the Nanking government is a prerequisite to an understanding of the aims and undertakings of Americans in China, private citizens and diplomats alike. The ten years of the Nanking government form a unique and relatively cohesive political unit in pre-Communist Chinese history in the modern era. To be sure, neither their uniqueness nor their cohesiveness were apparent to observers caught up in the turmoil of the times. As late as mid-1933 the

American minister was reporting that "the Nationalist Government has no government, for there is disunion here in the North, and there is disunion in the South, and there appears to be no possibility of any agreement among the Chinese leaders whereby this disunity may be dispelled." [9]

Yet time endows the inchoate data of the present with shape, if only by contrast with what comes before and what follows. So viewed, the Nanking decade reveals certain unifying qualities. In the first place, the government established in April 1927 did survive. None of its years were free of military strife, whether through the rebellious activities of ambitious *tuchun* (warlords), Kuomintang factionalists, Chinese Communists, or Japanese militarists. But the degree of political and military control—of national hegemony —exercised by the Nanking regime exceeded anything China had known since the brief republican interlude of 1912. Not only did the government survive, but by weathering the incessant assaults it was so measurably stronger by 1937 as to have forced basic changes in the strategy of its two most serious opponents.

In the second place, the Nanking government bore little resemblance to the *opéra bouffe* regimes of Peking that had preceded it. This was no "tuchunate." Military power was its foundation, to be sure; but there the similarity ended. Far from being a warlord's court, this was a party government equipped with political principles, a political ideology, and elaborate forms of political organization, however deficient any of these might be.

Third, Chiang Kai-shek, the enigmatic "Red General" of early 1927, was himself no warlord. Whatever his limitations, he sought above all other objectives the creation not of a regional bastion of private power, but of a strong national state. To be sure, elements of warlordism persisted throughout the decade and beyond; and Chiang's own power was rooted in a de facto regional base. Yet the central aim and, more and more, a central achievement, was national unification.

Fourth, the Nanking regime marked not only a break with northern political authority in the warlord era; it signified as well a turning point in the Nationalist revolution itself. With the anti-Communist purges of 1926–27, the Kuomintang severed its own Marxist flank and sent its Russian advisers packing. For ten years, in the period between the two United Fronts, it made war on the

Chinese Communists. And its leaders searched elsewhere than the Marxist-Leninist canon for solutions to China's problems.

Finally, it can be argued that the decade had its natural termination in the events of 1937. The outbreak of the Sino-Japanese War and the formation of the second—if tenuous—alliance with the Communists indicate the intrusion of a new overriding concern: national salvation in the face of the foreign invader. It was a concern whose roots lay in the Manchurian Incident and before that in the anti-Japanese riots of the years since 1915. Yet not until 1937 did the threat from Japan loom large enough to bring a temporary truce in civil warfare and the evacuation of the national capital. The move to Hankow and Chungking detached the Kuomintang from its miltiform base of support in the east. The regime which conducted a debilitating seven-year holding operation in the Szechwan hinterland could be at best only a refugee shadow government. Its productive years lay both behind it and, conceivably, in the postwar return to the east.

The Nanking decade, then, can be viewed as a proper testing period for the Kuomintang government. Its years stand apart from what preceded them and what followed. They are joined by the aspirations, programs, and activities of political leaders who held effective power and created an increasingly viable regime. In the chaos of China between 1911 and 1949, they are a period of transitional semi-stability. And in the span of modern Chinese history they are a cohesive unit of time.

## The Problem of Leadership

The Kuomintang government at Nanking was a child of schism. Its origin lay in Chiang Kai-shek's decision to break with the political commissars who had joined the Left Kuomintang in establishing a coalition government at Wuhan in early 1927. In March the vanguard of the revolutionary troops entered Nanking and plundered the foreign community, causing several deaths. Days later Chiang found himself under pressure from the foreign powers and the Shanghai business community. His successful bid for supremacy took the form of a coup against the Communists in mid-April; on April 18 he proclaimed the formation of a new national government in Nanking and the infant Kuomintang regime was launched. Within a year came the promulgation of a new organic law. And in 1931 the period of "tutelage" was formally begun with a new "Tutelage Constitution."

The guiding political principal of the new government was that of one-party dictatorship. This was the meaning of tutelage: political guidance by the ruling party, guidance toward eventual representative government of an indeterminate nature. Two basic structures overlapped: the Kuomintang as a party, and the national government. On the basis of interlocking personnel, however, the Kuomintang essentially *was* the government, and the government was the Kuomintang. No other political parties were permitted in the first decade.[10] Yet factionalism was rife within the Kuomintang. Meanwhile, the party itself kept to the forms of Sun Yat-sen's reorganized structure of 1924: this meant democratic centralism on the Soviet model, with a hierarchy of decision-approving bodies including a National Party Congress, a Central Executive Committee, a Standing Committee of the Central Executive Committee, and (after 1938) a Party Leader.

The government, too, followed Sun Yat-sen's prescription. The result was a complex five-power government, which added to the Western three branches (executive, legislative, and judicial) two Chinese innovations, the departments of examination and control. These five *yuan* or branches operated under a national council; above the council stood a president. Such a complicated structure was originally designed to avert dictatorship.[11] Its chief effect, however, was to make even more cumbersome the process of bureaucratic government. Political power existed apart from the forms.

Any search for the locus of power in Kuomintang China must lead at once to Chiang Kai-shek. In his person lay the greatest strengths and weaknesses of the Nanking government. If not the conscious objective, the ultimate drift of democratic centralism is one-man rule. But the machinery of Kuomintang decision making gave confirmation, not foundation, to Chiang's political control. His power base lay outside the central party apparatus: it resided in the Nationalist army, and in particular, those divisions led by graduates of the Whampoa Military Academy, where Chiang had served as commandant in 1923–1926. It was the loyalty of these lieutenants to their old commanding officer that carried Chiang to victory over the recurrent challengers to his authority. In the chaos of factionalism and political intrigue, these men were the few in whom he could place his trust. Yet in this very source of strength lay one of the regime's great weaknesses: chronic cronyism and the rigidity of the military mind tended to permeate the upper circles of Kuomintang administration.[12]

Nor did his strong military foundation immunize Chiang against rivals, both generals and politicians. Between 1928 and 1937 his paramount position was challenged by six separate military revolts and as many more major political conspiracies.[13] Victory was generally achieved through a process of negotiation and compromise rather than all-out warfare. But each new success saw the generalissimo's authority increased. The hero of the Sian captivity in late 1936 was a figure of considerably altered national stature from the regional commander who bought off Marshall Feng Yü-hsiang in 1929.

In the first years of the decade the chief political challenges came from the "leftist" Wang Ching-wei and from the "rightist" Hu Hanmin. Although Chiang's fortunes reached a nadir in late 1931 with his "retirement" from politics as a result of such factional squabbles, the expanding Japanese threat in Manchuria required his return to power. As one Chinese scholar has noted, the man "who was in control both of the armed forces and the financial interests of the country had become indispensable to any unified government." [14]

Chiang's recall to active service in early 1932 as the chairman of the Military Affairs Commission signaled the beginning of an uneasy four-year partnership with his rival Wang Ching-wei. The latter occupied the post of president of the executive yuan, and Lin Sen served in the purely ceremonial position of president of the republic. Not until Wang's wounding by a would-be assassin in November 1935 did Chiang return to the leadership of the executive yuan and the post he had held before the end of 1931. But his unique and indispensable base of personal power remained intact throughout, and it was strengthened immeasurably by his control of both the Central Political Institute and Central Military Academy.[15]

Strictly political rivals were, of course, the least of Chiang's problems. Of greater seriousness were the legacies of warlordism. They remained with him throughout the Nanking decade. The origin of the problem lay in the meeting of the Northern Campaign generals in July 1928 where attempts to achieve disbandment of the armies came to naught.[16] Large enclaves of troops loyal to regional chieftains remained a potential and sometimes actual source of rebellion against Nanking. Though nominally contained within the national armies, the independent forces of Feng Yü-hsiang, Yen Hsi-shan, and Li Tsung-jen made for a decentralization of authority. To them were added, after 1931, the refugee troops of Chang Hsüeh-liang from Manchuria, eager for a return to their homeland. Finally, the southwest, Szechwan, and the northwest were the battleground of competing petty *tuchun* until as late as the mid-thirties. Here Kuomintang control was feeble at best until the pursuit of the Communists on the Long March introduced Chiang's troops into these areas.

The maintenance of political power in the midst of a militarily fluid situation required artful strategy as well as an army. Chiang Kai-shek had both. A key to his survival was the deft political footwork which assured him command of the middle ground. Coalitions, pensions, and brute force—all were directed toward occupation of the center and isolation of the opponent. Yet Chiang seldom pushed so far as to annihilate the rival. Frequently he lacked the strength to do so. More important, he seems to have considered most of China's political groupings—with the exception of the Communists—as potential supports for national unity. It must be added, as well, that the existence of such havens as Hong Kong and the French and international concessions at Shanghai provided safe centers for political action by scores of dissident Chinese throughout the decade.

The political instability of Kuomintang China was heightened, of course, by two ultimate challenges from an internal and an external enemy. The operations of both Chinese Communists and Japanese had important effects on Nanking policy. Inevitably, the problem of leadership was compounded by this dual threat. Buffeted by rivals within his own party and by would-be warlords, Chiang was also the focus of fire from both Tokyo and the Chinese Soviets after 1931. At best his control could only be tentative and geographically contingent.

This complex of continuing politico-military crises seems to have played on the generalissimo's own limitations as a person. These limitations were several.[17]

In the first place, Chiang's training was exclusively that of a soldier; he was no intellectual, no theoretician. The son of a Chekiang gentry family, he commenced his education at the Paoting Military Academy in 1906, then moved on to four years of study in Japan at the imperial military college. Except for an obscure interlude as a stockbroker in Shanghai during World War I, he never left the soldier's profession. It was from his position as head of the Whampoa Military Academy that he succeeded to the leadership of the Northern Expedition. It is clear, then, that his training both in traditional Chinese studies and in Western civilization was minimal.

Moreover, Chiang was a military man by temperament as well as by education. Professional observers have frequently cast doubts on his skill as a military strategist; indeed, military errors constitute a fundamental factor in the Kuomintang's postwar collapse.[18] Yet there can be little doubt as to Chiang's dedication to the military ideal. For him, China's two greatest heroes were the third-century strategist, Chu-ko Liang, and the gifted suppressor of late Ch'ing rebellions, Tseng Kuo-fan. Such feelings seem to have been intensified by his studies in Japan in the years after the Russo-Japanese War. To the young Chinese officer, the concept of *bushidō* (the way of the samurai) assumed profound significance in the wake of Japan's victory. With its influence came insistence on the military virtues of personal loyalty, courage, sincerity, and asceticism. His penchant for moralizing on such virtues suffuses his writings of the period; it is particularly explicit in his statements on the New Life Movement after 1934.[19]

Finally, Chiang was a man with virtually no first-hand knowledge of the world outside Asia. His only travel abroad prior to the Cairo Conference of 1943 included the Japan years between 1907 and 1911 and one brief trip to the Soviet Union in 1923. The latter resulted from his dispatch by Sun Yat-sen on a three-month military mission. In Moscow, Lenin lay in a coma, but Trotsky was willing to talk. The upshot of the visit, according to Chiang, was his disenchantment with the Comintern. He returned with deep distrust of the Communists.[20] To the extent that he was to develop any understanding of the West, it had to come through the few Western associates he took into his confidence and, most particularly, through the American-educated family into which he married in 1927. The Soongs—Mei-ling, her brothers T. V. (Tzu-wen) and T. L. (Tzu-liang), and her brother-in-law H. H. Kung (Kung Hsiang-hsi)—were to be his chief channels of contact with the unknown world of Europe and America.

The impact of politico-military instability on a man of limited experience, of authoritarian personality, and of military training, seems fairly predictable. To maintain his tenuous control Chiang Kai-shek was forced to view all save his family and military intimates with thorough-going suspicion. Able, imaginative men who bore no personal obligation to him could be trusted only within limits. So it was that the rightist intellectual Hu Han-min ceased cooperation after his detention in 1931 and died a political exile in 1936; that the brilliant, ambitious Wang Ching-wei broke under long-term political frustration and died a Japanese puppet premier in 1944; and that Sun Fo, Li Tsung-jen, K. C. Wu, and many others experienced demoralization with the denial of true responsibility.

The problem of leadership, then, was essentially the problem of Chiang's leadership. He it was who commanded the support of the powerful First Army and, to some extent, of Shanghai business interests. He it was who isolated, outmaneuvered, and bought off military rivals, who finally drove the Communists out of their Kiangsi fastness, who kept the Japanese at bay through sometimes humiliating compromise. He it was, in short, who gave China a period of progressive unification and increasing stability.

Yet the very process by which such unification and stability were achieved frustrated the emergence of other men of ability, men who might act creatively within the framework of relative peace that Chiang had provided. The means he used—whether products of his character or forced upon him by events—were means that could only negate the democratic ends prescribed by Sun Yat-sen for the period of "tutelage." By 1937, at the end of the Nanking decade, the American ambassador was forced to conclude that Chiang was a lonely man with no friends, a man who "lives like an Oriental despot, isolated from his own people who cooperate with him through fear and because they want the national unity for which he stands." [21]

*Three Fundamental Quests*

For all his limitations, it must be said that Chiang Kai-shek retained a clear view of certain objectives he sought to achieve within the overriding aim of national unity. The pursuit of these objectives involved three basic lines of action.

The first of these was a quest for national dignity. The Northern Expedition of 1926–1928 had fallen heir to the anti-imperalist agitation that had permeated China after the post-May Fourth era, and Chiang's coup against Wuhan and the Communists only modified somewhat the anti-foreign demands of Kuomintang agitators. Foremost among the new Nanking government's aims was revision of the unequal treaties in emulation of Japan, where such indignities had been discarded as early as 1895. Revision meant, explicitly, tariff autonomy and the abolition of extraterritoriality. In the early years of the regime, these aims were packaged within a general "Rights Recovery Movement."

The success of this movement was moderate. By 1933 the Chinese had regained complete tariff autonomy. Along with this came full control over the Salt Revenue Administration, the Maritime Customs Service, and the Post Office system. Extraterritoriality, however, posed a special problem. In the chaos of 1926–1928 a few foreign territorial concessions had been returned to Chinese rule. Indeed, by 1937 the original maximum of thirty-three such concessions had been reduced to thirteen.[22]

But an end to foreign legal immunity required some adjustments in Chinese law. The Nanking government early produced a modernized law code and a new system of law courts.[23] Negotiations on extraterritoriality were making progress by the outbreak of hostilities in Manchuria. The Japanese attack there and at Shanghai in 1932, however, made Western powers reappraise the value of their special arrangements in a China under seige. Nanking itself now realized the usefulness of foreign concessions and immunities in the deepening struggle with Japan. With the replacement of Britain by Japan as the number one imperialist bogey, negotiations on the unequal treaties were quietly suspended. Nor was extraterritoriality abolished until 1943.[24] By that time abolition was a purely symbolic gesture to a wartime ally; not only had all foreign concessions passed under Japanese rule, but, in addition, the removal of legal immunities actually affected only the civilian personnel of the allies, or some 2 per cent of their nationals on Chinese soil at that time.[25]

In sum, the objective of rights recovery was pursued by the Nanking regime to the degree that such recovery aided the emergence of a strong national state. When Japanese encroachment interjected itself as a new factor on the scene, rights recovery became a consideration of diminished importance relative to other pressing internal and external problems.

A second major concern in the years of the Nanking government was the quest for economic stability. The Kuomintang assumed control of the nation after a period of economic chaos. It inherited a substantial debt, 80 per cent of it owed to foreigners. Yet a strong national state required a firm economic base.

Initially directed by Mme. Chiang's brother, T. V. Soong, an energetic Harvard-trained economist, Nanking's economic beginnings were promising. The government abolished the tael, unified the currency, and eventually adopted a managed foreign exchange currency. It set up a central banking apparatus which, though unwieldy in its fourfold structure, provided a modernized fiscal vehicle. It took control of tariff policy with considerable efficiency and experimented with annual budgets.[26]

Furthermore, from April 1931 the Nanking government embarked upon a program of technical cooperation with the League of Nations. One prerequisite was the formation of a National Economic Council to plan for "national reconstruction." [27] The NEC, under the chairmanship of T. V. Soong, was potentially a major planning body for economic development. Between 1931 and 1936 China was visited by 26 League advisers, specialists in such fields as agricultural rehabilitation, highway construction, cotton and sericulture, and water conservation. Not until 1933 did the NEC achieve a firm base, and in that year the League appointed a technical liaison officer, Ludwig Rajchman, for its relations with Nanking.[28]

League cooperation with China resulted in many pilot projects, considerable road construction, and a degree of genuine economic planning. It also resulted in the NEC's rural reconstruction program for Kiangsi province and the government's piecemeal attempts to reduce land rents.[29] Yet, continuing high military expenditures diverted funds that might have been used to finance the operation of such plans. T. V. Soong himself seems to have experienced sufficient disillusionment to resign from his post as finance minister half way through the decade; his brother-in-law and successor, H. H. Kung, lacked the training and ability that Soong had brought to the job.[30]

Indeed, as preliminary studies of Kuomintang policies have shown, the overall picture presented by the Nanking decade is largely one of economic stagnation.[31] The powers of the government were used neither to provide financing of economic development, nor to induce technological change, nor to encourage institutional reform. In a country that required massive savings in its agricultural sector to support industrial development, agricultural output between 1932 and 1936 probably increased by less than 1 per cent. And meanwhile national defense gobbled up 45 per cent of the annual budget.[32]

The major fault lay in Kuomintang tax policies. The Nanking government was simply unable to raise enough money to accomplish either real unification or reconstruction. Rather than tax either the landlords or the upper urban classes and risk their disaffection, the government relied on taxation of trade and industry—the very areas it needed most to develop. Fifty per cent of its revenues came from the Maritime Customs alone, and this meant export tariffs as well as import tariffs.[33]

Even so, revenues fell short of expenditures. The chosen solution was to borrow from the large east coast banks. Such borrowing was done at uniformly high rates of interest, and control of these same banks resided with key officials of the Nanking government.[34] The upshot of such policies was a lucrative business in government bonds, short-term high-interest loans, and in speculation. A concomitant result was the nonexistence of urgently needed long-term low-interest credit for farmers and would-be industrialists.

In short, Kuomintang fiscal and financial policies made the government a parasite on the modern sector of the economy in the style of Ch'ing bureaucratic capitalism.[35] The old collusion between officials and merchants was as stagnating to the economy as usual, and as profitable as usual to the handful of men who combined both roles. Thus, Kuomintang economic policies were never able to create the "pre-conditions" for economic development. They were never able to produce the savings and investment necessary for self-sustaining growth.

Such is the case despite highly ambitious paper programs for economic expansion. The last of such schemes, a Three-year Plan in 1936, was stopped short by the Sino-Japanese War.[36] It is doubtful that its success would have been any greater than that of earlier plans. Kuomintang economic theory had no conception of the government's role as a catalytic agent; Nanking's view was that either the government must do everything itself—or nothing gets done.

The third of the regime's major concerns in the Nanking decade was the quest for a unifying ideology. This was no new search. Since the fall of the empire—perhaps even before that time—the problem of Chinese thought might be termed the problem of the vacuum: once the all-encompassing ideology of the Confucian state had been swept away, what could be put in its place? This question underlay the search for universal values in the May Fourth Movement. It underlay the patriotic ferment of the twenties and the rise of Marxism-Leninism. And it was at the root of the Kuomintang's concern in the thirties.

The quest had two stimuli: first, the obvious deficiencies of Sun Yat-senism as a producer of loyalty or as a guide to action; and second, the undeniable successes of the Communists in commanding strong support from many in the territories they overran. The Nationalist search for a unifying ideology led the theoreticians of the Nanking government into a partial revival of neo-Confucianism itself. To be sure, the Kuomintang leaders made use as well of alien elements in their ideological improvisation. Yet in its deepening struggle with the Communist wing of the Chinese revolution, Nanking sought to strengthen itself with many of the traditional theoretical supports of Chinese political authority.

This shift in concern from revolution to restoration served not only to compound the break with the Communists, but to isolate Nanking increasingly from the nation's reformist intelligentsia, who had long since put traditionalism behind them.[37] At the same time, one major instrument of this shift—the New Life Movement

—was destined, ironically, to become a means of forging closer ties with American reformers resident in China. A source of weakness in one respect became a source of strength in another.

## The Double Malaise

No picture of the Nanking government is complete or comprehensible without attention to the double malaise which afflicted the regime acutely from 1931 onwards. The role played by Chinese Communists and Japanese expansionists in undermining the Kuomintang was decisive. For the Nanking decade was one in which the government's energies were devoted much of the time to fending off both threats.

The means employed by the government were, of course, radically different. The Japanese challenge became overt with the Manchurian Incident of September 1931. Against Japan, Nanking relied on negotiation, conciliation, appeasement, and gradual retreat. One major exception to this pattern was the heroic defense of Shanghai undertaken by the 19th Route Army in early 1932. By and large, however, Sino-Japanese relations in the period were better typified by the Tangku Truce of May 1933, which sealed the loss of Manchuria and Jehol by establishing a neutralized region between the Great Wall and Peiping; and by the Ho-Umezu Agreement of June 1933, which advanced Japanese interests in North China through the removal of anti-Japanese officials and the suppression of anti-Japanese agitation.[38]

Such attempts at appeasement were designed to extend the life-expectancy of the Nanking regime by giving it time to erase centers of domestic opposition and to build up its German-trained forces. Although their effect was to permit the incorporation of North China into the economic sphere of "Manchukuo," they also gave Nanking precious breathing-space in its conflict with Japan between 1933 and 1937. Against the Chinese Communists, Nanking's response was that of brute force: increasingly efficient German-trained ground forces supported by an American- and Italian-trained air arm. Progress against the Communists was nonetheless slow.

Forced from the cities in the "white terror" of 1927, the Chinese

Reds had first attempted a series of abortive urban insurrections as pawns in the Kremlin power struggle between Stalin and Trotsky.[39] The failure of this program drove them into the countryside where their major remnants were able to regroup in the mountains of Kiangsi. In 1931 they declared the formation of the Chinese Soviet Workers' and Peasants' Republic, with its capital at Juichin. Until late 1934 they were able to hold this border territory against repeated government assaults. It was only the Fifth Campaign of "encirclement and annihilation" that succeeded in driving them westward on their famous Long March. For nearly a year, from October 1934 to the autumn of 1935, they fought their way through Kweichow and Szechwan into Shensi. There they lodged themselves in the area around Paoan, a tattered but battle-hardened residue of their initial 100,000.

Communist strategy had a profound effect on the Nanking government starting in 1931. In the first place, the Reds early seized upon advocacy of resistance to Japan as a potent propaganda weapon. From Juichin's "declaration of war" against Japan in early 1932 onwards, they were able to project a highly patriotic image by their denunciations of the new imperialist menace. Their tactics forced the government into a vulnerable and uncomfortable middle position between the Scylla of Japan and the Charybdis of Juichin; it made Chiang appear to some not only a "reactionary" but a "lackey" of the Tokyo expansionists.

A second area in which the Communist threat shaped Nanking's destiny was that of military action. The Soviets forced Nanking to modernize its armies and experiment with tactics to a degree that it would not otherwise have attempted. The lessons learned may have been limited; yet they did much to prepare the government's forces for the major war ahead. Furthermore, pursuit of the Communists into the southwest and Szechwan brought Nanking's hegemony to these provinces for the first time. In a sense, the unification of the country was actually advanced by the need to destroy the Communist armies.

In December 1936 both the Japanese and Communist threat to the security of Nanking merged in the dramatic detention of the generalissimo at Sian, because Chang Hsüeh-liang's mutinous troops sharply posed the dilemma of a nation wracked by civil war at a time when the greatest danger came from an alien invader. The

Sian kidnapping marked Nanking's shift from a policy of "unity before resistance" to "resistance above all." Through the intervention of the Communists (under pressure, it seems, from Moscow) the generalissimo was released.[40] But the clamor for his release stemmed from yet another consideration: by December 1936 it was clear to Russians, Chinese, and Japanese alike that the greatest force for resistance to Japan lay in the person of Chiang and in the unity he had forged.

When the news of the generalissimo's release was broadcast to the nation on Christmas Day 1936, the rallying of public support was dramatic and universal. Overnight, Chiang had come to personify the nation and its destiny. Yet herein lies a considerable irony: this apex of fame was reached through the actions of Japan and the Communists; and the victory granted to Chiang by his two chief adversaries was pyrrhic in the light of later events. Japanese and Communists, who had brought him to this peak of power, were shortly to dash him and his state to destruction in protracted warfare. Like countless dynasts before him, Chiang Kai-shek was destined to defeat under the double assault of external aggressor and internal rebel.

# Chapter Two
# Americans and the
# Nanking Government

## Policies and Stakes

The Nanking decade of Sino-American diplomatic relations commenced with U.S. recognition of the Kuomintang government in July 1928 and ended with that government's retreat to Hankow in 1938. It was a decade that opened in revolutionary turmoil and closed in all-out Sino-Japanese hostilities. It was a period of time overcast, from 1931 onwards, by what foreign statesmen termed "the Far Eastern Crisis."

This decade had as its wider context a tradition of American sympathy with Chinese aspirations but exasperation with Chinese performance since the turn of the century. Enthusiasm for the revolution of 1911, for Sun Yat-sen, and even for Yüan Shih-k'ai had given way to disappointment and alarm over the disorders of the warlord era. The stable and sovereign China envisaged at the Washington Conference of 1921–22 failed to emerge. The China of American hopes—united, democratized, and Christianized—seemed further away than ever. The realities of the twenties were civil war, banditry, political chaos, and, most alarmingly, the rise of an intense nationalism directed against the treaty powers. Most exposed to the turbulence of the era were Christian missionaries living outside the foreign concessions; nationalist "anti-imperialism" was infused with antiforeign and anti-Christian passions, and the mission enterprise itself seemed in grave jeopardy. As a result, America's policy makers and citizens had their traditional sympathies severely strained—especially after the May 30th Incident of 1925. Yet despite strong provocations—widespread destruction of foreign property and even lives by the Nationalists and their Leninist allies —and despite pressures for a forceful response from treaty-port businessmen and some diplomats on the scene, Washington held to a policy of restraint and neutrality. Sixteen months after the violent assault on Nanking's foreign community in March 1927, Washington was ready to recognize the government whose troops had wrought that violence.

Between 1928 and the Manchurian Incident, the American government pursued a policy based on what Dorothy Borg has described as Secretary Kellogg's "simple almost instinctive reaction" to the plight of China: a desire—shared apparently by public opinion, according to samplings of the American press—to assist the Chinese toward full independence and equality with the West.[1] To this end, and despite the misgivings of some American diplomats, Washington acquiesced in Chinese tariff autonomy and moved slowly toward gradual termination of extraterritoriality. It did so in continuing adherence to the two main tenets of the traditional Open Door policy: the integrity of China and the equal treatment of all foreigners there.

With the Japanese seizure of Manchuria, however, American supporters of the Open Door were put to a test and found wanting. To the flagrant violation of China's territorial integrity the U.S. government was prepared to offer only a rhetorical response in the form of the "nonrecognition" doctrine.[2] Nonrecognition's negativism was soon to be buttressed, under Cordell Hull, by the doctrine of noninterference in Sino-Japanese hostilities. Together, these two concepts provided the doctrinal setting for an essentially negative phase of American diplomacy: a period in which moral disapproval of Japan's expansionist policies was tempered by a desire to avoid provocation of the Japanese militarists.

After 1931, then, the Japanese threat was the chief concern of the architects of America's Far Eastern policy. This is not to suggest that there was any unanimity within the government as to how to cope with the threat as it affected China. Indeed, the deliberations of the Roosevelt administration were marked by a continuing struggle between spokesmen for two divergent schools of thought, albeit a struggle between men of unequal power and of unequal proximity to the making of foreign policy.

On the one hand, Secretary Hull and his chief Far Eastern adviser, Stanley K. Hornbeck, gave prior valuation to the folly of provoking Japan. Despite Japan's aggression in Manchuria and Shanghai and the creeping encroachment on North China, the State Department remained convinced that our interests in China were not great enough to justify measures that might focus Japanese hostility upon us.[3] As Japanese aims came gradually to be seen as a potential threat to the independence of the United States, as well as China, the Department began to place new emphasis on the need to strengthen American naval power. The proponents of caution now made the construction of an effective Pacific navy the prerequisite to any deviation from the course of nonprovocation.[4]

The views of Hull and Hornbeck generally prevailed between 1933 and the Marco Polo Bridge Incident. And there is evidence that they were supported by substantial sections of public opinion in America during this period.[5] Yet they were hotly contested throughout by other voices in the administration. Chief among them was that of Treasury Secretary Henry Morgenthau, Jr., whose sympathies for the Chinese were intense and persistent. It was Morgenthau who pushed through the US$50 million Reconstruction Finance Corporation loan to T. V. Soong in the spring of 1933, despite the objections of Cordell Hull.[6] And it was Morgenthau who eventually found a way to repair some of the damage inflicted on China by the Silver Purchase Act of 1934: when China was forced off the silver standard in late 1935, Morgenthau turned the silver purchase program to China's advantage by paying the Nationalist government in gold or U.S. dollars for 500 million ounces of silver. Once again, Hull was reluctant.[7]

One key to Morgenthau's small but significant degree of success in bypassing the State Department was the goodwill of his chief. Franklin Roosevelt himself seems to have shared some of the Treasury secretary's instinctive sympathies for the Chinese people and tended to give him quiet encouragement in his tiffs with Hull and Hornbeck. The President's concern for the condition of China was manifested even in the turmoil of the New Deal's first Hundred Days, when he called in John Leighton Stuart of Yenching University for White House consultation. Roosevelt reminded Stuart of the Delano family's connection with the Canton clipper trade. "He wanted to know what America could do short of war to prevent the Japanese from overrunning the whole of China." [8]

The President's lively interest in the subject was also shown in a memorandum to Morgenthau late in December. "Please remember," he wrote, "that I have a background of a little over a century in Chinese affairs . . . China has been the Mecca of the people whom I have called the 'money changers in the Temple.' They are still in absolute control." China, in his view, had to press its anti-imperialist revolution a little farther: "It is better to hasten the crisis in China—to compel the Chinese people more and more to stand on their own feet without complete dependence on Japan and Europe—than it is to compromise with a situation which is economically unsound and which compromise will mean the continuation of an unsound position for a generation to come." [9]

The President's somewhat amorphous sentiments were an asset to Morgenthau in his struggle with the State Department, a struggle not essentially over objectives but over tactics. They helped him to bring a measure of assistance to the Nanking government, most of it in the realm of currency stabilization. But the fundamentals of the Hull-Hornbeck China policy remained unshaken throughout the Nanking decade.

These fundamentals may be clearly grasped from the Far Eastern Division's memorandum to Hull of May 1934, a document offering "Suggestions in regard to Sino-American Relations with a view to Avoiding Friction with Japan." The memorandum's conclusions—Hornbeck's conclusions—were several. It suggested first—with a gloomy eye to the recent RFC loan—that "no further financial assistance be rendered to China by the US Government or by agencies thereof" (unless it be done through international action). Second, an attempt should be made to discourage American citizens from offering their services as military advisers to the Chinese government. (The proposal for the renewal of an American air mission of private citizens who were reserve officers had recently died in the State Department.) [10] Third, Washington should continue to control rigidly the export to China of arms and munitions with "no attempt . . . to foster such trade." Fourth, the U.S. government should carefully scrutinize any new American "projects, or departure from the usual" in China "with a view to avoiding the creation of issues which may unnecessarily antagonize Japan." Fifth, China's best interests would be served by being treated as "an adult member of the family of nations" and being forced to "stand upon its own feet." Finally, the U.S. government should continue to help rehabilitate China, either alone or with other powers, but should do so "along strictly practical lines and in such manner as to make it amply clear that it is the friendly action of a good neighbor, and . . . not in any way dictated or prescribed by Japan or by a desire to assist China to the detriment of any other nation." [11]

To a depression-ridden America, struggling to put its own economy back in order, the risks of a more positive China policy seemed too great a price to pay in terms of national interests—despite sympathy for China, despite commercial and missionary interests in China, and despite the significance of China in an East Asian postwar peace system. At least they seemed too great a price until such a time as the United States possessed the naval strength to support such a policy.

One perspective on the "national interests" involved can be achieved from an appraisal of the U.S. commercial stake in Kuomintang China. If the diplomatic context of American involvement in the Nanking decade was largely negative, the economic context was even more so. To some extent, as the arguments of Hull and Hornbeck indicated, the one followed from the other: U.S. interests in China were simply not large enough to risk provocation of Japan. Nor was the American stake passing through a period of substantial growth. On the contrary, the Nanking government came to power on the eve of the Great Depression. The economic contraction forced upon foreign governments and private firms alike made the decade one of wholesale cutbacks in operations and personnel.

During the 1930's, America's total investment in China averaged between US$200 and US$300 million. This figure was roughly equal to American investment in Japan; unlike our financial relations with Japan, which largely took the form of Japanese bonds, the American stake in China was mainly direct investment.

In 1931 U.S. investment in China amounted to US$196.8 million.[12] By 1936, it had risen to US$287.6 million; one reason for the increase lay in American acquisition of two major Shanghai utilities.[13] These funds were distributed as follows (in U.S. $1,000):

| | |
|---|---:|
| Banking and finance | 53,411 |
| Manufacturing | 9,400 |
| Public utilities | 55,946 |
| Import and export | 94,465 |
| Shipping | 5,072 |
| Aviation | 1,036 |
| Communications | 14,102 |
| Railway loans | 11,581 |
| General government loans | 42,589 |
| | 287,602 |

The small size of American economic involvement in the Far East as a whole is seen in the fact that the nation's investment in both China and Japan amounted to only three quarters of a billion dollars. This figure amounted to only 5 or 6 per cent of total U.S. investment abroad. Furthermore, America's share was less than a tenth of the total foreign stake in China. Whereas British and Japanese investments were each over a billion dollars, the U.S. figure was barely one fifth of the British, and two thirds of American financial interest was concentrated in Shanghai.[14] In terms of persons and firms, the United States also ran a poor third. In 1933–34 the 8,637 American businessmen representing 559 firms were vastly outnumbered by their Japanese and British competitors.[15]

As John K. Fairbank has pointed out, an examination of foreign trade figures in this decade is "no more encouraging to the theory of economic determinism as the sole source of our policy than an examination of America's financial interest in China." [16] U.S. trade with Japan accounted for 8 to 9 per cent of the nation's total foreign trade, and the trade with China constituted less than half that amount.

America's economic involvement with Kuomintang China, then, was less than substantial. Nor was it growing. Private firms such as the British-American Tobacco Company, the Standard Oil Company of New York, and the four U.S. banks with branches in China maintained their operations during the decade; but none of them were in a period of growth. In 1935, an American business mission under W. Cameron Forbes came to China to explore the possibilities for expansion of trade; although this mission was enthusiastic about opportunities for U.S. traders, it failed to convince American businessmen back home.[17]

As for the economic participation of the American government, the struggle between the State and Treasury Departments has already been noted. The RFC's US$50 million credit to the Chinese government in June 1933 was negotiated at President Roosevelt's urging despite the misgivings of the State Department. The actual wheat and cotton credit used by the Chinese was US$30 million, and most of this went to T. V. Soong's currency stabilization program.

After 1933, Hull and his advisers were able to prevent further outright loans and grants to China until the early part of 1939, when the Sino-Japanese War was well under way. But Morgenthau was nonetheless able to give further assistance to Soong's monetary reforms through successful manipulation of silver-puchase legislation between 1935 and 1939. In 1937–1939, for instance, it is estimated that the Treasury paid US$184 million in gold or dollars for silver sold to the United States by the Kuomintang government.[18] In 1939–1941 three new loans were made to Chiang's refugee regime. All-out American economic assistance did not begin, however, until the massive and unrestricted US$500 million credit was granted to the Chungking authorities in February 1942. With that grant, American aid became official and substantial as it had never been during the preceding decade, and Sino-American relations entered a new era.

## The Foreign Service Evaluation

In the years of the Nanking government, Secretary Hull and Stanley K. Hornbeck had only to read the dispatches of diplomats on the scene to find confirmation for their analysis. It is a notable and often neglected fact that American diplomats in China viewed the Nanking government, its leadership, and its future with virtually unmitigated gloom from the Manchurian Incident on through the summer of 1936. From 1931 until the Sian Incident, Foreign Service officers generally despaired of the Kuomintang's ability to unify China, let alone govern it.

The chief American representative in China throughout this period was Minister Nelson T. Johnson, who became ambassador in 1935 when the legation's status was finally raised. Johnson was a man of lengthy China experience and of patient, philosophic laissez-faire temperament. He admired Chinese culture but was wearied, bemused, and made cynical by the intricacies of Chinese politics. He viewed political chaos as endemic to China and most regimes as transitory. The defects of the Nanking government were not lost on him.

In early 1933, Johnson reported to the outgoing secretary of state that the government to which he was accredited was "factional rather than national," that it showed "little evidence of having a constructive mind of its own and has allowed affairs to drift more or less aimlessly."

Meanwhile, the prestige of the Kuomintang was "at low ebb . . . the People have lost faith in it because it failed to take advantage of its exceptional opportunities and was unable to redeem its specious promises." What of alternatives to the Kuomintang? Regional armies continued to be the bane of China. And there was yet another peril: "The shadow of Bolshevism will lie over parts of China until a thoroughgoing program of rural economy has improved the lot of the masses and an efficient administration has produced a sense of security in the interior." [19]

A year later, the Tangku Truce had brought a temporary respite from Japanese encroachment, and the fifth anti-Communist campaign was under way. Yet Minister Johnson's pessimism had deepened: "At no time in my experience have I felt the domestic political situation to be so discouraging." The Kuomintang, he reported, was "increasingly impotent. Its leadership is divided and has deteriorated . . . The party remains for many merely a rice bowl that is badly cracked." What of China's emergent strong man? Chiang Kai-shek's control extended only to the handful of Yangtze provinces; to Johnson there appeared to be "little if any hope that Chiang can unify China." Meanwhile, the country as a whole seemed engulfed in disillusionment. In his report to the secretary of state, the minister groped for hopeful signs and found a few. The government appeared to realize "the importance of economic and agrarian developments for political stability," and the people themselves seemed to realize the need for reform; but such realizations were "defeated by disillusionment," and the government had accomplished nothing of any significance.[20]

Six months later, in July 1934, Johnson found no change in the fundamental situation. He did note a growing understanding of China's needs by the nation's leaders; but still lacking was evidence of a will to act on the basis of such understanding, and without such action there would be "little reason to view the present situation in China with other than pessimism." Still untouched and a continuing potential source of "subversive movements" were the terrible burdens under which the masses labored. As for the recently inaugurated New Life Movement, the minister noted merely that it placed "more emphasis on the evils of tobacco than on the evil of opium." [21]

In January 1935 it was Clarence E. Gauss, the chargé d'affaires in Peiping, who dispatched the semiannual report to the Department on the state of China. By this time the Chinese Communists had been driven from Kiangsi, the National Economic Council had launched its reconstruction program, and Japan was still largely quiescent in the north. Yet Gauss could only conclude that there was "small cause for genuine optimism with regard to the future of China under the present regime and grave cause for pessimism." The grounds for pessimism were familiar: despite a growing realization that unity could only be achieved through a solution of China's basic economic and financial problems, the Nanking government's efforts in this regard remained ineffective through inadequate implementation of programs, insufficient capital, and insufficient technical skill. The chargé's gloom was deepened by the fact that Chinese officials "continued to be as perverse as previously in negotiations over questions pending or arising between China and the U.S." Yet ironically enough—and with serious implications for the future—he also found evidence that the Chinese Communists "were adopting a policy more anti-foreign than formerly because of assistance allegedly given by foreigners to the established regime of General Chiang Kai-shek." [22]

The persistent pessimism of Johnson, Gauss, and other Foreign

Service officers in the China field continued unchecked through 1935 and the first half of 1936. At first glance, this might seem surprising, for these were the months during which Chiang Kai-shek extended his control to eleven out of 23 provinces through his westward pursuit of the Communist armies; Szechwan, Kweichow, and even Yunnan were now brought under Nanking's rule. However, this increase in national unity was more than offset, Johnson felt, by renewed Japanese pressure, by increasing economic and financial ills, by the continued existence of the Communist threat, and by the rising antagonism of Chiang's anti-Communist rivals. In July 1935 he reported once again that the lack of any competent program to cope with economic problems meant progressive deterioration of the nation's economy. Nor did China's economic and political plight cause any improvement in the perverse attitude toward Western nations which Gauss had noted previously. There was no evidence, Johnson wrote, "that she has any real respect for any of them; that she would not play one off against another when opportunity presented itself; nor that she would not make concessions to Japan which could only be made at the expense of other nations." [23] Six months later, in January 1936, the ambassador found the nation's condition "even more precarious . . . in respect to national unity, . . . Sino-Japanese relations, communism, finance, and economy." Caught between the Japan-sponsored "autonomous movement" in North China and the extraordinary outburst of nationwide student agitation for resistance to Japan, the Nanking government appeared more impotent than ever. Even the drastic monetary decree of November 1935 seemed late and ill-prepared; and furthermore, "the situation of the masses was not improved." [24]

Meanwhile, a very few Foreign Service officers had attempted to keep the ambassador and the State Department informed on the Nanking government's major internal enemy, the Chinese Communists. After the fall of the Wuhan government, the first full report on the location and activities of the Communists was a 123-page dispatch from Oliver Edmund Clubb, a vice-consul in Hankow, in April 1932. This remarkably thorough document identified seven large Soviet areas in China, covering one sixth of the country. It emphasized that the policies of the Chinese Reds were grounded in the orthodox Leninist tenets shared by Communists elsewhere; anyone who doubted this fact, Clubb added, would be led into "completely disastrous" action. Nelson Johnson thought well of the report—though he seemed to miss some of its implications—and urged the vice-consul to keep up his research.[25]

A year later Johnson himself had occasion to comment on the Communist movement in a letter to a friend in America. In the ambassador's opinion, "so-called" communism would continue to plague the Nanking government until some action was taken to solve the problem of land tenure; he had witnessed appalling conditions of tenancy in his many years of consular service in the hinterland. "The remedy for all this has seemed to me plain," Johnson wrote. "The Government, however, has been unwilling to use it for reasons best known to itself." The ambassador had pressed his views one evening in a long conversation with the generalissimo's brother-in-law and financial adviser, H. H. Kung: "We discussed the so-called communist movement in Hupeh, Hunan, and Kiangsi, and the apparent ineffectiveness of the effort then being put forward by the Government to suppress the so-called communists by force. The thesis then adopted by the Government appeared to be that the strength of the rural communities rested upon the old gentry, and that at all costs the power of the gentry should be restored." In reply, Johnson had argued that "the power of the gentry, based as it was upon ancient methods of taxation now discarded, was gone"; and he proposed a plan for redistribution of lands to former tenants and compensation of former landlords through government bonds. "But," added Johnson, "I never got anywhere with Dr. Kung." [26]

Foreign Service interest in the problem of the Soviet rebels was heightened during the period of the Long March in 1934–35. Initially, the consuls found their cynicism about the Kuomintang intensified by the "practically unopposed parade" of the Red Armies through the south and southwest despite the government's vast military advantages.[27] Then, as Chiang Kai-shek used his pursuit of the rebels to establish control over heretofore autonomous provinces, the foreign observers' optimism began to rise. Furthermore, a small source of additional hope was the reconstruction movement which the generalissimo and his wife introduced into Kiangsi province after the expulsion of the Communists. One effect of the Long March, however, was to make more difficult Foreign Service access to information about the Chinese Reds; reporting from the field became increasingly spotty and confused. As a result, the idea that the strength of the Communists was so depleted after their exit from Kiangsi as to make them a negligible factor persisted even after the Long March was completed and influenced the thinking of many foreign observers in China.[28] Increasingly, the focus of Foreign Service attention was now the Nanking government alone. And there a combination of circumstances was soon to make for a marked shift in the views of diplomatic observers.

The turning point in the Nanking embassy's evaluation of the Chinese Nationalist government was sudden and unforeseeable. It came with little or no warning in the autumn of 1936. Its causes lay deep in the mounting drama that culminated in the Sian Incident.

As late as July 1936, the American ambassador was still despairing of the Kuomintang regime. Although Chiang's dictatorial powers had increased, the southwest was now in all but open revolt. The "Liang-Kwang" uprising (by generals in Kwangsi and Kwangtung) threatened to topple Nanking on the pretext of resistance to Japan; indeed, nearly all the major developments of the past six months were judged to be factors contributing to the disintegration of China.[29] To nearly everyone's surprise, however, August brought a peaceful solution to the southwest revolt. At the same time, the internal Kuomintang split between pro-Japanese and "resistance now" groups seemed to have been tempered by the generalissimo's increased sense of confidence and strength. In his futile negotiations with the Japanese, Chiang became more firm and artful; he began to use the explosive term "national salvation," with all its anti-Japanese implications; he conferred with military leaders toward the rapid achievement of unity. On October 12, the central government endorsed a strongly worded patriotic manifesto signed by 66 leading Peiping intellectuals.[30] And in late November Chinese troops defeated an attempt by Japanese puppet forces to take over Suiyuan in Inner Mongolia.

At long last, Chiang was moving into closer harmony with an aroused public opinion. The effects were soon apparent. The celebration of the revolution's anniversary on October 10 showed more nationwide enthusiasm for the regime than any previous Double Ten (tenth day of the tenth month) since the Mukden Incident. Three weeks later, foreign observers were astonished at the genuine national acclaim that the generalissimo received in honor of his fiftieth birthday on October 31; fifty military aircraft were presented to him through popular subscription as a birthday present, and the degree of oversubscription in many provinces and cities was surprising.[31] More and more, Chiang was coming at last to embody the nation's growing determination to resist further Japanese encroachment. The culmination of this development did not occur, however, until the dramatic and totally unexpected detention of the generalissimo at Sian on December 12 by mutinous Manchurian troops, who were eager to stop fighting Communists and start fighting Japan. The almost universal denunciation of the Sian kidnapping—from Moscow as well as Nanking and Tokyo—caught both Chiang's captors and the Chinese Communists by surprise.[32] And the generalisssimo's ultimate release on Christmas Day produced an outburst of national rejoicing such as China had never before experienced. The groundwork was now laid for national unity against Japan under Nanking's leadership.

These stirring events of late 1936 caused an important shift in the outlook of Nelson Johnson and his colleagues. In January 1937 the ambassador wrote that the developments of the preceding six months had "definitely tended to unify and strengthen the Republic and even to cause the Japanese at least temporarily to adopt a decidedly less aggressive policy towards China." Johnson specifically cited the denouement of the Liang-Kwang uprising, the celebrations of October 10 and 31, the Suiyuan victory, and the Sian outcome. He viewed the China scene with cautious but growing hope.[33] Five months later, on June 10, the ambassador confirmed his new appraisal in a report of a conversation with a Nanking official. Old unsolved problems remained, to be sure, but there was now one big difference: a "change in the Chinese themselves." It was somehow a spiritual change, an almost tangible new national élan. "The unification of China no longer depends entirely upon what military force the Government, or the principal leader of the Government, can command. The ideal of national unity is rapidly becoming a part of China's national consciousness." And among the most hopeful expressions of this idea were the negotiations under way between the government and Communists in the northwest.[34]

Too soon, in less than a month, China's new unity was put to its ultimate test, one destined to last eight years. With the outbreak of the undeclared Sino-Japanese War, American policy toward China moved into a new phase: one in which the old tensions between U.S. concern for China and unwillingness to provoke Japan were increased to the breaking point. A new factor that strengthened the China supporters both in Washington and in the field was the emergent prestige and power of Chiang Kai-shek as a national symbol. The old pessimism and even despair of the diplomats gave way to an admiration undoubtedly intensified by the astonishment factor: only a year or two earlier, few if any could have predicted such an outcome.

There were many, of course, who recalled that it was largely the Japanese threat that had catapulted the generalissimo to such pre-eminence, who understood that the immense accumulation of unsolved economic and political problems provided an unsteady foundation for the nation's apparent unity. Diplomatic observers needed only to reread their own reports to realize that their eleventh-hour confidence in the Chinese state was based, not on the Kuomintang nor the Nanking government, but on one man and on the national will to resist that had made him its symbol.

Many years later, in accounting for the notable shift in America's view of the Nanking government between 1931 and 1937, Stanley K. Hornbeck himself bluntly commented, "It was not a case of the Nationalists doing better, but of the Japanese doing worse." [35] Such a summation does little justice to the complexities of U.S. East Asian policy in the nineteen thirties; yet it highlights a point of critical importance.

## The Agents of Reform

It is clear that four major factors combined to deter American policy makers, diplomats, and businessmen from any calculated effort to influence the course of China's internal and external development under the Nanking government. These factors, which varied in significance from one year to the next, were: an unwillingness to risk provocation of Japan, a low valuation of American interests in China, a deep skepticism as to the viability of the Nationalist regime, and the impact of the worldwide economic depression. One might well add to these factors two continuing preoccupations in the United States itself: the New Deal's efforts to combat the economic crisis at home and the dramatic rise of fascism and Nazism in Europe.

Against the passive backdrop provided by the noninvolvement of officials and merchants, one group of Americans stood out by virtue of their intense activity in China throughout the decade. By the nature of their calling, they were men and women dedicated to the production of change in human attitudes and—inevitably—change within the social order as well. This group was the American Protestant missionaries. To them was left a scope for action; yet it was a scope whose dimensions were deeply affected by developments both in China and at home.

China had long been the largest and most important missionary field for American Protestantism.[36] But the Nationalist government swept to power in 1926–28 on a wave of violent antiforeignism that caused a sharp break in the 93-year effort of American missionaries. Prior to 1949, no crisis ever placed as great a strain on missionary relations with the Chinese as the May 30th Incident and its aftermath in 1925.[37] And the tensions of those months were soon compounded by the antiforeign excesses of the Northern Expedition. Even the many missionaries who, by 1926, were sympathetic to the aims of the Nationalists and who favored treaty revision found their situation untenable. As the revolutionary armies pushed northward to the Yangtze, left-wing components disrupted one mission station after another; indeed, the Nanking Incident of March 1927 was only the most famous in a series of upheavals. The result was a collective trauma: lives endangered, possessions looted, property destroyed, and a mass exodus. Several hundred foreign missionaries and their families fled from the interior to the coast and from the coast to Japan, the Philippines, and the United States.[38]

In 1925 there had been 8,300 Protestant missionaries at work in China, of whom the greatest number—nearly five eighths—were Americans.[39] The troubles of 1926–1928 temporarily decimated these ranks, however, and the peak figure was never again matched. By 1936, the last "normal year" of the thirties, the Protestant total stood at 6,020, and it is estimated that 2,808 of these workers came from the United States and Canada.[40] Because of substantial variations in statistical methods among mission boards, however, no exact figure is available. One leading authority, M. S. Bates, who places the average interwar total for Americans at 3,000–4,000, makes some useful subdivisions of the total. Of this group, one third were single women, one third were married women (missionary wives, who served as part-time or full-time teachers and nurses), and one third were men. In addition, the three general subdivisions of missionary endeavor found approximately 600 Americans engaged in medical work, 1,200–1,500 in educational work, and 1,200–1,500 in various forms of evangelism. Finally, several hundred more Americans were engaged in other types of Christian enterprise—publications, YMCA and YWCA, social work, institutions for the blind and the deaf, industrial work, and the like.[41]

The sharp drop in the number of China missionaries by the early thirties was caused only in part by the exodus of 1926–1928. After the nationalist agitation of the post-1925 period, mission boards had accelerated the "devolution" of church and college duties from foreigners to Chinese Christians. Furthermore, some missionaries who had lived through the tensions and acute difficulties of the late twenties had "had enough" and felt they could be of greater service at home in America or in another mission field. The outbreak of Sino-Japanese hostilities in 1931 was an additional factor in dissuading missionary families from returning to China. But most compelling of all were financial problems that deeply affected the entire mission enterprise.

The Great Depression had a calamitous impact on the receipts of all church organizations and charities. From 1931 onward, the correspondence and minutes of mission stations were heavy with grim references to repeated salary cuts, reduction of personnel, and curtailment of activities. No board was untouched by such setbacks. Universities, hospitals, agricultural experiment stations, famine relief, as well as the ordinary parish—all were hit by months of unrelieved bad news from the financial officers back in America.

Nor was the depression the only reason for a loss in income. Foreign missions themselves had become a focus of controversy not only in China but in the United States. The postwar rise of theological liberalism had subjected traditional mission methods to severe criticism; and the development of a continuing liberal-fundamentalist debate caused deep divisions within the ranks of supporting congregations.[42] By 1926 the recruitment of new missionaries was becoming more difficult. At the same time, American journalists in China were adding their voices to the antimissionary criticisms of Chinese nationalists and intellectuals. Their books and articles fed the growing body of skepticism among one-time contributors to missions. In addition, China's foreign business community—and the English press that generally articulated its views—was hostile to the growing body of missionaries who argued for a revision of the "unequal treaties" and a return of the concessions. The "high water mark of Protestant liberalism" and the peak of Christian criticism of missions was the Laymen's Foreign Mission Inquiry of 1930. Under the chairmanship of Harvard's William Ernest Hocking, a commission representing seven denominations prepared a searching analysis entitled *Re-Thinking Missions,* a document supported by seven volumes of *Fact Finders' Reports.* Although these publications themselves were subjected to vigorous and widely publicized criticism, they provided additional fuel for those who either disapproved of missions or desired their reorientation.[43]

The cumulative results of the depression and declining home support forced limitations on the activities of those missionaries who remained in Kuomintang China. Physical hardship, economic distress, political uncertainty, native hostility—none of these were unfamiliar conditions for men and women who had chosen careers of Christian service in the turbulence of modern China. But to many in the early thirties it seemed particularly ironic that the mission enterprise should be deprived of personnel and resources just at a time when the opportunities for significant achievement in a reunified Chinese nation appeared greater than ever before.

By the middle of the Nanking decade, the reports from mission stations were graphic. The secretary of the Congregationalists' Tientsin Station wrote in August 1934: "And so we come to the end of the year's work, our foreign force reduced 50 per cent, two unfilled resignations from our evangelistic staff, the last payment of appropriations for the Stanley School received, facing further reductions in general funds beginning with the fall. Yet there is much cause for gratitude." [44] In the same months, another missionary reported the results of a station meeting at Lintsing, Hopei, where the new financial cuts meant that "the Educational work could hope for no more than a pittance, and must abandon hope of increasing the primary day school beyond three grades; the hospital must find substantial help towards its support outside of regular appropriations or gifts from the U.S.A.; the training School must abandon hope of having a physician regularly on its staff; the Evangelistic Department must cut down its staff, at however great cost to the work; AND the missionary group must move to Techou, and that pending a reduction in the numbers of the combined group." [45] Such drastic contractions, coming as they did in the midst of an era of rising hope for China, caused a profound sense of frustration. As one missionary wrote in the encouraging summer of 1934, "The attitude toward the church and the opportunity for work has been the best which has obtained for many years . . . With this remarkable openness to our message it is to be regretted that so much of our time and energy has, perforce, been given over to discussion of ways and means of meeting cuts in funds and withdrawals in personnel." [46] To such expressions of regret the board secretaries in New York and Boston could only reply with further gloomy predictions, as did the supervisor who wrote in the spring of 1933, "It seems improbable that for many years the giving of American churches will return to the 1925 high level upon which our program until 1929 was based." [47]

Despite these hardships, American missionaries were successful in maintaining much of their major work in evangelism, medicine, and education during the years of the Nanking government. To some extent, it should be added, the economic crisis forced the Christian Church in China to look increasingly for indigenous support; indeed, one healthy by-product was the firmer rooting in Chinese soil of those projects and parishes that were able to survive at all. Chief among the vital institutions of the missionary enterprise were the thirteen Christian colleges and universities, with a total enrollment of 6,475 students in 1934–35. In addition to programs in the arts and sciences, these institutions maintained three medical schools, seven colleges of theology, and two major agricultural colleges. At the secondary level, the missions also supported 260 Christian middle schools, with an enrollment of 50,000 in 1934–35.[48]

To some degree, this educational establishment owed its continued survival to contributions from private foundations as well as from American congregations, via the mission boards. Between

1913 and 1933, the Rockefeller Foundation had spent a total of US$37 million in China—a sum second only to the US$117 million spent by the foundation in the United States and far exceeding the US$14 million granted to the third largest beneficiary, Great Britain.[49] Fully US$33 million had gone toward the advancement of medical science in China through the consolidation of several mission institutions into the Peking Union Medical College, in 1921, and its regular support thereafter. As for the remaining US$4 million, it had been disbursed to several institutions, including nine of the Christian colleges, for the strengthening of premedical education and natural science programs. By 1934 it was estimated that the foundation was still contributing US$100,000 per year to the various Christian colleges.[50] Other private groups, as well, were giving significant aid. Among them were the China Foundation for Education and Culture (the remitted American Boxer Indemnity Fund) and the Harvard-Yenching Institute.[51] But foundations, too, found their incomes reduced in the depths of the depression, and their assistance was limited. In Peiping, Shanghai, New York, and Boston, their officers and representatives watched with apprehension and hope, trying to understand the unfolding chaos of China and trying to devise more effective ways to contribute toward the peaceful modernization of a nation.

If the uncertainties of the late twenties and early thirties caused missionaries and their Chinese associates to despair, there is little evidence of it. Many had viewed the Kuomintang with suspicion in the days since the formation of the first United Front, because its antiforeign orientation was all too clear. Yet missionaries also felt a growing sense of identification with the forces of Chinese nationalism, and many were outspoken in their denunciation of the unequal treaties that had done so much to make their presence possible.[52] Once Chiang Kai-shek had split with the Communists, he still seemed an enigmatic figure, perhaps just another warlord; the missionaries waited, their judgment withheld.

For a while the prospects were unclear. Mission institutions found themselves hampered by the rigorous application of registration laws—regulations that virtually forced Westerners out of the field of primary education and severely limited their middle-school activities. In addition, the government continued to acquiesce in the periodic harassment of missionaries and the destruction or occupation of mission property by Nationalist troops. Indeed as late as April 1931 the counselor of the American legation still suspected that Nanking was "deliberately working toward the conscious end of rendering impossible the carrying on in China of all foreign missionary activities with the possible exception of medical work." [53]

Nonetheless, within the first three years of the Nanking government, four unexpected developments gave new hope to the foreigners. The first was Chiang's marriage to the American-educated Methodist, Soong Mei-ling: here, perhaps, lay the basis for a softening of the Kuomintang's hostility toward Christians and the mission enterprise. The second was Chiang's gradual success in consolidating his rule. To be sure, the progress was slow; but the chaos of the twenties had given Westerners a longing for an end to tuchunism and for the emergence of a strong central authority. In the third place, no event was more effective in deflecting and transforming the Kuomintang's strong current of anti-imperialism than the Manchurian Incident. As one observer puts it, "It was easier for American missionaries to understand Chinese nationalists wanting to defend themselves against Japan than to understand their attacking all Americans as imperialists." [54] Finally, in 1931, many missionaries were heartened by the news of the generalissimo's conversion to Christianity. Harassments continued; yet the fact that the regime's strong man had accepted Christianity was a source of great consolation and considerable hope.

By 1932, then, the nature of Kuomintang leadership and the direction of Chinese nationalism seemed to suggest a widening sphere of opportunity for constructive Christian activity. At the same time, missionaries were now aware of the growing menace of Japan in the face of Nanking's weakness. And many among them were equally aware of the threat from communism. This combination of dangers instilled in some a sense of urgency: a sense of now-or-never, a belief that time was not on their side, that this might be their last chance, perhaps the last chance for China.

Of the two threats, that from Japan was more immediate; but the threat of communism somehow touched a deeper chord within many mission workers. Their reaction was complex: outrage at its godlessness, revulsion from its brutality, but sympathy for its note of social protest, and respect for its desire to change the world. In the troubles of 1926–27, foreigners had witnessed Marxism's explosive power; in the next seven years missionaries in Kiangsi, Fukien, and Hunan came to know it far better; and throughout the nation's universities the works of Marx and Lenin were arousing young minds. To an increasing number of articulate mission leaders, as they tried to gain perspective on their revolutionary surroundings, communism began to appear less simply as a threat and more fundamentally as a challenge: a challenge to put Christ's teachings to work in China among the poor, the sick, and the oppressed; a challenge to transform the social order or risk final expulsion by the tide of a stronger faith that promised to do much of what Christians had left undone.

Missionary journals and yearbooks exuded this sense of challenge in a variety of forms. "Communism challenges Christianity everywhere in the world," wrote one churchman in June 1934, "to make more effective in social, economic and political life the brotherhood that it proclaims so that all men who desire to live the better and more abundant life will be helped in doing so." [55] Another missionary, writing at the same time, judged that "Communism and Christianity have accepted the challenge of the present social crisis, which is driving them forward into new and unexplored fields. Their starting points are far apart and they have many differences as well as points in common. But both are sincerely trying to find the right way, and to the extent that they are successful in this, their paths will come together." [56] Such ingenuous predictions may not have been widespread among missionaries, but the theme of communism's challenge was deeply persistent.

Three factors, then, seemed uppermost in the minds of American missionaries by the first years of the thirties: the threat from Japan, the challenge from communism, and—more and more—the possibility of unity and progress under a stable central government. Together, these elements of danger and promise instilled in missionaries a mood of urgency. It took as its focus the task of national reconstruction: reconstruction of the spirits, bodies, and villages of the Chinese people—reconstruction while there was yet time, however inadequate the mission resources.

In these years, the fundamental concern of the reconstructionists was the welfare of the rural population, for it was here that the need seemed greatest and the Communist challenge most intense. It was inevitable that as they came to perceive a similar concern on the part of the national government, they would permit themselves to develop close ties with that government. And it was perhaps equally inevitable that these ties would have wider implications, as the decade progressed, than the reconstructionists were able to foresee.

# Chapter Three
# Christians and the Rural Crisis

## Background: The Crisis

The rural efforts of Americans in the decade of the Nanking government were focused on a deeply rooted affliction of modern China's countryside: acute peasant poverty and demoralization.[1] China's continuing rural crisis had a number of causes. One factor was undoubtedly the extraordinary population rise of the Ch'ing dynasty—a probable doubling between 1650 and 1800—a rise which apparently exceeded the rate of expansion of land under cultivation. In a later phase, between 1873 and 1933, the nation's population was estimated to have increased by 31 per cent while the area of farmland remained almost unchanged. Nor did the mounting population pressure find release in industrialization: the process of industrialization in China was severely hampered by factors that lie beyond the scope of this study.[2] The resulting decline of rural living standards was drastically accelerated, moreover, by natural and man-made disasters: floods, famine, rebellion, economic dislocation, civil strife, and banditry in the last century of the Ch'ing and in the warlord years that followed. The traditional farm handicraft economy was increasingly disrupted by the flow of factory goods; and such calamities as the great northwest famine of 1920–21 deepened the rural crisis.

Central to this crisis were three persistent phenomena. First was the widespread factor of land tenancy, particularly in South China. Between 1911 and 1949 China experienced a marked and continuous trend toward an increase in tenancy; and by 1937 it was estimated that "almost two thirds of Chinese farmers rented land from others, to whom they must pay heavy rents." [3] What was particularly severe for the tenant farmer was not so much the fact of tenancy but the prevailing conditions of tenancy—high rents, insecurity of tenure, excessive charges, and an absence of written agreements. As one authority has noted, "Tenancy is not in itself necessarily evil, but if the landlord happens to be avaricious it provides him with an effective tool for exploitation." [4] And with the breakdown of the old Confucian order, the sometimes benevolent landowning class—the rural gentry—was replaced by absentee landlords far removed from paternal concern for the peasant's condition.

A second ingredient of the rural crisis was heavy and inequitable taxation. The corruption of late Ch'ing rule had subjected the peasant proprietor, and particularly the poor peasant, to varieties of graft and "squeeze" in the collection of the land tax. In the years of the warlord era, the tax burden was steeply increased for support of provincial armies. The heavy "rent burden of the tenant farmers was matched by the tax burden of the small farm owners." [5] Increases took a variety of forms. In the absence of effective land surveys, the basic tax rate had often lost any relation to reality; literate tax collectors were able to press illiterate peasants into payments on the basis of old high evaluations. Furthermore, the basic tax was generally increased many-fold by the universal evil of surcharges. Such surcharges were added at the whim of governors and local officials all through the twenties, and inevitably these charges weighed most heavily on poorer farming areas. Finally, these burdens on the peasant were compounded by special military levies (through corvee, payment in kind, or money), by corruption on the part of officials, by evasion on the part of the rich, and by advance collection of future taxes. In some parts of Szechwan, indeed, it was reported that taxes had been collected as much as fifty years in advance.[6]

A third major ingredient of the crisis was the scarcity of rural credit at reasonable rates of interest. Given the burdens of land rent and land tax, it is little wonder that rural indebtedness was extensive and constant and that the moneylender was the scourge of the peasant. Sources of rural credit were more often personal than institutional, and loans invariably involved exorbitant interest rates—set by "the borrower's need, which is always dire." [7] In normal times, money loans would bear interest of as much as 5 per cent per month, and the rates for grain loans would run even higher. One important aspect of the credit problem was the use to which such loans were put in village China. By far the largest percentage would go for nonfunctional conspicuous consumption—for weddings, funerals, ceremonies, and the like. For this reason, rural credit in China was not merely a problem of economics but one of education as well. [8]

### The Village Pioneers

In their efforts to treat the rural crisis, Americans in the decade of the Nanking government built upon a foundation of piecemeal experimentation which extended back through the twenties and even earlier. In some particulars, the experience of their Chinese and foreign precursors fed directly into the work of the missionaries and philanthropists.

Throughout the troubled decades of China's "response to the West," from the Treaty of Nanking through the Boxer Rebellion, it is notable that no Ch'ing scholar or high official ever proposed the reform of land tenure as a solution for agrarian discontent. [9] It remained for Sun Yat-sen to be the first to treat the problem directly by proposing a radical solution: the equalization of land ownership. This he included as the fourth cardinal objective in the 1905 Manifesto of the KMT's predecessor, the T'ung-meng-hui (United League). "The good fortune of civilization," Sun said, "is to be shared equally by all the people of the nation." After an assessment of all land value, the unearned increment of the land would revert to the state of Henry Georgian principles. [10]

A year before Sun's manifesto, modern China's first rural reconstruction center had been established in Chechengts'un, Tinghsien, Hopei, by a father and son, Mi Chien-shan and Mi Ti-kang, who devoted their efforts to agricultural improvement and village education. [11] The Mi enterprise was modest and short lived, but its location was destined to become in later years the heart of a national rural reconstruction movement.

Not until World War I and its aftermath were associations formed to administer to the needs of the villager. In 1916–17, two private groups were organized: the Chinese Rural Association and the Chinese Vocational Education Association. Both were dedicated to the promotion of self-help among the rural population; but it was ten years before these groups actually established rural training centers, in Kiangsu and Chekiang.[12]

Meanwhile, the floods of 1917 and the five-province drought-famine of 1920–21 had produced extensive help from foreign relief agencies, and especially from the American Red Cross. The recurrent nature of such disasters was a stimulus to the formation of a permanent multinational relief organization. In the autumn of 1921, under American leadership, seven such societies were joined in a new nonsectarian and nonpolitical body, the China International Famine Relief Commission (CIFRC), with headquarters in Peking. To a large extent, Christian and missionary influence lay at its roots; its long-time executive secretary was Dwight W. Edwards of the YMCA, and most of its directors were missionaries, Chinese churchmen, and YMCA personnel.[13]

From the beginning, the aim of the commission was famine prevention as well as relief; it was "a service organization rather than merely a philanthropic body," and its basic principle was that— except in emergencies—relief was to be given only in exchange for a fair return in labor. In its first fifteen years of existence its preventive accomplishments were impressive. Despite the political and military instability of the twenties and early thirties, the CIFRC by 1936 had constructed 2,000 miles of new roads in 14 provinces, had repaired 1,300 miles of old roads, had dug 5,000 wells, three large irrigation canals, 300 miles of drainage canals, and had built nearly a thousand miles of river embankments. Its greatest institutional accomplishment lay in the field of agricultural credit. Beginning in 1924, the Commission provided loans in Hopei for the establishment of credit cooperatives, as well as brief training programs in cooperative management. In the building of cooperatives and the digging of wells, the CIFRC gave most abiding assistance to farmers. By 1936, 20,000 farmers were members of cooperatives in several provinces, most of them north of the

Yangtze. By that year, too, some $50 million had been expended on the commission's various programs.[14] Despite such achievements, the CIFRC's major role was that of a stimulus and a model; for in the face of China's needs, one private agency could do little more than point the way. It was through the work of the commission, however, that many missionaries and officials were given a first lesson in what, specifically, might be done for and by the peasant to hold off his supreme enemy, famine. In the process, they participated in a "modest pioneering attempt to modernize China's economy." [15]

By the mid-twenties, Sun Yat-sen had reemphasized his land program as a fundamental part of his third great principle: livelihood. Sun's message was infectious. In the ferment of the waning *tuchun* era, several Chinese seized the initiative in various parts of the country and attempted to help villagers improve their own lot.[16] One of these experimenters was P'eng Yü-t'ing, who organized a peasant militia in Chen-p'ing, Honan, during the troubles of 1927; by 1930 P'eng had created a system of local self-government. In 1927, as well, a Kuomintang leader named Shen Hsüan-lu, who had formed a peasant association six years before, resigned his other posts to devote full attention to a village reconstruction project. Another pioneer of the same era was the noted educator T'ao Hsing-chih (H. T. Tao or W. T. Tao); in early 1927 he set up a teachers' school in the village of Hsiao-chuang, near Nanking, and tried to show how literacy could be introduced with a minimum expenditure.[17]

The political instability that stimulated such experimentation in the late twenties ultimately stifled it as well. In the post-1927 period of counterrevolution, or at least suspended revolution, the experimenters fared badly: P'eng Yü-t'ing and Shen Hsüan-lu were both assassinated, and the Hsiao-chuang school of T'ao Hsing-chih was closed down in 1930.[18] Rural improvement was clearly a hazardous business.

Two pioneers, however, fared better than others, and both were destined to have a profound influence on the development of the rural concern in the decade of the Nanking government. The first was Liang Sou-ming, born of a Kwangsi family, who was lecturer in Buddhist philosophy at Peking University. In 1924 he resigned his post to put his teaching theories into practice. During the troubles of 1925–1927, he experienced a radical internal transformation: "I repudiated the entire Western bag of tricks and was not again to be tainted. What did I believe in? I believed in our own way of setting up our country and was not again to be intimidated." [19] Liang's outlook became that of a Buddhist social reformer; Western influences played little part in his motivation. His concern was the recovery of the traditional Chinese values he found disintegrating under the impact of the modernizers, and as the basis for such a recovery, he looked to the reconstruction of village life. After preliminary work as head of the Kwangtung-Kwangsi Reconstruction Committee, he joined with Liang Chung-hua, the son of Honan gentry, to establish the Honan Village Government College. Four years later the college was closed down. But the Liangs now moved on to Shantung, whose progressive governor, Han Fu-chu, became their patron. There they founded the Shantung Rural Reconstruction Institute, and in the village of Tsouping (Chou-p'ing), near Tsinan, the institute undertook a variegated program with a Peasant School at its center. By 1933 Tsouping was a gathering point for rural reconstructionists from many parts of the country.[20]

The second outstanding pioneer was a product of strong Western influence. By 1929 James Y. C. Yen (Yen Yang-ch'u) was the prominent leader of a mass literacy movement and founder of a unique village experiment at Tinghsien, in Hopei. It can be asserted that no other rural project in China ultimately had as great an impact on as wide and influential a group of Chinese and foreigners alike; after World War II, indeed, Yen's methods were adopted in other parts of Asia as well.[21]

The roots of Tinghsien lay in the France of World War I. It was there that James Yen, a Yale graduate serving with the YMCA's program of assistance to the Chinese Labor Corps, developed a simple "thousand-character" approach to the teaching of illiterate workers. In 1923 he organized—with foreign support—a National Association of the Mass Education Movement in Peking, and three years later he made plans for a model literacy project in a rural Hopei hsien. Like many other émigrés to the countryside, however, Yen's initially narrow concern began to expand; for literacy was clearly only one of the peasant's needs. By 1929, the focus of the movement had begun to shift "from extensive promotion of literacy to intensive study of life in the rural districts"; Yen's approach was "that of a research student," and his laboratory was the "hsien-unit." [22]

In his Tinghsien laboratory James Yen diagnosed four basic weaknesses of Chinese life: ignorance, poverty, disease, and "civic disintegration." [23] As a treatment he and his colleagues prescribed a fourfold program of reconstruction in the areas of culture, economics, health, and politics. This program was carefully planned as a supplement to the threefold literacy process the movement had already developed.[24] The total project seemed to Yen to embody Sun's injunction to "awaken the masses." In 1930 the Tinghsien center had accumulated a staff of nearly 200, including families, virtually all of them city-bred and Western-oriented. Both qualities made it essential to avoid what Yen termed the "two pitfalls in our path: first, the fatal error of assuming a patronizing attitude towards the people, and second, the danger, as we say in Chinese, of 'Raising the level of consumption without raising the level of production.' " [25]

Within a year of Tinghsien's new policy, the Nanking government expressed its interest in the project by inviting Yen to the capital. There the reformer met with Chiang Kai-shek, who desired to have his native Chekiang village of Chikow transformed into a model community "as an adequate expression of his love for his birthplace." Yen visited the village and made recommendations; but as he discussed the project with the Chiangs and told them of the Tinghsien work, it is reported that "they were particularly struck with the significance of a correlated program such as ours for the national reconstruction of China with the hsien as a unit." Chiang invited Yen at once to address both the Government Institute for Sons of the Revolution and the Central Military Academy. At the latter institution the generalissimo himself gave an exhortative address in which he asserted that projects like Tinghsien "would bring into realization the Three Principles of Dr. Sun." Chiang concluded his negotiations with Yen by arranging for the dispatch of representatives from the military academy and other government institutes to Tinghsien for training in the principles of rural reconstruction.[26] Shortly thereafter, Yen traveled to Mukden where Chang Hsüeh-liang made elaborate plans for the creation of a model district at Shen-yang. To Yen such enthusiasm from government officials seemed to herald a new day; his infant project, "which at first glance may seem calculated to benefit the population of a few small villages in a remote district," appeared destined to be a pilot light to kindle the fires of a rural awakening throughout the country.[27]

By the end of the 1920's, however, Yen's impetus was only one of several. Inevitably, such pioneers were drawing the attention of an increasing number of churchmen to the condition of the Chinese peasant. The development of their concern can best be traced through the deliberations of the National Christian Council of China (the NCC).

## The NCC and Rural China, 1928–1933

Christian concern for the condition of rural China was hardly a new phenomenon. From their earliest decades of activity, Christian missionaries had striven for freedom of access to the Chinese countryside. In a land where over 80 percent of the population lived in villages, it was inevitable that the agents of evangelism would seek to penetrate the hinterland. To the extent that xenophobia, banditry, and disease would permit, missionaries had searched diligently for the village convert.

But if the rural concern itself was not new, it had at least undergone a subtle change by the first years of the Nanking decade. During the political and economic upheavals of the twenties, the condition of the Chinese villager had visibly declined. As the "social gospel" began to infuse the thinking of new missionary recruits to the China field, Christians urged greater attention to the social and physical welfare of the people to whom they preached. As early as 1922 the delegates to the National Christian Conference, which resulted in the establishment of the NCC, had decreed a formidable objective for future Christian social policy: it was their conviction, they said, "that the application of the Gospel to social problems means nothing less in the long run than the complete abolition of poverty." The conference went further than generalized injunctions; it directed its recommendations explicitly to the plight of the peasant. What was needed was a comprehensive church program for rural areas, new emphasis on agricultural education and improvement, and a study of the possibilities of cooperative finance.[28] At its first meeting, in the same year, the NCC voted to create a Committee on Rural Problems and the Country Church; and in its first annual report this committee warned of the urgency of the rural situation.[29]

Such warnings were to be perennial. Yet the next eight years saw almost no progress toward a coherent Protestant program for the Chinese countryside.[30] Indeed, a Conference on Christianizing Economic Relations in 1927 produced only ten pages of discussion on rural economic problems, in contrast to the thirty pages devoted to industrial conditions.[31] At the same time, the NCC's Rural Committee itself admitted to being "tired of too many meetings and little action." [32]

While China was passing through the turmoil of the nationalist revolution of the late twenties, a conference in the Middle East gave worldwide Christian rural reconstruction powerful support. In 1928 the Jerusalem meeting of the International Missionary Council received a comprehensive report from the noted agricultural specialist and university president, Kenyon L. Butterfield, on the Christian role in rural cultures. Butterfield urged a "rural community parish" approach to the villager in Asia and Africa, and the conference heartily endorsed his recommendations.[33] A few months later the NCC invited Butterfield to visit China and formulate a specific program for the Chinese countryside. Butterfield arrived in China in November 1930 and stayed through the following April.[34]

The Jerusalem Conference was only one of several factors, however, which moved the Chinese church from fruitless discussion to action. In late 1927 the NCC had procured the services of a rural secretary of great ability in the person of Chang Fu-liang, an educator and agricultural specialist trained at Yale and the University of Georgia. The vigorous development of Christian rural reconstruction after 1929 was largely attributable to the leadership of Chang; indeed, his departure for service as director of the Nanking government's rehabilitation program for Kiangsi in 1934 was a severe loss to the church program.[35] It was Chang Fu-liang who initiated the invitation to Butterfield. It was also Chang who created a vitally important bond between the NCC and the noted pioneer in mass education, James Yen, who was married to the sister of Chang's wife.

In the context of Yen's background and Tinghsien's prominence by 1930, it is no surprise that churchmen as well as politicians were taking note of his enterprise. As a Christian, Yen had early despaired of the church's interest in rural China and had moved off on his own course of action. He had severed his formal connection with the YMCA, and religion played no part in the Tinghsien experiment. Indeed, Yen had lost patience with most missionaries. Despite the fact that 50 per cent of Chinese Protestants were illiterate, the church seemed to him to be paying "little or no attention to methods developed by the Mass Education Movement" throughout the twenties. But as it was the problem of literacy that had drawn Yen to the countryside, so it was literacy which finally drew the church to Yen.

In fact, the church's small rural beginnings had preceded Yen's: Hugh W. Hubbard and his Congregational associates of the Paoting area had begun to experiment with thousand-character lessons among villagers as early as 1923–24, on the basis of Yen's initial efforts in urban areas.[36] In due course Hubbard and Yen made contact and began to assist each other's enterprise as Yen, too, moved into the countryside. By 1930 Yen's rural work was known to a significant group of North China churchmen.[37] And in that year the NCC requested him to send some mass education experts to Shanghai to advise on expanded church literacy programs. Although he could spare no specialists at the time, Yen welcomed the NCC request and suggested instead that the council send its own delegates to Tinghsien to observe mass education in action. It seemed to him that, at long last, "the strenuous opposition to the Christian Church occasioned by the new nationalistic feeling brought home to them the urgency of literacy education." [38]

The two-week Tinghsien Literacy Institute of April–May 1930 was one major turning point in the history of Christian concern for rural China. Evangelism had originally brought the Christian to the countryside; the illiteracy of the rural convert now brought the evangelist to Tinghsien. But Yen was already several strides ahead of the church, and it was at Tinghsien that a few Christian leaders received a vivid impression of the possibilities for rural social work beyond mere literacy education. Yen himself believed that the institute's "real significance" lay in the stimulus the 90 delegates received from the project's educational, economic, and citizenship divisions "to evolve a new program for the Church to meet the needs and demands of the new China." [39] Yet at the November meeting of the NCC executive committee, the general secretary's report emphasized exclusively the literacy problem. The "attempt to eradicate illiteracy from the Christian Church" on the basis of Tinghsien methods, he said, had "aroused remarkable interest and met with hearty approval"; indeed, if every Tinghsien delegate would carry his enthusiasm into action, "we have every reason to believe that illiteracy in the Christian Church can be removed in the not distant future." Meanwhile, the secretary added, "The cry of the young China today is 'Go to the people,' and the people of China are to be found mainly in the country." [40] After 1930, Christian cooperation with the Tinghsien experiment was expanded and intensified; all future church efforts in rural reconstruction bore the imprint of James Yen and his colleagues.

If one vital spur to Christian rural reconstruction was the Tinghsien example, another came from the visit of Kenyon L. Butterfield, who arrived in China in November, seven months after the literacy institute. Fresh from a study of village communities in India, Butterfield toured the Chinese countryside with Chang Fuliang and offered far-reaching recommendations to the NCC. At the core of his proposals stood a multi-faceted "community-parish, with a self-supporting rural church, indigenous in its methods, led by a specially trained pastor" who was to be both "a preacher and a community leader and builder." Such a pastor should be aided by volunteers, specialists, and "organized groups of institutions." [41] Butterfield saw the growing literacy movement as a "heaven-sent" impetus to rural consciousness. "But literacy is not an end," he warned, "it is only a tool . . ." As a follow-up, he urged that the NCC provide an agency for closer cooperation among the various infant projects in North China rural reconstruction. Throughout China the reconstruction movement seemed to him to suffer from a patchy development, from a lack of coordination of effort.[42] Before he departed from China in the spring of 1931, Butterfield addressed the NCC's biennial meeting in Hangchow. In its recommendations on rural problems, the meeting urged the formation of a North China Rural Committee to help guide the activities of Christian workers who had already gathered in two conferences at Tsinan and Peiping earlier in the year.[43]

In May the NCC took action to carry out Butterfield's recommendations. It reorganized its Committee on Rural Work under Chang Fu-liang and voted to establish provincial branch committees in Hopei and Shantung to coordinate reconstruction projects in those two provinces.[44] The tie-in with provincial units was the first step toward the formation of a system of regional Christian Rural Service Unions. Although plans for the first of these, a North China Christian Rural Service Union, had been drawn up as early as the summer of 1930, it was nearly a year after the Hangchow meeting that this union took shape. But the Hangchow sessions seemed to one veteran observer to indicate nonetheless that Christianity was finally "beginning to cooperate with the socially reconstructive movements in China."[45]

Meanwhile, four developments were destined to make the year 1931 of decisive significance in the history of rural reconstruction in China. These were the catastrophic Yangtze and Huai River floods of the summer, the Mukden Incident in September, the establishment of the Chinese Soviet Republic in November, and the impact of the worldwide depression. Together, they produced the most critical year that the Chinese countryside had experienced in the century. The havoc wrought by floods, invasion, and depression was to throw its shadow over the remainder of the decade. At the same time, the challenge posed by rural revolutionaries was to goad both government and church into intensified activity.[46] The cumulative disasters required, initially, an emergency response. Long-term planning was rejected in favor of relief for the victims of flood and warfare. It was estimated that the floods alone had affected 25 million people in 131 hsien of five provinces, with a material loss of two billion dollars.[47] Christians were invited by the National Flood Relief Commission to preach to flood refugees "with a view to helping keep up their spirits."[48] More tangible assistance came from the NCC in the form of flood rehabilitation loans to needy farmers grouped in mutual aid societies.[49]

But by May 1932 the executive committee was once again struggling with the role of the church in the continuing rural crisis. What was needed, it was felt, was first, further promotion of the Butterfield survey and recommendations. Second, the North China rural service group should work out "a compassable program" for a rural church. Third, denominations should be encouraged to experiment with Butterfield's proposals and should cooperate to develop one or more rural service groups similar to the one in North China. These suggestions were added as corollaries to the NCC's Five-year movement, begun on January 1, 1930; this movement had included in its objectives the spiritual deepening of Christians and the doubling of their numbers, but no mention had been made of a rural program.[50]

Not until September, however, could the NCC rural secretary report the formation of the long-awaited North China Christian Rural Service Union (NCCRSU), on which future regional reconstruction groups were to be modeled. This union was a very loose association of six missions and church groups and three Christian institutions in Hopei, Shansi, and Shantung. Its purpose was "to pool the expert personnel for the service of the rural churches in North China" in accordance with the Butterfield recommendations.[51] In a period of budget cuts and personnel demobilization, however, the NCCRSU was slow to become much more than a paper federation.[52]

Meanwhile, the NCC Rural Life Committee had decided on the need for a second Tinghsien institute. This time the gathering would emphasize rural improvement as well as literacy, and it was hoped that delegates would see to it that regional institutes were organized as a follow-up to the Tinghsien sessions. The objective was still the discovery of the elusive "practical program" of rural reconstruction which Christians might pursue to implement the Butterfield suggestions of two years before.[53]

The Tinghsien Institute on Rural Reconstruction took place during the second two weeks of April 1933. Although 80 delegates had been expected, 180 appeared—36 of them foreigners, the rest Chinese. Together they represented 14 provinces. The main discussion question of the institute was, "What is the Christian Church's task in Rural Reconstruction?" To arrive at an answer, the delegates were exposed to instruction in a vast array of topics: the history and significance of mass education, organizing and teaching the thousand-character classes, alumni clubs of the people's schools, cooperatives, agricultural projects, rural health work, home education, citizenship, rural survey, drama and art.[54]

From the literature of the time, it is clear that the impact of the second Tinghsien Institute far exceeded that of the first. Christians

from all parts of China saw in Yen's experiment a compelling answer to the agrarian misery and chaos they saw about them. Hugh
W. Hubbard of Paotingfu presented the delegates' reactions in a report to the NCC's biennial meeting in May: "What did we delegates
get out of the Tinghsien Institute? . . . We got an inspiration, a
vision, and a practical program." In the first place, he wrote, "We
were inspired by the example of a group of men, highly trained,
keen, utterly devoted, seeing clearly problems, patiently and scientifically experimenting, working in perfect teamwork at the gigantic
task of transforming old China, individual and masses." Second,
"We were inspired and touched by having these men welcome us as
comrades in a common task. They convinced us, if we needed convincing, that with the Christian dynamic, the Christian Church
might play a great part in the rebuilding of the. nation." A third
source of inspiration was "the wonders that can be performed in a
comparatively short time with the raw material to be found in the
villages." It seemed to Hubbard that the Christian responsibility
was clear—to "make real Christians, but intelligent, healthy, public
spirited, patriotic, economically independent, cooperating Christians." The alternative was for the church to go the way of Nestori-
anism. Hubbard was impassioned in his conclusions: "It is time to
act. Let us do something before it is too late. We have no time to
lose." For Japan's attack would inevitably strengthen the ties between China and Russia. "Another wave of Communism is sure to
sweep the country sooner or later. How many years have we in
which to make good—two? five? ten?" [55]

Nor was Hugh Hubbard's reaction atypical. In a symposium on
"The Church and Rural Reconstruction," 13 other missionaries
joined with him in joyous reports of the new vistas Tinghsien had
opened to them. One, indeed, saw Yen's experiment as a major step
toward "bringing in the reign of Christ on earth—a true Christian
Communism." [56] To a Christian community which had heretofore
seen no "way out" for China, Tinghsien was enormously significant.

Two weeks after the end of the institute, Chang Fu-liang presented a long and careful report to the NCC's biennial meeting at
Sungkiang. It was a report on the state of the church in its rural
mission; its tone was sober, stern and impelling. For Chang was
only too aware of how little of tangible significance had been ac-

complished in rural reconstruction since the Jerusalem meeting, despite five years of conferences and institutes. Chang noted the grim dimensions of the continuing national crisis. Yet what was the church doing? Not only were half the Chinese Christians still illiterate; but the Five-year Movement was failing to appeal to the vitally important student groups. "At the same time," he wrote, "the Communistic program for national salvation strongly appeals to many of the idealistic and unselfish young Christians." The alienation of Christian youth was compounded by the alienation of leadership as well; both James Yen and T'ao Hsing-chih were Christians, "and yet they went outside the Church and Christian institutions to begin their work in rural reconstruction." Where was the challenging program that the church should be producing? The Jerusalem meeting, the Butterfield visit, and the Hangchow conference—"all have pointed out to the churches in China rural reconstruction as an answer to the present crisis confronting us." But with a few exceptions, the response had been indifferent. Certainly, Chang continued, the church had a continuing responsibility for increasing literacy. But along with this, he wrote, "Let us frankly recognize that man's spiritual life and physical life is a unity; and the more abundant life which Christ came to bring is meant to set mankind free from many of the physical disabilities under which it has so long struggled." [57]

The Sungkiang delegates responded to the Chang Fu-liang report by adopting a series of recommendations which went further than any previously voted by the NCC. In the first place, they agreed that parishes should recognize "literacy work as one of the church's major tasks," since mass education was the best foundation both for religious education and for "a more comprehensive church program of rural service." Second, they urged that each member church experiment in at least one rural community parish and train rural workers. Third, they asked that churches and Christian institutions in a given area pool their expert personnel in rural service unions on the pattern of the NCCRSU; such unions were particularly needed in Fukien, Kwangtung, east, central, and west China. Fourth, where such a service union was not possible, they urged that mission stations give aid to rural parishes. And finally, they voted a further reorganization of the NCC Rural Life Committee with an enlarged membership composed of representatives from regional unions, important institutions training rural leaders, and others.[58]

The Tinghsien Institute and Sungkiang biennial meeting of 1933 were jointly a milestone in the history of Christian rural reconstruction in China. For the first time since the Jerusalem meeting of the International Missionary Council, the NCC found itself a coordinating agency for scores of Chinese and foreign Christians who had become converts to the gospel of rural reconstruction. All over China men were eager to work out a synthesis that partook of both the rural community parish of Kenyon Butterfield and the model hsien of James Yen.

Along with these developments, a visiting British economist had done much to turn the attention of Chinese intellectuals toward the nation's agrarian crisis. In 1930 R. H. Tawney had made a study trip to China at the invitation of the Institute of Pacific Relations. Tawney's findings, first presented at the institute's Shanghai Conference in 1931 and then published in his classic, *Land and Labour in China,* had a major impact on the Chinese intelligentsia.[59] Nor was the political climate unfavorable to a new venture in rural reconstruction. The Tangku Truce in May 1933 brought China a period of relative release from the formidable Japanese pressure to the north. The emergency measures necessitated by the Yangtze floods and the Shanghai warfare had given way to a stage when a longer-term strategy to cope with the rural crisis could be profitably discussed. The time was ripe for a major Christian initiative in rural reconstruction.

*Origins of the Government Invitation*

In the summer of 1932 a group of American Protestant missionaries vacationing at the international mountain resort of Kuling in Kiangsi, near the Yangtze River port of Kiukiang, came together to discuss the problems posed by communism in China. Ever since the upheaval of 1927, an increasing number of missionaries had been forced to grapple with this issue. The existence of the Soviet Republic and the exploits of the Red Army made communism a continuing national vexation. Most disturbing to foreign educators, however, was the vigorous growth of Marxist-Leninist thought among Chinese students and intellectuals.

The Kuling discussions of 1932 produced no tangible results. They were considered so useful, however, that it was agreed to hold a second seminar on the subject during the following summer. In the intervening months the northern Kiangsi mountain top assumed a new significance: with the establishment of the generalissimo's military headquarters at Nanchang, Kiangsi, in early 1933, Kuling became an informal summer capital for the Nanking government. At the same time, Chiang Kai-shek's contacts with Kiangsi missionaries became closer and more frequent; in April he and his wife rented a house belonging to the Nanchang Methodist Mission as their temporary home.

Chiang's presence in Kiangsi related, of course, to the persistent Communist threat from the Juichin Republic. With the signing of the Tangku Truce in late May, the generalissimo was ready to embark upon another campaign of "encirclement and annihilation" during which he hoped to apply his new formula of "30 per cent military, 70 per cent economic" measures, a formula which had recently been used with considerable success in Hupeh.[60] Plans were under way for large-scale rehabilitation of the former Communist areas, and in June the necessary funds were procured with the successful negotiation of the US$50 million loan in wheat and cotton from the Reconstruction Finance Corporation in Washington.[61]

In Nanchang, meanwhile, one of the missionary participants in the 1932 Kuling discussions had developed a friendly and portentous relationship with Mme. Chiang Kai-shek. William Richard Johnson, a Methodist from Illinois assigned to Nanchang since 1910, was the superintendent of the Nanchang Academy and, on behalf of the mission, the Chiangs' local landlord.[62] Johnson had been deeply concerned with the plight of the villager, and since 1928 he had been on part-time loan to the China International Famine Relief Commission. By 1933 he was acutely aware of the desperate need of war-ravaged Kiangsi for thorough-going rural rehabilitation. But like all missionaries of the time, Johnson discovered that this period of rural crisis had caught the home boards at the height of depression cut-backs; funds from America had been so curtailed that his own academy was in danger of closing its doors. At the end of May 1933, William Johnson journeyed to Nanking to attend the annual meeting of the CIFRC. During his visit to the capital and Shanghai, he made a determined effort to locate new ways and means to supplement the income of the academy in order to keep going.[63] Johnson's search was encouraging if not conclusive. He found the two cities astir with confidential plans for rural reconstruction. The planning centered in the University of Nanking, the national government, and the Rockefeller Foundation.

A month before, Johnson had met with Professor Harry H. Love and Dean K. S. Sie (Hsieh Chia-sheng) of Nanking University's College of Agriculture, on their visit to Nanchang. Love, a Cornell agriculturalist who had taught at Nanking and was now consultant to the Ministry of Industries, was advising the governor of Kiangsi on problems of rural rehabilitation. In Nanking Johnson pursued this acquaintance and tried to persuade the two specialists to include the Nanchang Academy in any scheme for rural training; his institution owned 200 *mou* of undeveloped land which might be used for agricultural experimentation. Both Love and the dean were receptive to the suggestion. It was conceivable, Johnson reported, that the academy might develop an extension station under the College of Agriculture and also serve as "a base for such mass education and rural reconstruction work" as might be planned in the region. In this way the academy could teach its student body "some of the fundamentals of agricultural work for the masses." When Johnson learned that the university was about to receive a US$600,000 endowment fund, which had previously been held in America, and that this fund was to be spent in reconstruction work over the next twenty years, he immediately requested that Love and Sie include in their program a US$3,000 annual appropriation for the academy's experiment station. Dean Sie was encouraging but gave no promise.[64]

It was in Shanghai, however, that Johnson learned of much larger sums of money that might become available for rural reconstruction. There he called on a vice president of the Rockefeller Foundation, Selskar M. Gunn, who had been sent to China to study the rural situation and was rumored to have "some millions at his disposal." Johnson argued that the foundation should channel a part of its program into already existing institutions supported by Americans rather than allow them to shut down in the depression. He told Gunn in particular of the confidence expressed in his mission's work by Mme. Chiang and by Colonel Huang Jen-lin, the director of the Officers' Moral Endeavor Association; the two of them had been so impressed with Methodist efforts in Nanchang, it seems, that they had made a "recent arrangement to introduce our evangelistic work into the military hospitals, etc." From S. M. Gunn, Johnson learned that one of the Rockefeller Foundation's chief interests was "to back the Provincial and Central Governments' plans and to stimulate them to undertake an adequate program for this kind of work." Gunn was in close touch with H. H. Love, and Johnson hoped that Love's support would bring results from the foundation. For Love had said that "his prime motive in accepting this present position with the Government was that he might help to bring the missions into closer relation with the Government in plans for Agricultural Reconstruction." To his bishop, Johnson wrote that the objectives of Love and the presence of Gunn were "a fortuitous set of circumstances which at least has in it a possibility of definite results for our work." [65]

William Johnson's trip down the Yangtze had uncovered new possibilities for saving the academy, but his return to Nanchang brought a development of far greater significance. On the day after his arrival, Johnson received a visit from Mme. Chiang Kai-shek. The generalissimo's wife had two requests to make. The first was that Johnson help her find a missionary couple to take charge of the orphanage at Nanking in which she had long been interested. The second concerned rural reconstruction: "She asked me if I would study the problem and outline for her a program for rural reconstruction in Kiangsi on a large scale, and plans whereby such a scheme might be carried out under Mission auspices." [66] Here was the genesis of an unprecedented project: an invitation from the Chinese central government to foreign Christian missionaries to undertake the rehabilitation of former Communist areas.

Before Johnson could give the news more than the briefest attention, the following day brought a second call from Mme. Chiang. Her initial request seems to have envisioned Christian operation of the entire reconstruction program for Kiangsi. But overnight she had learned that "the government funds being prepared for such a program have already been allocated, and that it is too late to bring the Missions into it on the large scale she had hoped." Nonetheless her request for a study remained intact, "but the plan to be formulated must now be on a smaller scale. She still hopes that the mission or missions can be brought into the work, and she still wants to back such a program financially." Johnson's reply was that such a study would take considerable time and effort: he must first examine in detail the work at Tinghsien, at Nanking, and at the Kiangsu Provincial College of Education in Wusih. Mme. Chiang at once agreed to underwrite a substitute for Johnson in his mission's summer building operations, and within ten days the missionary had departed on a study tour of Nanking and the north.[67]

Before he left Nanchang, however, William Johnson reported the entire episode to his superior, Bishop Herbert Welch in Shanghai. In Johnson's view, Mme. Chiang's request seemed to require that the church "consider most seriously just what we are prepared to undertake in the field of agriculture, assuming the personal backing of General and Mrs. Chiang for an annual grant for a period of, say $10,000 Mex. for this kind of work." Furthermore, Johnson wondered about the possibility of interesting Gunn and the Rockefeller Foundation in the project; in Shanghai Gunn had said that he would be invited by Mme. Chiang to look into the problem of rural reconstruction in Kiangsi. The essential point, however, was to "act with reasonable promptness"; Johnson wrote, "Mrs. Chiang feels the urgency very much," and unless the church responded speedily, it might "find her interest waning or turned elsewhere." [68]

When the missionary leaders returned to their Kuling vacation seminar in the summer of 1933, they received a confidential report of Mme. Chiang's request from William Johnson. During the course of their summer study on Christianity and communism, Johnson pursued the peripatetic investigations he had agreed to undertake. In August, as he put together his findings, it seemed to him imperative that the Chiangs discuss their request with the wider circle of missionaries assembled on the mountain top. At his suggestion, the seminar participants invited the generalissimo and his wife to join them for a special session on August 13. Chiang himself was away from Kuling, but Mme. Chiang attended. To the seminar participants she is reported to have reaffirmed her conviction that "those areas in Kiangsi Province which had been reclaimed from the Communists presented a real challenge to the Christian Church to put forth the best efforts of which it was capable in reconstruction work." She felt sure, she said, that "the Government would welcome any suggestion which the Church might have to make in regard to a practical program for these areas." She suggested that the conferees consider this request and meet with her again in a week's time.[69]

An offer from Chiang's wife bore the full weight of Nanking's authority. A sub-committee of the seminar decided on August 18 to pass the news at once to the NCC in Shanghai; Bishop Logan Roots of the Episcopal church, bound for Shanghai on his way to America, was made their confidential messenger. Should the NCC decide to cooperate, it was agreed that special attention must be given to land tenure, agricultural improvement, cooperative and rural credit, dike repair, communications, and literacy.[70]

On August 19 Bishop Roots and two others met with Mme. Chiang at her summer home to report their interim decisions. This time she named the particular Kiangsi and Fukien hsien in which the church might operate. All were still under Communist rule, but their reconquest was expected imminently.[71] Chiang's wife once again urged that Christians accept the reconstruction task. She is reported to have said that "If our Christianity were vital, it should prompt us to render such service." At the same time she agreed to press for a survey of land tenure. As for the structure of the service organization, she suggested a Nanchang local committee, of which the Chiangs would be members; the national governing body would be composed of the NCC's Rural Life Committee.[72]

On the next day a slightly enlarged group gathered for tiffin with Mme. Chiang.[73] At this final conference William Johnson outlined the program he had been preparing since her first approach to him in June. The Johnson report included a plan for two-phased reconstruction: intensive short-term rural improvement by a team of experts in a delimited area and extension of such services to a wider area through the training of local leaders.[74] His program borrowed heavily from a variety of sources: from the report of the 1928 Jerusalem meeting, from the Butterfield findings of 1930–31, from the Tinghsien experiment, Nanking Seminary's project at Shenhuachen, Cheeloo University's project at Lungshan, and Yenching's demonstration center under J. B. Tayler at Chingho. But of greatest influence on his thinking was the Kiangsu provincial government's rural project at Hsuchow under F. T. Shih. Unlike the other projects mentioned, each of which had stressed a particular aspect of rural reconstruction, Hsuchow's aim was sufficient self-sustaining growth so that specialists might be withdrawn within three years and the program would continue under local workers, "with only occasional visits from the specialists who will then be moved on to another cultural unit to repeat the program." Another unique feature of the Hsuchow experiment also appealed to Johnson. Most rural projects commenced with a program of mass education, then tried to induce improvement through the formation of local alumni associations. But Johnson had observed that mass education had two drawbacks as a starting point: it appeared to be hard to convince farmers of the need for literacy; and literacy programs tended to arouse the immediate opposition of the gentry. Hsuchow, therefore, adhered to "the principle of first projecting into the villages that form of service most calculated to bring immediate material benefits to the largest possible number in the community." First came wheat-seed improvement, then, with the harvest season, the formation of cooperative societies and the extension of loans; later, the organization of an anti-bandit corps; and so forth. The result was that the friendliness of the workers and the value of their service program was so quickly demonstrated that everyone was won over, including the influential gentry.[75]

Using the Hsuchow plan as his guide, Johnson proposed several points of emphasis for rural reconstruction in Kiangsi: first, an agricultural experiment station should be established in cooperation with the University of Nanking; Johnson was quick to recommend his own academy's 200 *mou* of land for the station's site. Second, a team of specialists, preferably college graduates, should set to work in a delimited area, the cultural unit—a market town with its contiguous territory. Third, a possible modification of this second method would involve an attempt at once to develop a program in a larger area by extensive training of local workers. As final points of emphasis, Johnson cited two important preparatory phases: the selection and training of specialist personnel and the survey and research work necessary for an understanding of the territory and people concerned. As for the particulars of the reconstruction work itself, Johnson analyzed the village needs under the headings of economic improvement, health and sanitation, literacy and continuing education, home improvement, religious education, and recreation and play.[76]

The Johnson report was notable for its thoroughness and scope.

Yet it was also notable for a few key omissions. Three major areas of economic life had been explicitly exempted from the discussion in the early paragraphs of the study. "No effort will be made in this plan," he wrote, "to deal with such fundamental problems as transportation, land tenure, and taxation, the solution of which is regarded as belonging entirely within the realm of government activities." [77] The exemption of land tenure is particularly surprising in view of the emphasis placed on the subject in the two previous meetings. Indeed, Johnson was careful throughout to demarcate the roles of church and government in the proposed project; the activities of the church, he said, "are intended to supplement those of the government, and these activities are in no sense competitive with the government or with any government department or agency. The government has primary responsibility in this field. The church enters it solely in the spirit of service in the carrying out of its duty to serve humanity." [78]

William Johnson's proposals provoked lengthy discussion at the luncheon meeting of August 20. One major concern was finance; it was estimated that the project would cost $200,000 per year for three years, a prohibitive sum for depression-hit mission boards. The church must look, therefore, to "the cooperation of General and Mme. Chiang" and the Rockefeller Foundation. Although finance was a problem, however, it was agreed that the greatest difficulty of all lay in the area of personnel; for there was clearly "a great scarcity of men trained along the lines required." Yet it was precisely here that the church might be able to make its greatest contribution to the project. Meanwhile, the first essential was a preliminary survey by four or five men who should meet in Nanchang in mid-September, then confer with Mme. Chiang in Kuling. At the close of this final Kuling meeting, Bishop Roots called for a policy of "cooperative independence" between the government and the Christian movement; "freedom of initiative and action" must be maintained within a working relationship of "the closest harmony and understanding." The bishop's suggestion drew unanimous approval.[79] The Kuling conferences ended with the dispatch of Bishop Roots downriver to Shanghai. Three days after Mme. Chiang's tiffin, Nanking's unprecedented invitation to the Christian church was in the hands of the NCC.

*The NCC Response*

The news of the government's request reached the executive committee of the NCC toward the close of the summer holidays. The Tinghsien Institute and the Sungkiang biennial meeting had brought the council's members to a new peak of expectancy on the subject of rural reconstruction; but no further action had been initiated in the ensuing three months. Indeed summer was a time of forced inaction through much of the oppressively humid Yangtze valley. Informal conferences at such vacation spots as Kuling, Peitaiho, Tsingtao, and Mokanshan took the place of normal administrative procedures; it was the season of review and refreshment, when missionaries traded religious insights and political gossip with their brethren from other stations.

Word of the significance of Logan Roots' message had preceded the courier's arrival, however, and five members of the executive committee had joined with the four staff secretaries to await the bishop's coming. On August 26 these nine met with Roots at the council's headquarters.[80] The bishop explained the circumstances leading to the calling of the meeting and then read a memorandum that summarized the sessions with Mme. Chiang. After considerable discussion of such matters as financial support, manpower, and the church's proper relationship to the government, it was agreed that the bishop and the council's chairman should write Mme. Chiang "stating the nature of this meeting and the steps which may be taken to secure official action by the NCC with regard to these proposals in view of the very deep interest and sympathy which they have evoked."[81] Roots then left for the United States on other business. Two days later the NCC staff took further action; in a special meeting it voted to send Chang Fu-liang first to Nanking to consult with Dean Sie and Dr. Love, then to Nanchang and Anking to see W. R. Johnson and others who had participated in the Kuling conferences. At the same time the staff voted to ask George W. Shepherd of the Fukien mission of the Congregational church to come to Shanghai and report on conditions in West Fukien and Kiangsi, areas close to the hsien suggested by Mme. Chiang.[82]

During the next two weeks the NCC discreetly sounded out its constituent elements in north and central China. While Chang Fu-liang was upriver, one of the council's associate general secretaries, E. C. Lobenstine, journeyed to Tsinan and Peiping to consult with mission bodies there. On September 18 the NCC staff met to hear their reports. Lobenstine had found general agreement in both cities "that the invitation was a challenge which could not well be ignored." Two dangers were inherent, however, in an acceptance of the request: first, that the Christian group might become "too closely related to Government authorities" (a regime whose popularity and life expectancy were necessarily uncertain); and second, that the church might "appear to be standing for a particular economic theory" (that is, that of Nanking's planners). Of the North China leaders it was reported that President John Leighton Stuart of Yenching and Professor William B. Djang of Cheeloo were "most enthusiastic." On the other hand, the North China Christian Rural Service Union's leading figure, Hugh W. Hubbard of Paotingfu, was cryptically reported to be "more hesitant." It was significant that of all the people interviewed, Hubbard had had the widest experience in rural reconstruction.[83]

Chang Fu-liang reported his findings at the same meeting. He had changed his itinerary and gone right to Kuling, because the missionaries he sought were still there. At the mountain resort he had interviewed T. V. Soong and Sun Fo as well as Mme. Chiang herself. Chang admitted that on his way upriver he had not felt "very enthusiastic as to what the Christians could do." He was immediately convinced, however, "of the sincerity of Madam Chiang and returned believing that we must certainly do something." Interestingly enough, the generalissimo's wife still seemed to hope for the large-scale Christian effort she had first suggested to Johnson. Indeed, she discussed the possibility of a plan whereby the church would put twelve reconstruction teams to work in both Kiangsi and Fukien for a three-year period at a cost of a million Chinese dollars. Would such a plan, she wondered, "free the Government from other responsibility for this work?" Chang's answer: not at all. At this she turned to a discussion of a more limited budget; she was still prepared, she said, to ask the government for a financial grant for the church project. Chang Fu-liang also reported that the generalissimo had invited H. H. Love to prepare an agricultural plan for Kiangsi. In conclusion he suggested that whatever the final arrangement, Mme. Chiang should be chairman of the Christian project's supervisory committee. Although the NCC staff continued its discussion of the problem of church-state relations at this meeting, there is no indication of any decisions on the matter.[84]

The following day, on September 19, the results of these negotiations were presented to a formal meeting of the NCC ad-interim committee. Lobenstine reported on the steps taken thus far, and he read a reply from Mme. Chiang to his letter on behalf of the council. At the same time, William Johnson's proposals, now available in mimeographed form, were presented in full as a basis for discussion. The minutes of this meeting provide an interesting glimpse of the consensus of NCC opinion:

Following discussion, it was noted
1) That something should be done
2) By some independent body
3) With a strong Christian control
4) Without Government subsidy if possible
5) With assured personnel
6) With support secured in advance
7) In a strictly limited area
8) With plans not too ambitious at the beginning.[85]

The ad-interim group then voted to create a sub-committee of four to investigate and report back "regarding possible field, program, staff and finance required." [86]

It was a week before the sub-committee met to consider the problems raised by the government invitation; exactly a month had passed since Bishop Roots had first presented the request to the Shanghai members of the executive committee. Yet, all the major questions remained unresolved. The sub-committee explored with particular care the troubling intricacies of church-state relations. Should the missions accept financial aid from the government? If they did, would such a subsidy make "impossible or undesirable specifically 'evangelistic' work on the part of those working under the committee in charge? " But without an outside subsidy, how could the churches finance such a project? Among the most interesting questions raised, however, was one whose cryptic wording in the sub-committee's minutes leaves its implications unclear: "In what ways can the position of the church be safeguarded in its relation to the economic theories of Communism?" Undoubtedly, the question harked back to Lobenstine's concern lest the church appear to give its blessing to a particular school of economic thought, that is, whatever program the national government was offering as an alternative to communism.[87]

After a good deal of deliberation, the sub-committee arrived at four conclusions. First, the NCC should express its "willingness to aid the Government in its rural reconstruction work through the means of Christian personnel." Second, "it would be better not to seek for a Government subsidy in launching a distinctly Christian program." Third, any Kiangsi project should be linked to the rural work of the NCC as a rural service union; "Kiangsi would then fit into the general plan of developing rural reconstruction units," and such a program would not prejudice appeals for help from other sections of the country. Finally, a group should proceed at the earliest moment to Nanchang to make concrete plans; those suggested were Bishops Herbert Welch and Daniel T. Huntington, Chang Fu-liang, NCC Chairman R. Y. Lo (Lo Yun-yen), E. C. Lobenstine, George W. Shepherd, and one representative each from the national committees of the YMCA and YWCA.[88]

On September 28 the sub-committee reported back to a special meeting of the ad-interim committee. After discussion, the enlarged group voted "to put on record its profound sympathy with the purpose in view and its readiness to encourage the Christian forces to cooperate in such ways as may later be determined." The committee further agreed to send Chang Fu-liang and two or three other experienced rural workers to Kiangsi to study the local conditions and formulate proposals. Meanwhile, the NCC should obtain full information on any rural plans contemplated by the government and others "with a view to making the proposed Christian project a contribution to the entire program." It was important to discuss with local Kiangsi Christians precisely which hsien—"one or more" —should be chosen, the nature and extent of the program, its staff, financial arrangements, organization, and relationship to the NCC. After such investigations had been completed by Chang and his colleagues, an enlarged group from the NCC executive committee should join them in late October and consult with the Nanchang leaders and Mme. Chiang "with a view to bringing definite recommendations to the Executive Committee at its November meeting." Those named as possible fellow investigators with Chang Fu-liang were Frank W. Price of Nanking Theological Seminary, George Shepherd of Fukien, and Josephine Brown of the YWCA.[89]

In short, the ad-interim meeting showed that it would be nearly three and a half months from the time of the Kuling conferences before the ponderous machinery of the NCC could produce a definite response to the surprising request from the government. Despite five years of thought on rural reconstruction and despite the strong recommendations of the Sungkiang biennial meeting, the leaders of the NCC evidently harbored grave reservations as to the ability of the church to move into a Kiangsi project. In a letter to George Shepherd at the end of August, Lobenstine himself had warned that "We should be foolish indeed if we thought a band of Christian workers here were in a position to undertake reconstruction work on a big scale." Lobenstine noted that Hugh Hubbard of the NCCRSU "says that after all his years of work he is at a loss to know how really to face the problem of rural reconstruction"; even the experience of James Yen seemed to Lobenstine to "show the exceeding difficulty of the task." [90]

Whatever the council's misgivings, they were somewhat alleviated by the events of late October and early November. On October 18 Chang Fu-liang and George Shepherd had arrived in Nanchang for two weeks of intensive negotiation, and by the 31st a Kiangsi Christian Rural Service Union had come into existence. When the full executive committee of the NCC held its second meeting of the year in Shanghai, Chang and Shepherd were ready to report the results of their trip. At this meeting, Chairman R. Y. Lo revealed that Generalissimo and Mme. Chiang had sent their "hearty greetings" and "their hope that Messrs. Shepherd and F. L. Chang might be set aside to develop the project." At this point, Lo introduced George Shepherd, who spoke on the nature and operations of communism as he had witnessed it in Fukien. Then came a full statement by Chang Fu-liang on the outcome of his investigations.[91]

Under the title "The Christian Rural Reconstruction Project in Restored Communist Areas," Chang's report outlined the essential features of a Kiangsi program. At its core stood a "traveling normal school of experts" who were to train indigenous leadership through "service-in-training and supervision of work." Although Chang noted that such a vehicle had been successfully used in Mexican folk schools, it also seems to have derived from the Hsuchow experiment as described by W. R. Johnson. Under two executive secretaries, a Chinese and a missionary, this traveling normal school would undertake five distinct lines of work: (1) village organization (self-defense, recreation, and so forth); (2) agricultural extension (liaison between the people and an experiment station); (3) public health (with a doctor and a nurse); (4) village industries; and (5) religious training. Within a selected area—a *ch'ü*—a literate, respected local leader would be chosen from each village to be trained for one month by the specialists. Upon his return to the village, the leader would conduct a rural school for children in the mornings, mass education classes for women in the afternoon, and for men in the evening. "In short," commented Chang, "the whole approach selects education as the fundamental process in rural reconstruction." Here, at least, the program deviated from Johnson's Hsuchow example. While the classes were in operation, the specialists would visit the villages, assisting and supervising the work; and at the end of a four- or five-month term, new meetings would be held with the local leaders to plan new projects for the next term. "Thus the training-in-service and the village education program alternate, always introducing new ideas and new ways into the village and making life in the country richer and happier." Chang's hope was that the program "may so commend itself to the rural folk that they may be willing to eventually support it so far as possible financially." [92]

The expenses of the project would be minimal. The local leader would receive an annual honorarium of $50–100, plus travel and entertainment allowances during the training-in-service. Voluntary service to the community, Chang argued, was an old and honorable practice in rural districts, which the NCC project "should conserve and enhance." Although the project as a whole would operate under a regional Christian rural service union affiliated with the NCC Rural Life Committee, its future would depend on a finance committee of well-known Christian leaders. The estimated budget for a five-year program was $100,000. [93] To meet such a goal Generalissimo and Mme. Chiang Kai-shek had already agreed to subscribe $50,000; this left an equal amount to be pledged by other prominent Chinese Christians.[94]

As for operating principles, Chang Fu-liang listed six paramount aims. The program should be "people-centric, rather than institution or government-centric." It should concentrate on the "training of indigenous leadership, rather than importing specialists from outside to do local work." It should proceed by testing and adaptation of the results achieved. It should operate in a limited area and cooperate with the government. It should assist local leaders to carry out a program of service "within the economic capacity of the people to support." And it should give the Christian religion "an important place in serving the whole man and the whole community." [95]

Chang Fu-liang presented his findings on the morning of November 8. The executive committee at once gave its blessing to the report. In the afternoon session it voted its satisfaction with the organization of the Kiangsi Christian Rural Service Union (KCRSU) and its approval "in general" of the plan agreed upon in Nanchang as embodied in the reports of Chang and Shepherd. It further voted to request that Shepherd's mission employers loan him to the Kiangsi project as an executive secretary "until furlough or if possible for a year and a half beginning January 1, 1934." And it recommended that Chang Fu-liang "give as much time as may be found necessary to insure the successful inauguration of the plan." According to the minutes of the meeting, it was voted to spend the rest of the afternoon session "in discussion of the Communist challenge and the church's answer to it." Regrettably, no transcript of these significant proceedings remains for the student of history.[96]

Three more months were to pass before Shepherd and Chang finally returned to Nanchang to commence the operation of the Kiangsi project. Meanwhile, the NCC staff members continued their discussions of the arrangements. By November 15 they had received a formal request from W. R. Johnson, as chairman of the KCRSU executive committee, for action by the NCC. Johnson warned that "Mme. Chiang felt she had done her share." Chang Fu-liang now reiterated his conviction that the Christian project should be entirely independent of the government. Lobenstine feared, however, that the people within the church-operated district might well feel the NCC project had deprived them of government assistance. It was decided that Chang should go to Foochow to persuade Shepherd's mission to release him; and Reverend Y. Y. Tsu (Chu Yu-yu) should journey to Nanchang to make yet another study of the local situation.[97]

On the 29th, the staff met to discuss a letter from Tsu, which enclosed the constitution of the new KCRSU. Tsu wrote that Johnson had been authorized to approach Mme. Chiang for a first installment of $5,000. A disturbing factor during this staff meeting was a newly arrived letter from John H. Reisner, former dean of Nanking's College of Agriculture and now director of the recently formed Agricultural Missions Foundation in New York. Reisner's letter in response to material sent him in September is said to have emphasized "how ill-prepared the Church is to face a rural problem of any magnitude." [98]

A week later Y. Y. Tsu had returned to supplement his written reports. There was some discussion of a possible approach to H. H. Kung, Mme. Chiang's brother-in-law, for financial assistance; but it was decided, somewhat cryptically, that the NCC must first "learn what the situation is and the relations with Mme. Chiang." Other possible sources for a Chinese subsidy were mentioned: C. T. Wang (Wang Cheng-t'ing), the eminent diplomat, and K. P. Chen (Ch'en Kuang-fu), the banker. At any rate, the NCC was itself in no position to provide funds. As for the administration of the project, Tsu felt that the council "must recognize Johnson's leading position and the fact that this will probably become a Methodist project." [99] This was the first suggestion during the three months of negotiation that one particular denomination might assume control. It seems to have been an outgrowth not only of Johnson's catalytic role in the project but perhaps of the Chiangs' Methodist affiliation as well. As matters developed, Methodists and Episcopalians seem to have held dominant positions in the executive committee of the project, although the first two foreign executive secretaries, Shepherd and Hubbard, were both Congregationalists.

The organization of the Kiangsi project held the attention of the NCC staff members at two further meetings after the beginning of the new year. In the first week of January 1934, Y. Y. Tsu underscored the problem of the long time-lag since the Kuling conferences: there was growing criticism of the NCC in Kiangsi, he reported, for failing to make any concrete proposals on the operation of the project. The experiment in Christian rural reconstruction remained only a paper scheme despite the passing of seven months since Mme. Chiang's original approach to W. R. Jŏhnson. It lacked even an executive secretary; although the Foochow mission had agreed to furnish the services of George Shepherd, Fukien's rebellion against the Nanking government had kept him immobilized on the South China seacoast. One encouraging development was the cooperation offered to Lobenstine by James Yen. Yen would be willing to provide a mass education team; but he felt that the project would need more assistance from the personnel of the YMCA and YWCA.[100]

On January 22, George Shepherd finally broke loose from Fukien and arrived in Shanghai. He spent that day with the NCC staff on their New Year Retreat. The two overriding questions were, first, how deeply the NCC was to be involved in the project, and second, how to find a Chinese executive secretary. No one seemed better qualified for the latter post than Reverend Robin Chen of Anking. The first task was to obtain the services of Chen and a Tinghsien team. Shepherd was leaving that night for Kiukiang and would henceforth give half to three quarters time to the Kiangsi project.[101]

With the departure of Shepherd for Kiangsi, the Christian experiment in rural reconstruction entered a new phase. The role played by the NCC became secondary to that played by Shepherd and the leaders of the KCRSU. To be sure, the council maintained a loose consultative relationship with its affiliate. For the first three months of 1934 this relationship was strengthened by Chang Fu-liang's close cooperation with Shepherd in the initiation of the project. Whatever his earlier misgivings, Chang had come to believe strongly in the value of the undertaking. In a Christmas letter at the end of November 1933, he had termed the government invitation as "one of the biggest challenges that has come to the Christian movement in China in recent years." Paraphrasing Mme. Chiang, he wrote that a successful response to the challenge might well "vitalize our Christian religion." More than that, it would then "point the way to our idealistic youth, full of the spirit of adventure and patriotism, to service in the country. In rural reconstruction we hope that the church will find an adequate and concrete answer to the challenge of communism." [102]

Chang Fu-liang, however, was destined for even more important duties. In early April the NCC received an urgent request from Finance Minister H. H. Kung that Chang be loaned to the government to manage its own large-scale program for the rehabilitation of Kiangsi province.[103] The National Economic Council, buttressed by the US$50 million RFC loan, was about to move into the former Communist areas with an elaborate plan that dwarfed the minute experiment of the Christian church. Chang's release was voted by the NCC executive committee on April 17. Thereafter, though the council's indirect role in Kiangsi was vast indeed, its control of policy in the Christian experiment was minimal. Deprived of the services of its rural secretary, the NCC failed to play an active part in the rural reconstruction movement. Its period of catalytic significance had been the months between the Tinghsien Institute of April 1933 and the establishment of the KCRSU in November. For an understanding of the nature and development of this Christian experiment in church-state cooperation for rural reform, it is necessary to examine the role of George W. Shepherd, because the project at Lichuan in south Kiangsi was largely a product of this man, his outlook and experience.

# Chapter Four

# The Missionary as Rural Reformer

## George Shepherd's Background

Among the Americans who developed close associations with the Nanking government's reform efforts, George William Shepherd played a role of unusual significance. This Congregational missionary was chosen by the NCC and by Chiang Kai-shek personally to direct the Christian rural reconstruction experiment in Kiangsi; later on, the generalissimo brought him to Nanking to revitalize the New Life Movement. By 1939 Shepherd had achieved brief renown in the American press as the "one trusted American" in Chiang's "innermost circle"[1] and, second only to the Australian W. H. Donald, as the "closest white collaborator of Mme. Chiang."[2]

George Shepherd was actually American by adoption. Born in New Zealand in 1894, he first came to China as a missionary of the fundamentalist Plymouth Brethren in 1917. His preparation for the assignment was minimal: one year of high school, seven years as a hardware salesman in New Zealand, and two years at Chicago's Moody Bible Institute. It was not long before he realized "what a fool" he had been "not to take a college course."[3] A voracious reader and able student of Mandarin, Shepherd found his horizons rapidly enlarged by his new learning, the impact of China, and the American physician he married in 1921. In the process, he felt himself increasingly alienated from the Plymouth Brethren, a "reactionary" group that preferred, he charged, "to remain a back eddy in the stream of the Christian program." [4] In 1925 George Shepherd arranged his permanent transfer to the more liberal and socially activist American Board of Commissioners for Foreign Missions (ABCFM), a Congregational enterprise with headquarters in Boston. For one year he studied intensively at the then Harvard Theological School. In 1926 he returned to China under the new sponsorship, convinced, he wrote, "that this generation must help solve the world's problems by carrying the Gospel to other peoples." [5]

Shepherd's mission post was the town of Kienning in the Shaowu region of northwest Fukien near the Kiangsi border. This was a field he had come to know during his previous years of service, and his assignment there was rural evangelism. But the Shaowu region proved to be a precarious base for operations. In the spring of 1927 the advancing forces of the Northern Expedition drove foreigners out of Fukien. Returning a year later after flight to New Zealand, the Shepherds found themselves harassed first by intensified banditry, then by the new menace of communism. Over the mountains from Kienning, Red troops under Mao Tse-tung and Chu Teh had come together to form an infant Chinese Soviet Republic. By 1931 all of Shaowu was in Communist hands, and the Kienning missionaries had escaped to Foochow.[6]

*Impact of the Communists*

The successive Communist incursions into northwest Fukien in 1931, 1932, and 1933 had a profound effect on the thinking of George Shepherd. They forced his attention to the inadequacy of Nanking's administration, the nature of the Communist appeal, and the potential role of Christian missions. In the process, he gained a deepened awareness of agrarian discontent as China's chief political and social problem. To be sure, the rural crisis was no new concern to a Shaowu missionary. Shepherd's first contribution to the foremost missionary journal, the *Chinese Recorder,* had been an article in early 1931 entitled "The Unmet Rural Challenge." [7] In it he noted the dearth of trained workers for rural parishes; and he deplored the "city-minded" outlook bred by Christian institutions.

"Until missionaries, church officers, and Christian schools make a psychological adjustment, throw away their prejudices . . . , and decide to give the toiling masses trained leadership," he warned, "the situation amongst 80 per cent of China's population, so far as the Church is concerned, must remain unchanged." [8]

Nor was Shepherd alone in his concern. This was the period of the first Tinghsien Institute and the Butterfield visitation. Shepherd had applauded the Butterfield recommendations for a rural community parish. Yet he also gloomily commented that vast quantities of young leaders would have to be produced "if anything approaching Dr. Butterfield's suggestions are to be carried out." [9]

It was at the same time, then, as the rising rural interest among missionaries that the Communists established their Kiangsi border state. To Shepherd their success in 1931 was a judgment, first and foremost, upon the men of the Kuomintang: Nanking's "policy, or rather the lack of it so far as the provinces are concerned, . . . has been suicidal the past three years. They have not shown the slightest appreciation of all China's great rural past, and they have almost completely ignored this growing group of communists in South China, so that the people have nothing to gain by leaning over toward Nanking." With millions of peasants now suffering from a "scourge . . . as disastrous as many famines put together," the uncomprehending government had "mustered its entire army for an attack on a social problem." But the social problem would remain unsolved, and the church would continue to founder, "until the government really carries out a constructive program for these inland rural regions." [10]

Shepherd felt that the Communist assault contained a lesson for missions as well: it marked a new day in the relation of the church to the Chinese. With the destruction of the Shaowu buildings, "We are now forced to admit that the mission and the church must be prepared to face the same conditions as all Chinese citizens." [11] Gone were the days of special protection for missionary property; and indeed, Shepherd added, "This is as it should be under the circumstances." [12] The church was now "taking its place with the smitten afflicted people, and upon this foundation of identification with the halt, the blind, the oppressed and the imprisoned, the Chinese Church will begin to build a fellowship close to the needs of the people and to the heart of its Founder." Affliction had created new bonds between missionary and Chinese: "We are now inseparably linked together." [13]

Deeply enmeshed in Shepherd's reaction to the destruction of his mission base were questions about the methods and aims of the destroyers themselves. From the outset he seems to have been possessed of a profound and growing ambivalence toward the Communists. In simplest terms, on the one hand, he resented their intrusion, condemned their doctrine, and abhorred their cruelty; to this extent they were a destructive menace. But on the other hand, he admired their success, marveled at their tenacity, and approved of many of their aims; to this extent they were a creative challenge. A sense of the challenge was already implicit in his Annual Letter of September 1932. "Communism as a solution to the social problems of China," he wrote, "is still commanding the attention and serious study of many students. Does Christianity offer any such crusade against the entrenched evils of society? This is a question that many are asking." In the first of many such admonitions he warned, "It will be disastrous for us all if we lack leadership and daring." [14]

Some weeks later Shepherd made his first inspection trip back to the Shaowu area, newly cleared of Communists and bandits. The destruction at Kienning appalled him: "This town has been hard hit, and will not recover in this generation." Nonetheless, he noted, "Many farmers and workers frankly say that the communists are the friends of the poor." Shepherd admitted "not the slightest doubt but what the communists have swept away a lot of rubbish," yet in so doing, they had been "cruel beyond comprehension, and they have also destroyed much that was the flower of thousands of years of culture." [15] A few days later they nearly destroyed George Shepherd as well: a new Red drive suddenly engulfed the whole region, and the missionary's escape down the Min River to Foochow was narrow indeed. [16]

In his coastal exile that autumn Shepherd brooded over the relationship between communism and Christianity. Others in China were being drawn to the same perplexing subject, and their discussions were to bear results within a year. Meanwhile, Shepherd told the mission board in Boston of his discoveries upriver. One leading Christian at Kienning, it seems, had survived Communist rule with particular success, for no citizen would come forth to accuse him, and "The communists cannot condemn a man for whom the people stand firm." Herein lay a lesson, he felt: "I think the communists put us to the real test. They ask the people on the streets and in the fields what kind of men we are." [17] As for the nature of the Reds, "There is much that is good in their program, and they certainly get rid of a lot of parasites and corrupt officials." But once again the deep-seated ambivalence showed itself in the conflict over means and ends: "Their program is cruel beyond words, and is too drastic for the followers of Christ." So drastic, in fact, that by now "deeds have probably been burnt in huge piles . . . How fortunate," he added, with the landlord's sigh of relief, "that the Mission deeds have been removed to Foochow." [18]

### Rural Reconstruction in Fukien

The Communist successes in 1932 seem to have produced a subtle shift in George Shepherd's views on the rural role of the church. Although he retained a concern for the evangelical tasks of a village parish, the economic and social needs of the villager were pushing to the forefront of his mind. In the summer of 1932 he had opposed those of his Foochow colleagues whose outlook was still strictly evangelical. "What we need," he had written, "is not a Bible School so much as a Rural Service Training Institute that will be a Bible School and more. A new field of operations is opening to the Chinese Church, and there will soon be a call for men to meet the demands of the new program." It was once again Kenyon Butterfield who gave direction to his thoughts; Shepherd told the mission board that the Butterfield Report was "bringing new vision to us all and our institutions are beginning to realise that Community Uplift is going to bring new vigor into all our activities." [19] In December the NCC sent Chang Fu-liang to Fukien to win support for the Butterfield proposals. Chang persuaded the Mid-Fukien Synod to hold a Rural Training Institute in Foochow during July 1933. [20]

The months of exile on the coast had caused George Shepherd considerable frustration. He longed to get back into the countryside where he could throw himself into a new type of village work. An initial opportunity came in early 1933 when the mission board appointed him temporarily to the town of Yangkow, half-way up the river toward the old Shaowu territory. There a combination of circumstances made the outlook for rural reconstruction seem bright.

In the first place, Yangkow was close enough to Communist territories to make church workers aware of challenge as well as threat. During a series of February "fellowship meetings," Shepherd noted an interesting social attitude: "A great many looked upon the communist movement as containing a few elements of value. It was said again and again, 'God's time of reckoning with corrupt officials, land-grabbers and money-lenders seems to be near at hand.' " [21] Chinese Christians were being forced to consider the church's role in a new revolutionary context.

A second factor of importance was the presence in Fukien (since July 1932) of the government's 19th Route Army, now famous for its heroic stand against Japan in defense of Shanghai. Removed from close contact with Nanking, the leaders of the 19th had linked themselves with "progressive Canton"; [22] in March the announcement of a Kuomintang reconstruction program that excluded Fukien seemed to strengthen that link. [23] Shepherd reported, "The future of Fukien is much brighter since the new government has come into office," because "long established systems of corruption have been swept away over night." [24] Although the 19th Route Army's ultimate plans remained unclear—indeed, by late March it had withdrawn to southwestern Fukien—Shepherd viewed it as a potential force for reconstruction and reform. Any program that held "the welfare of the people as its main objective, will yet prove to be a more powerful weapon against communism than bombs and bullets." [25]

The reform impetus supplied by the Communist challenge and progressive local government was compounded by a third development. In the spring of 1933 George Shepherd took a trip that marked a turning point in his China career. He traveled north to attend the NCC's second Rural Reconstruction Institute at Tinghsien. There he saw for himself the thriving pioneer experiment conducted by James Yen. He went north an enthusiastic inquirer; he returned an ardent convert.

"I have just spent the two most inspiring weeks of my life," Shepherd told the mission board. "Jimmy Yen accomplishes all of the Red program, and more, in a way that is Christian and acceptable to all who still believe that Christ's principle of love and sacrifice is more powerful than violence and the sword." [26] To Shepherd,

Tinghsien embodied "the only answer to Communism that has yet appeared." Yen and his staff taught, worked, ate, drank, and lived with the villager. "It gave us a new kind of thrill to sit under PhDs who have identified themselves with the people." With wonder and approval he reported, "This experiment has no headquarters in Peiping or Shanghai." And with hearty concurrence he quoted Yen's admonition that "religion which cannot recreate men is not true religion. Merely teaching something out of a book is no contribution to the needs of humanity. Our Tao [way] must become flesh if it is to become intelligible to the people." [27]

George Shepherd's response to Tinghsien was a five-point proposal for an immediate rural reconstruction project in the Min basin from Foochow up to Shaowu. In certain carefully selected village areas he intended to combine the "Educational Program of Jimmy Yen and the Rural Parish of Dr. Butterfield" as a two-pronged "answer to communism." Mrs. Shepherd, a trained physician, would supervise the project's health division. But the urgency of the matter could not be overestimated, for throughout Fukien the church leaders were said to be "discouraged and without a program in the face of today's challenge." For Shepherd it was now or never: "Yesterday has gone forever, and only today is ours. And what a day it is! Communism in the South, invasion in the North, division between Canton and Nanking, and on top of that the effects of the world depression." [28]

Such a project required a crash program to train Chinese leaders for village work. Too many of the mission schools and colleges were channeling their graduates into business, politics, teaching, and urban medicine. What was needed was to give the Fukien students "a first hand knowledge of this rural life around them and the Christian answer to communism . . . To say that the boys themselves are interested," he added, "is to put it mildly. Scores of them believe that communism has the only way out for China. They will rise like pop corn when given the chance. Nobody can answer all their questions, because the answers have not yet been found." But the chief objective of the mission schools must be "to set these boys working on finding their own answers." [29]

Shepherd's trip north had done more than fill him with the gospel of Tinghsien; it had increased his awareness of the alienation of the student class from both Christianity and the Kuomintang. On the trip back to Fukien he spent many hours in discussion with young Chinese intellectuals. "These fellows," he wrote, "were students full of communism and enjoyed the chance to cross swords with someone who knew and understood both sides. There were no reservations on my part or theirs, and I think they appreciated meeting someone who saw the good in the communist movement, was seeing it in action, and still believed in the Christian program of love." [30]

In one further respect—a matter both curious and extraordinary—the northern excursion contributed to the education of George Shepherd. On the way home he had had a confrontation with the enemy himself. "While in Shanghai," he reported to the mission board, "I had a secret interview with the agent of the Kiangsi-Fukien Soviet Government. I discussed the matter of a passport for missionaries and church workers, and although favorably disposed he inferred that the time is not quite ripe. He will, however, take up the matter with the Kiangsi Soviet Executive Committee." The encounter had an unsettling effect on the American missionary: "These first hand contacts with communism at work make a fellow think furiously. Are they right, or are we?" And then he adds, "I honestly believe that Jimmy Yen has the only answer." [31] The Boston office of the ABCFM found Shepherd's secret interview "decidedly interesting." The China secretary replied: "It was to be expected that communism in China would be largely different from communism elsewhere, and I hope that you will find that it is possible to work out compromised solutions which to a westerner would probably seem impossible." [32]

Upon his return to the south, Shepherd went to work with vigor in the Yangkow area. At the begining of June he completed his first village literacy survey on the Tinghsien plan and was "surprised to find the men 50 per cent literate, and the women 20 per cent. This means that with many of them we shall be able to commence on second year work." The pressure for speed was great, for "just above us the communists have a big start on a similar program with a revolutionary basis." [33] By mid-June he could report that the Yangkow Chinese staff had been won over to the Tinghsien approach.[34] Meanwhile, the semi-independent 19th Route Army had returned to firm control of the region and had begun to apply its own reform program under the slogan "A New Fukien in Five

Years." The leaders of the 19th had taken over much of the Communist program, while rejecting its objectionable features, Shepherd wrote. At the core of their reforms were the establishment of a farmer militia and large-scale village improvement. Their program seemed to him the most far-reaching plan for reconstruction in China.[35] But who was to administer such reforms? Here Shepherd now saw "the golden opportunity of the Church";[36] "if it turns out that the government is really going into this reconstruction program, we shall have a grand opportunity to train men for it."[37]

And yet, for all his optimism, the ever present threat across the frontier could not be ignored. In late May George Shepherd had written the mission board a letter heavy with foreboding and prophecy. From the plateau of historical self-consciousness to which the northern trip had lifted him, he could view the China of 1933 in troubling perspective.

"The communist movement is spreading," he wrote, "and the government seems powerless to stem the tide. Communism is certainly a force to be reckoned with in south China, and to live right next door to it makes a fellow think furiously. Its ranks are full of Christians who claim that at last they have found the movement, great and noble, for which they can gladly spend themselves. Its methods are cruel, but its aims are identical with ours in some particulars, and it fearlessly puts into practice some of the things that Christianity might have stressed some more. It does not interfere with the faith of individuals, but it crushes the life out of organized Christianity. We can no more ignore it than we can the sun and the moon."

During his rural survey, Shepherd had found the cooperation of the villagers deeply encouraging. "Such a response is heartening," he continued, in the same letter, "but as I walked the top of a mountain and viewed the villages along this beautiful winding river, I kept wondering if we are too late. Only God knows that, so we shall work intensively in the Yangkow and Tsianglo fields. I am going up to Tsianglo next week. Beyond that is the domain of our most powerful rival in the Orient. We are now on the frontier." And then, in closing, the troubling cosmic question that had clearly become the driving force of George Shepherd's life: "Shall Christ or Marx win?"[38]

By mid-summer Shepherd's hopes were rising. But in late August catastrophe struck. "The worst has happened," he wrote: north Fukien was suddenly engulfed by "hordes of Red soldiers . . . by far our most disastrous invasion . . . This Red Revolution is gaining momentum." As he contemplated the wreckage of his infant project from a second Foochow exile, he wondered, "One blow after another, how do these people stand it?" [39]

## The Call to Kiangsi

George Shepherd's forced return to Foochow coincided with the last of the Kuling conferences. On August 26 the NCC received the report of Bishop Roots; on the 28th it summoned George Shepherd to Shanghai. The council needed a first-hand picture of conditions in the Communist areas, and few missionaries had acquired as much knowledge of the Kiangsi border regions. The invitation from the north reached Shepherd in the wake of the Yangkow debacle. It brought him his first word of the Kuling proceedings along with the request that he attend the NCC meeting of September 19. The new Communist drive, however, had thrown Fukien's transportation into a turmoil, and there were no boats to Shanghai in time. Instead, Shepherd remained in Foochow and studied the Kuling memorandum. Its implications intrigued him.

Mme. Chiang's proposal itself seems to have drawn mixed reactions from the Foochow Christian community. Several Chinese were outspoken on the perils of cooperation with the government. But Shepherd shared the more widespread view that "this may be the greatest opportunity that the church will have in this generation." Even so, his enthusiasm was tempered by the fact that "all the hsiens mentioned, and as many more, are as Red as the old barn door. Chiang Kai-shek will have to win this time, or South China will go Red." [40]

To E. C. Lobenstine, who had conveyed the NCC invitation, Shepherd was candidly pessimistic. "The important factor in the whole situation," he wrote, "is that Communism is growing in both Fukien and Kiangsi, and the Government has been powerless to control it." Noting that his own village project at Yangkow had "quite recently been taken over by the communists," he warned that unless the provincial governments "get on the job within the near future, we expect a few more of our rural reconstruction units to fall into the hands of these young enthusiasts." The sad truth was that Christians were "very young and immature in all our rural programs" and also "fearful about undertaking reconstruction on a large scale." Not only did he find his colleagues timid, they were clearly tardy as well: "We are a little late in entering this field, some think we are too late." [41]

If anything, George Shepherd's cautious response endeared him to the executive committee of the NCC. Lobenstine himself was overwhelmed with doubts. Nonetheless, he had felt that the Shaowu missionary was "better qualified than anyone else I know to advise us as to the feasibility of work being undertaken in the area." [42] On September 28 the NCC voted to send Shepherd and Chang Fu-liang to Nanchang. Two weeks later Shepherd left Foochow for Shanghai en route to Kiangsi.[43]

George Shepherd's trip to Tinghsien marked his conversion to rural reconstruction; his trip to the Yangtze valley gave him a new view of the Nanking government. For the first time since the Kuomintang's accession to power, he began to see the regime as a potential modernizing force equipped with power and direction. From the isolated semi-autonomy of the Fukien enclave, he emerged into a thriving river basin where substantial material progress was visible. Shepherd's enthusiasm for the Kuomintang had never been great; indeed, he had frequently despaired of its ability to rule China. But from the evidence of the Yangtze valley he now began to feel that this was "a government of young men, and everywhere they are making progress" and that after his seven-year absence, the improvements were quite noticeable. Chekiang, Kiangsu, Anhwei, Kiangsi, and Hunan, he wrote, were now covered by "a network of roads. Apart from Kiangsi the Church leaders are everywhere enjoying the new facilities for travel." Nor was the villager entirely neglected: "Rural reconstruction is everywhere under discussion and both government and church are thinking in terms of a peaceful prosperous countryside." [44]

Shepherd's judgments derived only in part from tourism. From the moment of their arrival in Nanchang on October 18, he and Chang Fu-liang were more officials than sightseers. For there they found provincial and national bureaucrats remarkably responsive. All doors were open, and Chinese and their foreign advisers alike extended pleas for church assistance in reconstruction. Shepherd was surprised to find provincial officials eager for a Christian rural program in areas shortly to be cleared of communism. At National Army headquarters the invitation was even more cordial. The sincerity of the government's desire was overwhelming: the commissioner of education, Ch'eng Shih-kuei, a former pupil of Methodist Bishop John Gowdy, is reported to have said, "I need three hundred young village teachers tomorrow, can you provide me with Christian men who have the spirit of service?" "What a challenge!" Shepherd exclaims, "It sent us home in a thoughtful and prayerful mood." [45]

The major significance of the Nanchang journey lay not, however, in the sights of the river valley or the welcome of functionaries, but in a momentous encounter. "I am returning from the strangest kind of a mission," Shepherd later reported. For it was in Nanchang that George Shepherd first met Chiang Kai-shek. Their meeting was the culmination of a series of preparatory conferences. Shepherd and Chang Fu-liang had consulted with lower officials. Then Lobenstine and Y. Y. Tsu arrived on the scene, and the enlarged group conferred. The final steps in the process were "three tiffins and long interviews at the Generalissimo's headquarters." [46]

From the outset, Chiang seems to have singled out the Fukien missionary for special attention. "Knowing that I have been in close touch with these communist areas," Shepherd wrote, "he questioned me minutely on all things of interest to him, but more particularly on the possibilities of the Church getting under way, and into the business of character building right away." Chiang was insistent that the church move in "right behind the armies." With military directness, the generalissimo is said to have announced, "We must organize the local Christians as soon as the armies enter a district. The Christian farmers and workers will be our right hand men in establishing law and order." As for a specific program, Shepherd reported that both Chiangs were well pleased with the new plans submitted by William R. Johnson.[47]

The interviews were wonderfully encouraging. But there was, said Shepherd, a "fly in the ointment." With remarkable restraint he now told the mission board of the trip's most important news for his own future: "They have requested Chang Fu Liang . . . and me to set up this work in an area yet to be determined." The invitation was still informal, but an official request for both men was to be made to the November meeting of the NCC executive committee. Meanwhile, Shepherd had already advanced a suggestion for the project's geographic location. Not suprisingly, it was an area close to his beloved Shaowu, "the fifth district of Lichuan, in which Kienning has a church, and in which work accomplished will serve the communist controlled areas of both Fukien and Kiangsi." [48] The exile's ulterior motive was clear but understandable.[49]

Nanking's request seems at first to have filled Shepherd with awe and misgivings. The project "depends so much upon the success of the government suppression campaign," he wrote, "that I am at a loss what to say or think about the proposed plan." Peace was essential. Chiang had said that it would probably take three years to eradicate communism in South China. Nonetheless, Shepherd felt, "The Reds . . . have lots of kick left." [50] Perhaps his chief reaction was a sense of unreality about his extraordinary mission to Nanchang. "It seems strange that after all the opposition that we encountered seven years ago in this very same region the government is now asking us to lend a hand." [51]

With George Shepherd, introspection generally resolved itself in action rather than paralysis. Such was the case, once again, with the impact of the Nanchang journey. No sooner had he arrived back in Fukien than he produced his own program: an outline for "Rural Reconstruction in the Communist Devastated Areas of Kiangsi and Fukien." [52] The two major subdivisions were relief work and permanent reconstruction. Under the second heading came three points: a demonstration or work area; an agricultural experiment station; a rural middle school. His prospectus quoted from H. H. Love of Cornell, a chief proponent of Kuomintang reform: "To conquer communism we must have another program of social organization . . . a program, then, that appeals to the people more than the program of communism." [53] Considering such an explicit aim, it is significant that Shepherd's prospectus made no mention of the problem of land reform.

To this outline Shepherd added a statement of his own conviction. In a way the words constituted his personal credo for Christian rural reconstruction: "We can help the world's toilers," he wrote, "as we toil with them and bend together on the dusty road. This, after all, in the spirit of our Master, may be our most lasting contribution. Others may reorganize villages and rural communities, teach self-defense, train the young, teach morality and religion or completely ignore them, improve agriculture and village industries, impart the principles of healthful living, organize cooperatives and self-governing units, solve the agrarian problem, etc., and we may do some or all of these, but only as we manifest the spirit of Him who went about doing good from early morn till late at night regardless of His own rights or comfort, and eventually gave up life itself in the interests of the people, shall we make this a truly Christian project and an answer to those who advocate coercion as the only road to social reorganization." [54] The missionary was still, emphatically, evangelist as well as social reformer.

The Kiangsi Christian Rural Service Union was formally launched in November 1933. Four cooperating Christian bodies formed its core, and Shepherd was urged to move at once to Nanchang.[55] Once again, however, a familiar obstacle upset his plans: a new rebellion against the central government at Nanking. This time the rebellion was led from Foochow itself. For some months the 19th Route Army had been a center of dissidence and radicalism as well as military efficiency, for its leaders had fallen under the influence of their Communist neighbors. In the autumn the army government announced a new program of *sheng ch'an* or "creative productivity" for Fukien. By December Li Chi-shen, Ch'en Ming-ch'u, and Ts'ai T'ing-k'ai had led the province into open revolt against Nanking; the rebels appealed to Canton for support and sent out feelers to the Communists.[56]

Shepherd was at first tolerant of the new regime. Its program appeared to be "some kind of State Socialism" with "much talk of a real rural program . . . for Fukien and the other provinces in the south." This seemed to him all to the good as the land redivision the rebels had promised was long overdue. He wistfully hoped that the 19th Route leaders had in mind "the formation of another Party, and not a declaration of war upon the National Government." [57]

Such was not the case, however, and by January Nanking's new American-trained air force was bombing rebel installations.[58] Shepherd's patience with endemic political chaos was now at an end. "How did we Get into the Mess?" he asked, in a mimeographed broadsheet sent to his friends in America. Answer: "Through a pack of professional revolutionists, who decided to organize another revolution. Yes, another revolution . . . Can you beat it? As if this country needed another revolution!" The 19th, he feared, had been deceived into believing that rebellion would "deliver the country from its present rural bankruptcy." But the truth was that deliverance would only come through "decades of national unity and far-seeing reconstruction." Nor, as far as he could tell, did the rebels have the support of the people of Fukien. Whatever Nanking's shortcomings, Fukienese wanted peace above all.[59]

By the end of the month, the rebellion was over, and Nanking's victory was complete. The outcome, Shepherd wrote, had given the national government very great prestige and power. Indeed Chiang Kai-shek's "display of military strategy and equipment probably foretells the end of the communists in Kiangsi and Fukien," for never before had the government coped so successfully with a military uprising. As for the rebels, Shepherd felt a touch of regret over the fate of his erstwhile reformer friends: "We are sorry for the 19th, but there was nothing else to do, after they rebelled." Their alleged alliance with the Communists, he said, had been their undoing; as a result, even the Canton dissidents had held aloof.[60]

With the suppression of the Fukien Rebellion, George Shepherd was now free to become associate general secretary of the Kiangsi project. He could do so with a new sense of confidence in the Nanking government and a new contempt for its rivals; the rebellion's outcome had confirmed his recently acquired faith in the goal of national unity under the hegemony of a reformed Kuomintang. In late January the Shepherd family left Foochow to set up residence in Kuling.

## The Lichuan Project: Preparatory Phase

For ten hectic months, from February until December 1934, George Shepherd threw himself headlong into the organization of the Kiangsi Christian Rural Service Union (KCRSU). Many weeks were spent on endless quests for personnel, funds, and ideas in Nanking, Shanghai, and Peiping. Driven by a haunting sense that time was running out, he labored nearly indefatigably. By June his health was impaired, and his physician-wife ordered a one-month rest. And by the end of the year, when the mission board decreed home leave for him, Shepherd reluctantly complied.

In January Shepherd had explored the problem of funds. With Chang Fu-liang, he interviewed a group of leading Shanghai bankers assembled by K. P. Chen (Ch'en Kuang-fu). Shepherd found them intensely interested in the Kiangsi experiment; they "asked a million questions" and promised cooperation. A later interview with the manager of the Bank of China filled Chang and Shepherd with optimism: "Those of us interested in helping the farmers and workers have merely to stick together and influence public opinion at every opportunity in order to lift the burdens of the masses." The value of their semi-official status was becoming clear to them. With a touch of surprise and elation, Shepherd wrote, "We all have access to the National leaders, and instead of starting another revolution we shall put our efforts into changing what we already have." [61] Revolution from above was a concept fraught with new possibilities. Shepherd discussed them at length with his Shanghai host, Frank J. Rawlinson, as well as with the staff members of the NCC. Rawlinson, the editor of the *Chinese Recorder* and long an outspoken proponent of Christian social action, found Shepherd "an interesting fellow." The Shaowu missionary would "have to walk carefully between the influence of both Whites and Reds," Rawlinson thought; but if he could really "put over a rural rehabilitation scheme, it will have great significance for the future." [62]

By March Shepherd had finally reached the heartland of Kiangsi. During that month he and Pastor Liao from Shaowu roamed through rural areas, following in the path of Chiang's armies. The German-directed fifth campaign of "encirclement and annihilation" was proving highly effective, and the Communists were being expelled from districts they had held for four years. Shepherd and Liao soon determined that Lichuan hsien would indeed be a feasible site for their project, as they had hoped.[63]

In the countryside, George Shepherd found his reception surprisingly cordial. "We cannot begin soon enough for those who are urging us to make the contribution," he reported. But as he surveyed the villages, the vastness of the task continued to grow upon him: "There never has been presented such a challenge to the Church, and we might daily pray that our smallness and petty divisions, added to our own limitations, may not hinder us answering with a united front." [64] On one matter, however, his prayers went unheeded: the outstanding Chinese candidate for general secretary of the KCRSU was Reverend Robin Chen (Ch'en Chien-chen) of Anking; to Shepherd's despair, however, Chen's appointment was soon to be blocked by Episcopal administrators in New York who disapproved of ecumenical projects. [65]

If Shepherd was staggered by the challenge of the Kiangsi countryside, he was encouraged by the response he saw in the Kuomintang. On February 19, Chiang Kai-shek announced in Nanchang the launching of the New Life Movement. This operation, Shepherd wrote, was "a large scale program to modernise China and attain equality in the family of nations, through *making* China progressive and the equal of her neighbors." It seemed to him that "the breaking up of old China by the communist revolution and now by the 'New Life Movement' " made Christian rural reconstruction "not only possible but imperative." [66]

Shepherd had seen enough to know what the Kiangsi project required. Leaving two Chinese colleagues in Lichuan to make preparatory contacts, he now journeyed to Nanking. All of April was to be given to the recruitment of personnel. In the mission universities, colleges, and theological schools of the east coast he sought for the ideal volunteer—"physically robust, able to endure hardness as a good soldier of Jesus Christ, . . . clean in mind and body, willing if called upon to sacrifice personal ambition for the higher value of team work, and day in and day out . . . devoted to the welfare of the farmer and worker." [67] High salaries were out of the question, of course; all the project could offer was "hard work, and a small living allowance, with an annual opportunity to follow special lines of research at some suitable institution in China." [68]

In Nanking Shepherd discovered what seemed a good solution to the problem of staff. Mission universities were thinking of assuming responsibility for certain aspects of the project; the result would benefit both the institutions and the KCRSU. The University of Nanking, with a high reputation for agricultural extension work, might take over the areas of agriculture, forestry, and economic survey. [69] Yenching's president had already promised to send two full professors for a few months of service. [70] Nanking Theological Seminary offered to take responsibility for religious education in the work area; Ginling College's Department of Sociology was sending a volunteer to work among women and children.[71] Nor were Shepherd's efforts restricted to mission institutions: offers of assistance poured in from the national government's Departments of Health and Education, from the National Economic Council, and from the Kiangsi Provincial Agricultural Institute.[72] At the same time, the missionary was able to induce subscriptions from such diverse sources as H. H. Kung, Sun Fo, Chang Hsüeh-liang, the Standard Oil Company of New York, and the British-American Tobacco Company.[73]

In many ways Chiang Kai-shek's invitation to the Christian church to pioneer in Kiangsi reconstruction had been surprising. Even more astonishing, however, was a second invitation now forthcoming. At the urging of League of Nations experts, the government had been preparing its own program for large-scale rehabilitation of the Communist areas. In mid-April the National Economic Council asked Chang Fu-liang to assume direction of the entire government project with an annual budget of two million dollars.[74] Shepherd was overjoyed with the turn of events. "It is a staggering challenge," he wrote, "but he will have many strong backers, and has had much experience . . . We already have worked out the closest relations with the government, and this will be a step farther in the right direction." [75] Henceforth some sort of coordination between the KCRSU and the government's program of rural welfare centers could be expected through the Shepherd-Chang relationship.

Chang Fu-liang's last act as NCC Rural Secretary was his report on the progress of the Kiangsi experiment to the April meeting of the NCC Executive Committee. This report outlined the steps taken since the formation of the KCRSU. Optimism was enveloping the infant project. Both mission institutions and government agencies were cooperating to the fullest degree. Provincial leaders "impressed us as genuinely interested in the constructive planning and endeavor of remaking Kiangsi." Furthermore, Chang could find no trace of anti-Christian feeling in the province. Indeed, the major difficulty was "for the Church and Christian institutions to live up to the high expectations of the local leaders . . . 'Come to us! Come quickly!' was their cordial invitation." Chang reminded the council of Mme. Chiang's hope that the Christian effort in Kiangsi might both contribute to rural reconstruction and revitalize the church itself. "I believe," he concluded, "that the Kiangsi Christian rural project is on the road to the fulfillment of this two-fold purpose." [76]

George Shepherd was present to participate in the NCC's discussion of the Chang Fu-liang findings on April 18. He told of his own efforts to secure personnel for the project. He spoke glowingly of Lichuan's challenge both to youth and to the church. He described what seemed to him the government's wholesale conversion to rural reconstruction. The New Life Movement was one symptom of this conversion, he said; the revolution had at last really come, and there were men actually capable of carrying out a program of reconstruction. [77]

Shepherd's remarks about the government seem to have been received with some skepticism by the able Anglican Bishop Ronald O. Hall. The bishop was quick to call attention to "the un-Christian system of land-tenure which obtains in South China whereby the tenant farmer does not reap a sufficient reward for his labor." What remedy did Nanking offer in its program for Kiangsi? In reply, Shepherd is reported to have "outlined the plan proposed in Kiangsi by which absentee landlords are to be bought out by farmers' cooperatives." In addition, the NCC Chairman, Dr. R. Y. Lo, himself a member of Nanking's legislative yuan, came to the defense of the government. A commission had been appointed by the Ministry of the Interior, he said, to study the question of land tenure; furthermore, the provisions in the draft constitution decreed the abolition of absentee landlordism and usury. The executive committee thereupon voted to express its deep appreciation for the Lichuan progress reported. [78]

One final preparatory step now remained for George Shepherd. Toward the end of April he journeyed northward to revisit the scene of his conversion to rural reconstruction. Running through his mind as he traveled to Tinghsien were the words of Bishop Hall, who had spoken forcefully on communism and Christianity during the Shanghai discussions. Shepherd reminded Chang Fu-liang of Hall's warning that "the only way to combat communism is to realise that this protest against the Church is warranted, and the only road for Christians to travel is the same one that the communists are travelling—love of the poor." For Shepherd, "everything he said rang true to the standards of Christ." [79] In his battle against the evangelists of Marxism, Shepherd continued to feel some of the ambivalence that had troubled him in the days of his Foochow exile.

At Tinghsien James Yen and his associates carefully studied Shepherd's plans for the Lichuan project. Assistance from the Tinghsien leaders was essential, for in Kiangsi there was a dearth of men trained in rural education techniques. "To carry away a few ideas is one thing, and to have men come down and put over an already well tested program is quite another." Yen approved Shepherd's Lichuan program and promised to help in every way possible.[80] All was now ready for the move to south Kiangsi itself.

Between Peiping and Tinghsien Shepherd wrote an important letter to a former Shaowu colleague, Walter H. Judd, a medical missionary then on prolonged furlough in the United States.[81] The gist of the message was an appeal to Judd to throw in his lot with the Kiangsi project rather than return to North China. Conditions had radically altered, he wrote, since Judd's departure for America in 1931. The most significant changes in the modern history of China were transpiring. Many factors were responsible: "The Christian forces have had some part, the communists another, and current events in various parts of the world" had left their mark. Together they had produced a new outlook among Nanking's leaders, who were at last convinced that "they must busy themselves with the welfare of the common people." This change of heart was having far-reaching consequences: "All progress in reconstruction and gains on the battle field may be traced to a changed attitude on the part of China's prominent leaders."

Shepherd described the Kiangsi project for Judd. As its unique characteristic he cited the nonpayment of salaries. "We are asking men and women to serve as the communists do—for living expenses only. The response has been overwhelming." Of course, the church could only do so much; "Reconstruction is essentially not the business of private institutions in any country. It is the business of the government." But the church's role was to pioneer and experiment, then pass on its results for extensive application by the government. Meanwhile, Shepherd had become convinced that "work put into Chinese institutions and personalities is permanent. All other efforts for a man of your qualifications and accomplishments will be only second best."

Shepherd's appeal to Judd to join the Lichuan enterprise was wholehearted. "In all events," he said, "if we make a success we open doors everywhere for the Chinese Church and its institutions to remould the life of the people. If we are a failure, we let the whole movement down. *Shih pu shih?* [Right?] Our work will be a centre where young men and women will catch the spirit of sacrifice as a sort of post graduate course, or internship. They are rarin' to come for the experience. What else can we give them? Does Christianity really have an answer to communism? Prove it. There are lots of young people who are anxious to come and try." Any earlier misgivings Shepherd had harbored were a thing of the past: "No better opportunity ever came to any man or to any Christian organization to demonstrate to the world how genuine and how practical are all our braggings about Christianity being the way out." [82] There is no record of a reply from Walter Judd; nor did he join the Lichuan project on his return to China in 1934.

By the middle of May, George Shepherd had taken up residence in Lichuan. The preparatory phase was over.

# Chapter Five

# Lichuan: The Church on Trial

*The High Tide of Rural Reconstruction*

In the spring of 1934, as the Lichuan experiment began, China stood on the verge of a nationwide movement for rural reconstruction (*hsiang-ts'un chien she*). Its institutional roots were manifold: national, provincial, and district; public and private; Chinese and foreign. By 1935 it is estimated that over 690 agricultural institutions were acting as agencies of reform. Only 109 of these were privately sponsored; the remaining 84 per cent operated under the direction of national, provincial, and district government bureaus, with the largest number initiated by the provinces.[1]

The proliferation of projects produced increased communication among the reformers. In July 1933—three months after the second Tinghsien Institute—a National Conference of Rural Reconstruction Workers brought 60 participants, from 35 organizations to Tsouping in Shantung. The next year, in October 1934, a second National Conference, this time at Tinghsien, attracted 150 delegates from 76 agencies; and at a third conference at Wusih in October 1935, the figures would rise to 200 delegates, 99 organizations.[2]

The reasons for this remarkable burgeoning are not difficult to discover. Rural China was in a state of acute crisis. To the population rise and the breakdown of village society was added the chaos

of the twenties.[3] The resulting rural decline was drastically accelerated, moreover, by the natural and man-made disasters of 1931–
32. Floods, Japanese aggression, rebellion, and worldwide depression all combined to strike at China's economic and political
existence within the space of a few months. The impact of this
catastrophe on the Chinese countryside can be seen in two statistics:
the quantitative index of imports fell from 130 in 1931 to 77 in
1935; and the land value index in rural areas under Nanking's
control fell from 100 in 1931 to 82 in 1934. Despite an urgent need
for agricultural credit, the Shanghai silver stocks continued to soar
until new U.S. policies suddenly produced a dangerous drain of the
metal away from China.[4]

And yet it was not the intensity of the crisis alone that was significant in the years between 1931 and 1937. Famine and discontent were indeed endemic to the countryside throughout much of
Chinese history, and the nineteenth century had had its massive
share of both. What was new in the first years of the thirties was not
just the clear and present need, but the mounting concern over the
plight of the Chinese peasant. As already noted, this concern had
diverse origins: the writings of Sun Yat-sen, the relief work of foreign agencies, the convictions of Chinese idealists, and the compassion of churchmen.

It need hardly be emphasized, however, that the concern had a
more recent and explosive cause as well, dramatized in 1933–34
by the plight of Kiangsi province. With the collapse of the Stalinist
strategy in China in the years after 1927, Chinese communism had
been forced into the rural hinterland—and was pressed, as it developed, into an immensely useful alliance with the peasantry. To
be sure, the alliance was less than a winning combination in the
days of the embattled Juichin Republic. Nonetheless, the words and
deeds of Chinese Communists in 1931–34 inevitably transformed a
latent and chronic social question into a not so latent political
question. What George Shepherd had seen and felt in Fukien was
only the sharp point of a sword whose ominous shadow had troubled many, both missionaries and officials, since the collapse of the
first United Front. It was the actions of the Communists that had
forced the Nanking government to provide a rural program for the
reclaimed territories of Kiangsi. And it was the government's resulting initiative that had suddenly put the Christian church on trial at
Lichuan.

In the context, then, of the decade's interlocking crisis and concern, the Christian experiment in rural reconstruction at Lichuan was by no means unique. Throughout the country, efforts to improve the lot of the peasant were under way. Such efforts covered a wide spectrum, from the militant expropriation program of the Communists to the pilot projects of James Yen and Liang Sou-ming and the paper plans of the national government. And Americans were involved in varying degrees in several of these efforts. Of longest life, apart from educational institutions, was the CIFRC, which celebrated its fifteenth anniversary in 1936.[5] Equally important were the pioneering agricultural projects of the University of Nanking under John H. Reisner and J. Lossing Buck.[6] At the same time, various mission stations were attempting patchwork responses to the need for "rural improvement"; the most successful were those of Nanking Theological Seminary at Shenhuachen and of the NCCRSU near Paotingfu.

Nor was Lichuan necessarily the most important undertaking of foreigners striving to provide a model for rural reform. Yet in its origins, nature, and development, Lichuan illustrated both the opportunities and the limitations the missionary agents of rural reconstruction faced in Kuomintang China.

## Lichuan in Operation

In the third week of May 1934, George Shepherd finally reached Lichuan itself. The experiment was in progress, and it was "a joy to be on the field" at long last.[7]

The site of the Christian rural experiment, once envisioned as covering twelve hsien, then one or two, actually comprised the fourth district or *ch'ü* of Lichuan hsien. This district lay in a fertile stream-fed valley of southeast Kiangsi. Barren hills cupped the level land, but behind them towered high wooded mountains. These mountains had supported the once thriving paper industry of the region. Otherwise, its economy depended on rice and some tobacco. Lichuan would normally have ranked as a backward region; the national government brought the hsien its first vehicular road in the spring of 1934. But Communist occupation, warfare, and economic blockade had intensified its backwardness. During this time the hsien's population was reduced from 110,000 to 90,000;

in 1934 the figure for the fourth district stood at 1582. In the hsien as a whole, only 2.5 per cent of the people were literate. In the project's central village, no school had existed for three years. Illiteracy, poverty, and isolation had left their mark upon the citizenry. One observer termed them "conservative and superstitious far beyond the average of interior villages." [8] Added to this was a linguistic peculiarity: in this border region between Kiangsi and Fukien the villagers spoke a patois that Mandarin speakers and Fukienese alike found incomprehensible.[9] It is not surprising, therefore, that George Shepherd's successor at Lichuan was to term "the human material of this section . . . one of the most difficult problems of our work." [10]

In later years Shepherd wrote that he had really had no idea of what the invitation to Kiangsi would involve. And as his duties developed, they struck him as "quite different from my earlier idea of the work of the average missionary." One of his first tasks, indeed, "was to help run to earth a guard of soldiers which had cruelly and secretly murdered a young farmer in order to gain possession of $240 that he carried in his bundle." Meanwhile, the imported staff of 14 volunteers adapted themselves to the depressed condition of their surroundings. Shepherd reported, "None of us has had any heart to do more than make our own surroundings sanitary, while the people around us continue to live in such poverty and squalor. We have accustomed ourselves to the neighbor's chickens and pigs roaming at large through our rooms and seemingly for ever under our feet." Their way of living became rapidly "a life of 'having all things in common,' " a life strikingly similar, he thought, to "the New Testament's description of Christian communism." [11]

The energetic experimenters at Lichuan in the spring of 1934 were only a small pocket in a vast area of change. Kiangsi province was in the process of transformation under the two-pronged impact of a provincial and national assault. The agents of the former were a young and ambitious Japan-trained governor, Hsiung Shih-hui, and his largely Japan-influenced staff. Nanking's men were the administrators of the National Economic Council (NEC), most of them returned-students from America. The ultimate form of rehabilitated Kiangsi would be a hybrid product of these two forces. But behind them, and uniting them to the best of his ability, was Chiang Kai-shek.[12]

To Shepherd the atmosphere was exhilarating. All about him he discerned signs of progress; "The government is using technically trained men where it once had only politicians," he wrote, "and that simple change is making the difference." The change he attributed to one first cause: "The determination of General Chiang Kai-shek to remould the life of the people, and his willingness to pay the price himself, is at the bottom of all this amazing progress." The result was immediately apparent. "You don't have to wait years for action. Subordinates who fail to measure up to the new standards are dismissed with lightning rapidity." [13]

Like the winner of a sweepstakes, Shepherd was still overwhelmed by the turn of events. He continued to write much about the challenge Lichuan presented. And he found the circumstances of his Kiangsi employment slightly unbelievable. "Think of it," he exclaimed to the mission secretary, "Chinese leaders have already turned from communism and Russia to the Christian Church." As soon as he arrived in Lichuan, the NEC suggested that he apply for a $10,000 health clinic grant; at the same time the provincial education commissioner volunteered the information that he had $3,000 available for mass education purposes—Shepherd had only to name a school superintendent and send eight men for summer training.[14] To a man who had been driven out of his mission station four times since 1927, such treatment by Chinese officialdom was intoxicating.

In the midst of progress, however, one development deeply depressed the reformer. News had come of the New York Episcopal mission board's veto of Robin Chen's appointment as general secretary. This was particularly distressing as Mme. Chiang herself had greeted Chen's nomination with great enthusiasm. To Shepherd, it was "plain suicidal" for the church to make such errors. "I hang my head in shame," he wrote, "when I bump into the narrow-minded stupidity and lack of vision on the part of our Church leaders in some parts of the world." It seemed to him that the lessons of recent history clearly showed the dangers of such idiocy: "Dr. Sun Yat-sen turned to [the Soviet advisers] Borodin and Galen when American and British and European governments gave a deaf ear to his entreaties for help. I don't need to go into details on the cost of that folly. It has cost China and the Church more than any other act in the history of modern China." Indeed, the memory of Michael Borodin's role lay heavy on Shepherd's mind. In the battle

for China's soul, Marxism had employed a gifted emissary; did it
lurk in his thoughts, perhaps, that history might make of him a
Christian Borodin? There is later evidence to support such a con-
jecture. At any rate, the blunder over Chen presaged no good for
the Christian enterprise. And there were other non-Communists
lurking in the wings, he warned, men eager to step in if the Christians failed. "Hitler is already in very great favor out here, and his
men are coming into places of tremendous influence." [15] But no
further mention is made of such competition from the right for another three years.

By mid-June the news of both government and church projects
in Kiangsi was spreading to other regions of the country. From
Nanchang, on his way to a one-month convalescence in Kuling and
Japan, Shepherd noted frequent and favorable comment in the Chinese press.[16] And his own report at the April NCC meeting had
gained wide circulation among Americans. Earle H. Ballou, secretary of the ABCFM's North China Mission, wrote that this report
contained "among the most encouraging pieces of news that I have
heard about this country in a long while." Ballou marveled at the
government's alleged conversion to rural reconstruction. What impressed him most was Shepherd's account of the revolutionized
yamens "where the farmer can now walk right in by the door-
keeper and talk with the magistrate in person if he has real business
to be attended to." [17] Apparently, Shepherd was already showing
the publicist's skill that he was later to use in America for the cause
of Free China.

Others were also promoting the cause of Lichuan in the latter
part of 1934. At the annual meeting of the Methodist Episcopal
church's Kiangsi Conference, W. R. Johnson's Rural Reconstruction Committee termed the project "one of the most significant
rural enterprises of our times." Never before had an "almost exclusively . . . city church" faced such a challenge: the challenge of a
"constructive rural program, Christian in motivation and scientific
in method." Furthermore, "Seldom if ever in China was such official recognition given to Christian missions, or has there been extended to the Christian Church more practical official cooperation
and support." [18] Any dangers inherent in official patronage seem
to have eluded the committee; its main concern was with the unpreparedness of the Methodist church for such an opportunity, for few

if any of its pastors had been "trained even in the rudiments of agricultural economy or in the elementary principles of rural sociology, cooperative endeavor, or in the special problems of the rural church." The committee's recommendation was that the Kiangsi Methodists use Lichuan as a laboratory for such training.[19]

George Shepherd's Japanese vacation in the summer of 1934 refreshed him, and by September he was back at work in Lichuan, where Mrs. Shepherd had started the project's medical program by setting up a clinic in July. For several months, however, his mission board had urged him to take a year's furlough; it was feared that the long period of uprooted living, political crisis, and civil warfare had taken their toll on him and his family. But now Shepherd could not bear to leave the project; it seemed to require his constant presence. He did agree to send home his wife and children, and they departed at the summer's end. The mission board was adamant, however, and a new concern dominated their thoughts. Of Shepherd's character and native ability they had no doubts; but of his educational limitations they were well aware. Here was a rural reconstruction leader with not one iota of professional training in agriculture.

The China secretary had been frank and explicit in a letter to both Shepherds: "For the present, George's assets are his intimate knowledge of the communist ridden areas, his abounding energy, his ability to work with others and to get things done, and a certain amount of rural background in New Zealand with a large amount of practical common sense, added to the Christian spirit of devotion which makes all these things usable in the finest way." But this was still not enough for leadership in rural reconstruction; further training was necessary for his further success.[20] The secretary's prescription: a year of study at the Cornell School of Agriculture.

The argument, of course, was unanswerable. Shepherd was aware of his limitations. Yet the Robin Chen debacle had left Lichuan without a Chinese general secretary; Shepherd remained an indispensible man. Before he could think of leaving, he must arrange for his replacement by a man of experience and ability. Faced with such a need, Shepherd turned at once to one of his Congregational colleagues, Hugh W. Hubbard of Paotingfu.[21]

Hugh Hubbard was no stranger to rural reconstruction. Since 1923–24 he had experimented with rural literacy programs; and since 1927 he had moved toward broader village work. In the next two years he and his colleagues cooperated with James Yen, whose Tinghsien project lay within the Paotingfu mission field. In 1930 his mission loaned him for one year to the NCC to expand the council's literacy program; it was Hubbard who played a major role in organizing the Tinghsien Institutes of 1930 and 1933. In the same period the Butterfield proposals had induced him to experiment in the rural parish; since 1932 he had centered his work in the village of Fanchiachuang, near Paotingfu. It was Hubbard, as well, who had done much to make the NCCRSU something more than a paper scheme for rural reconstruction.[22]

Hubbard's credentials, then, were as good as those of any churchman. The problem was to negotiate his loan from the North China mission for one year. It must be added that financial difficulties had already forced the ABCFM to recall 18 of its North China missionaries during the past year. Any such loan would therefore be a substantial sacrifice.[23] The KCRSU approached Hugh Hubbard in mid-October. At the same time he received supporting pleas from Shepherd, from Chang Fu-liang, and from the KCRSU's Secretary, Eugene A. Turner of the Nanchang YMCA. Each one emphasized the urgency of the need and the uniqueness of the opportunity.

Shepherd knew that the request would sound peculiar in view of the North China mission's plight. But the rapid development of the government's own program in Kiangsi made it "imperative that the Church utilize the best men in China in its own approach at Lichuan." What Lichuan needed desperately was mature guidance. "To fail," Shepherd warned, "is to influence the trend of events, so far as the Church and the government are concerned, for many years to come." Chang Fu-liang was equally insistent: "There is too much at stake for both the country and the Church for anything less than a one-hundred percent success." [24]

Hubbard's reaction was cautiously favorable. It should be recalled that he had been highly dubious about the Kiangsi possibilities at the time of the original government invitation.[25] Yet he was attracted by the offer for three general reasons. First, now that the project had been launched, with support from the Chiangs, the NEC, and the Mass Education Movement, it constituted "a major challenge to the whole Christian movement in China to see it through properly." Second, his own Paotingfu work would profit in the long run from the experience and contacts Lichuan would offer. And third, "My own experience, my interests, and, I believe, my future lie in the direction of Christian rural reconstruction. This requires intensive experimentation such as I cannot undertake with my present duties in the Paoting field." [26]

Negotiations between the KCRSU and the Paotingfu mission dragged on during the autumn of 1934. In early December, however, the Boston office of the ABCFM added its pressure to the pleas from Nanchang. The China secretary cabled, "Regard Lichuan primary strategic importance whole Christian movement Urge loan Hubbard immediately." [27] At the same time, an emphatic summons to Shepherd from the mission board extricated him from the project. In January 1935 he was back in America. In the same month Hugh Hubbard arrived to take over the Lichuan operation.

## Development of the Project in 1935

George Shepherd was away from Kiangsi between December 1934 and October 1935. During the first few weeks of his absence, Eugene A. Turner of the Nanchang YMCA kept the enterprise moving as acting general secretary. At the end of January Hugh Hubbard became the project's director, new to the scene and still lacking a Chinese counterpart. Not until August 1935, in fact, did the KCRSU finally acquire the services of P. C. Hsu (Hsü Pao-ch'ien), dean of the Yenching University School of Religion, as the project's general secretary. Meanwhile, Hubbard was required to make at least two inspection trips back to his Paotingfu village base. Despite his earnest efforts, it seems clear that Lichuan was handicapped by Shepherd's absence.[28]

Under Hubbard's direction, the Lichuan staff now included 22 volunteers, eight of them college graduates. These workers lived on payments of $30 per month plus food, although a number received additional allowances from the institutions they represented. The major cooperating bodies, by April 1935, were Yenching (two staff members), the National Committee of the YMCA (one member), Nanking Theological Seminary (it planned to send graduate students for training), and the Mass Education Movement (a team of four came to Lichuan, three of them staying for two months to start education work). In addition, the Nanchang Hospital offered medical services; the NEC provided a $5,000 grant for rural industries; the Provincial Agricultural Institute gave trees and seeds; the Provincial Bureau of Education registered the schools as "Special Education" institutions eligible for monthly grants; and the hsien government aided in a social survey.[29]

Despite these facilities, reconstruction work proceeded slowly. The experimental center itself had not been organized until the fall of 1934. Its first effort was directed toward "village-unit-experimentation"; the aim was to rehabilitate several villages in the fourth district. With the help of the Tinghsien representatives, a "construction committee" was organized and an experimental "tutor-student system" was initiated. Staff workers were divided into two departments: research and experimentation, and training and extension. Yet, these techniques, which had proved so successful in the more prosperous Tinghsien area, brought meagre results at Lichuan. The backwardness of the region thwarted even the least complex schemes for rural improvement.[30] Indeed, two visiting Methodist ladies from Nanchang were appalled at the condition of the Lichuan peasant. Their report was graphic: "The people are deeply superstitious; they are against education; they know how to raise very, very few vegetables; most of them are ill with malaria, swollen feet, trachoma, and other disease; they know nothing of sanitation; they cannot knit; and they are simply in darkness as far as the light of Christ is concerned." Nonetheless, the visitors were delighted to find, as a small but important beginning, that "knitting is proving the key which is opening the door to the confidence of many of them!" [31]

Hugh Hubbard himself found the situation discouraging. In his report to the biennial meeting of the NCC in April 1935 he could tell of 10,000 trees planted, of vegetables introduced, of studies to assist village industry. But the project's three village schools, with an enrollment of 350, had a daily attendance of only 150. The chief problem in education, Hubbard said, was "to develope among the local people a sense of its value." Nor were the results significantly better in public health; these villagers had more than a usual lack of faith in Western medicine. Attendance at clinics was minimal; a goodly number, 600, had been vaccinated; but the project could report the care of only two cases of childbirth. (A later survey was to show that 84 per cent of all the children born in this district died of lockjaw within a week of birth.) [32] As for evangelism, Lichuan city had a small and weak Chinese Methodist church, but the project's chief village contained not one local Christian. The staff was attempting, Hubbard said, to approach religion through such character-building enterprises as Boy Scout troops. In other areas of activity, eight or ten women were attending a daily vocational class; posters, movies, and plays were being circulated through the area; and the project was cooperating with the hsien authorities on a survey of one ch'ü.[33]

Such an account made gloomy reading. It also pointed up the urgency of the project's needs. For Lichuan was caught in a national spotlight and must produce far better results. Hubbard knew this well. "Throughout the whole nation," he wrote, "Lichuan has come to represent the entire Christian movement." This attitude was partly due, he noted, "to publicity beyond our control"; but nonetheless, "It is a fact." It was therefore of the utmost importance, he warned, "that Lichuan be made worthy of this great responsibility." [34]

So far, it was clearly less than worthy. Its weaknesses, Hubbard said, were primarily the immaturity and inexperience of the staff. Though each of the NEC's Kiangsi welfare centers was equipped with four high-grade specialists, one in each major field, Lichuan still had no such assistance. The comparison between Christian and government project could escape no observer. Hubbard gave highest priority at this April meeting to the appointment of the still-missing Chinese general secretary. In addition, it was essential that Lichuan procure a first-class agriculturist, an education expert, and a trained specialist on cooperatives. His closing plea was emphatic: Lichuan's only hope was that *the leading Christian educational institutions of the nation back us up with the personnel we sorely need.* [35]

Hugh Hubbard's report to the biennial meeting produced new resolutions of support from the NCC. The conference's rural committee agreed on the strategic importance of the project; "Its success or failure," they said, "may greatly affect future relations" between the church and the government. The committee therefore voted that the leading Christian institutions be urged to assist directly by providing the needed leadership and that the Rural Life Department of the NCC give special attention and help to the project.[36] The council's Rural Life Department, however, had all but vanished with the departure of Chang Fu-liang for service with the NEC in Kiangsi. Although the value of Chang's government employment was emphasized at some length—"an especially favorable position to test many of the ideas for rural improvement which were proposed at the Jerusalem meeting"—his absence left the NCC reasonably impotent as a support for Lichuan.[37] Indeed, the NCC staff found their present plight a distinct "let-down from our advertised program in rural work." [38]

While Hugh Hubbard labored to keep the Kiangsi project alive, George Shepherd was preparing to attend a brief summer session of the Cornell School of Agriculture. To this extent, at least, the missionary followed his board's furlough prescription. Most of his time and energy were given, however, to extensive speaking throughout the country; he had too much to tell to sit still and study. In March his wife scored a major success: an offhand request that the Ford Motor Company contribute an ambulance to Lichuan was granted at once. "It came so easily, it has just about taken away our breath," she reported.[39] Acquisition of the ambulance now heightened the Shepherds' desire to leave for China at the earliest moment. And in July George Shepherd received a new stimulus in the form of a letter from Mme. Chiang Kai-shek urging his speedy return. Enclosed with her plea was an outline of the recently announced People's Economic Reconstruction Movement, which seemed to Shepherd very promising if carried through.[40] In one respect Shepherd's stay in America may have given a new dimension to his enthusiasm for the reform programs of the Nanking government: he learned of the intensity of anti-Kuomintang feeling in some American circles. This was the era of the pro-Communist magazine *China Today*. And as Shepherd surveyed the Chinese scene from across the Pacific, he was increasingly aware of the doubters and their views. "There is much to be hopeful over," he wrote, "but there are also many questionings. Some of the latter are in China, and a great many of them here. It is surprising how many of our intellectuals in America are opposed to Chiang Kai-shek and his program." [41] This was Shepherd's first glimpse of a problem that would come to vex him considerably in later years. By the end of the summer, the mission board found it could no longer restrain him. Meanwhile, the KCRSU's directors had voted to request his early return to Lichuan.[42] By autumn the Shepherds were back in Kiangsi.

In mid-October, the newly returned Shepherds joined with the directors of the KCRSU in a four-day retreat to take stock of their progress to date. The conference received a report from Lichuan's Chinese staff in which the objectives of the project were reviewed and restated. The primary purpose remained "the establishment of a Christian Rural Community by uniting kindred minds in a common effort and life, on the basis of a Christian self-sacrifice, love and service, combined with scientific methods." The program was based on four steps to be carried out in three years: research, experiment, training, and expansion. "The first year is educational in nature, utilizing research and experiment. The second is for training, and the third for extension" from the individual village to the entire hsien.[43]

One major problem confronted the conferees. This was an unexpected request from the generalissimo's close associate, the provincial governor, that the project assume political responsibility by naming its own candidate for *ch'ü chang* (district administrator). In terms of the original Kuling policy of "cooperative independence," Governor Hsiung Shih-hui's invitation was fraught with complications. So far, the KCRSU had kept itself aloof from political ties; the naming of a *ch'ü chang* would inevitably mean direct involvement in provincial politics. The project's Chinese staff had concluded, however, that "certain political contacts must be established and utilized with the spirit of social workers, where necessary." With some misgivings, the directors put themselves on record as "in favor of nominating a suitable person for the position of Chu Chang . . . for the 4th District of Lichuan Hsien." [44]

The directors' action on this matter had no immediate consequences. Indeed, by December, with no nominee yet in sight, Governor Hsiung became impatient. He called in Shepherd and bluntly accused the Christian forces of being afraid to tackle the corruption of politics and thereby to help assure that reconstruction be permanent. Though not a Christian, the governor met Shepherd on his own ground with consummate skill. He argued, Shepherd reported, that "Christ never turned his back on a human being suffering from an incurable or loathesome disease. He asked us to explain why Christians of our day are giving themselves to the nice pleasant tasks of social welfare and refusing to tackle the giants of evil and corruption." Shepherd was defenseless. "Of course we cannot explain," he wrote. "We know how ready we are to wash our hands of everything that looks like a political mess." [45]

This was not the missionary's first encounter with the insoluble problem of the church's role in politics; nor was it to be his last. The issue underlay his thinking about the Chinese Communists; as Nanking's leaders increasingly assumed social responsibility, it also infused his thoughts about the Kuomintang. How much political involvement did the social gospel require? How much political involvement would religious commitment permit? A perplexing dilemma; but Shepherd's answer to the critics he knew he must face was firm: "We have no apologies to offer any one. Our farmers might just as well have good government as bad government. So far as we are concerned, we prefer them to have it within a system that guarantees freedom of thought and worship, and the Three Principles of Dr. Sun Yat Sen, who lived and died a Christian, answer the needs of the people of China." Then, finally, with a touch of defiance, "If anyone wants to inquire further, tell him that we have no use for communism as it exists in China today." [46] The old ambivalence was resolving itself.

In mid-December the KCRSU bowed to the governor's request. The project's director of religious work was appointed to the position of *ch'ü chang*.[47] "The news that the Union has gone into politics," Shepherd wrote in January 1936, "is sure to cause a stir in certain circles . . . Our communist friends will be right up in the air and will be setting their dogs on our trail. Of course," he added, "those gentle little darlings never seize political power." George Shepherd's tone was hardening. And there was good reason, he felt, to be firm: "We are in the position of 'riding the tiger' in this business of Christian Rural Reconstruction. If we slide off now, what will become of us; and if we hold on, where will the tiger take us? We have decided to hold on." [48] Holding on meant, for the moment, yet deeper political involvement: in February 1936 Governor Hsiung called a conference of representatives of all the Kiangsi reconstruction units, government and church alike. A major recommendation of the conference was the establishment of a Provincial Rural Welfare Commission, with the governor as its chairman, to simplify and unify reconstruction work in Kiangsi.[49]

Meanwhile, political involvement on the district level meant intensive training in practical politics for the members of the Lichuan staff. All around them they found indications of deeply entrenched corruption. The district police force, for instance, was graft-ridden; but on eight dollars a month, as Shepherd commented, a man "must squeeze somebody in order to live." Shepherd found the artfulness of official corruption wondrous to behold: "Four thousand years of experience has taught them so many tricks that not all the books that have been written could describe them in detail." But Shepherd brought to crime-busting the same zestful optimism that generally characterized his responses; to him, unraveling the skein of rotten government was an exciting business. Nor was he surprised at the obstructive tactics of gentry and petty officials; "The Chinese farmer's greatest need is good government, and anyone who sets out to get it for him is asking for trouble." In his battle for good government, Shepherd did find higher officialdom hearteningly cooperative. One of the reformer's first discoveries was that "the district administration which we had taken over had no audited accounts." But the mere mention of this fact to the provincial government had allegedly set a lot of machinery in motion.[50]

Political questions were only a few of the problems facing George Shepherd on his return to Lichuan in the autumn of 1935. As early as May, staff members of the NCC had begun to show disquiet over another aspect of the Kiangsi project: Lichuan had been in operation for more than a year, and yet its directors had still made no provision for a religious program.[51] In September Ronald D. Rees reported to the council on his recent visit to Kiangsi. At a staff meeting early in the month he raised the question as to whether Lichuan should merely be one of several projects similar to those undertaken by the government, or whether it should instead attempt to build a solid rural parish.[52] A week later, Rees elaborated on his misgivings at a two-day staff retreat. He reported that the project suffered from two problems. In the first place, P. C. Hsu had encountered difficulties in producing the spirit of teamwork on the part of his staff that he had sought to develop as the captain of the team. A second and deeper ailment concerned Lichuan's ultimate objective. Was it to be turned over in 3 or 4 years to the government or rather "something to be integrated with the Church to build up the Church"? The project's administrators were evidently still unclear in their own minds.[53]

In the course of the NCC discussions it was noted that the July minutes of the KCRSU showed a large number of resignations; was this to be interpreted as further disquieting evidence of instability? Chester Miao (Miao Ch'iu-sheng), a participant, spoke to this point. He saw undue boosting of the project as a distinct liability at this juncture; too many young people were going to Lichuan for experience and training with different motives, and there existed no church unit to act as a stabilizing nucleus for these young workers. Until the NCC could find itself a dynamic rural secretary to take the place of Chang Fu-liang, all it could give to the project was ineffective moral support, for it was equipped with no expert counsel.[54]

One of the Chinese secretaries, T. C. Kuan (Kuan Ts'ui-chen), saw Lichuan posing different problems from the normal rural parish; as a region that had known no church previously, it required an entirely new approach. But as to what this new approach might be the NCC deliberations gave no indication. L. D. Cio (Chu Li-teh) re-emphasized, in conclusion, Lichuan's significance for the church: he had had real doubts as to the wisdom of attempting such a task in the first place, "but as the undertaking is on, we must carry it on to success and give it a most wholehearted support." The church was on trial in the public eye, and it must produce tangible results.[55]

## The Unsolved Tenure Problem

While Christians debated Lichuan's problems of political and religious responsibility, there remained one area in which Shepherd himself was increasingly conscious of failure. As early as May 1934 missionaries in the Kiangsi field had acknowledged that the greatest problem any reconstruction scheme had to face was that of land tenure. An annual letter from three Methodist missionaries in that year had pointed out that "under Communism, land was held for the common interest, and the need of most of China is just that."

These observers were encouraged by the fact that the government proposed to reduce the amount of land an individual might hold by "heavy graduated taxation of holdings above a small unit, thus removing the profit from large holdings and putting a premium on sales which when made are to be made not to individuals, but to cooperatives which will rent land to its members for personal use only." [56]

There is no evidence, however, that the government's program was ever put into effect in Kiangsi province; nor was it applied anywhere else outside of a model hsien or two and, for a brief period, in Chekiang province.[57] Indeed, by mid-1935 it was clear that the most important aspect of government policy in Kiangsi was, in fact, neglect of the land problem. George E. Taylor, a keen academic observer who visited the province at that time, warned that such neglect meant that the real causes of communism had not yet been touched. Taylor perceived an underlying assumption on the part of Nanking that "the way to defeat Communism is to strengthen, both politically and economically, those classes of the population that have most to fear from Communism . . . Strategically considered, therefore, the Government policy is directly opposite to that of the Communists, who sought to strengthen the poor against the rich." Taylor found that officials who, two years before, had been worried about the land problem were now totally indifferent to it. "In other words," he wrote, "by a policy of masterly inaction this thorn in the side has been removed; the *status quo ante* has been restored and everyone is happy, except perhaps the landless." To Taylor, such a situation was fraught with danger for an agricultural nation: "If the reconstructed national state does not provide for the thousands who cannot maintain life under present agrarian conditions, then the cause of Communism, though it may be hopeless, will hardly be dead." [58]

By no means a trained political analyst himself, George Shepherd seems nonetheless to have shared some of Taylor's misgivings. It will be recalled that land tenure had been discussed at one of the NCC meetings during the birth of the Lichuan project. A partial survey of the Lichuan area revealed that, prior to the Communist invasion, a quarter of the farmers owned 75 per cent of the land. Under Communist rule, these landlords had been driven out, their land redistributed. But they returned on the heels of the Nationalist army and recovered their land.[59] By 1937 Shepherd could only report, "We are constantly pushing for action on the pressing problem of land tenure." [60]

Quite clearly, action was not forthcoming. One common but specious excuse for inaction in this field was the alleged need for a comprehensive land survey—a cadastral survey—as a "prerequisite" to land reform. Such an aerial survey for Kiangsi alone, it was argued, would cost $11 million.[61] Yet surveys of this sort were in fact a prerequisite only to land tax reform, not to the reform of land tenure arrangements. For a more valid explanation of Nanking's failure to act one must look elsewhere: to the hardening lines of policy detected by George Taylor, to a fear of alienating gentry support, to an abhorrence of reforms that smacked of communism. In no province would land reform have been less difficult to effect than in Kiangsi, for the Red occupation had already caused the death of many landlords and the destruction of title deeds. Yet the will to reform was lacking. And beyond the reasons already suggested lay one additional factor of fundamental importance: an ebbing sense of urgency. As Taylor reported, Kiangsi officials had —two years before—been deeply concerned about the land problem; but by 1935 complacency had returned. What was the cause of such a shift? The answer lay, ironically, in the rising fortunes of the Kuomintang. The very success of the fifth anti-Communist campaign in the autumn of 1934 spelled failure for those who were convinced that Nanking's long-run survival would depend on a national reform of land tenure. As the Long March finally removed the Red Army from the mountains of East China that November, so it removed the one most pressing impetus to land redistribution in Kuomintang territory.

In early 1936, rural reconstruction in Kiangsi underwent its most severe test to· date. League of Nations advisers had been largely responsible for the government's decision to apply a comprehensive rehabilitation program to the recovered areas in 1934. In November and December of 1933 three foreign experts had visited the province and submitted recommendations that formed the basis of the NEC program. Now, in January 1936, one of these advisers, Dr. Andrija Stampar of Yugoslavia, revisited Kiangsi to evaluate the progress of reconstruction. Stampar's long and thorough "Report on Rural Welfare Activities in Kiangsi" was a milestone in the history of the rural reconstruction movement.[62]

The League of Nations adviser focused his attention at once on the heart of China's agrarian crisis: land tenure. However admirable the objectives of Kuomintang and private reformers alike, Stampar confirmed Taylor's opinion that none of the reformers had faced up to this problem. His criticism was particularly stinging in view of his own previous recommendations: "When, in company with two other foreign experts, I visited the province in 1933, we formed the opinion that the chief cause of unrest was the tenancy system." There were other causes as well, of course; but "if the problem of the landlord, and the problem of rural credit, could be solved, the position of the farmer would be immediately improved." What had happened in the ensuing years? "In 1933 . . . my colleagues and I presented a scheme for land reform. This the government has not carried out. In the areas recaptured from the Communists, the old order has been restored." In the remainder of his 1936 report Stampar made many suggestions for increasing the efficiency of welfare centers and rural reform projects. But his overall conclusion remained unshakable: whatever the accomplishments of welfare centers and experimental hsiens, "I am of the opinion that no radical improvement can be made in the position of the farmer without a land reform." [63]

Although Stampar's chief interest was the NEC enterprise, his report made two specific mentions of the Lichuan project: the first was the statement that its annual expenditure per head of population was the lofty sum of eleven dollars, considerably more than that in any other center; the second was a generous footnote concerning Lichuan's director. "The moving spirit in the work of this centre, Mr. Shepherd," Stampar wrote, "has in my opinion a very good understanding of the problems of Kiangsi." [64]

This heartening reference aside, the Stampar findings might well have proved discouraging to George Shepherd. He forwarded them to the mission board, however, with the statement that the report, "up to the time of his visit, is correct, and in my opinion, his criticisms of all our welfare centres in Kiangsi are just. Fu-liang and I travelled to many of them with him and admitted everything. We greatly appreciate his criticism and wise counsel. We must make our work less expensive, and enlarge our work areas still further." Shepherd noted two recent changes that would decrease the per capita expense and produce greater coordination with other projects. And he added a personal comment on Stampar's view of missions. "Christian leaders take note," he urged, "that Dr. A. Stampar is opposed to missions in China, after two and a half years experience in all the provinces." Why? ". . . very largely because missions have been training an intellectual group of men and women, most of whom have refused to become a part of an agricultural civilization and to work and sacrifice for the uplift of the farmers." [65] The views were those of the antimission Stampar; yet they sounded remarkably similar to the convictions of missionary Shepherd.

George Shepherd promised to take the Stampar criticism to heart, to strive "to enlist more of the intelligentsia and the products of our Christian colleges in this grand work of rural reconstruction." [66] Yet even while he wrote, forces were at work that would effectively detach him from further rural reconstruction in Kiangsi. In March 1936 Shepherd moved to Nanking, at the generalissimo's invitation, to serve as an adviser to the New Life Movement; thenceforth his connection with Lichuan was to become increasingly nominal. Later in the year, Chang Fu-liang, who was serving in the dual capacity of NEC Kiangsi director and KCRSU chairman, departed for a seven-month trip to Europe. Meanwhile, the entry of the Rockefeller Foundation into the field of rural reform had shifted the focus of American participation away from Lichuan and its Christian experimental district to North China and a substantially new approach.

### Lichuan: Its Fate and Significance

In 1939, a year and a half after the beginning of the Sino-Japanese War, the Lichuan experiment ended its first five years of operation. Despite the outbreak of hostilities, the project had been able to maintain most of its work and had added to its facilities an orphanage and refugee camp. Directed now by Kimber Den (Teng Hsu-k'un) of Nanchang, it continued to operate beyond the Japanese lines throughout the war.[67] Its wartime activities, however, were considerably narrowed by the national crisis; they lie beyond the scope of this study. A tentative appraisal of the project can be made on the basis of Lichuan's relatively "normal" years, from 1934 until the resignation of P. C. Hsu, the KCRSU general secretary, in June 1937.

In retrospect it can be said that the Lichuan experiment faced grave problems in the realms of site, personnel, and policy. The region chosen by the Christian reformers was, to begin with, more than challenging; in many ways it was forbidding. The backwardness and abject poverty of the people of southeastern Kiangsi made them "hostile, doubtful, passive, and non-cooperative" in the extreme.[68] Such local attitudes were compounded by the linguistic barrier which the curious regional dialect erected against outsiders.

These local conditions made for two important results. First, grimly spartan living conditions dissuaded trained university experts from joining the project. Despite George Shepherd's high expectations in early 1934, it is surprising how few qualified specialists responded to Lichuan's call. Shepherd himself complained bitterly in 1936 that "institutions like the College of Agriculture at Nanking University and the Medical Schools have been extremely slow in joining with us." [69] Indeed, one of the center's greatest problems was to find a Chinese doctor who was willing to work in such a depressed rural region. Shepherd met one candidate who said that "during his entire course in a Christian medical school nobody ever brought up the subject of what a Christian doctor might do for the great masses of people in need of better ways of living." [70] On the other hand, such rural experts as Dean Sie of Nanking University felt that Lichuan's planners erred in "thinking they can get good men to work at great sacrifice over long periods," because "in five years they will make only a small impression." [71]

A second result of Lichuan's backwardness was the inhibition placed on those experts who did join the project. As was noted earlier, the mass education team from Tinghsien found the community so poor in manpower and economic resources that at least two of James Yen's techniques, the construction committee and the tutor-student system, failed to operate with success. Tinghsien methods were too sophisticated for the suspicious and apathetic Kiangsi peasantry. In lieu of the expertise so urgently required, Lichuan had to be satisfied with recruits, many of whom had never been to college. Their inexperience and immaturity led inevitably to grave problems of morale. P. C. Hsu complained that for the first two years the spirit of cooperation was poorly developed in the young workers of the project. "Factions, prejudice, and personal differences among the workers" plagued the center. By 1937, however, Hsu reported that such problems had been almost entirely eliminated.[72]

Morale problems undoubtedly accounted, in part, for another of the project's personnel afflictions: its very high rate of turnover in staff. Aside from the external factors that resulted in the leadership succession of Shepherd, Hubbard, Hsu, and Den, younger workers came and went at a rapid rate. Shepherd wrote rather lightly of the matter: with the initial call for volunteers, he said, "They came tumbling in upon us in sweaters and slacks, bringing with them the atmosphere of the campus and the enthusiasm of youth. Some got tired of the work in the first three months; others fell in love and went off to establish homes in more suitable surroundings; a few have stayed with us through two years of bitterness and joy." [73] The rate of turnover was such, however, that the NCC emphasized in February 1937 Lichuan's urgent need for men who would stay in the work and build a permanent base.[74]

In the realm of policy undoubtedly the greatest continuing problem was the project's relationship to government, provincial and national. Although the planners' original intention was to avoid political connections, the staff discovered in its first two years that without government aid the work could not be carried far.[75] Attendance at the village schools, for instance, was meagre indeed in Lichuan's first two years of operation. Only with the transfer of the district administration to the project's leaders were they empowered to force school attendance.[76] Effective action could now be brought, as well, against corrupt officials. P.C. Hsu saw a Christian obligation to improve politics in the course of reconstructing rural life. Yet he admitted that "Whether the center will be master or slave of politics remains, of course, to be seen." [77] The political issue clearly contained an old dilemma: without political support, nothing basic could be accomplished; yet an alliance with the state could compromise the reformers by identifying them with the policies of the state. And in this case, of course, the state's aim seems to have been to maintain the economic status quo. Christians might have desired otherwise; but in the battle between proponents of revolution and defenders of the status quo in the Chinese countryside, the Lichuan reformers found themselves firmly placed in the ranks of the latter. From July 1936 Lichuan carefully integrated its reconstruction work with the Kiangsi government's threefold three-year plan of "educating, feeding, and protecting." [78] George Shepherd might write, "One fundamental difference between the missionaries of Lenin and the missionaries of Christ is that we come not to destroy but to fulfill, not to take life but to restore it in all its fullness"; [79] but the fact remained that what was being fulfilled and restored throughout Kiangsi was an economic situation that left the region a fertile field for future Leninist conversion.

Lichuan found its relationship with the state a problem, but it fared little better in its relationship with the church. In accepting the governor's invitation to political responsibility, the project's leaders seem to have shocked some churchmen.[80] By the autumn of 1936, however, the criticism was more far-reaching: Lichuan, some said, was hardly a Christian enterprise at all; it was not church-centered; it was merely a social welfare experiment. In June the NCC's worry on this count had begun to deepen.[81] L. D. Cio and T. C. Bau (Pao Che-ch'ing) of the staff visited the government and the church projects in Kiangsi. Though impressed with the NEC achievements, they were appalled at the Lichuan conditions: the backwardness and poverty of the region and the difficulty of the local dialect, which made all the workers—Chinese and Americans alike—foreigners in terms of the Kiangsi countryside. They were particularly disturbed that no religious program had yet been attempted, that P. C. Hsu and his colleagues were opposed to direct evangelism, and that the indirect approach (that is, regular devotions and diligent Christian service on the part of the workers) had resulted in no religious inquiries from the villagers. The NCC visitors were agreed that there was need for some religious program if the work was to be differentiated from that of the government. Meanwhile, they emphasized that Lichuan should not be considered in any sense a training ground for Christian rural work; nor should outsiders be encouraged to visit the project for the time being.[82] As a result of the report of Cio and Bau, the ad-interim committee requested a clarification of policy from the Lichuan authorities.[83]

In November the NCC's executive committee heard a report on "some of the problems of the Lichuan project, particularly whether the project is to be definitely Christian or merely a social project." [84] Two weeks later the council's staff seems to have sought further clarification through a conference with George Shepherd and Chang Fu-liang. Shepherd, now deeply involved in New Life Movement affairs in Nanking, was optimistic about the Kiangsi experiment; it had lived up to the expectations of the Chiangs, he said, and the time had come for the project to be fully church-centered. Chang Fu-liang demonstrated the KCRSU's ambivalence on the subject, however. "We must encourage," he said, "whatever groups are prepared to carry on our service work, and not insist that they follow any cut and dried program, whether they prefer the religious or the social motive and method as dominant." [85] A month later a second conference on Lichuan showed a continuing indecision as to the degree of Christian proselytizing that the project should undertake. It was agreed at this session that Lichuan's "unique contribution so far is the evidence that the church cares and that college men can work in such a project." Still, there were those who felt that "the more valuable contribution yet to be made is the introduction of the vital Christian element." [86]

By January 1937 this series of inconclusive conferences with Lichuan officials had produced only agreement that increased religious emphasis was needed and that further visits to Lichuan by the NCC would be advisable.[87] A month later Dr. Herman Liu (Liu Chan-en), president of the University of Shanghai, who had attended a KCRSU meeting on behalf of the NCC, urged that Lichuan's work be made less expensive and that its program "be worked out so as to make a distinctive Christian contribution," perhaps through the assistance of Nanking Theological Seminary.[88] It seems clear that Lichuan's Christian fathers were increasingly uneasy at what they had sired.

By the outbreak of the Sino-Japanese War, then, the Kiangsi project found itself criticized by churchmen for worldliness, by outsiders for ineffectiveness. There is some evidence, as well—George Shepherd to the contrary—that its most eminent patrons were less than happy with its results; at any rate, Generalissimo and Mme. Chiang discontinued their annual contribution in 1939.[89] Certainly, Mme. Chiang's high hopes for Christian rural reconstruction as a revitalizing force for church and nation had not been realized. What she had originally hoped Christians might accomplish in a dozen hsien the reformers had been barely able to manage in a single district. At the root of the failure was the formidable unpreparedness of the church for the role it had been called upon to play. For leadership in comprehensive rural reconstruction, it was clear that China must look elsewhere.

# Chapter Six
# From Models to Training Programs: The Rockefeller Effort

## The Need for a New Approach

Writing in April 1937, a Chinese social scientist gloomily surveyed the plethora of rural reconstruction efforts that had marked the decade of the Nanking government. "What, after all these strivings, has been accomplished?" he asked. "When the total needs of China are considered, all these efforts are small indeed." [1]

The truth was that ten years of models and pilot projects had produced little but a series of fragmentary and disjointed indications of good intentions. Indeed, one major problem of reconstruction in China was the lack of coordination among the scores of public and private agencies; this condition persisted despite periodic institutes and conferences on the subject.[2] The national government's own network of programs gives clear evidence of the defect. Since 1928 a National Construction Commission had tried to spread irrigation through electric power. A National Famine Relief Commission of the executive yuan had existed since 1929. In 1931 a National Flood Relief Commission was established. But with the preparation for the National Economic Council, this commission was dissolved. The NEC itself, formally inaugurated in November 1933, took over projects from the CIFRC as well as the

National Flood Relief Commission; but its major effort was directed toward Kiangsi. Meanwhile, the Ministry of Industries had operated its own National Bureau of Agricultural Research since April 1931. The executive yuan had established a Rural Rehabilitation Committee for planning and promotion in May 1933; with the reorganization of the yuan in early 1936, this committee became a Citizens' Economic Planning Council. In addition, the Ministries of Industries and Interior had departments and organs that were active in the rural reconstruction field. Finally, the legislative yuan was responsible for a series of laws regarding land ownership, cooperative societies, and other rural reforms between 1929 and 1934. With so many agencies overlapping in responsibility and competing for less than 3 per cent of the national budget, it was obvious that the net results in terms of achievement would be meagre.[3] At the same time, the often grandiose bureaucratic blueprints which such agencies produced bore little relation to China's striking deficiency in basic services—communications, credit facilities, and the like.

Lack of coordination was not the only problem. China's reformers were faced with a formidable dearth of effective manpower. As the economist Franklin Ho (Ho Lien) wrote in 1936, "Most of the work in China's rural economic reconstruction is being carried out by inadequately trained personnel." Even the foreign experts who came to China were less useful than one might have hoped. They stayed too short a time, Ho said, and they emphasized carrying out particular projects rather than training. Indeed, too often they served "no other purpose than the satisfaction of having added another paper plan to the government archives." [4]

A final problem in these lean depression years was the lack of adequate finance. In 1931–32, only 0.2 per cent of the national budget went for rural rehabilitation; in 1933–34 the figure was 0.5 per cent; in 1934–35, with the activities of the NEC, it rose to 3.9 per cent; and in 1935–36 to 3.7 per cent. To be sure, the provincial picture was more encouraging: roughly 16 per cent of the expenditures in the provinces went for the rural sector. But, as Franklin Ho pointed out, much of this money was derived from local surcharges, which squeezed the peasant even harder.[5]

Meanwhile, throughout China little or nothing was being done to relate three vital areas to one another: the college classroom, the village, and the local yamen. With few exceptions, colleges were not equipped to coordinate their teaching with large-scale field work in the intensely backward countryside. At the same time, such projects as Lichuan and Tinghsien, which had no direct and continuing ties with institutions of higher education, were unable to benefit from academic expertise. Finally, both the urban student and the untrained field worker found their hands tied by local political officials who had little sympathy for reconstruction schemes that might alienate the landowners.

How much could Nanking's College of Agriculture do on its own toward improving the plight of China's 300 million farmers? How much could a Lichuan do? Indeed, how much could a Tinghsien do? The dimensions of the problem were so vast as to require a combination of funds, specialists, students, village laboratories, and government sympathy such as no one of these institutions—or the several hundred other agencies of rural reconstruction—could hope to provide. What was needed was a new kind of program which would build upon the base that had been constructed through the long and tireless efforts of Chinese and foreigners.

The most obvious candidate for such a large-scale creative role was the Chinese government itself. Yet by the mid-1930's the Nanking government had lost its zeal for comprehensive rural reconstruction. George Taylor's observations showed this to be true in the one province where the Kuomintang had the greatest incentive to attempt fundamental changes. The Japanese and Communist menace kept revenues channeled into purely military enterprises throughout the decade. It should be noted again that the Communist Long March to the northwest removed an earlier stimulus to thoroughgoing reform. And the studies of Douglas Paauw have demonstrated that the neglect of the rural crisis stemmed as well from fiscal policies to which the regime remained deeply committed.[6]

Chinese reformers had to look elsewhere for a rural reconstruction effort that would be more than just another model hsien, an experimental parish, or an agricultural extension service. They had to look elsewhere for an agency that would furnish not only the incentives but the funds to build an inter-institutional program for the remaking of rural China—a program that might ultimately provide in large enough numbers the trained student-cadres required for such a formidable objective.

## S. M. Gunn's Investigations

In May of 1933, William R. Johnson of Nanchang had learned of the presence in Shanghai of a Rockefeller Foundation vice-president who was alleged to have a vast sum of money available for the purposes of rural reconstruction. Despite intensive efforts, however, Johnson was unable to interest this foundation official in his plans for a Christian rural training program in Kiangsi under the patronage of Mme. Chiang.[7] Selskar M. Gunn was already embarked on a search for a new kind of reconstruction program that might utilize the best of currently existing Chinese institutions. Simultaneous wth the second Tinghsien Institute and the genesis of the Lichuan experiment, an alternative Sino-American effort was under way.

S. M. Gunn had first passed through China in the fateful summer of 1931 on his way home from Paris to New York.[8] Since 1917 he had been serving with the International Health Board of the foundation in Europe; since 1927 he had held the title of vice-president; and in 1930 he was also named associate director for the social sciences in Europe. Gunn's initial stay in China was brief; it lasted seven weeks, from June 9 to July 30, 1931. During those weeks, however, he visited more than 40 academic institutions, hospitals, and government bureaus from Canton to Mukden; and he had interviews with over 130 leading Chinese and foreign officials, advisers, doctors, educators, and businessmen.[9] As a public health expert, Gunn was particularly interested in the medical and scientific work being undertaken by various groups. But at the urging of Edmund E. Day, director of the foundation's social sciences division, he also observed James Yen's demonstration center at Tinghsien (now a focal point in the budding rural reconstruction effort), Yenching University's program in rural sociology, and Nankai University's program in rural economics and political science.[10]

These visits and interviews had a decisive impact on S. M. Gunn. In a letter to foundation president Max Mason, he termed his China trip "unquestionably one of the most interesting experiences of my life." Mason, he predicted, would be "intrigued and somewhat staggered by the complexity of China and her problems." But the complexity itself provided a vast opportunity and responsibility for American philanthropy: "I feel very certain that the Foundation cannot neglect this tremendously important part of the World." The paramount need was for the development of "the machinery which will keep our organization in contact with the constantly changing conditions existing in China." The overriding fact of the situation was that "China has become plastic after centuries of rigid conventionalism." [11] This concept of China's "plasticity" seems to have deeply affected the officers of the foundation. The term was to recur in their references to that nation throughout the decade, and it was this factor above all others that eventually led the trustees to approve a new Rockefeller program for China.

Rockefeller involvement in China was, of course, no recent phenomenon. As noted earlier, the foundation had spent a total of US$37 million in China since 1913, the highest figure for any foreign recipient.[12] Almost all this money had gone toward the advancement of medical science in China through the Peking Union Medical College (PUMC) and funds variously distributed by the China Medical Board, Inc. One small but significant exception was the sponsorship of a Cornell-Nanking University project since the mid-1920's for the improvement of Chinese agriculture; this project eventually involved eleven cooperating experiment stations.[13] This Rockefeller infusion made Nanking University central to the hopes of such rural reformers as George Shepherd, Hugh Hubbard, and Chang Fu-liang.

However, medicine, public health, and agricultural improvement were only discrete and uncoordinated elements in a program of national development. And it was of the need for something broader and deeper, firmly rooted in Chinese institutions, that Selskar Gunn became convinced in the wake of his first visit to China. His informal report to President Mason of September 8, 1931, was a long and frank appraisal of the strengths and weaknesses, the promise and inadequacies, of the institutions he had visited throughout China. No sentimental predilection for American-sponsored colleges marred his cool objectivity. Indeed, with a few notable exceptions, he was dubious about the value of further foundation investment in mission institutions and saw the national universities as the institutions of the future—although they were currently in a phase of considerable instability.[14] He was glad to discover at Nanking that in the continuing atmosphere of anti-imperialism, the foundation was "not included in the Missionary Group." [15]

Gunn turned an equally skeptical eye, however, on the government itself. It was chronically unstable; it actually collected revenues from only three of the 20-odd provinces over which it proclaimed sovereignty; and 90 per cent of its funds seemed to go to the military. "Stories of prodigious graft are rife," he wrote, "and probably there is much truth in the rumors." He was amazed at the amateur approach of the Nanking regime: "I had the feeling it was more like a group of youngsters running a high school society rather than the affairs of a country of 450,000,000 people." [16]

The visitor was well aware of his own limitations as a seven-week expert on the Chinese situation. He commented wryly that everywhere he went "both Chinese and foreigners stated that China was too complicated to warrant one's having an opinion. Having made such a statement the individuals then proceeded to give most decided opinions on all questions." [17] Gunn's own opinions were tentative and guarded; he would require a return to China and months of further investigation before they could be otherwise. But within the "plasticity" of the scene, two major facts seemed to stand out: first, that "China has decided to use and adopt, with probable modifications, much of Western civilization"; and second, that such able leading figures in the Nanking government as T. V. Soong and C. T. Wang showed great cordiality toward the foundation.[18] These two facts were basic to the foundation's opportunity. At the same time, however, Gunn was aware of countervailing forces as well: not only the already noted shortcomings of the government, but also the fact that simultaneously "Western civilization is under fire in China" and "many intellectuals, often trained in the United States or Europe, are among its sharpest critics." [19] Between the Westernizing tendencies of friendly government officials and the viewpoint of the intellectuals lay an ominous gap.

Such a gap seemed to be uppermost in S. M. Gunn's mind throughout his discussion of individual colleges and universities, whether mission-supported or Chinese. In listing their assets and liabilities he was groping toward some channel by which Western techniques could be made more immediately relevant to China's pressing problems. He took full note, for instance, of the deficiencies of Chinese students returned from abroad: too often their research plans were overly based on foreign theories and methods not applicable to China.[20] And he was likewise dubious of the value of the overly detached Chinese Economic Society and the Academia Sinica.

In the course of Gunn's travels, certain institutions did seem to be relating themselves to the national need—among them, the Agriculture College of Nanking University and Nankai's Institute of Economics. But it remained for Tinghsien to fire his enthusiasm as nothing else he saw in China. As with others before and after him, it was James Yen who caught his imagination. "It was one of the most inspiring accounts of any activity that I have heard," he wrote. "This movement is one worth watching with the greatest possible care. It may conceivably bring the answer to many of the problems in China in the course of the years to come." Here was a place where higher education finally came to grips with the heart of China's needs; here was a place where Ph.D.'s "actually ended up by being students of the peasants rather than their leaders." [21]

To S. M. Gunn, Tinghsien's guiding spirit loomed as "truly a remarkable man. He combines idealism with great wisdom in judgment and the ability to place himself practically in the attitude and mind of a peasant." To be sure, Yen had his detractors: "No one seems to doubt his sincerity, but a number of people believe that his program is too idealistic and doomed to failure. In China idealism is rare." Gunn was nonetheless steadfast in his appraisal: "My own guess is that Yen and his group are going to be successful." As an afterthought he added the comment that Yen's program had much in common with the one suggested by Andrija Stampar for Yugoslavia.[22] Two years later it was Stampar who was to suggest a similar program for Kiangsi.

In the concluding paragraphs of his 1931 report, S. M. Gunn unwittingly wrote his own ticket for a return trip to China. The Rockefeller Foundation's present approach to that country seemed to him inadequate in view of China's importance. He was convinced, on the basis of his findings, that the foundation must pay more attention to the Far East. The prerequisite, he said, was "a broad gauge man" on the scene—perhaps in Shanghai, where he

would "not be too closely tied up with the Nanking government"—
a man "with a fine personality who would keep in touch with important Chinese and foreigners engaged in all kinds of activities." [23]

Max Mason wholeheartedly agreed; and the perfect candidate,
he judged, was S. M. Gunn himself. By the spring of 1932 Mason
had secured the approval of the trustees. It took additional months
to lay the groundwork for the return trip. But back to China went
Gunn in the autumn of 1932, this time as the foundation's special
representative, commissioned now to plan the structure of a new
program for consideration by the Rockefeller officers. In this
assignment he had the solid support of Mason, for the 1931 report
had greatly stirred the president's imagination. As Gunn later reminded Mason, "Your letter of May 2, 1932, in which you discussed the question of my going to China stated that you had long
felt that a major weakness in the Foundation's organization, or
rather, in the functioning of its organization, was a tendency to become static, settling down to rather long continued programs."
What the president wanted was more fluidity of purpose, a willingness to devise a new program "of unquestioned value, whether that
program is one that falls into the previous work of the Foundation
or not." [24]

Selskar Gunn's arrival in China in October 1932 occurred at a
turning point in Kuomintang fortunes. The tragic nadir of
1931–32 was about to give way to a season of hope. The spring of
1933 brought not only the Tangku Truce, but the RFC loan and
the second Tinghsien Institute as well. As before, Gunn sought the
advice of hundreds of leaders; but this time he made a special effort
to study the many Chinese and foreign projects in the field of rural
reconstruction. He took note of the marked lack of coordination
among agencies at work in the rural sphere. He learned of the extraordinary dearth of leaders trained for village work. He listened,
noncommittally, to the proposals of missionaries like W. R. Johnson, who had begun to focus on Chinese rural needs in 1932–33.
He perceived that demonstration projects were largely in the hands
of men of boundless good will but very little specialized training.
Even such pioneers in rural reconstruction as James Yen, Liang
Sou-ming, and Chang Fu-liang were men of strikingly limited academic expertise: Yen was briefly trained as a political scientist,
Liang as a professor of Indian philosophy, and Chang as an expert

in forestry. Their work, however admirable and important, lacked both the facilities and the prestige of the university. Meanwhile, the universities and colleges remained a world apart from the villages and woefully deficient in field-work facilities.[25] Selskar Gunn's 15 months of observation and planning resulted in a 97-page report to the president and trustees of the foundation in late January 1934. A month later he returned to America to argue in support of his far-reaching proposals.

### *"China and the Rockefeller Foundation"*

The Gunn report of January 23, 1934, entitled "China and the Rockefeller Foundation," is a document of major significance for an understanding of American influence on the development of Kuomintang China. Based on the state of the nation in 1933, it constitutes an evaluation both of China's modernizing process at the mid-point of the Nanking decade and American efforts to assist that process. It also constitutes a prescription for future action. In keeping with the foundation's chief interest, Gunn concentrated his attention on institutions of higher learning. By so doing, however, he was also concentrating on the major channels of Western influence.

Gunn's premises, in simplest terms, were a strengthened version of his earlier report to Max Mason: that China's plastic condition provided an opportunity unmatched elsewhere in the world for constructive assistance by the foundation; that the foundation's previous activities in China were no longer adequate to the times; and that it should therefore embark upon a radically reoriented program better suited to the pressing needs of the Chinese people.

Throughout his discussion of institutions and programs, Gunn seemed to be asking three persistent questions. First, how directly did these offerings relate to the welfare of the Chinese citizen in general, the villager in particular? Second, how well equipped were they to weather the forces of Chinese nationalism? And third, how closely did they approach Western standards of academic excellence? Inevitably, some that met the first and second test were deficient in the third; and others that maintained lofty standards seemed too little rooted in China's rural soil. The latter judgment

Gunn applied to the Rockefeller enterprise itself, and to its long efforts in the field of medical science. "While the Foundation has undoubtedly accomplished a good deal in China along lines which at the time appeared to be significant," he wrote, "I am thoroughly sincere in my belief that that program is no longer in touch with the times or the best we could find." [26] Of PUMC he was forced to conclude that "important as it is in its own sphere, [it] has had a very limited effect nationally." [27]

Gunn began his report to the trustees by disposing of one potential roadblock to foundation approval: the chronically unsettled condition of China. He indicated no illusions about the effectiveness of the Kuomintang regime. But, "If one waits for stable government and unification of the country, one might wait until a time when the Foundation would no longer be in existence." Indeed, the complications of the Chinese political scene seemed to him "added reasons why our collaboration is desirable at this time. It is not stretching the imagination to state that the Foundation may play an important role in helping to stabilize, at least, certain activities." Gunn was quick to acknowledge that no one could guarantee the course of events, and that unforeseen circumstances might make foundation cooperation difficult, if not impossible. But he remained insistent that political uncertainty per se was not a valid objection: "I do not consider . . . that we would show statesmanlike qualities if we postpone the development of a new program and wait for a Utopian condition which none of us will live to see." In short, he was convinced that the foundation was "singularly well adapted, as demonstrated by its history of accomplishment, to take a significant part in helping China in its struggle for stability and progress." [28]

Having dealt with the political context, Gunn next turned his attention to the country's two sets of major universities, the mission and national institutions. Here again, his initial impressions of 1931 had been strengthened. Too many of the mission universities were mediocre by American standards, in fact not really "universities" at all; too much of their income came from exclusively Western sources; and the depression had produced revenue cuts which further limited their offering. "Without prejudice," he wrote, "I think it can be fairly stated that the majority of the mission colleges have reached a point where their significance in China is definitely on the wane." As a result, "I am definitely of the opinion that the future emphasis of the Foundation in China in higher education should be in connection with Chinese institutions. These are the institutions of the future." And the national universities, he noted, had made great strides toward stability since his previous visit. Gunn added a proviso, however, which formed the basis for continued foundation assistance to certain phases of mission-sponsored higher education. Though it would be useless for the mission colleges to compete with the national and provincial universities, he felt that some of these colleges "should be continued indefinitely, but only on the basis that they be small, that their programs be limited, that they excel in such programs, and that they demonstrate their importance to the country to the extent of interesting the Chinese authorities and public to contribute toward their maintenance." [29]

The discussion of alternative channels of assistance now took Gunn to the heart of the old Rockefeller China program: the fields of medicine and public health, into which the foundation had poured some US$37 million since 1914 (US$33 million of it to PUMC). For this program's past he posed a question, and for its future a sober injunction. Gunn was a public health man himself; and PUMC was the pride of American humanitarianism in East Asia. Nonetheless, he felt impelled to ask if the results achieved were really commensurate with the effort over the past twenty years. His answer: "Frankness forces me to state that I cannot feel satisfied that the huge contributions to the PUMC have been warranted in terms of accomplishment in China." Furthermore, in terms of the nation's needs, it was equally clear that the foundation's contribution to China's public health had not been great.[30]

Such a judgment could not but be disillusioning to the foundation's trustees. Yet it had to be made, if Gunn was to persuade them to move from complacent satisfaction to a renewed and redirected effort. His criticism of the old program, then, was coupled with a suggestion for the reorientation of medical and public health assistance. What was needed was, first, "a contribution to a program of National Reconstruction of which a Unified Medical Policy should be a part"; and second, some method to assure "the continued value and significance of the large investment already made." In other words, "The time is past when medicine and its applications in public health should be considered separate entities." The requirement, instead, was a fully integrated approach to the manifold problems of China, an integrated approach in which medical science would play its proper role. And here for the first time Gunn gave a clear glimpse of the new type of program toward which his report was gradually moving, in the footsteps of James Yen and the American rural reformers: "A rather unique opportunity presents itself to us, to integrate activities of this kind with other branches of human endeavor, looking toward a general raising of the economic and social level of the masses." [31]

The Gunn report now surveyed the general condition of the natural sciences, the social sciences, and the applied sciences in the institutions of Kuomintang China. These were fields in which the foundation had made a series of small grants in past years. In the natural sciences, the picture was "distinctly discouraging . . . One is depressed with the low quality of teaching and research in the natural sciences in all institutions in China." Despite kind words for Yenching, Lingnan, and Nanking Universities, Gunn suggested a general reallocation of the foundation's customary grants in this field with the aim of a slow decrease in aid to mission colleges and an increase in aid to government universities.[32] As for the second division of learning, "If the natural sciences in China are weak, it must be acknowledged that the social sciences are weaker." Here again, he singled out three institutions for special praise in an otherwise dismal picture—Nankai in economics, Yenching in sociology and political science, and Nanking in agricultural economics.[33] It was in the applied sciences that Gunn saw a special opportunity for a reoriented program of foundation aid. In the past, the Rockefeller effort had been largely in the natural sciences and as part of the premedical program. But the time had now come, he felt, for emphasis, above all, on the applied sciences in the field of agriculture. Here it was Nanking University, again, that was leading the way. Fully 90 per cent of the 300 graduates of its College of Agriculture were actively engaged in agricultural work. This in itself was a marked deviation from the normal pattern in other universities where the "vast majority of the graduates, for various reasons, have not followed their professions on graduation." Of the other mission universities, only Lingnan seemed to have a promising agricultural program; no government university was strong in this field, but National Central, Chekiang, and Wuhan had made the most encouraging starts.[34]

Inadequate career use of college training was a problem in the applied sciences, but it seemed to Gunn an even more ominous drawback in the foundation's fellowship program for study overseas. "Observation leads to the belief that a great deal of money has been wasted in this activity." On their return to China, cut loose from their professors abroad, the majority of fellowship holders "settle down to a life of teaching which too often becomes merely a routine business. Their imagination, if they had any, seems to have been destroyed." Gunn's indictment of the returned-student-become-professor was severe: "There is altogether too much importance placed on higher degrees obtained in foreign countries, and the kudos of being a Doctor of Philosophy of an American or European university leads to people being put in positions which they are incapable of filling adequately, and the old scholar tradition of China elevates them to a position of conceit entirely unwarranted on the basis of their mental equipment."[35]

What was wrong—and how to correct it? For Gunn the answer was clear: drastically reduce the fellowships for study abroad, develop advanced training centers in China, and concentrate instead on local fellowships. Study abroad too often made cultural mongrels of the fellowship recipients; the institutional structure for the proper placement of college graduates was difficult enough—and foreign study only tended to intensify the institutional defects. Gunn pointed out that the training that returned students obtained abroad was academic and Western in character. He reported the widespread view that "the majority of Chinese fellows, on their return, are found to be unsuited to fit into the local situation. They have lost a good deal of their Chinese point of view and background and have picked up something of Western life but insufficient to make them really Western in their outlook. Many are disgruntled," he added, "and become the leaders of radical movements."[36]

Chinese society, then, had not yet developed the institutional mechanism to make effective use either of its best trained local products or of the scores of returned students. And this fact related directly to the problem of foreign experts, a subject to which Gunn next turned his attention. He noted, first, the long tradition of visiting experts—"Government offices are full of reports made by all kinds of experts, from highly competent to very mediocre." Such reports had prompted the formation of the NEC; but of the council's future Gunn was none too sanguine. As far as he could see, experts came and went, and there was little to show for their efforts; once again, the institutional structure for proper utilization of their expertise was defective. Gunn's own opinion was that "the experts who can really make a contribution are those who come to China not merely for the purpose of making a study and report but who stay for a period of at least three to five years and participate actively in the implementing of their report and carrying out of technical work."

Once again, the Rockefeller representative was well on the way to writing his own return ticket to China—this time for a longer tour of duty. Gunn's final comment on the role of foreign experts dramatized the predicament of would-be reformers among the Chinese themselves. Many Chinese, he said, were equipped to give an expert opinion on China's problems. "Too frequently, unfortunately," he wrote, "they have lacked either the courage to say what they thought or the power to put through their recommendations. Consequently, it is often the Chinese expert who is anxious to have a foreigner come to China who will officially recommend what the Chinese already have in mind." [37]

Having delivered his comments on the problem of visiting experts, S. M. Gunn was now finished with preliminaries. Section X of his 1934 report was entitled "National Reconstruction (With Special Reference to Rural Problems)."

It was here that he laid the groundwork for a series of far-reaching proposals. His dissatisfaction with the foundation's current program had been detailed with care. What was needed now was an equally specific case for an alternative. If the foundation's old modes of activity were so patently ineffective or irrelevant, what precisely *could* be done in the hopelessly complex morass of Kuomintang China? Gunn came right to the point: "If there is one thing on which all intelligent persons and all warring political interests are agreed, it is the need of a program which will raise the educational, social, and economic standards of the Chinese rural population. All over the country one hears of plans for national or provincial reconstruction and with particular reference to the rural problems. This is natural as it is estimated that over 85 percent of the population is rural. The opportunities for the Foundation's cooperation in China lie in many directions but I urgently insist that a considerable part of any future aid which we may give be devoted toward activities the benefits of which will be felt by the rural population." [38]

Here, then, two and a half years later, was the clear result of a seed first planted by James Yen and others during Gunn's visit to China in the summer of 1931. Here, too, was a logical outgrowth of Gunn's preliminary report to Max Mason. But the intervening months had given him more than simply a heightened enthusiasm for the Tinghsien approach. Gunn had also visited—as did William R. Johnson in the summer of 1933—other major reconstruction efforts as well: at Tsouping in Shantung, at Chingho in Hupeh, at Wusih in Kiangsu, and at Hsuchow in Anhwei. And he had returned with several firm impressions about the inadequacies of the rural reconstruction movement.

In the first place, he was troubled by the total lack of cooperation between workers engaged in these various regions—a situation, he noted, that had recently resulted in the creation of a nonofficial clearing-house, the Rural Reconstruction Institute. Second, he was struck by the appalling shortage of trained personnel for rural work. "In general," he wrote, "it is fair to say that the educational institutions in China have signally failed to train any serious number of people for work in the many fields involved in a rural reconstruction program." Third, even in those few places where such education was available, it "has been given in theory only. The outstanding problem is the lack of personnel trained along practical lines." And it was in this third area that Gunn perceived an outstanding opportunity for Rockefeller cooperation. It seemed to him axiomatic that effective training for rural service could not be provided solely within educational institutions but rather must be combined with practical field experience. For an example, he once again returned to a case close to the hearts of the trustees: "It is doubtful if the stereotyped medical education now being given at Peking Union Medical College is really meeting the medical and public health needs of China." [39] Gunn summed up his general argument with an almost impassioned plea. "Is it necessary," he asked, "to further stress the importance of activities which have as their object the welfare of the rural population in China? If anything is fundamental it is the raising of the level of all aspects of the life of the country people. It therefore seems entirely reasonable that the Foundation should take an active part in this program." [40]

Perhaps so; but what specifically did he have in mind? Selskar Gunn's actual proposals took the form of a "Program for North China," described in Section XI of his report to the trustees. In brief, he proposed that the foundation coordinate and underwrite the activities of six institutions that had already shown initiative, imagination, and durability in the field of rural reconstruction; and that in so doing the foundation move to fill the gaps between piecemeal and integrated reconstruction and between academic training and field-work experience.

Of the six cooperating institutions, five were familiar to the trustees from Gunn's survey of the China scene, and the sixth had already been a Rockefeller beneficiary. First came Yenching's Institute of Rural Administration: "Its function is to train men and women for rural service in China . . . the result of a rather remarkable evolution in the minds of those who are responsible for Yenching University." Next was James Yen's Mass Education Association center at Tinghsien: its role in the program was to serve as the field laboratory for teachers and students of the new Yenching Institute. The third component was Nankai's Institute of Economics: "The direction of the Institute is keen to place at the disposal of the Tinghsien group the facilities of the Institute. This makes the talented men of Nankai immediately available to carry on thorough-going studies of the major economic and political problems of Tinghsien." Fourth was the College of Agriculture of the University of Nanking: given the lack of an adequate agricultural college in North China, this University, in Central China, would make available its experimental farms in the north and cooperate with Tinghsien. The fifth component was the Department of Preventive Medicine of PUMC—a department already cooperating in Yenching's demonstration area at Chingho. The final component would be the North China Industrial Institute, an outgrowth of the old North China Industrial Service Union, organized initially by missionaries under the NCC and now utilizing the faculties of Yenching, Nankai, and Cheeloo Universities in the field of village industrial development.[41]

Gunn's proposals constituted a carefully designed plan to utilize the best institutions available for a coordinated attack on the problems of the countryside in North China. The choice of region was dictated by the location of the institutions. The program's administration would require a relatively autonomous three-man team of foundation representatives, preferably in Shanghai. And the cost would amount to approximately US$300,000 per year, with US$50,000 allocated to fellowships (almost entirely local rather than overseas), US$35,000 to a research and development aid fund, and the remaining US$215,000 to the major reconstruction projects.[42]

Selskar Gunn summed up his recommendations for the trustees in compelling terms: "We have, therefore, a program for both training and research in rural work which involves (1) four of the leading educational institutions of the North (to which the Foundation already has made large appropriations—Yenching, Nankai, Cheeloo, and the Peking Union Medical College), (2) the foremost rural experiment county in China (Tinghsien), (3) a new organization particularly designed to handle the weighty problems of village and home industries, and (4) the best agricultural college in China (Nanking University). It brings into intimate relationship a number of the best Chinese and Westerners who are technically well-equipped, and who have the greatest leadership and inspiration in the work which is being done. This is a first-class opportunity and I strongly recommend that the proposals, which are presented separately for the Institutions involved, be given favorable consideration."[43]

In March of 1934 S. M. Gunn presented his report to the trustees of the Rockefeller Foundation. At that session the 97-page document was tentatively adopted but referred for further study to the Committee on Appraisal and Plan. This group was made up of Raymond B. Fosdick (destined to succeed Max Mason as president in 1936), President James Rowland Angell of Yale, and New York financier Walter W. Stewart. At the December 11 meeting of the trustees, it submitted its own report. There could be little question, the committee felt, "that Mr. Gunn's program represents a realistic approach to present difficulties in China." China was evidently "bound by few hampering traditions, and the plastic condition of her life and institutions at the present moment is an inviting challenge to a positive kind of service." The challenge was particularly appealing because "There is a sense in which China might become a vast laboratory in the social sciences, with implications that would be international in scope." On the positive side of the ledger, it was clear that the Gunn program would help to "conserve and revivify the work" of PUMC by tying it "more intimately to the life of China." [44]

But the committee nonetheless harbored certain reservations. It viewed the suggested annual expenditure of US$300,000 as too modest; "a plan aimed at raising the educational, social, and economic standards of rural China" was clearly no small undertaking, and the foundation must face this fact realistically. The program's length was also a matter for consideration: "If we embark, we embark for the voyage, and we must contemplate a trip of considerable duration if any significant contribution is really to be made." [45]

The committee had other doubts. It was worried about the advisability of operating two programs, one in Peiping and one in Shanghai; also, the relation of the foundation's International Health Drive to the program: "Are we to have two techniques in public health—one for the rest of the world and one for China?" A final consideration was the overall allocation of funds: China was already the foundation's largest beneficiary abroad. Was this further support for Chinese institutions justifiable? "Is the welfare of mankind best served by enlarging our investment in China? Is China the outstanding strategic point in which we ought to push our attack? Is there no other sector of the world where we can hope to obtain as large a return in human happiness and welfare as we can in China?" [46] The questions briefly touched the core of America's curiously persistent humanitarian concern for the Chinese above all others.

Yet the reservations, the doubts, and the questions were not enough to dissuade the trustees from enthusiastic endorsement of the Gunn recommendations. At the meeting of December 21, 1934, they voted to appropriate US$1 million for a three-year experimental program in rural reconstruction. By the following July this program was under way.

## The North China Council for Rural Reconstruction

In January 1935 Selskar Gunn returned to China to lay the groundwork for the foundation's bold effort to aid the multitude of public and private agencies now attempting "to reconstruct a medieval society in terms of modern knowledge." [47] He was accompanied by Raymond B. Fosdick, of the Committee on Appraisal and Plan, and their travels took them to the sites of several rural reconstruction projects. Most impressive to Fosdick were the literacy classes of Tinghsien and the "evangelical zeal" of Yen and his associates. In the early months of 1935, China was enveloped in an aura of hope. Among the Nanking officialdom Fosdick noted a high idealism; they were "so intelligent and forward-looking," and at the same time "they just overwhelmed us with their hospitality." [48] A year and a half before, George Shepherd had been similarly intoxicated by Nanking's atmosphere.

The results of the Gunn-Fosdick survey were a series of appropriations in July 1935. The largest of these—$150,000—went to Yen's Chinese Mass Education Movement as the base of a three-part North China program. It was felt that the Tinghsien experiment was "now ready for extension through the launching of a program to train personnel"; the goal would be the "broad application of this knowledge to the country at large." In the ensuing months the Mass Education Movement set up a special training commission, and the foundation endowed 37 local fellowships in education, health, local government, agriculture, and economics. In the process, Tinghsien was used as the central experimental laboratory and the headquarters of the training program. Techniques were developed for country-wide application, and within a year plans were under way to extend Tinghsien's program to ten hsien in Kwangsi, as well as to Hunan, Kwangtung, Szechwan, and perhaps Honan. [49]

The second part of the North China program was a grant of $37,500 to Nankai's Institute of Economics. Under the leadership of Franklin Ho, Nankai planned "to extend its graduate instruction and research to the problems of rural reconstruction and to establish close cooperation with the Mass Education Movement." Such cooperation was effected by making Tinghsien a training ground for some of the graduate students. A two-year post-graduate program was established, with eleven fellowships provided by the foundation. This training was designed to qualify men for administrative posts in the field of rural reconstruction.[50]

The final grant of the North China program was a $77,325 disbursement to Yenching University. The university's responsibility was to lie in the realm of education and the natural sciences, and a committee of representatives from Tinghsien and Nankai were to meet with the Yenching personnel to plan a cooperative arrangement. Meanwhile, Yenching's natural science program was being redirected in part toward rural problems.[51]

The rest of the first year's funds were channeled to Nanking, where two major aspects of rural reconstruction were embodied in a Public Health and Medical Program and an Agricultural Program. Grants in the first category were made to the central government's National Health Administration and Commission on Medical Education (a total of $108,750). Agricultural grants were made to the University of Nanking ($83,500), to National Central University's animal husbandry and veterinary programs ($34,-600), and to the insect control program of the National Agriculture Research Bureau ($34,300).[52]

This first series of grants under the new China Program was noteworthy for the variegated character of the recipients—three government bureaus, one national university, one private nonmission university (Nankai), one Chinese association (Yen's MEA), and two mission universities (Yenching and Nanking). The program's immediate impact was considerable not only on these recipients, but on those foreign and Chinese Christians who had been attempting to advance the cause of rural reconstruction since the Butterfield visit of 1931.

At the NCC's biennial meeting in late April 1935—when Hugh Hubbard reported on Lichuan's bleak beginnings—the associate general secretary took special note of the foundation's rural program as a significant "new actor" in a period when rural reconstruction "is becoming a driving force, awakening a new sense of social responsibility, and finding new forms of expression." The foundation's entry upon the field was profoundly encouraging to "the Christian colleges that are now preparing, or are desirous of preparing, students for rural service." Indeed, "Several of these are

expecting substantial permanent help from this source." [53] Because of the special achievements of such mission institutions as
Yenching and the University of Nanking, Gunn's general view that
the foundation should de-emphasize its aid to Christian colleges had
been modified in keeping with his own suggested proviso. What his
program was able to do, however, was to correlate the efforts of the
best Christian institutions with those of secular agencies; and this
was no small achievement. By the following April, Gunn could tell
the trustees of "general approval both on the part of Chinese and
foreigners of the fact that the Foundation is directing its attention
to the rural problems of China." [54] He already felt, indeed, that the
foundation's efforts had stimulated Chinese leaders to produce "a
very much better group definition of the aims and scope of rural reconstruction." [55]

On one major question S. M. Gunn remained silent in April
1936 —as he had been silent in his report of January 1934. Nowhere was there mention of the critical matter of the reform of land
tenure. Nor do the foundation records available indicate any attention to this problem in later years. It is doubtful that he was blind to
the problem. More likely Gunn the trainer of men and Gunn the
pragmatist chose to by-pass or postpone the matter in the hope that
a new breed of trained leadership would eventually force change on
old patterns of rural injustice.

The major institutional accomplishment of Gunn's China program was not evident until April 2, 1936. On that day there
emerged from the painstaking negotiations of the previous months
a new body: the North China Council for Rural Reconstruction. In
many ways this council was the most promising fruition of a generation of foreign and Chinese efforts toward an effective response to
the rural crisis. The North China Council was an outgrowth of the
coordinating committee which had been established in early 1935
by the Mass Education Movement, Nankai, and Yenching to determine the most effective service that Yenching could perform as a
part of the Rockefeller program. In the course of the committee's
discussions it was felt that the greatest need was for a field laboratory
"which would bring their teaching and their students into direct
contact with the vital problems of rural reconstruction." The result
of the committee's quest was the decision to enlarge the group of
cooperating institutions and to establish two field headquarters. The

first would be at Tinghsien, where the institutions could make use of Yen's project; and the second would be at Tsining, in Shantung.[56]

Perhaps the most notable result of the coordinating committee was the degree of cooperation achieved among several institutions. The members of the newly formed North China Council were six in number, and each member would guide and operate a particular phase both of training and field work. As a new participant, National Tsinghua University now assumed responsibility for rural engineering; as previously determined, Nankai would be responsible for economics and local government, Yenching for education and social administration, PUMC for social medicine, Nanking for agriculture, and the Mass Education Movement for literacy. In each case, the field units would be staffed by members of the relevant departments of the cooperating agencies. As to allocation of tasks between the two field laboratories, Tinghsien would specialize in education and social medicine, and Tsining would bear the brunt of economics, agriculture, engineering, and civil and social administration. One remarkable achievement of the council in its early days was the securing of permission from the government to nominate its own personnel to official administrative posts at Tsining; this power had already been granted to the Tinghsien leaders in 1933. The semi-official nature of the council was furthered by full recognition from the Division of Higher Education of the Ministry of Education, so that a liaison officer from the ministry attended all council meetings.[57]

The significance of the new council cannot be over-emphasized. Here was an opportunity for students from the best national and private institutions of China to combine their academic training with intensive field work under expert guidance; at the same time, this field work was designed to produce immediate practical results. For the first time the coordination which rural reconstruction had so badly needed was available; and so were the necessary funds. As the foundation report for 1936 rightly concluded, "This form of organization, in making it possible for personnel of high technical quality and strong moral responsibility to develop well conceived and practical programs for social reconstruction and public administration, is of potential significance not only for China but possibly for other countries as well." [58]

In 1936 the foundation allocated US$342,540 to this new China Program. Of these funds, nothing went directly to the North China Council; instead, the foundation provided nine grants to separate activities of the council through the member institutions. For the aim of the foundation was "to unify the major projects, and to stimulate the separate agencies to seek, of their own accord, to coordinate their efforts." [59] At the same time, the foundation maintained its grant of the previous year to the Mass Education Movement for its move from a phase of concentration to a phase of expansion. Indeed, it seems to have been the demand on Yen and his associates for trained leaders to extend the work that constituted the strongest impetus for the formation of the North China Council. And now, with the North China Council's program under way at Tinghsien, the Mass Education Movement had transferred its headquarters to Changsha where it sought to develop Hengshan county as a province-wide training center in rural reconstruction. Meanwhile, James Yen's native province of Szechwan still demanded a similar extension. The snowballing effect of a coordinated reconstruction movement was already becoming apparent.[60] At the same time, as Japan's pressure began to make itself felt through the "autonomy" movement among North China provinces, both Yen and others found it wise to shift their base of operations to the south and west.

Other Rockefeller funds in 1936 maintained the Nanking programs both in agriculture and public health. Also of considerable importance were the 289 fellowships which the foundation granted in all phases of its China Program. Of these, 106 were in public health, 54 in agriculture, 32 in nursing, 23 in rural education, 21 in rural economics and sociology, and so forth. The new rural orientation of what had heretofore been largely a medical program was striking.[61]

In early 1937, as he surveyed the first results of a year and a half of the new endeavor, Raymond B. Fosdick, now president of the foundation, could not but be filled with high expectations. The Sian crisis had come and gone; the new spirit of unity was infectious. In his president's review for 1936, he announced that "China today stands on the threshold of a renaissance." Fosdick did not underestimate the problems of the modernization on which the Chinese were embarked, for "the impact of Western civilization upon the East is not without the possibility of grave danger . . . A high degree of selection is called for if China and her neighbors are to preserve without contamination their own great civilizations." But nonetheless the West did have something nontoxic to give: "Western medicine and sanitation and perhaps the inductive methods of Western science do seem to offer unchallengeable means for promoting the well-being of mankind around the world." In this conviction, Fosdick looked to China, in her selection process, to avoid some of the difficulties of the West and "thus make a unique contribution to the future, a contribution which the ability and high quality of her people seem clearly to promise." [62]

The second full academic year of the program, from July 1, 1936, to June 30, 1937, gave further stimulus to the foundation's hopes. Only a few days away lay the beginnings of a long and terrible war, and within a few weeks six of the eight major projects of the foundation would have to be relocated in other parts of the country. But in 1936–37, nonetheless, much had been accomplished. Although the North China Council continued to cooperate with the health program of the Mass Education Movement at Tinghsien, most of its energies were devoted to the Rural Institute conducted at Tsining. The work of the institute was carried on under seven departments: civil administration, economics, social administration, agriculture, engineering, social medicine, and education. In the district of Nan Chia Ts'un the council maintained a station for intensive experimental work. The relentless aim was training—of the staff, the students, and the villagers themselves. The project was infused with a sense of urgency as the pressure from the north continued to mount. Meanwhile, the cordial relations with the political authorities resulted in the appointment of staff members as *k'o chang* (section chief) and below; in addition, there were temporary interchanges of personnel between the institute and the hsien government; and such cooperation produced the welcome addition of $600,000 to the council's treasury in the form of local tax-derived funds.[63]

In terms of the North China Council's human output—the trained personnel graduated or in preparation—the results at Tsining were promising. In 1937 a first class of ten graduate students obtained their master's degrees after two years of study and direct practical experience. In 1936 a second class of eight began such training. At the same time, and perhaps more significant, 165 undergraduates from the several cooperating institutions were enrolled in the Tsining program. The demand for such trained personnel was evident in the fact that all ten master's degree holders and all 23 graduating seniors moved immediately into jobs with important private or government rural reconstruction agencies.[64]

Meanwhile, the foundation's support for the expansion of the Mass Education Movement was also bringing tangible results. At the new Hengshan headquarters near Changsha great progress was made in mass literacy training through the establishment of an Experimental Rural Normal School. But it was in Szechwan that the movement proceeded with "perhaps its most ambitious undertaking, the economic and political reconstruction of the province as a unit, to be completed in a period of three years." [65]

In February 1937, S. M. Gunn returned to America for the first time in two years to report on the progress of the new China Program. In the wake of the Sian Incident, he was able to speak both of the program and of China's development with fresh confidence and optimism. In his view, the work of the North China Council was an undertaking of the utmost significance. This organization—more comprehensive and effective than he had dared hope for originally —might well "prove to be the major justification of the experiment in a coordinated program which led to the present China Program." And meanwhile, both in Kiangsi and elsewhere, China itself had "evolved through a partial political unification in bringing about the beginning of a comprehensive national program of rural reconstruction." Gunn viewed this parallel course of Rockefeller and Kuomintang development as inherently complementary. On the one hand, there was substantial evidence that the government's reconstruction work would be quantitative rather than qualitative. Nanking, he thought, would find it necessary "for political expedience . . . to carry on activities in many places and over wide areas." But the ultimate success of the government program would be "proportional to the ability of China to develop qualitative work which necessarily will depend on the availability of trained leadership." And "Here it is," he stressed, "that the Foundation may be crucially important." [66] The experience of the past two years, it seems, had convinced Gunn and his colleagues that the Rockefeller role lay in qualitative reconstruction. For the diffuse quantitative efforts of national and provincial governments had moved "in many

directions with generally inferior results. Our program in emphasizing quality," he wrote, "is already attracting attention and gives
indications that the government is recognizing the weaknesses of its
quantitative program and is beginning to take counsel from the organizations which we are helping to build up." [67]

Gunn brought with him one illustration of his program's new
prominence: a testimonial from Mme. Chiang Kai-shek. In a letter
dated February 5, she told Gunn that the foundation's "change of
emphasis . . . has just recently come to the attention of the
Generalissimo and myself. Your efforts in the field of rural reconstruction are highly commendable," she wrote, "and embody the
spirit and the aims of the New Life Movement . . . Henceforth
the Generalissimo and myself will hope to keep in close touch with
the activities of your Foundation." She closed with an offer to "do
everything possible to make this program of rural reconstruction an
outstanding success." [68]

So far, it seemed to Gunn, the contribution of the new China
Program to the process of national reconstruction had been two-
fold. First, facilities for investigation and training for public administration and service in rural work had been developed. And second,
steps had been taken "which give an opportunity to demonstrate
how universities' activities in the Social Sciences can be developed
along sound lines, maintaining university standards but permitting
them to have more realistic value and to be of actual use in assisting government in developing organization and techniques for rural
reconstruction." [69]

On the basis of such specific achievements and the more general
national impact of the Rockefeller effort, Gunn saw no reason for
substantial increases in the foundation's appropriations. Recalling
the worry expressed in 1934 by the Committee on Appraisal and
Plan—a misgiving about the massive investment which the new
program would almost certainly involve—Gunn reaffirmed his own
original view. Indeed, he felt strongly that further foundation aid
for the China Program "should be for a definite period of time, on a
tapering basis, and with an even heightened interest in the quality
of the work aided." [70] Once again, his consuming aim was to root
Western assistance in Chinese institutions and only to stimulate,
never to envelop, constructive indigenous efforts. The concept of
qualitative pump-priming was basic to Gunn's outlook; if justifica-

tion was required, he need only point to the achievements of the past two years and the happy augury for the future.

And yet the solid achievements and bright hopes of early 1937 received a devastating setback with the resumption of Sino-Japanese hostilities in July. One of the first acts of the Japanese aggressors was to strike at the heart of the North China Council's efforts by razing Nankai University itself. Within a few months the entire program seemed to have collapsed. President Fosdick could only recall with bitterness his forecast of China's imminent renaissance and write, "This proud ambition, in which the Foundation was participating, has been virtually destroyed by the events of the last six months . . . The work, the devotion, the resources, the strategic plans of Chinese leaders for a better China, have disappeared in an almost unprecedented cataclysm of violence." [71]

## The Rockefeller Effort: Its Fate and Significance

Despite Raymond Fosdick's gloomy epitaph for rural reconstruction in early 1938, the foundation's China Program joined many of the nation's leading middle schools and colleges in showing a remarkable survival power. Though the U.S.-sponsored Yenching was able to maintain an uneasy existence in occupied territory, Nankai, Tsinghua, the Mass Education Movement, and the North China Council itself became refugee institutions in the southwest and Szechwan. The council—now the National Council for Rural Reconstruction—continued its Tsining program, first at Kweiyang in Kweichow, and after 1940 in Chungking, where it allied itself more closely with the Mass Education Movement.[72]

During this period of wholesale relocation and readjustment under wartime conditions, the foundation maintained its annual appropriation of over US$300,000. By 1942, indeed, it had contributed a total of nearly US$1.9 million to the cause of rural reconstruction in China.[73] After 1937 some of these funds were allocated directly to the Associated Boards for Christian Colleges in China in the form of emergency assistance. Ultimately, however, the program received a fatal blow not from Japanese aggression, but from the forces of spiraling inflation which the war unleashed in

China. By 1943 economic chaos had effectively suspended further New York appropriations for the program.[74]

Like Lichuan, then, the Rockefeller effort was the victim eventually of circumstances far beyond its own control. Unlike Lichuan, however, the program had pointed the way—albeit briefly—to a new gradualist approach to China's rural crisis. Lichuan illustrated not only the possibilities but some of the severe limitations which the evolutionary alternative faced in China; but the North China Council showed what incisive leadership and adequate funds could accomplish in utilizing the potential of the Chinese scene.

What Selskar Gunn did not do was to inaugurate yet another new experimental hsien or demonstration center. It may be all the more surprising that he avoided the temptation when one considers the impressive results the foundation could have obtained by the expenditure of US$1 million on one model district. Nor did he attempt to create a new PUMC for rural reconstruction—a vast Western-sponsored institution to train high-powered specialists in plant breeding, veterinary medicine, pest control, and rural sociology. Indeed, it was above all Gunn's sober realization of PUMC's isolation from the Chinese village that impelled him to seek a more viable alternative. The medical college was the finest of its type in all of Asia. And yet its highly trained doctors and nurses were necessarily removed from the village by virtue of the urban life they had lived and the urban demands for their services.

What Gunn did do, instead, was to use Rockefeller funds and imagination as leverage in an attempt to coordinate and expand the rural reconstruction movement. The foundation's China experiment became, as Fosdick was later to write, "an attempt to awaken the Chinese universities and other native authorities to the means of national reconstruction that were available through improvement of the rural economy." Such an experiment, Gunn and his associates well knew, would require decades of time and patience before large-scale results would be visible. Even so, the brief life of the experiment yielded as tokens of value at least two things: "the coordination of several fragmentary native efforts into a united movement to improve the lot of the Chinese peasant" and "the discovery of leadership material among the youth." [75]

In S. M. Gunn's own words—on the threshold of hope, in early

1937—the foundation's China Program had "contributed (1) by bringing some of the universities into an intimate contact with problems in the field which they have previously largely ignored, (2) by stressing the qualitative side of activities in rural work, (3) by making it possible to train, in a relatively short time, a large number of young Chinese for rural reconstruction, (4) by giving moral backing to Chinese leaders in these fields, and (5) by emphasizing the significance of this type of work to the interested ministries and government offices." [76]

If, indeed, there ever was a gradualist alternative to violent revolution in the Chinese countryside, the program of the Rockefeller Foundation came closer to it than any previous effort by the many would-be reformers in Kuomintang China. It eschewed social revolution—and most notably was silent on the issue of land reform. But it provided unique support for those who sought to change the conditions of life in village China. Yet gradualism required time; and time was the one element denied to the rural reconstructionists by external aggressor and internal rebel alike.

# Chapter Seven
# Americans and Ideological Reform: The New Life Movement

*Context of the Kuomintang Ideological Quest*

American reform efforts under the Nanking government followed two frequently converging paths. On the one hand, as we have seen, Americans joined with Chinese activists in recognizing the crucial significance of the Chinese village; they sought to resolve the rural crisis by direct participation in rural reconstruction. On the other hand, Americans also joined with Chinese in recognizing a continuing crisis in ideology; as bearers in a general sense of "Western civilization" and as specific purveyors of the Christian religion, they sought to fill a perceived ideological vacuum or at least give form and direction to ideological flux. It would be misleading, however, to separate neatly the rural concern from the ideological concern. In the minds of many missionary reformers the one grew out of the other: the aim was a "Christianizing" of economic and social relationships in the countryside as elsewhere. Nor were the two areas clearly divorced in the minds of Chinese reformers: In the tradition of Wang Yang-ming, the Ming dynasty neo-Confucian idealist, Liang Sou-ming and James Yen saw their work as the identification of thought and action; rural reconstruction was, for them and their colleagues, the vital core of a political and social credo, however much they might differ among themselves as to the credo's particulars.[1]

It is not surprising, therefore, that missionaries who began to cooperate with the national government in rural reform in 1934 soon discovered a related sphere of ideological reform and character rebuilding in which their services were demanded. The specific context of their ideological activity, however, was surprising. For the movement to which they were called by the government was a hybrid composite of Confucian, fascist, Japanese, and Christian elements, which could not help but appeal to certain sections of American Protestantism. The strength of this appeal caused a significant shift in the relationship between many missionaries and the Kuomintang regime. At the same time, the movement itself bore increasingly the mark of mission influence. The development of this interaction between American Christians and the so-called New Life Movement forms a perplexing but significant chapter in the history of Kuomintang China.

During the years of Sun Yat-sen's life, the Kuomintang had found cohesion and unity chiefly in the force of his charismatic personality. After Sun's death in 1925 the cracks in the United Front deepened, although an uneasy truce between Right and Left prevailed through the first months of the Northern Expedition. With Chiang Kai-shek's anti-Communist coup in April 1927, however, the Nationalist Revolution was divorced from its Leninist flank. Thereafter, the Kuomintang was forced to rely for ideological justification on Sun Yat-senism. Yet, deprived of the founder's magnetic presence, the philosophy of Sun Yat-sen was thin fare. It was vague and fraught with contradictions; but most important of all it was largely nonoperative—it failed to spell out coherent plans for organization and action. As a result both of this ideological weakness and of the continuing challenge from the Communists, the Kuomintang quickly took steps to demonstrate its own legitimacy.

Mary Clabaugh Wright has ably traced the process by which the Nanking government strove to make itself the heir to Chinese tradition.[2] The First and Second Congresses of the Kuomintang, in 1924 and 1926, had produced revolutionary anti-imperialist proclamations. But at the Third Congress, in 1929, the Communist rebels were now the chief enemy. Meanwhile, the public veneration of Confucius had been resumed in 1928. In 1931 his birthday was proclaimed a national holiday. And in 1934 the sage was recanonized.

The attempted Confucian revival in these years was clearly directed toward the re-establishment of public order in a time of continuing disorder. At the same time, Chiang Kai-shek himself seems to have regarded the loyal Confucian generals of the T'ungchih Restoration (1862–1874) as his personal models for emulation. He looked with particular favor on Hu Lin-i; by 1932 the cult of Tseng Kuo-fan was intense. Restoration did indeed replace revolution as the overriding concern of the Kuomintang regime, and it is not surprising that it should do so in these first years of recurrent threats to Nanking's leadership. Yet it would be a mistake to conclude that the T'ung-chih example was the only influence affecting Kuomintang development. Of considerable importance as well was the role played by the Japanese military training of many Kuomintang leaders, Chiang in particular. The generalissimo's obsession with military obedience and personal austerity seems to have derived as much from his experience of late Meiji *bushidō* as from his Ch'ing Confucian predecessors.[3] Nor should it be assumed that the Kuomintang's reversion to traditionalism meant a denial of nationalism. On the contrary, for Chiang Confucianism was imbued with a romantic nationalism; in such warrior-heroes as Chu-ko Liang he saw the Chinese ideal. His was a nationalism that looked to the Confucian past for inspiration. It was a nationalism that permeated his writings.[4]

Yet Chiang himself personified the curiously hybrid quality of the emerging Kuomintang ideology. In 1927 he had married the Wellesley-educated Christian daughter of a successful Methodist merchant; and in 1931, reportedly after four years of Bible study, the generalissimo was baptized a Methodist. Chiang Kai-shek's conversion to Christianity is a subject of much speculation and little established fact. From 1931 to 1933, a period of continuing antiforeign and anti-Christian agitation, he remained largely silent about his new faith. The events of 1934, which brought him closer to the missionary community through reconstruction enterprises, also produced at least one public expression regarding his religious belief. In a commencement address at Ginling College that year, Chiang assured the students that religion was essential to life, that without religion life was "aimless," and that religion would enable one "to struggle with a definite purpose toward a final goal." He further described Christianity as a religion with "a definite goal and a lofty purpose," whose founder "was a revolutionary in his conception of living and society." Sun Yat-sen's Three Principles, said Chiang, had "evolved from the philosophy of Jesus Christ." Finally, he argued that China was now in particularly dire need of the "Christian spirit of service." [5]

Meanwhile, Mme. Chiang was under less compunction to de-emphasize her Christianity than her husband, and it was through her that missionaries were introduced to the Chiang household after 1927. There developed, as early as 1931, a regular series of Sunday evening religious services in the generalissimo's Nanking home at which a visiting missionary was often asked to lead meditations.[6] Such interaction with the foreign community must have left its mark on Chiang. But of the precise nature of that mark—and, indeed, the importance of his faith—one cannot judge. Suffice it to say that he gradually came to view the church as an effective force for maintaining the social virtues he admired in Tseng Kuo-fan, Hu Lin-i, and the Japanese samurai. He seems to have regarded it as an ally in his struggle to achieve social stability and popular discipline.

## Origins and Nature of the Movement

The Kuomintang's attempt to buoy up Sun Yat-senism with an infusion of neo-Confucian and foreign elements must be viewed against the background of domestic and international politics. Confronted after 1931 with relentless Japanese encroachment from the north, the Nanking government sought unity but achieved at first only further factionalism. Bickerings within the party itself were compounded by the unpredictable machinations of regional warlords and by the Communist revolt in the border areas of Kiangsi, Hupeh, and Fukien. The very unity and seeming indestructibility of the embattled Communists clearly acted as a goad to Kuomintang strategists: communism filled its adherents with a dynamism and oneness of purpose woefully lacking in the incomparably larger but fragmented anti-Communist elements. Somewhere, somehow, the Kuomintang must regain its lost fire. It must evoke the moral allegiance of a united people as Mussolini had done in Italy. It must produce a militant awakening and an enthusiastic modernization as Atatürk had done in Turkey. Such thoughts certainly ran through the minds of Chiang Kai-shek and many of his advisers as they pitched from crisis to crisis in the months after the Mukden Incident. They clearly lay at the roots of the Kuomintang's curious ideological innovation of 1934.[7]

In the evolution of the New Life Movement, Kiangsi province played the same catalytic role it had filled in the birth of rural reconstruction. Here it was that communism posed its most decisive challenge in the early thirties. The national government faced a double necessity: to instill its troops with an effective fighting spirit and to infuse the population of former Soviet regions with an ideology that would guarantee their loyalty. As the military requirement took precedence, it is not surprising that a precursor of the New Life Movement was an organization designed to encourage discipline and upright behavior among the military elite, the Officers' Moral Endeavor Association (OMEA). Established in 1929, the association was led by Colonel Huang Jen-lin, a Christian and former YMCA secretary who was a son-in-law of the prominent YMCA general secretary, David Z. T. Yui (Yü Jih-chang).[8] Colonel Huang was a close associate of Mme. Chiang Kai-shek and was later to play a significant role as her chief representative in the New Life Movement. With the generalissimo's support, he modeled the OMEA program to a large extent on the YMCA's character-building procedures.[9] It was Huang, too, who arranged in the spring of 1933 for the Nanchang Methodist mission to extend their evangelistic work to military installations with Mme. Chiang's blessing.[10] Kuomintang utilization of missionaries was not altogether new at this time; since the crises of 1931 the government had made several surprising approaches to foreign Christian groups. In the autumn of that year both H. H. Kung and Chiang had assembled missionaries for informal consultation on national affairs. At the same time, the National Flood Relief Commission had invited Christians to preach to flood refugees with a view to keeping up their spirits. In addition, Chiang is reported to have endorsed heartily the suggestion that the noted evangelist, Sherwood Eddy, come to China each year for five years between 1931 and 1936 to conduct religious campaigns.[11]

The approach to the Nanchang Methodists by J. L. Huang in

1933, however, represented an extension of officially approved moral uplift from the officer corps to soldiers in general. Together with the invitation from Mme. Chiang to large-scale Christian participation in rural reconstruction, it indicated the degree to which missionary methods and personnel were being considered for application to the problems of Kiangsi. Such moves presaged a far larger effort to revive the spirit of the province and the country. With the conclusion of the Tangku Truce and the end of the Fukien Rebellion, Chiang Kai-shek was now ready to attempt such a revival.

On February 19, 1934, Chiang made a speech to a Nanchang mass meeting in which he called for "a movement to achieve a new life." [12] To the assembled citizens he cited the examples of Germany and Japan; such nations were strong because they had developed the proper way of life. What China needed in order to achieve strength was "to militarize the life of the people of the entire country." Between March 5 and 21, Chiang explained the movement's aims in four more addresses. On the 11th, after ten days of feverish preparations, the movement was officially launched in Nanchang at a gigantic meeting of 100,000 people representing 142 organizations.[13] Governor Hsiung Shih-hui and the provincial commissioner of education joined the generalissimo in calling the citizens of Kiangsi to a new struggle for orderliness, cleanliness, simplicity, diligence, and propriety. Six days later the movement's Nanking branch was opened under the auspices of Wang Ching-wei and other government officials, and on the 18th Peiping followed suit with a mass rally addressed by two generals and Peiping University's Chancellor Chiang Mon-lin.[14]

The precise origins of the New Life Movement are unclear. At the time, the press reported that it had originated in "an accident": while motoring through Nanchang, Chiang Kai-shek had come upon a "boy of 20 in student's uniform with a cigarette in his mouth quarrelling and fighting in the street." Deeply depressed by the sight, Chiang had meditated on the subject and "thought he perceived one of the main causes why some foreigners appear to despise the Chinese people." At once he ordered his "subordinates" to organize a movement to improve the life of the Chinese people in general, and that of Chinese youth in particular.[15] It seems probable, to be sure, that Chiang himself was the movement's originator. His own addresses, since 1931, had stressed the need for character improvement, self-discipline, and "sincerity." [16] But the role of the unnamed "subordinates" was substantial, and chief among them were party ideologues Ch'en Li-fu and Tai Chi-t'ao. According to one observer, it was Ch'en "who gave Chiang the theoretical foundation of the New Life Movement and transformed it from a hygienic regimen into a philosophy." [17]

The hygienic regimen envisioned by the generalissimo was simple and puritanical. His objective was clean living among his men—the soldiers and potential soldiers of China. Cleanliness, temperance, and physical fitness were the crux of the matter. Chiang wanted men to brush their teeth regularly, wash their bodies and clothes, abstain from alcohol, opium, and tobacco, and take daily physical exercise. So far, none of this was unexpected from a commanding officer with an admiration for Spartan virtues; Chiang himself was already noted for the simplicity and frugality of his life. Indeed, his speech of March 11 had included the revelation that his parents had early inculcated in him the habit of keeping clean. "This early training, stern as it was," he added, "has made me what I am." [18]

The theoretical foundation supplied by Ch'en Li-fu, however, extended the injunctions from the soldiery to the citizenry and bound the movement to the already evident Confucian revival. To the soldier's hygienic code were added four ancient Confucian virtues, *li, i, lien,* and *ch'ih* (or, as Chiang himself interpreted them, correct behavior, justice, integrity, and honor). The re-emphasis of these virtues in what was planned as a spontaneous nationwide movement would produce—Chiang hoped—"the social regeneration of China." As for procedure, the movement was to be confined, in its first year of operation, to two campaigns: orderliness and cleanliness. To endow the virtues with precision, 96 specific rules for their application were announced in regard to food, clothing, shelter, and action. The focal points were personal hygiene, the destruction of pests, and punctuality. [19] And why did such a program deserve top priority in the mind of generalissimo? Chiang's answer, in 1934: "The poverty of our nation is primarily caused by the fact that there are too many consumers and too few producers. To remedy this we have to emphasize the four virtues, and we have to make people work harder and spend less, and the officials be honest." And, as an afterthought eminently worthy of a Ch'ing bureaucrat, he added: "This was the secret of success of the two ancient kingdoms Ch'i and Ch'u. It is also the primary cause of the strength of modern nations." [20] To the examples of Germany and Japan Chiang soon added those of Italy and Turkey; his paramount aim remained, as in all things, the creation of a strong national state.[21]

From its inception, the New Life Movement embodied two major paradoxes. In the first place, the campaign was repeatedly labeled a people's movement and not a government organization; yet its sponsorship came from the top of the government pyramid, and its extension from city to city resulted from the diligent efforts of party functionaries. Its nature was therefore initially ambiguous. Within two years, it was transformed into an official national organization with headquarters in Nanking. Yet throughout its existence it lacked either the mass appeal of a Communist campaign or the coercive power of Atatürk's decrees. A second paradox involved the movement's explicit intention to affect material and economic aspects of life: the generalissimo wrote in 1934 that New Life would remove "beggary and robbery," would make officials "honest and patriotic," would terminate "corruption," and cause the people to "pursue more productive enterprises." [22] And yet to accomplish such admirable economic results the movement relied entirely on a psychological remolding through the reform of personal habits. The economic causes of beggary, robbery, dishonesty, and corruption were blithely ignored. For conditions of economic distress the movement prescribed purely moralistic remedies. A mass campaign for national regeneration was to be built on the toothbrush, the mouse trap, and the fly swatter.

At the outset, to be sure, the New Life Movement had been tied in with the government's new program for the rehabilitation of Kiangsi. Nanchang was selected as a model city, and in the spring of 1934 city-wide clean-up campaigns produced sensational results. Lectures, lantern processions, posters, and entertainment rallies aroused the populace. A thousand citizens were selected as honorary detectives whose duty it was to inspect homes and remind people to be clean and orderly. Indeed, a certain esprit-de-corps was developed locally in the first months of the campaign. The chief impetus seems to have come from the presence of the generalissimo; in 1935 a shrewd Western observer described his personality as "the most impressive thing in Kiangsi today." [23] Furthermore,

New Life Voluntary Service Groups were organized to visit the countryside in conjunction with the establishment of NEC welfare centers. In Kiangsi, at least, New Life was girded by a substantial government effort to improve the economic condition of the farmer as well as the manners of the city dweller. It operated there as the psychological branch of the two-pronged government effort described earlier: the fascist-influenced activities of the energetic provincial authorities and the American-influenced program of the NEC.[24]

As the movement was extended beyond the unique Kiangsi situation, however, it seems to have lost all touch with the countryside. Divorced from the Communist challenge, from the generalissimo's personality, and from rural reconstruction efforts, it degenerated into a perfunctory urban operation. The New Life promotional associations of the country's major cities were staffed and supported largely by party regulars, as they had originally been sponsored by local officialdom. Nor were they ever removed from strict Kuomintang control. Their activities became increasingly restricted to campaigns against spitting, smoking, and "the littering of public places with watermelon seeds." [25]

Between 1934 and the outbreak of the war in the summer of 1937, the NLM passed through three stages. In its first year of existence it achieved some success in terms of enthusiasm aroused within Kiangsi and growth outside the province. By its first anniversary, the generalissimo was well pleased. Critics had already attacked the movement's superficiality, however, and in April 1935 Chiang announced the inauguration of a People's Economic Reconstruction Movement. Allegedly a long-planned adjunct to the NLM, this second operation quickly joined the ranks of Kuomintang paper programs.[26] The second year of the movement produced profound pessimism. By 1935 many writers were assailing the NLM both for its close party connection and its focus on symptoms rather than causes. Japanese encroachment in the north made New Life seem increasingly irrelevant to the crisis at hand. Its lack of spontaneity was particularly apparent against the backdrop of the extraordinarily spontaneous Student Movement in the autumn months. At the second anniversary celebration in February 1936, the generalissimo made no attempt to conceal his irritation and disappointment.[27] Thereafter, the government shifted its approach.

The movement was reorganized in Nanking as an overtly government-directed drive. Plans were made for "Military Discipline, Increased Production, and Cultural Training." An NLM Inspection Corps, staffed by 136 graduates of the government's Central Political Institute, undertook to examine "the efficiency of public servants" as to their observance of NLM principles and to investigate "people's organizations" and "social education." In addition to the departments of administration, promotion, and training, a Students' Department was created to arrange for "practical service" and student research "into the economic and social problems of farmers and workers." [28] As the generalissimo became increasingly involved in problems of internal and external security, leadership in the movement passed to Mme. Chiang, who occupied the post of director-general.[29]

The transition of 1936–37 produced a significant shift in the relationship of the NLM to foreigners and to the Christian church. In April 1936, Chiang Kai-shek had asked George W. Shepherd to move to Nanking as an adviser to the movement. Within a few months Mme. Chiang was making urgent public appeals to Christians to give their support to the movement. Both developments had their roots in the earlier phase of the NLM. These roots had major implications for the role of the American reformer in Kuomintang China.

## The YMCA's Dilemma

The New Life Movement came into being at a time when Christian leaders were moving from a dark night of pessimism into what appeared to be a promising dawn. The trauma of 1927, with its explosive xenophobia and anti-Christian agitation, had been followed by the disasters of 1931. Despite patent disunity, the Nanking government, of which many had despaired, somehow survived. The undeclared war ended in the spring of 1933, and foreign Christians sensed a change in climate. Japanese had replaced Westerners as a prime target for national hostility, and the debacle of Chinese resistance in the north had chastened many who once blamed all the nation's misfortunes on outsiders. From all parts of the country, the spring of 1933 brought reports of a shift in national attitudes: a new tendency to ascribe China's plight to weaknesses in the "national character," a tendency toward national introspection. Outside of Kiangsi and Fukien, post-Tangku China experienced its quietest and most orderly months in many years.

In Nanking, at the end of May, the local YMCA secretary sensed a growing pro-Christian attitude on the part of the national government and attributed it to the "spiritual effect of national adversity." Kuomintang leaders were making statements which would have been unthinkable a few years before. At a Boy Scout conference, Chiang's ideological adviser Tai Chi-t'ao warned that it would be "a great mistake . . . if religion were left out" of scout training programs. A few days later, Ch'en Li-fu told a YMCA audience that neither the government nor the party would be able to save the country "without religion as the guide and support of character." [30]

From Peiping, at the same time, another YMCA secretary reported similar changes. The recent military defeats and continued Kuomintang factionalism had produced in that city "a lessening of the talk concerning anti-Imperialism and a turning of the blame for China's troubles upon the government and upon one-self." There was a decided lessening, too, of opposition to religion and Christianity. The association, he felt, had a duty now to stress the reasons for China's weakness, "namely selfishness, lack of cooperation, etc. —in a word, lack of character." [31] The YMCA's Peiping student secretary confirmed his colleague's report. He found that the young intellectuals seemed "to hunger for something which can give them hope and courage." They were increasingly convinced that "there must be basic weaknesses in Chinese personal and racial character"; indeed, to many students the supreme test of Christianity was whether it could "help to make the Chinese race a strong and respected equal with all other races in practical world affairs." The secretary qualified his optimism by noting that "their acceptance of Christianity is made much more difficult by their own feeling that Christianity is not consistent with the development of strong nationalistic loyalties, and especially the use of those military methods which they feel China is now forced to adopt." Meanwhile, students were "passionately eager to find a movement in which their lives will really count for something." [32]

In these same months, YMCA secretaries were also beginning to be aware of the persistent student attraction to communism. The Shanghai executive secretary reported in May 1933 that "Communist ideology, spread through all kinds of literature and in other ways, is taking hold on increasing numbers of people." [33] Also in May, Kiang Wen-han, the national committee's student secretary, warned that "the Communist undercurrent among the students remains torrential" and that communism therefore "challenges us to a fundamental reconstruction of the social order." [34] Another YMCA figure, Y. T. Wu (Wu Yao-tsung), the editor of the Association Press, wrote in January 1934 that "Communism is fast spreading in many parts of the world and most significantly in China." Christianity had an obligation in China to work "towards the pulling down of the old order in its manifold aspects and the building up of a new one." To the extent that Christianity failed to meet this obligation, communism's "social passion, its sacrificial spirit, and its methodical efficiency ought to bring humiliation to Christians who stand by and watch." [35] One need only recall the debates within the NCC and the writings of George Shepherd in Fukien to realize how widespread were such views as those of Kiang Wen-han and Y. T. Wu among Christians in 1933–34. Post-Tangku China confronted at least the socially conscious and activist branch of Protestantism with a sense of opportunity and of danger: the national government was becoming more approachable, more friendly, while the Communists waited ominously in the wings. Indeed, some missionaries perceived a hopeful implication in the fact that the Chinese word for "crisis" was made up of the two terms "danger" and "opportunity." [36]

Such was the setting for Christian response to the NLM in early 1934. Its initial impact was limited to Kiangsi. There, in the excitement of early March, the movement's leaders called on "all civic and church organizations" to cooperate. [37] Such cooperation with the YMCA, at least, was institutionally easy: the generalissimo appointed as the NLM's first general secretary of the Nanchang headquarters Paul Yen (Yen Pao-han), a man who had been YMCA Secretary in Mukden prior to the Japanese occupation. At the same time, the generalissimo "drafted" the local YMCA organization "for considerable help" in connection with the NLM program. Eugene A. Turner, the American secretary stationed there since January 1, became one of the movement's staunchest supporters and advocates.[38] Meanwhile, George Shepherd had come to the province at the end of January to start the organization of the Lichuan project. One of the first recorded missionary reactions was his. As previously noted, Shepherd linked the NLM together with the Communist revolution as two major forces causing "the breaking up of old China." In a letter dated March 17, he described the movement as "a large scale program to modernise China and attain equality in the family of nations, through *making* China progressive and the equal of her neighbors." He reported Chiang's conviction that "all such progress must be based on knowledge and character, and knowledge and character that has truly become a part of the people." [39] A month later, Shepherd told the NCC that the movement had grown up very largely to meet the needs of the farmers behind the front lines; it showed, he thought, "a very definite conversion of the Government in its attitude to the farmer." [40]

The *Chinese Recorder,* unofficial journal of the Protestant missionary enterprise, made no comment on the NLM until its May issue in 1934. At that time, its editor took note of the fact that "a revival of China's own ethical consciousness is under way." The editorial viewed the "paradoxically" named movement as "an expression of the Chinese conviction that China should put her own house in order in terms of her own understanding of what that order should be." It spoke approvingly of the government's recognition that right conduct and character were fundamental to "the successful mastery of modern problems." And in an unintended but remarkably close paraphrasing of the dictum of the late Ch'ing "self-strengtheners," the writer described the NLM as a process "whereby the Chinese will use what they learn from the West in terms of their own ideas of how they should be rightly used. It shows that China is not going to be entirely westernized, but that she will strive to be herself in a modern way." Concluded the editor: "That this movement is needed is obvious." [41]

It was not until October that the *Recorder* once again discussed the movement's progress. By this time the NLM's outlines had become more clear. It had assumed at least four concomitant forms. Besides the overall drive to "stiffen the moral, communal, and national backbone of the people," the NLM had also resulted in a recrudescence of heretofore discouraged folk festivals and superstition, in a "Purity Drive," and a "Return to Confucius Movement."

Of all save the Purity Drive the editor was amiably tolerant: "China must build her new life upon these permanent principles of character already known to her people." But the puritanical aspects of the movement—restrictions on dancing, women's dress, mixed bathing, and the like—seemed "not usually constructive" and even "regrettable." Particularly distressing were attempts to push Chinese women back toward their traditionally inhibited state; such acts were a "misdirected attempt to make the New Life work." When all was said and done, however, the movement still appeared to be "a re-awakening of China's self-consciousness" and "a reassertion of China's determination to settle her own destiny." [42]

Throughout the development of Christian attitudes toward the NLM, the role of the YMCA was uniquely significant. It is hardly surprising that a Christian organization devoted primarily to character building rather than evangelism should find most speedily a common ground with the movement. An apparent overlapping of aims was furthered by an overlapping of personnel: by 1936 one-time YMCA Secretary Paul Yen had been succeeded as the NLM's national director by one-time YMCA Secretary J. L. Huang of the OMEA.[43] In the national government, meanwhile, other key figures had also once served as association secretaries. Among them were the generalissimo's brother-in-law and finance minister, H. H. Kung; the former foreign minister and high Kuomintang official, C. T. Wang; and Philip Cheng, director of field work in charge of the NEC's Kiangsi welfare centers.[44] An organization that emphasized activism, social service, and the "well-rounded man" over theology, dogma, and conversion was easily adapted to the hybrid aims of the movement.

Such was the view not only of Paul Yen and J. L. Huang; it was, as well, the view of the generalissimo. As the movement began to falter in its second year of operation, both Chiang and his wife were to turn increasingly to Christian organizations for support. A revealing insight into the generalissimo's thinking, however, can be obtained from an earlier document. In the latter part of 1934, E. A. Turner of the Nanchang YMCA had been asked to assist in the translation of reports and minutes of the NLM's local office. In the course of this work, Turner came across a confidential statement by Chiang Kai-shek to the movement's executive committee. Its contents astounded him; they were so flattering to the YMCA that he desired to see the statement widely circulated. Without clearance, however, such a release would be impossible. Turner thereupon edited Chiang's remarks in the form of a news story to the Associated Press, sent it by air mail to Mme. Chiang together with a covering letter; Mme. Chiang was to read it and send it on to the wire service only if she wished. In January Mme. Chiang forwarded the release to the Associated Press and wrote Turner a note of thanks.[45]

Chiang's *in camera* statement was clearly newsworthy. In it he explained the motivation for the NLM as he had done nowhere else. "The great need of society in China," Chiang had said to the movement's directors, "is an integrating force. In England and America this force is furnished by churches and kindred social organizations, and in Italy and Russia by the dominant party. Our own national party has in many places lost public respect and cannot function as the needed force." In former times, China's classical scholars had been the leaders of the people; now the country must look elsewhere—to every possible agency, and especially to the churches, for the leaders of the churches "are already up to the standards of the New Life Movement." For this reason, Chiang decreed, "Officials, teachers, students, military and police should cooperate with the Young Men's Christian Association, for that is the clearing house of service for the churches in our large cities. Where there is no YMCA, a plan of cooperation with the Churches directly should be worked out." In addition, "Western church leaders in our midst ought also to be utilized. Their attitude toward life is sane and sensible." Chiang added one qualification lest he be misunderstood: "I am not urging that we become foreignized, that we eat foreign food, wear foreign clothes and live in foreign houses, but rather that we live the rational sane life that the Movement and its principles call for."[46] E. A. Turner termed Chiang's remarks "unprecedented";[47] and indeed they were. The generalissimo had clearly revealed his view of the YMCA as a model for the New Life Movement, a producer of social cement in a fragmented society.

Many months before the discovery of this document, however, the YMCA's national leaders had already felt the impact of the movement. Its overtones seemed to them familiar, yet vaguely suspect, and the association's proper attitude in the matter became a subject of considerable discussion. At a Hangchow meeting of general secretaries from the major cities in June 1934, the Chinese representatives were outspokenly skeptical. One said that the movement was "not being promoted by the right kind of people." Another argued that "no valuable result has been accomplished because it is being promoted without enthusiasm or sincere spirit by political workers." A third noted that "the words and actions of the movement do not correspond." A discussion ensued as to the real motivation of the NLM. President J. Usang Ly (Li Chao-huan) of Chiaotung University outlined the two current theories as to its origin. Some said that the movement was an accidental outgrowth of Tai Chi-t'ao's efforts "to put flesh onto the bones of Dr. Sun's Three People's Principles"; others claimed that it was a carefully constructed attempt to "lay a foundation for Fascism." The secretaries then discussed how the YMCA might "do the work of the New Life Movement." Ly's suggestions: by evangelism, by a social program, and by organizing for action. The association should work, he said, "for the real aims and objectives of the New Life Movement, but it should retain its liberty of action and not be tied up to the political organization of the Movement." [48]

At the end of this conference, the meeting's secretary summed up the discussion: "The YMCA may maintain toward the New Life Movement an attitude of sympathetic approval of the objective; it may recognize in it a scheme for *sheng-huo chiao-yu* (education for life) in the promotion of which we may cooperate. The YMCA, however, should adopt its own methods for promoting the movement, and not relinquish its liberty by being too closely involved in the outside local organization of the movement." One participant added that the association would do well to get "the members of its groups to actually practice the virtues advocated by the New Life Movement." The national committee's acting general secretary, S. C. Leung (Liang Ch'ang-shu) closed the discussion by suggesting that the two organizations supplement each other. It was true, he said, that the YMCA actually stressed the promotion of the virtues advocated by the NLM; but the former dealt with "more fundamental issues and concerns than the latter, and should furnish a spiritual dynamic which the latter needs." [49]

It is clear that the NLM's inauguration in 1934 placed the YMCA in a delicate situation. Prior to the Nanchang mass meetings, many officials of the association were increasingly aware that the YMCA's appeal had been undercut by the influence of communism among young people everywhere. With the coming of Chiang's new movement, the association now found itself hemmed in from the right as well as the left. Cooperation with the NLM would not only threaten to immerse the association in something vast and not explicitly Christian; it might also serve to identify the association in the public mind with the less savory aspects of the Kuomintang. Within an increasingly polarized situation, the YMCA leaders were highly uneasy about yielding to the call of their new would-be bedfellow. Yet the elusive middle ground—the "third alternative"—was becoming less and less tenable. With both the Communists and the New Life spokesmen they claimed to share objectives: the creation of a more just, happy, and prosperous society. The Communists sought to accomplish this by transforming the material environment, while Chiang looked to the transformation of the individual character. Uncontestably, the YMCA traditionally stood closer to Chiang's intended method than to that of the Communists. Yet, how might they cooperate with a party-sponsored, party-staffed movement and still preserve their separate identity as Christians and democrats? The question was to plague the association through the next 15 years until its own leadership followed China into acute polarization.

In July 1934, the national committee's executive secretary, Eugene E. Barnett, brooded over the complexities of the association's role. In his administrative report that summer, he noted that the year had brought a new concern with deeper social, economic, and cultural developments in place of the old political issues. The NLM he viewed as one expression of this change. It had produced, to be sure, a mixed reaction: "Many question the appropriateness of its claim to be a *new life* movement since its emphasis is placed mainly upon a revival of the personal virtues handed down from China's immemorial past." The movement, too, was "significantly suggestive of Italian Fascism in which an effort to modernize the industrial and economic progress of society has been combined with an endeavor to revive the ancient spirit of Rome." One such suggestive product was "the Blue Shirt Movement, generally believed to be the military counterpart" of the NLM. Barnett was more enthusiastic about the country's economic progress under the NEC and the various rural reconstruction efforts. In political unity, as well, China had made strides with the suppression of the Fukien Rebellion and the new successes against the Communist troops. A new military spirit was abroad in the country: during the summer of 1934 college students were required to take military training for the first time in history; indeed this "militarization of the mind of China" might well prove to be the decade's most significant development.[50]

But within this situation of economic, political, and military progress, Barnett was deeply disturbed by the role of the church in general, the YMCA in particular. In the past, he recalled, Christianity in China had frequently been a liberalizing, even a radical movement; indeed, it had supplied "a good deal of the yeast" which created the present ferment in China. But now Christianity seemed to have "fallen into the rear." While the church was becalmed in indecision, complacency, and cutbacks, communism had entered the picture with "an aggressive missionary program." In the past ten years, this program had shown enormous appeal, "especially to idealistic youth, because of its 'thorough-going' revolutionary proposals which aim at the overthrow of China's 'feudalistic system' and also of the 'capitalistic system' which is seeking to establish itself in this country, and the erection instead of a fairer happier socialistic society." Perhaps communism in action had been greatly discredited in the eyes of the people; it certainly seemed so in Kiangsi and Fukien. But what was the church doing to provide an alternative? "The feeling persists," Barnett wrote, "that Christianity is altogether too vague and, therefore, ineffectual in its approach to the fundamental problems of the times." [51]

Eugene Barnett's views had evidently infused the 12th National Convention of the YMCA that spring; and at that convention, Barnett reported, the association's leaders were "just beginning to grope for light." One outgrowth of the convention was the decision to utilize the YMCA in rural reconstruction. This would mark a substantial shift in what was traditionally an urban-directed organization. Its American staff, in fact, were hesitant as to whether the association should even attempt such a shift; but the Chinese secretaries were overwhelmingly approving. As a result, the association had decided in May 1934 to try to provide leadership in rural communities, to bring experts to the countryside, and to make the urban memberships more intelligently aware of the rural situation.[52] Such decisions were almost irresistible in the climate of early 1934. James Yen had pointed the way. The Lichuan experiment had commenced. S. M. Gunn had probed the rural crisis for fifteen months and was now presenting his proposals to the foundation. "Rural reconstruction" was the watchword.

Yet the implementation of such decisions was easier said than done in any normal period of operation. And the YMCA, like all other American organizations, was in no normal phase; for it stood in the full shadow of the Great Depression. In 1922 its China staff had boasted 92 American secretaries. By 1935 the number had dropped to 17. Of these, only two were new arrivals since the earlier date.[53] Although such statistics sometimes indicated a healthy transfer of leadership to Chinese secretaries, the drastic reduction in staff and appropriations meant that any real extension of the association's work into the countryside was out of the question. The decision of May 1934 remained a hope rather than a program.[54]

### 1934–35: Christian Ambivalence

While the YMCA was attempting to tread a middle path in its approach to China's youth—a path between those of the Communists and the government—the NLM was beginning to make itself felt among other types of missionaries outside Kiangsi province. From Fukien, where Nanking had now replaced the 19th Route Army with more reliable administrators, Americans dispatched glowing accounts of the new ideological drive. Roderick Scott of Fukien Christian University reported that he had already made three speeches to 2,000 students on the NLM during his visit to Amoy, and "not without some success, I hope." Scott termed the movement no less than proof of Chiang Kai-shek's Christian interest. He found it significant for two reasons, whether or not it succeeded: "first, as a sign of renewed enthusiasm in the nation; second, as a sign that China looks to spiritual as well as to scientific sources (hitherto the exclusive emphasis) for revival." [55] Similar reports came from missionaries in the Fukien hinterland. From Diongloh, in the summer of 1934, Lyda S. Houston expressed her astonishment and delight at being appointed chairman of the local committee to plan and execute the NLM's inaugural festivities: "Try to imagine, if you please, a school in America handing over to a Chinese the planning for the exhibits for one of the most intensely patriotic parades of the times." The lady interpreted the gesture as a sign that "the unhappy time of intense nationalism was passing." As for the movement itself, she had no evident misgivings: "Would that other nations were emblazoning these four virtues, courtesy, righteousness, integrity, honor, before their young people." Furthermore, the movement seemed to have brought with it a new spirit of approval of the activities of Christian missionaries: the hsien magistrate came to Miss Houston's house for dinner in an "atmosphere of comradery, of mutual tasks and interests"; and at the NLM festivities a young official called on the assembled populace to examine the "Jesus Teaching" for the movement's four virtues. All this, the missionary noted, "would have been impossible five years ago." [56]

Toward the end of the year, the enthusiasm of the Fukien Christians had anything but abated. At its November annual meeting, the Mid-Fukien Synod of the Church of Christ in China voted to recognize that the NLM, "in reviving the original four principles of morals of the Chinese civilization, . . . is most commendable"; the 73 delegates further vowed to do all in their power to promote it. In addition to writing an expression of their approval to the NLM headquarters, these Fukien Christians decided that they should "in the Spirit of Christ see to it that steps are taken for promoting the Movement in every local Church." [57]

Even north of the Yangtze the movement's impact seemed to arouse some Christians. In the vicinity of Peiping, where the Japanese threat was paramount and the government was weakest, there were few reactions at all. But in Kaifeng, the local YMCA secretary felt that the movement posed a formidable challenge in showing what the association itself might have done. He reported that the NLM had "gripped the young men of the country," and he thought it indicated "the felt need for the more abundant life which the Association program stands for." The challenge provided, of course, an opportunity as well: "to show our ability to meet such a challenge by enlarging our program." [58]

By the autumn of 1934 Christians in most parts of China were aware that the year had brought a marked change in their status as a minority. In a November editorial, the *Chinese Recorder* found

China's current attitude toward Christianity an almost startling contrast to the bitterness of the recent past. "All this," the editor wrote, "is part of a growing cooperation between Christian and non-Christian agencies toward a common end—the welfare of the Chinese people." Among the major signs of Christian cooperation with the government were "the emphasis on Confucian ideals and the New Life Movement," for they both showed "a growing realization of the necessity of inculcating moral principles in Chinese minds as well as new economic and social ideals and practices." Here was an opportunity for "the Christian genius . . . to fit easily so as to enlarge its service to China." [59] It seems evident from such writings that Christians were slowly moving away from thoughts of a middle route between radicalism and the Kuomintang; a government infused with Christian leadership and at least semi-Christian ideals was a more promising vehicle for Christian reform efforts. Almost imperceptibly some elements of the Christian activist wing were sliding into an informal entente with the Nanking authorities.

At the time of the NLM's inauguration, it will be remembered, its sponsors called upon all civic and church groups to cooperate. The Nanchang churches in particular were invited to assist by lending their places of worship for meetings and lectures for the general public.[60] By the end of the year, however, the invitation to Christian cooperation had become more emphatic. The revealing document discovered by E. A. Turner in Nanchang was published widely in the early part of January. Meanwhile, Generalissimo and Mme. Chiang Kai-shek had embarked upon airplane tours of northern areas on behalf of the NLM. Wherever they went, they called upon missionaries and churches to lend their aid. At Taiyuan, for instance, the local Christian leaders, Chinese and foreigners, were assembled and addressed first by H. H. Kung, then by Mme. Chiang, and finally, briefly, by the generalissimo. Mme. Chiang reported extensively on government reconstruction work in Kiangsi; she is said to have supplemented her account with extracts from the letters of George Shepherd at Lichuan. Then she explained the movement and the meaning of its four virtues. She assured the Christians of its flexibility; "it takes in any local reform needed in any part of the country," including such diverse problems as opium, foot-binding, and flies. Some criticized the NLM, she acknowledged, and said, "It is no use to talk of these things when there is not enough rice to feed the people." But Mme. Chiang had an answer: "There is plenty of rice. But those who have it hoard it, and those who do not have it do not understand the dignity of labor. No work is too hard if one is honest." It is reported that the lady spoke persuasively, "in excellent English and with charm." [61]

The travels of the Chiangs were supplemented, early in 1935, by a circular letter from the NLM's headquarters to the officials of the National Christian Council, the YMCA, and the YWCA. This letter's appeal for more active cooperation caused considerable discussion. In January the NCC staff had already been considering "New Life" as the theme for the council's biennial meeting in May.[62] When the NLM request arrived, a sub-committee was appointed to read the movement's literature and make recommendations; it was agreed that the church could no longer ignore the NLM.[63] Meanwhile, it was voted to consult with the YMCA and YWCA before making any commitment. In late February the sub-committee of T. C. Kuan and H. H. Tsui reported its findings: the movement, with its 96 points of emphasis, was "good . . . in spirit and nothing contrary to religion, but cannot furnish a real dynamic for new life"; Kuan and Tsui would urge "Christians as individuals to follow its principles, but as a church to leave the movement alone, or there will be endless complications." [64]

At the March meeting of the NCC ad-interim committee, the YMCA and YWCA positions were reported. Both organizations were said to "have taken the attitude that the activities of the New Life Movement have largely appeared in the program of these associations, but that it does not seem advantageous to ally themselves officially with the Movement because it would involve them in reports, etc., and they have so written the headquarters." The NCC leaders decided to follow suit. It was noted that two activities of the movement were of special interest to the church: the anti-opium drive and the emphasis on rural life. But the council could do no more than "wish the Movement success and express sympathy with its general aims without officially allying ourselves with it." [65] NLM requests continued, however, to vex the NCC authorities. In April the movement's then general secretary, Paul Yen, asked to attend the biennial meeting. The council's staff foresaw embarrassment if Yen were invited, for he would desire to speak "and if he speaks he will doubtless urge cooperation with the Movement"; but not to invite him would be equally embarrassing.[66]

As for the YMCA, one full year of the NLM had brought the association's leaders no closer to a clear-cut decision. Certain foreign secretaries, among them E. A. Turner, were outspoken in their admiration for the operation; the revelation of the role played by the YMCA in the generalissimo's thinking filled them with pride and optimism. Turner's report to his friends at home in February 1935 was printed on the back of a New Life poster bearing the generalissimo's picture; to each copy was attached a Sung dynasty copper cash (representing, one assumes, the past) and a small Nationalist flag (representing the present). The movement's purpose, Turner wrote, was to preserve the best of China's past and to guide the nation to "new ideas and ideals, such as democracy, nationalism, patriotism, industrial and political revolutions, education and rights of the common man, which like mighty tides are flowing over the land." [67] In a later letter Turner revealed that his own activities on behalf of the movement in Nanchang had made him often wish "that I were trained in municipal government, city planning, and sanitation, for in spite of lack of training in such matters, one is called into frequent council." [68] Such intensive extra-curricular involvement seems, however, to have incurred the disfavor of the YMCA executives; a few months later, while on furlough in America, Turner learned that his failure to attend to the development of an effective YMCA program in Nanchang had deprived him of reappointment to the post. This was done despite his claim to having developed "a direct relationship with General and Mme. Chiang, which the Committee regarded as important in spite of its adverse effect on our local program." [69]

Turner's case was less than typical. Proximity to the heart of New Life enterprise had kindled an enthusiasm within him which was not fully shared by his colleagues elsewhere. The national committee's draft of a "ten-year policy" in the spring of 1935 showed one cause of their misgivings. At least in its impact upon students, the NLM was falling far short of success. The movement was making a bid for student participation; but the association noted that it had "failed as yet to arouse any widespread interest." Students were as indifferent to the encouragement of Confucian ethics as they were to the current Buddhist revival, and to the various eclectic movements. Where, then, did their interests lie? Once again, the answer was communism. "Socialistic and Communistic literature is being widely read. Russian writers are best-sellers. The policy of suppression seems to whet the appetite of students for such literature." [70]

Another cause for misgivings by 1935 was the NLM's patent link with the party's political apparatus. Whatever initial spontaneity the movement had contained seemed on the wane by the middle months of the year. Kuomintang officials were mouthing the slogans of the movement but showing no character change themselves. Where the generalissimo's example was absent, cynicism was an increasingly widespread response to the NLM. It was little wonder that YMCA officialdom pursued a path of caution in response to the pleas of the movement's directors. The NLM·was still clearly in its formative stage, as a YMCA observer from the U.S. national committee wrote; it reminded him of "the early days of the Fascist organization in Italy, although the 'castor oil-cure' has not yet been invoked." It was a movement, he thought, which might "easily become a great energizing and revitalizing influence in Chinese life." [71] But it was still a movement which the YMCA was determined to treat with discretion.

By the autumn of 1935, then, Christian opinion was divided as to the success of New Life and the precise relationship which the church should seek with the operation. It was viewed by some as exciting, hopeful, and highly Christian in aims; by others as superficial and irrelevant; and by still others as hyper-political and semifascistic. Of the three groups, those best disposed toward the movement were men who had known it in Kiangsi. It is not surprising, therefore, that as the NLM began to falter, Chiang Kai-shek reached into Kiangsi in his search for a Christian who might give the movement itself "new life."

# Chapter Eight

# Missionaries and the Kuomintang: The Gathering Entente

*The Call to George Shepherd*

In the late autumn of 1935 George W. Shepherd, recently returned from furlough, traveled to Nanking to discuss his Kiangsi project with Kuomintang leaders. In the course of his stay, he seems to have had five conferences with the Generalissimo and Mme. Chiang on the New Life Movement as well as Lichuan affairs. Despite the pressure of politics and Japanese aggression, the Chiangs asked him to spend a quiet Sunday with them in their country retreat. He found it encouraging, "after a year's absence and all that has happened," that China's leaders were "more deeply concerned than ever with the spiritual values and the realities of life." [1]

It was during this Nanking visit that the generalisssimo asked Shepherd to become a "director" of the NLM. P. C. Hsu, his associate at Lichuan, was given a similar title; in a way, this was not unusual, as Paul Yen, the current NLM general secretary, had earlier been made a director of the KCRSU. In Kiangsi, rural reconstruction and New Life were two sides of the same coin. Of what the title might mean Shepherd was unsure. "Perhaps it is nothing more than an honor," he wrote on his return to Lichuan, "a position that will involve a conference or two with the staff of the Movement." Any weightier interpretation did not appeal to him as he gazed wistfully toward his old Fukien pastorate: "I am finding it difficult to get any time for Shaowu, under existing conditions, and cannot welcome time-claiming National appointments." He did note, however, that the NLM's rural department was weak; "perhaps P. C. and I can give that a boost." They were already using the movement among the farmers as a means of getting them interested in community needs.[2] Shepherd's hopes for the movement had been high ever since its inauguration. In a contribution to the *China Christian Year Book* for 1934–35 he had described the NLM as "the first shot in a great social revolution that will go down in history." With its coming, he announced, "Radicalism and communism are dead." [3]

To his account of the Nanking visit Shepherd added an interesting postscript ten days later. It revealed, obliquely, the growing bond that was developing between the Congregational missionary and China's dictator. Shepherd reminded the mission office of his previous references to the Chiangs. "It has occurred to me," he wrote, "that they have frequently said that they do not want any publicity on the fact that they are Christians, since Feng Yü-hsiang is still referred to in the papers as the 'so called' Christian General." The reason for Feng's conversion had become widely suspect, and the Chiangs wanted no parallels drawn. "In all events," Shepherd continued, "it will be unwise for us to quote the Gimo or refer in either newspapers or magazines, to anything that I have written you." As an afterthought, however, Shepherd felt "It might be all right to discreetly refer to Mme. as a Christian and leave the Gimo out of the picture." [4] Proximity to power was breeding a new discretion in the outspoken rural reformer.

There is no indication that George Shepherd gave further thought to his NLM sinecure during the first two months of 1936. In March, however, his life was transformed. "Here is a strange letter from a strange place," he wrote in a long message to the mission board marked "Confidential." The place was Nanking, once again. The letter contained news of his appointment to the new full-time post of "adviser" to the NLM.

Shepherd had gone to Nanking to collect on pledges for the Lichuan project. There the Generalissimo and Mme. Chiang had summoned him and requested that he give them some time on the movement, which had just passed its gloomy second anniversary. "For obvious reasons," Shepherd explained, "the work of this movement has not been proceeding as they would like to have it." Part of the trouble lay with the "exigencies of the times," but more important was "the type of men who have had the responsibility of promotion." Increasingly, it seemed, the movement's direction had fallen into the hands of army officers. Actually, he said, the general-issimo wanted this to be a "civilian organized movement, and one which puts the needs of the masses foremost." That was where Shepherd was to fit into the picture.[5]

For the missionary, the new request was hard to fathom. "The only answer I can find is that our response to the invitation to do something for the stricken areas of Kiangsi has left the impression that the Church is prepared to be practical and meet the needs of the nation as they arise." His feelings were mixed and recalled his reaction to his first call to service: "I have the same strange feeling about this movement that both Chang Fu-liang and I had about associating with the government in Kiangsi." And what of his deci-sion? "I am not sure that I have done the right thing, but I have done the *only* thing possible in the face of such an invitation, which involves the church more than it does me personally, and I have agreed to stay by the Gimo and Mme. for the month of March." The Chiangs had shown their gratitude at a small Sunday service in the home of H. H. Kung, where they gathered that evening to study the 46th Psalm. In these surroundings any doubts Shepherd might have harbored seemed to vanish: "As one by one these lead-ers of the nation revealed their spiritual hunger, sang joyously the grand old hymns of the Christian Church, and united in prayer, I felt glad that I had not turned them down." To the China secretary, he exclaimed, "Think of it . . . they can't go to a church service openly. If they did they would lose their lives." [6]

George Shepherd's doubts about the rightness of the cause might disappear; but his self-doubts were persistent. "The New Life Movement is their answer to the needs of a modern China," he con-tinued, "and they are requesting a Christian missionary to be at the heart of it. The responsibility is staggering. When I protested that the burden might be too great, they answered simply, 'you know the needs of our people, you have done it in Kiangsi, you can do it here.'"

Even with such compelling evidence of trust, Shepherd remained troubled. There was Lichuan, still only a small beginning; beyond it, over the mountains, lay the Shaowu parish to which he longed to return. And here in Nanking, the engulfing vastness of a movement for national resurgence. "A man's commitments are ever with him at such a time as this," he wrote. "This question is ever before me, but right or wrong, I am here for a month. A month won't do this job, it merely gives me time to write to you, and then to pray, to consult others, and to think." And then, once more the Christian reformer looked back toward another who tried to change China, and the question fairly bursts across the page: "What would Borodin do with a chance like this?" And more softly, "What will the Christian Church do with it? What should I do about it?" In Boston, the China secretary was deeply moved. To his advice that Shepherd must follow his convictions, he added the comment, "Your sentence 'What would Borodin do with a chance like this' has come back to me again and again." [7]

Meanwhile, George Shepherd had briefly consulted with another Christian activist, Frank J. Rawlinson, editor of the *Chinese Recorder,* a man whose advice he had sought at the time of the Lichuan invitation. At the beginning of March, Shepherd stopped one evening to talk with Rawlinson in Shanghai. The generalissimo's request made the move to Nanking seem not so much an abandonment of Lichuan as a massive extension of the Lichuan idea: Chiang had been so favorably impressed with the Kiangsi work, it was said, that he would like to have "the same methods and personality at work in the New Life Movement." In Nanking Shepherd had had a chance to meet with the hundred young men specially trained under German advisers for leadership in the movement. Rawlinson warned the ABCFM China secretary that this "militaristic basis . . . would be one of the difficulties met in any attempt to reorganize the Movement." In Shanghai Shepherd encountered another of the difficulties: monumental indifference to the NLM on the part of the Chinese municipal authorities. Rawlinson's reaction was that "If George Shepherd or anybody else were going to help in a matter like this they had better care [*sic*] one province like Kiangsi and demonstrate what might be done." As for the editor's private view of the NLM—his public view, one assumes, was that of the *Recorder*'s editorial columns—he chose to define it quite simply, he said, as "an attempt at the regimentation of the moral life of the Chinese." [8] In a reply to Rawlinson's doubts in early April, the ABCFM China Secretary admitted that he himself had "not yet come to a conclusion regarding the wisdom or otherwise of George Shepherd's decision in response to Generalissimo Chiang's request." But conclusion or no, Shepherd was "very much in the situation of Booker Washington's Negro lady friend whom he asked 'Wha's yo gwine, Anna Liza?' and she replied, 'Ah ain't gwine no whar. I'se done been whar I'se gwine.' In other words, George was asked to put in the month of March in this way and it is now April!" [9]

Although he returned periodically to Nanchang and Lichuan, George Shepherd's time of service to both Shaowu and the KCRSU was over. The man who had expressed distaste for "time-claiming National appointments," who had rejoiced that Tinghsien had no big-city headquarters, now found himself the holder of a bureaucrat's job in Nanking. In their April meeting the Kiangsi project's directors took note of Shepherd's new commitment. "It is considered a great honor," they agreed, "that the Associate General Secretary of the Union may help in this important work." [10]

*New Pressures for Cooperation*

When George Shepherd moved to Nanking, in March of 1936, the New Life Movement had just finished its disappointing second year of existence. Nothing had more effectively dramatized the movement's irrelevance to the nation's articulate elements than the nationwide outbreak of student demonstrations in December 1935.[11] The artificial quality of the generalissimo's "mass movement" from above was underscored by the spontaneous formation of National Salvation Associations in the country's leading cities.

Chiang himself gave tacit acknowledgment to this fact in his anniversary address in Nanking on February 19. Although 100,000 workers were now participating in the NLM, there was a notable dearth of tangible results. This was especially true in the larger cities, Chiang said, where orderliness and cleanliness were conspicuous by their absence. Henceforth, the NLM would intensify its enforcement program for the promotion of upright behavior among officials as well as the people. Chiang's rhetoric in Nanking was buttressed by the "Christian General" Feng Yü-hsiang, who inveighed against the evils of smoking, drinking, prostitution, and gambling, and called for the preservation of Chinese virtues.[12]

As a result of the movement's reorganization—of which he was a part—George Shepherd found himself in an anomalous situation. On the one hand, the generalissimo was concerned about the NLM's close identification with the soldier-officials of the Kuomintang, an identification that made the movement distasteful to much of the citizenry. Shepherd was hired as a part of a "civilianizing" effort; and at the same time, the establishment of a Women's Advisory Board under Mme. Chiang marked the beginning of an administrative shift to the generalissimo's wife. On the other hand, Chiang's disappointment with the results achieved so far made him move instinctively toward greater militancy within the movement —toward widespread use of a semi-military Inspection Corps of young men schooled at the Central Political Institute. The conflicting courses of action were fueled, increasingly, from two divergent ideological camps: the American-oriented circles which looked to Mme. Chiang for support, and the axis-oriented products of German, Italian, and Japanese military training. More and more, it seems, the movement's hybrid origins were creating impossible tensions.

A further anomaly in George Shepherd's new employment was the nature of his particular assignment. Its general dimensions had been suggested by the generalissimo in their conversations during March: somehow to make the movement one which "puts the needs of the masses foremost." More specifically, Shepherd's role related to the final element in the NLM's revised program: the extension of its activities from the cities to the rural districts.[13] On the face of it, this was the paramount reason for bringing the Tinghsien convert and Lichuan reconstructionist to the Nanking headquarters. Yet quite a different purpose ultimately determined Shepherd's activities. For the generalissimo clearly saw Shepherd as much more than an enthusiastic rural expert: more significantly, he saw him as a vital link with the leadership of both the Christian church and the American missionary enterprise. In the months to follow, the "needs of the masses" were increasingly subordinated to the generalissimo's own needs for foreign support. The missionaries themselves might well become, in turn, a vital link with the American people and their government. The need for such a link would intensify in direct proportion to Chiang's growing determination to resist Japan with force.

George Shepherd's move to Nanking was coupled with the announcement that his assignment was to give the NLM a more adequate objective by connecting it with "the national reconstruction aim and motivation." [14] The assignment immediately brought him into contact with Mme. Chiang's relatives. "Two weeks ago," he wrote in the middle of March, "Mme. Kung [Mme. Chiang's sister] asked me to draw up a program of work for students during the summer. She said, 'just put in a small booklet a few simple things that students may do when they return to their homes in the villages.' " Proximity to political power meant proximity to financial resources as well: Mme. Kung had promised to meet the entire cost of the program. "It will be called 'The Summer Student Volunteer Movement' or something of that nature," Shepherd added.[15]

The second part of his assignment, however, was touched upon before the end of March. A week after Shepherd's assumption of the NLM duties, the generalissimo had spoken with him about the problem of liaison with the Christian community. It had already been the Chiangs' practice in Nanchang to invite Shepherd to dinner occasionally so that they might chat with him at leisure. "The Generalissimo," Shepherd wrote from Nanking in mid-March, "is about as talkative as Calvin Coolidge . . . so when he speaks it usually means something. Once in Kiangsi, and then again last night, he drew me aside and earnestly requested me to link the Church with this work for the uplift of the people. In this instance he wishes me to get every church group, and every school, solidly behind the NLM." [16]

In the initial months of his employment, Shepherd involved himself primarily in his reconstructionist role. One initial project was the production of literally floating models of New Life in the form of steamboat reforms on the Yangtze River, in cooperation with both the Shanghai labor unions and the China Merchants Steam Navigation Company. He also made some valiant attempts, under dangerous circumstances, to break up key opium gangs in Shanghai and Canton. Another important project was the preparation of a special training program in rural reconstruction for hsien magistrates "so they would return with a commitment to reform." By the autumn the first of several groups of magistrates had been gathered for NLM instruction, and Shepherd himself addressed them. Finally, he also undertook to arouse student enthusiasm, in Nanking and other cities, for the NLM's revival of "the essential values within Chinese civilization." "There was hope that the students could see it," he was later to recall, "but most of the students were so hell-bent on westernization that they couldn't see anything in China." [17]

In the course of these efforts, George Shepherd's contacts with the generalissimo and his wife became increasingly frequent. "I had many opportunities," he said, "to give him advice on the improvement of the life of rural dwellers." And indeed, he seemed to find Chiang receptive. "He came from the villages, lived simply and close to the ordinary village dweller," Shepherd reported. "His interest in the livelihood of the common man was deep. He longed for an honest administration in Nanking, and throughout the hsiens." But at the same time, Shepherd encountered a massive obstacle in Chiang's recurrent question: "Where are the honest men to appoint to these positions?" [18]

In one essential, the generalissimo's developing trust in the missionary took tangible and perhaps unique form. Although the Nanking government had made a practice of hiring foreign consultants for short-term duties, none had ever been given administrative authority within the Chinese government. With George Shepherd the generalissimo made his one and only exception. In the late spring of 1936 he wrote out a special commission and handed it to the missionary. In it Chiang specifically endowed Shepherd with "executive authority," a statement closely followed by the stricture that "this establishes no precedent for giving any other foreigner executive authority." [19]

As the storm clouds of civil war, mutiny, and invasion began to darken, however, such authority—flattering though it may have been—had little significance. With the generalissimo's attention drawn toward rebellion in the south and encroachment from the north, George Shepherd's liaison role became paramount. Among missionaries, Christian colleges, and congregations, he labored indefatigably as a spokesman for church cooperation with the NLM.

Shepherd's appointment itself had had no immediate impact on the Christian community in the early months of 1936. To be sure, he had already relayed the generalissimo's concern to the NCC in November 1935 after his initial Nanking conversation about the NLM. Chiang was ambitious, he told the council's staff, to "get the *Tao li* [principles] of the Movement into the hearts of the people . . . To have a movement which is a mere shell, outward conformity, will be a mockery. They wish to make it real for all sorts of people in all classes of society." Shepherd's message at least convinced the NCC to send one of its members to participate in a national conference of NLM leaders in early 1936.[20]

As for the YMCA, however, an informal conference of secretaries in mid-April produced the customary inconclusive discussion of the movement. Once again, secretaries voiced a variety of concerns: In Kaifeng, the NLM was "under the influence of the military who are not very progressive" and seemed to compete with the association for the people's time; in Nanking, the local association was under considerable pressure to cooperate more fully with the movement, and indeed had been treated with "an increasing coolness" by the generalissimo as a result of its failure to do so.[21] The recent reports of the NLM's imminent reorganization, however, were more encouraging. Henceforth it appeared that the movement would assume "a more military character"; but it would also come under the guidance of George Shepherd, who was known to be a believer in programs which attacked "more fundamental issues in the range of economics and politics." Some secretaries, nonetheless, still regarded the NLM "as really a blue-shirt movement, looking forward to the regimentation of the country under a sort of Fascist regime." The consensus of the conference was that the association should "give enthusiastic support to the Movement but should be very careful to avoid seeming to become an adjunct of the larger movement."[22]

Such was clearly a less satisfactory attitude than either Chiang Kai-shek or his missionary aide desired from Christian agencies. For the time being, the generalissimo's attention was diverted by an apparently serious threat to his rule, the Liang-Kwang uprising in the south. But the ominous revolt turned out to be as short-lived as it was bloodless; by the end of the summer Chiang's position was more secure than ever before. He was now ready to press with new vigor his courtship of the church and its members.

In September 1936 the NLM headquarters in Nanking extended an unprecedented invitation to the Christian community throughout China. It moved from its earlier generalized appeal to a specific series of recommended regulations for the establishment of "New Life Movement Service Groups" among all Christian organizations. Such service groups would be composed of the members of the Christian churches or organizations and would be led by the pastor, preacher, or executive officer. Each group was to be subject to the supervision of the local NLM association, and its program was to include the following: first, each member must "pledge his or her personal allegiance to all New Life principles"; second, each member must see to it that his or her family observe these principles; third, each group must strive to win all other members of their organization to "living the New Life"; fourth, they must extend New Life to all friends and neighbors; and finally, they must promote the NLM "in all church services and Christian assemblies." As an additional requirement, it was noted, all activities of the service groups must be reported to the local NLM Association.[23]

There is no record of an immediate Christian response to the terms of the September invitation. Yet the dramatic developments of the next six months were destined to produce solid new bonds between Nanking and the church.

### Sian and the Altered Climate

As noted in an earlier chapter, the autumn of 1936 was a period of confidence and consolidation for Kuomintang China.[24] With gathering momentum, the generalissimo seemed to be hardening in his attitude toward Japan. His personal popularity rose accordingly. As one Chinese observer commented in the *China Weekly Review* at the end of November, "After a long waiting and desperate search, we, to our great joy, have at long last found our Leader. The small bright figure which we first saw a few years ago has now grown to a real giant, and the erstwhile star has transformed itself into a radiant sun." [25]

Against such a background, the news of the generalissimo's kidnapping at Sian on the night of December 11 left large sections of the nation aghast. For thirteen days Chiang's life and the nation's unity hung in the balance. At Sian, Chiang's Manchurian captors and their Communist allies came and went in the room where the injured leader lay. And then, inexplicably, on Christmas Day the nation learned of Chiang's release and return to Nanking. The reaction was three days of frenzied national joy. China had "found" its leader.[26] The Sian Incident was a turning point of preeminent significance for the career of Chiang Kai-shek and the history of Kuomintang China. It had a special impact, as well, on the person of George Shepherd and the outlook of the Christian community.

For George Shepherd, Sian produced a sudden confrontation with ugly forces whose presence he had but barely sensed in the past. As soon as the mutiny occurred, Mme. Chiang had summoned the missionary to her side. In the next few days, Shepherd claims to have learned of a plot in Nanking to destroy the generalissimo by the bombing of Sian. To his astonishment, one center of the plot lay in the NLM itself, where "a General Teng" had set up an apparatus of young officers who were fascist sympathizers, trained under Germans and Italians. Teng was said to have sent his men throughout the country to prepare for a coup d'état which would install General Ho Ying-ch'in, the minister of war, as dictator "because he is easy to control." But pro-Chiang elements in Nanking were able to avert the bombing of Sian while negotiations took place. And during the ensuing days of waiting, Shepherd had maintained Nanking's contact with the generalissimo by means of messages exchanged with Chiang's Australian adviser, W. H. Donald, at Sian. According to Shepherd, the "Fascist groups" did their best to censor these telegrams and sever the communications entirely. When Chiang was finally released, the missionary was called to the ancestral retreat at Fenghua. There, in the company of W. H. Donald and Wei Tao-ming, he shared for eight days the generalissimo's self-imposed seclusion.[27]

If anything, the Sian crisis bred in George Shepherd a new sense of loyalty and urgency: loyalty to the person of Chiang Kai-shek, in the face of the threat from the Right; and urgency about the need for intensified support from the Christian community. In Shepherd's view, the only possible alternative to Chiang Kai-shek now was "chaos." [28] In such circumstances, the ideals of social reconstruction were soon superseded by concern for the public relations of his chief. Inevitably, in the first months of 1937, the reconstructionist gave way to the promoter.

In his promotional task Shepherd received two large pieces of assistance from the generalissimo himself. Christians had already joined in the national thanksgiving over Sian's result.[29] But Chiang's stature in their eyes was immeasurably increased that spring by two apparent revelations of the generalissimo's spiritual life. The first was Chiang's Good Friday message to the Methodists' Eastern Asia Conference on March 26. The second was the publication, in early May, of extracts from his journal under the title of *Sian: A Coup d'État*.[30] Both documents emphasized the paramount role of the Bible, prayer, and religious faith in bringing the generalissimo through the December crisis.

The *Chinese Recorder* greeted Chiang's revelation with unrestrained satisfaction. Chiang's message to the Methodists was something which "would have been unthinkable . . . twenty or so years ago." It showed simplicity and sincerity; it showed how the Bible had brought strength to the general; and there seemed to breathe through it a sense of fellowship with Christians. "Here and there," to be sure, "one may see how Confucian emphases are being carried forward into and supplemented by Christ's principles." But to the editor, the main point about the message was "its recognition that the Christian faith, being adventurous, meets the needs of adventurous people." [31] In the same issue of the *Recorder,* the editor concluded that China's current attitude toward religion was more hopeful than it had been for years: "There is an inarticulate feeling that economic, social and political changes are not enough. Thus for all kinds of aggressive movements the hour is propitious." [32]

Indeed, the hour was viewed as so propitious that Christian reservations concerning the NLM might be reexamined and withdrawn. The May issue of the *Recorder,* in which the two editorials above appeared, was itself chiefly devoted to the subject of "Christian Co-operation With the New Life Movement." The time had come, the editor announced, "for the churches to give it serious attention as a force in the life of China with which they can work . . . The fact that its purpose runs so nearly parallel with that of the churches indicates that the New Life Movement is a new channel through which the life that should characterize the churches may flow into more extended channels." [33] Other writers were similarly optimistic. Shepherd himself contributed two articles to the issue. In the first, he wrote of the natural harmony of aims between the NLM and the church. The movement was "not a rival of the church and cannot do the spiritual work that only the church is qualified to do." On the contrary, the NLM "gives the church a large place in Chinese society, and a standing that has not been previously so frankly acknowledged, but it grants this status believing that the church and its institutions have spiritual vitality." His closing injunction: "May the church take care that it does not let the New Life Movement down!" [34] In a second piece of promotional writing, Shepherd defended the objectives of the movement. It was important, he warned, to have all church members "live New Life." Of the virtues proclaimed by the NLM, the most significant, he announced, was honesty, for "at the heart of most of China's problems lies the matter of dishonesty." [35]

In the same issue of the *Recorder,* R. Y. Lo of the NCC argued that New Life meant a new birth, was therefore based on the fundamentals of Christianity, and should be promoted by all Christians. Lo saw the personification of the movement in Chiang Kai-shek: the reason he and General Feng Yü-hsiang were "so stable in their characters can be definitely traced to their profound faith in the Christian religion." [36] Mme. Chiang herself contributed an appeal for Christian assistance. The cross, she wrote, had always been "in the background of the New Life Movement." It had always been at the center, too, of the generalissimo's life and her own. Since Sian, Chiang had been giving "more and more time to the development of character" through the movement. "There was a time," she admitted, "when some thought they might make a political instrument out of the New Life Movement, but this can never be." It must remain "a movement within the hearts and lives of the people," and "if we Christians should be busy about any task, surely it is this." [37]

The logic of a tie-in with the church had already been stressed anew some weeks before in an edition of *The China Press Weekly Supplement* devoted to "Ten Years of Nationalist China." Writing in this issue, one C. Kuangson Young had foreseen a day when the movement would "act as the meeting place every Sunday of the villagers and the surrounding country folk." Such gatherings would "create a unifying force for the nation that cannot be paralleled"—

an effect similar to the "unity of purpose and thought" which the West achieved on Sundays, a unity "not to be found any other day." In the West, Young added, "The masses are told, in a nutshell, to do good. They are admonished to be unselfish. From these centers [that is, churches] social welfare work radiates." [38]

There were still some Christians, to be sure, who were far less enthusiastic; most of them were Chinese, not foreigners. The May *Recorder* included as well a brief symposium on the NLM in which three Chinese continued to emphasize the movement's "superficiality." Kiang Wen-han, the YMCA's perceptive student secretary, felt that the real question of the masses was still "one of livelihood," not manners. The movement's effectiveness, furthermore, was limited by its close connection with the government and official groups. The task of Christians, said Kiang, went much further than any tasks set by the NLM. Others criticized the movement's "odor of formality and external authority," its lack of spiritual force. "It gives us a lot of platitudes," wrote Z. K. Zia, "but it has no technique for the attainment of spirituality." [39]

Among Christians, however, such articulate critics were few by the spring of 1937. More and more the movement was being viewed in the bright new light shed among missionaries by the generalissimo's Christian affirmations; more and more, in fact, those Christian circles that admired the movement were coming to equate New Life with the generalissimo, and the generalissimo with the government. A large body of Christian support for Chiang and his regime was now rising out of a common stake in moral uplift. And the common stake was compounded by the post-Sian euphoria: a sense that China was on the threshold of unity and increased progress under a strong national leader.

The change in climate was perceptible in the deliberations of the NCC's various committees. In April the NLM was discussed at some length by a Sub-committee on Studies, which was preparing for the 1938 International Missionary Council meeting at Hangchow. In relation to "The Church and Its Environment," the NLM seemed an element of special significance; for "in it we have a Movement distinctly Chinese which has turned to the Church for aid." It was suggested that the NLM "might help to supply the solution of the social responsibility of the church by furnishing a center around which Christians could gather." At the same time, it should "be borne in mind that the Christian conception of human relations in industry and economics is inadequately dealt with by the Movement, and that fundamentally the Church had long stood for many of the things which the Movement is now advocating." It was voted to have two members join with Frank Rawlinson of the *Chinese Recorder* in preparing a memorandum on the NLM for the biennial meeting in May.[40]

As May approached, formal action on the NLM loomed as a growing necessity. One of the chief speakers scheduled for the biennial meeting was Mme. Chiang herself, and it was predictable that she would exhort the delegates to cooperation with the movement. By the NCC Cabinet meeting of April 27, George Shepherd had already approached the staff about the NCC's response. It was agreed that "we must be prepared for some formal action if Mme. Chiang speaks in advocacy of the cooperation of the churches." Preliminary action would include the elaboration of "two or three principles of cooperation" and a judicious announcement by the chairman after Mme. Chiang's speech that the subject would be fully discussed in the course of the conference.[41]

The biennial meeting took place in Shanghai on May 5–11, and Mme. Chiang, in her address to the opening session, did indeed demand full-scale Christian cooperation with the movement. In one of the ensuing sessions, the Rawlinson committee presented its memorandum. This document was a thorough review of the NLM's three years of life. Its premise was the desirability of "concrete plans . . . by which cooperation might be effected between the church and the state in a united effort for national reconstruction." [42]

The memorandum began by listing six general observations on the movement. Three years were "too short a period to evaluate its real influence"; yet it was "a move in the right direction and a worthy cause." As a movement "for the re-shaping of the people's modes and concepts of life and for the improvement of their social life," it was a social revolutionary force. It was also a "character-uplifting movement" in its promotion of a regulated life. It was "a noble effort to save the nation from degeneration and decadence" —and hence a rejuvenating influence. Finally and most significantly, "as the leaders at the headquarters of the movement are many of them Christians, the movement may be considered one possible expression of the Christian faith." [43]

This document did not stop with such generalized compliments, however. It proceeded to list seven criticisms of the NLM. The movement had "an odor of formality and external authority"; it was somewhat superficial; it was only "able to go forward because of the important forces behind it"; it failed to emphasize sufficiently "a change of heart, a spiritual re-birth, or a living of the life"; it lacked spiritual force, tended to fall back on platitudes, and had "no adequate technique for attainment." It included "apparently the militarization of the people for war." And it lacked "a central personality or an example for the people to emulate." [44]

The memorandum's concluding section was devoted to suggestions for church cooperation with the movement. Christians should first study the needs, meaning, and content of the movement. They should realize, moreover, that "Christianity is and has always been a New Life Movement," and that Christians should therefore emphasize the Christian way of living. Christians must uphold the "unique teaching and message of Christianity and make the Cross the centre of new life." Furthermore, Christians must "realize that the duty of the church is to impart the spiritual vitality desired by the New Life Movement." To fulfill this duty, Christians should pray daily for China, as the NLM requested: "Let the love of God and the love of country go together." Finally, Christians should "cooperate with the Movement without hesitation and carry out as many as possible of its activities in conjunction with the program of the church for reconstructive service." [45]

The generally sympathetic views of the Rawlinson memorandum dominated the atmosphere of the biennial meeting. The new general secretary's opening address was symptomatic of the new bond between church and state. W. Y. Chen (Ch'en Wen-yuan) noted that "the attitude of the people toward the Central Government is completely changed. Instead of suspicion they show faith." Chen cited the Sian Incident as the crucial turning point: Even those who formerly opposed Chiang Kai-shek had changed their attitude. In such a situation, the question for the church was simply, "What part can we Christians play in furthering the cause of national unity?" The answer lay in a united front with the NLM; Chinese leaders had discovered that the nation needed "the spiritual and moral bases for national regeneration," and "the New Life Movement is born in this search for spirituality." [46] Clearly, Christians and the Kuomintang could unite forces in such a quest.

It is no surprise, therefore, that the delegates to the biennial meeting accepted with enthusiasm the principles of cooperation with the NLM. The political motives which many had suspected in the movement seemed now to be absent. A fresh confidence had been inspired not only by the Christian professions of the Chiangs but by the participation of George Shepherd and by the movement's new secretary-general, Colonel J. L. Huang of the OMEA. By now four of the movement's top executives were former YMCA secretaries. The delegates formally approved cooperation with the NLM, "recognizing in the ideals of the New Life Movement many of the same objectives that Christians have always taught." [47]

"Cooperation" remained, of course, an imprecise term. When the NCC staff met to discuss implementation of the resolution, they found themselves lacking in specific recommendations. W. Y. Chen suggested that the best procedure would be informal church activities to Christianize the movement. Chen wanted Christians to address groups of NLM leaders as well as the reverse; he evidently saw the relationship as a two-way process. Action was deferred, however, pending conferences with J. L. Huang as to precisely what the movement wanted churches to do. [48] With the outbreak of hostilities in the north, nationwide church-state cooperation in support of the NLM remained a still-born scheme.

Meanwhile, the new outlook of the NCC was reflected in such reports as those dispatched by the YMCA's representative in Nanking, George A. Fitch, formerly of the Shanghai Foreign YMCA. Fitch, who had arrived in the capital in September 1936, found it "a city of extraordinary progress and change." He rejoiced that the NLM, now "taken out of politics," was "seeking the cooperation of the church and the YMCA." He was also delighted to report that Mme. Chiang had termed the YMCA and YWCA "one of our greatest aids in giving youth a zest for New Life." At the same time, the generalissimo's pro-Christian statements seemed to him to provide a great opportunity for establishing YMCA branches in government colleges, military academies, and the like. [49] But Fitch's enthusiasm did not restrict itself to New Life and the present. Like a good number of foreign Christians, he came to eulogize the man responsible for the present, the man who had ushered in the new day. "Some of our best papers," he wrote in early July 1937, "have persisted in referring to General Chiang as Dictator and as having won his position by the ruthless slaughter of countless thousands of communists. If you have read the Generalissimo's 'Sian Diary' and his Good Friday speech . . . you will realize how unjust and absurd these accusations are. Without a doubt he is one of the truly great men of the world today, and a great Christian." [50]

To be sure, the skeptics still remained—and were undoubtedly more widespread in the Christian and missionary community than the record would suggest.[51] Christian educators, in touch with student radicalism, were skeptical of the movement and its enthusiasts. And meanwhile a few Christian rural reformers were beginning to develop a friendlier view of the Kuomintang's old adversaries, the Chinese Communists; from the spring of 1936 onward the Communists had apparently suspended their anti-Christian activities, especially in North China.[52] Yet, in some circles, at least, the Kuomintang-Christian entente had become a mutual admiration society, and in the warmth of the new camaraderie certain hard facts of history were easily vaporized. In the process, the foundation was being laid for a relationship that would last through World War II and well beyond.

### Aftermath: The Reformer Bows Out

In the first half of 1937, George Shepherd was moving toward a similar equation of the NLM with the generalissimo, and the generalissimo with the government. As the promoter of the one, he became the promoter of all three. Inevitably, his initial function as a revitalizer of the movement underwent a transformation; it was a change that was eventually to prove his undoing.

Shepherd's close association with the Chiangs had early produced a delicate financial problem. In March 1936 the generalissimo had given him a "small Ford car." [53] By the autumn, he had offered to underwrite Shepherd's salary, and the missionary passed the suggestion on to the Boston authorities. But the China secretary's response was a categorical refusal. In so doing, he cited a statement Shepherd had earlier ascribed to Mme. Chiang: she had told him, it seems, that "one of the disappointing things about most missionaries is that they so often become like the Chinese and fail to make any distinct contribution to modern China." Shepherd's independence as a mission appointee, the secretary wrote, was invaluable. Any financial infringement of this independence "might compromise you in relation to any statements which you might make which were favorable to General and Madam Chiang." This danger, the secretary continued, suggested a second point. In a sentence which later seemed prophetic, he warned that "there is very great danger in your becoming a propagandist for the Chiangs either in China or in America." [54] Shepherd accepted the board's decision and later reaffirmed its wisdom. He continued to live on his ABCFM salary; the NLM imbursed him only for special expenses incurred in his duties.[55]

Since Sian, however, these duties included increasingly the function of privy counselor to the generalissimo and his wife. This role had its own promotional aspect, not only with the mission and church authorities, but with American officialdom at a time when diplomats were beginning to revise their old pessimistic estimates of Chiang's survival power. To such officials Shepherd began to serve as an informal conveyor belt, on Chiang's behalf.

One such interview, with the American ambassador, took place in May of 1937. In a conversation with Nelson T. Johnson, Shepherd spoke at length of the generalissimo's character and position. He told Johnson, first, of the attempted right-wing coup during the Sian Incident. His conclusion was that Chiang had become an indispensable man: for if he were to be removed, chaos and fascism would result. The generalissimo, he continued, was a lonely ruler with no friends. He was not on terms of enough intimacy with his own officers, indeed, to ask them to dine with him. Meanwhile, he was confronted with the growing problem of young officers trained in Italy, Germany, and the fascistic NLM schools. As a man, Shepherd felt, Chiang was a true revolutionary. He wanted genuinely to see an end to corruption; he desired to effect a full revolution for China. His attitude, nonetheless, was that of an "oriental despot"; this attitude, Shepherd added, was most clearly shown in his stubbornly held views on the expenditure and accounting of money.[56]

Shepherd's remarks made a good impression on the American ambassador. Johnson found the missionary both "modest and honest" in his attempts to guide the generalissimo's actions. The ambassador concluded that Chiang "is dependent on people like Shepherd and Donald . . . he lives like an Oriental Despot, isolated from his own people who cooperate with him through fear and because they want the national unity for which he stands." [57]

Despite Shepherd's success with missionaries and diplomats, however, Chiang Kai-shek's dependence on him could not survive the outbreak of Sino-Japanese hostilities in the summer of 1937. In the face of the generalissimo's military preoccupation, the American's contacts were now generally restricted to his wife. Meanwhile, the NLM itself was being rapidly transformed into a war relief agency. In late 1937 Mme. Chiang dispatched Shepherd on an air mission to the United States and Great Britain in behalf of relief work and the ideals of the NLM. On his return to China in 1938 Shepherd followed the refugee government to Chungking. His position was still that of NLM adviser. But by the end of the year it seemed that his usefulness might be greater on a fund-raising expedition to America. In January 1939 George Shepherd left China for the last time.

For some months, on his return to America, Shepherd made headlines as a spokesman for the cause of Free China and its generalissimo; his relationship with the Chiangs was by now a widely known fact. He stayed through 1939, then took a year's furlough in 1940 to get his children well situated in American schools. Yet despite his continuing efforts on behalf of the Free China government, it was not long before he fell prey to the professional perils of both privy counselor and impassioned publicist. Although he had not heard from the Chiangs since 1939, Shepherd expected to return to his NLM post in Chungking some time in 1941. From a third party, however, he learned that his commission had lapsed. Mme. Chiang, the Shepherds were told, "has felt rather resentful of the reports reaching her from America that George was appearing as her 'representative.' " There was "a general assumption," furthermore, "that this feeling would stand in the way of the resumption of the previous type of service." [58]

Meanwhile, in 1940, another missionary, James G. Endicott, had moved into Shepherd's job with the NLM. A Canadian with long experience in Szechwan, Endicott survived the wartime assignment for barely two years. Yet he in turn fell out with the Chiangs over their failure to support basic reforms, and he publicly broke with both them and their regime; in later years, indeed, Endicott was to become one of North America's leading apologists for the Communist government in Peking.[59]

George Shepherd's rebuff in early 1941 produced no such bitterness. As a minister, first in Illinois, then in Massachusetts, he was an indefatigable spokesman for the Chungking government during the years of World War II.[60] His public loyalty to the Chiangs and their regime remained unwavering, despite the disillusionment that began to engulf the U.S. press. As he was later to comment, "I was convinced all along—and am still convinced—that the nationalist government, with all its faults, held the door open to freedom— whereas the Communists did not." [61] By 1944, as a result, Shepherd found himself the target of a rising tide of anti-Kuomintang sentiment in America. Within Congregational circles, in fact, the estranged counselor was even accused of being in the pay of the Nationalists.[62]

The patent irony of the accusation was compounded by the fact that George Shepherd's private misgivings about the Nationalist regime had intensified markedly since his departure from China. In mid-1943 he reported to the China secretary on a trip he had taken to Washington for conferences with Chinese officials and private citizens. His discoveries there were deeply distressing. At Chungking, a marked deterioration had set in during the past four years. "The present narrow nationalistic clique that dominates the Chiang government," he wrote, "is at heart antagonistic to the Church and all liberal institutions . . . How much Chiang is in sympathy with this new trend it is hard to discover at this distance from Chungking." The ugly forces that Sian revealed had now moved into power. "It is this inside control of China's National Government by a small clique of ultra-conservative fascist minds that has compelled such a large number of Chinese liberal leaders, Christian and otherwise, to seek a haven in America for the duration of the war." [63]

In private Shepherd could only conclude that "Chiang is now a prisoner within the government clique that he has allowed himself to be surrounded with." [64] In public, however, he continued to urge all-out support for the regime and for the man he had come to see as its chief hope for salvation.

# Chapter Nine
# The Fate of Gradualism in
# Kuomintang China—I

## The Decade in Retrospect

By September 1937, in the last months of the Nanking decade, the Nationalist government of China had reached the zenith of its prestige among Chinese and foreigners alike. In its hour of gravest crisis, its support was well nigh universal. The cause of national resistance was a universal one in which parties, factions, and critics could wholeheartedly unite, suspending for a while old feuds, forgetting old wounds and misgivings. At its helm was Chiang Kaishek, onetime "Red General," onetime "butcher of Shanghai," onetime "lackey of the imperialists," onetime "dictator" and "Oriental Despot"—but now, transformed, the embodiment of national resistance, the symbol of national survival, the "erstwhile star" become a "radiant sun." As warlords and peasants, businessmen and intellectuals, missionaries and diplomats rallied to his side, so ultimately did his oldest enemies, the Chinese Communists, who formally entered a second United Front with the Kuomintang late in the month. For diverse reasons, and with varying expectations, the Chinese of the Nanking decade gave their allegiance, the foreigners their admiration, and under the shadow of Japan's expansionism, Chinese unity became a temporary reality.

But what, in point of fact, had changed? Two new elements had entered the picture: Japan's decision to move, and Nanking's decision to fight. But beyond this, what else? What of the old unsolved problems, now blurred by the national élan? What of the deficiencies in leadership, the confusion in goals, the divisions within society? What, in short, underlay the new unity? What was the record of accomplishment by the end of the decade, when national reconstruction moved out and national resistance moved in?

By contrast with what had come before, the achievements of Kuomintang reconstruction were considerable. Of particular significance was the regime's progress toward the recovery of full sovereignty, the creation of a modern army, the introduction of Western law, the development of a stable currency, the encouragement of industry, and the construction of basic communications.[1] In all these areas, China had utilized, from time to time, the advice of foreign experts—League of Nations technicians, German army officers, British and French postal personnel, and Americans trained in law, finance, and transportation.[2] In the Yangtze River basin, the results were especially impressive.

Beyond such accomplishments, however, lay two vast areas in which the ten-year record of Nationalist achievement was small indeed. The first was social welfare for the villager; the second was ideology for the citizen. In 1937, despite the efforts of a decade, all evidence from the countryside pointed to a worsening of the condition of the peasant. At the same time, in the schools and colleges of China, all evidence also pointed to the steady rise of the Kuomintang's ideological foe, the gospel of Marx and Lenin.

For a nation where four fifths of the population were peasants, the first area of failure had far-reaching implications. For a people in search of something to fill the vacuum left by the collapse of Confucianism, the second failure's implications were equally great. Waiting in the wings, ready to unite and meet both unmet needs, were the revolutionary practitioners of Maoism.

Such failures had implications, too, for Americans who had served in the China of the Nanking government. These would-be agents of reform—the missionaries, the foundation men, and the experts—had gradually come to recognize both needs. In trying to influence the development of modern China, they had eventually directed their efforts, above all, to two areas: to rural reconstruction, and to ideological reform—to the social welfare and attitudes of the Chinese people. They had done so as Christians and individualist democrats, and their concern was for the well-being and evolutionary reconstruction of China, soul by soul and village by village. In so doing, they had been the chief Western bearers of the gradualist alternative in China—the alternative of nonviolent evolutionary reform. Through their growing ties with the Kuomintang and their opposition to its enemies, Nanking's failure became, in part, their failure as well. In probing that failure, one probes as well the fate of gradualism itself.

### Rural Reconstruction: Three Unmet Needs

In February 1933, as communism perched on Fukien's doorstep, George Shepherd quoted Chinese Christians as saying, "God's time of reckoning with corrupt officials, land-grabbers, and money-lenders seems to be near at hand." In these three terms Fukien Christians had suggested the paramount economic needs of the Chinese countryside: tax reform, land reform, and agricultural credit. It is notable that throughout the years of the rural reconstruction movement, nowhere was action less adequate than in meeting these three needs. To be sure, China's peasants had other needs, too: among them, literacy, education, health clinics, agricultural improvement, rural engineering, village industrial aid, and training in politics and culture. But the first three needs remained supreme. And even in the other areas the decade's achievements were small.

*The land tenure problem.* As noted in Chapter 3, tenancy showed a continuous increase after 1911, and by 1937 it was estimated that almost two thirds of China's farmers were tenants.[3] The crux of the problem was not so much the fact of tenancy but the oppressive conditions of tenancy. One effective cure for the abuse of tenancy would have been the enforcement of an equitable level for the land rent, coupled with an increase in the per capita productivity and income of the rural population.[4] A more drastic solution would have been the eradication of tenancy itself by forcible expropriation and redistribution.

The Nanking government espoused both solutions and effected

neither. While paying lip service to Sun Yat-sen's objective of "land to the tiller," the government stipulated a land rent ceiling of 37.5 per cent of the main crop in its land law of 1930. This measure would have provided considerable relief for tenants accustomed to paying an average rental of 60 per cent. In no province, however, was redistribution ever attempted; and the rent ceiling itself was never enforced anywhere beyond a handful of "model hsien." [5]

To be sure, the government found itself subjected to repeated pressures to undertake a reform in land tenure. The most outspoken of Nanking's critics in this regard were the League of Nations advisers. As noted earlier, Stampar of Yugoslavia first pressed in 1933 and then again in 1936 for land reform in Kiangsi. "No radical improvement can be made in the position of the farmer," he had warned, "without a land reform." [6] Such attempts, however, were unavailing. The Nanking government was wedded to the landed gentry; as George Taylor had written from Kiangsi, Nanking was convinced that "The way to defeat Communism is to strengthen, both politically and economically, those classes of the population that have most to fear from Communism." [7] These were classes, furthermore, that often as not had official positions within the Kuomintang or close ties with important provincial governments.

Within the regime itself, of course, there were both agricultural specialists and politicians who dissented from the prevailing view.[8] Among the latter were such left-Kuomintang remnants as Wang Ching-wei and Sun Fo. Under the aegis of Sun Fo's Sun Yat-sen Institute for the Advancement of Culture and Education, such outspoken internal critics as K'ung Hsueh-hsiung singled out land reform and political reform as the key missing ingredients throughout the rural reconstruction movement.[9] Devoid of military power, however, the critics remained helpless in the face of the government's resolve. Because that resolve seems to have stemmed from the generalissimo himself, his outlook merits special attention.

In early 1934, the executive yuan met in Nanking to consider the reconstruction proposals of Stampar and his League of Nations colleagues. In anticipation of that meeting, Chiang Kai-shek expressed his own views emphatically in a telegram from Nanchang to the members of the yuan.[10] "The so-called agrarian policy of the Red bandits is merely their weapon of war, and nothing else," Chiang announced. Even so, he noted, there still seemed to be "some members of the Party who are aggrieved at the failure of the Government to emulate and enforce such a land policy." His reply to them: "If we wanted to adopt their policy, we would have to discard our Party principles and adopt a new name for our Party like the Fukien insurgents." The generalissimo proceeded to describe the Communist methods in the various stages of the expropriation process—all designed, he said, "to prolong the period of 'Red pauperism' so as to force the poor to join the ranks of the Red bandits and fight their battles"—and then asked, rhetorically, "Is our Party's programme for the equalization of land to be compared to this?" [11]

In Chiang's view, the telegram had continued, the agrarian question embodied two problems: first, the matter of redistribution, second, that of "exploitation and land readjustment"; and the latter aspect was "more urgent than . . . redistribution." In his discussion of redistribution, Chiang repeated the old objectives of Sun Yat-sen: the Party's "settled policy" was to realize "the system of equalization of landownership," and the ultimate goal object was to "give land to all tillers of the soil." But all this was to be accomplished by peaceful means, gradually, and without "class strife." And how should this be done? Chiang's plan involved a system of maximum limits on landholdings (with the excess land subject to graduated taxes), together with special land-purchase options for village cooperative societies, the purchases to be financed by loans from banking interests. "This will result," Chiang added, "in the gradual acquisition by these societies of all farms in the villages," and the societies themselves would distribute land in accordance with the need of their members. As a result of such a procedure, "the Government need not either float loans or take forcible measures for the acquisition of the land." Chiang closed his telegram with a warning: "I hope our comrades will not forget the stand of our Party vis-à-vis this particular question, nor allow themselves to be misled by Communist propaganda regarding the so-called agrarian policy." [12]

Caught between this message from their chief and the recommendations of the League experts, the members of the executive yuan had no alternative but to indulge in "careful deliberations" and arrive at no decision. The fourth plenary session of the

Kuomintang Central Executive Committee referred the matter back to the Central Political Council; a study commission was appointed; and the problem was discreetly dropped.[13] In brief, the generalissimo's views were in harmony with those of the landholding pillars of the Nanking regime. Even his own imprecise plan remained a dead letter: maximum limits were never enforced, and agricultural credit was virtually nonexistent. At the same time, government officials were quick to cite the prohibitive cost of a comprehensive land survey as an obstacle to action; a "reasonable estimate" in 1934 put the figure at $150 million.[14] Yet, as noted earlier, such a cadastral survey—of quantity and quality—was not essential to a reform in land tenure. Its importance lay in a second crucial area: that of land tax reform.

*The land tax problem.* In 1928 the Nanking government decreed a division of tax resources which may be compared with that which occurred in the period of the Taiping Rebellion. In the 1850's *likin* collected locally on goods in transit and goods sold, as a local tax, was left largely in provincial hands. Peking was not strong enough to take over this new revenue source. In 1928 Nanking was not strong enough to get control of the local land taxes in most provinces; it therefore announced that revenues from the land would go to the support of local and provincial government. Through this action the Kuomintang government lost all opportunity for the creation of a rational, centralized tax structure in which the land-tax burden might have been lessened and made more uniform. Not until 1941, when the refugee government found itself deprived of former revenues from the nation's "modern" sector, did the land tax revert to the central regime.

One result of Nanking's renunciation of land revenues was an intensification of rural indebtedness. In the absence of intervention and reform by the central government, provincial and local authorities continued the abusive practices of the previous decade: anachronistically high evaluations compounded by the recurrent imposition of surcharges. In many regions the old evils of special military levies, corruption, tax evasion by the rich, and advance collection of future taxes all continued unchecked by Nanking.[15] As usual, those who suffered most were the unprotected and illiterate poor—victims of corrupt officials, tax collectors, and their wealthier (and well-connected) neighbors.

To be sure, some attempts were made to conduct a nationwide cadastral survey during the years of the Nanking government. But by 1946 only 2.7 per cent of the total area of the country had been surveyed. And even in the most widely surveyed province, Chekiang, only 16.6 per cent had been covered.[16] Under such continuing conditions of land-rent and land-tax distress, it is little wonder that the third great need of the rural population in the Nanking decade was extensive facilities for agricultural credit.

*The rural credit problem.* According to Franklin Ho, statistics gathered in 22 provinces between 1938 and 1947 show that "at least one-half of the rural population was always in debt." Other data from the mid-thirties also indicate that the sources of rural credit remained, as before, more often personal than institutional. To meet his obligations to landlord or tax collector, the peasant had to look to the local money lender. And in village China the exorbitant interest rates of the past prevailed—5 per cent per month on money loans, in normal times, and higher rates for grain loans.[17]

One potential solution to the peasant's credit problem was the creation of rural cooperatives. Since 1924, the China International Famine Relief Commission had pioneered in the provision of agricultural credit. It had pointed the way toward the formation of rural cooperatives, and various government and private agencies attempted to extend this work in the thirties. Chief among them were the NEC, which collaborated with both the CIFRC and the National Flood Relief Commission in several provinces.[18] The normal cooperative institution was the credit society of 20–30 farmers with a working capital of $1,000–2,000 and shares ranging from $1 to $20; also widespread were marketing societies, consumers' cooperatives, and utilization societies.[19]

The Nanking government's efforts to create rural credit, however, fell far short of the peasants' needs. As noted above, it had been the generalissimo's expectation that the nation's private banks would go to the aid of villagers. To some extent, banks responded —notably in the Kincheng Banking Corporation's assistance to the Tinghsien cooperatives from 1933 and in the Shanghai Commercial and Savings Bank's work on rural credit in South China.[20] But the majority of the nation's modern banking institutions confined their operations to the more lucrative business of treaty-port finance and loans to the central government. The short-term high-interest opportunities in urban areas kept bank credit out of the countryside. As a result of such institutional failings, the nation's agricultural cooperatives succeeded in distributing only 1 per cent of the total rural credit extended between 1933 and 1935; and these funds went, in turn, to only 5 per cent of the farmers borrowing.[21] In 1935 the government established an Agricultural Credit Administration; but this agency had shown few results by the outbreak of the war.

By the end of the decade, then, the Nanking government's success in the three fundamental areas of rural need was virtually nonexistent. To be sure, its contributions to the agricultural development of China had been considerable in certain technical areas: notably in seed improvement, production increase, and crop rotation. In the development of pest control and the use of chemical fertilizers some progress had also been achieved. Through agricultural experiment stations, through research in 14 experimental hsien, and through the paper plans of a host of committees, many aspects of farming had been subjected to careful study. Among the more promising were the studies produced by the Rural Rehabilitation Commission of the executive yuan, the Central Bureau of Agricultural Research of the Ministry of Industries, and the Sun Yat-sen Institute of Culture and Education.[22] Nonetheless, by 1937, the basic sources of rural poverty and peasant unrest remained as yet untouched. And with the coming of the war, national reconstruction had become a thing of the past.

*Rural Reconstruction: The American Effort*

Americans who participated in rural reconstruction in the Nanking decade did so in a context of failure: the failure of China's leadership to attack the roots of rural distress. Yet, the American effort deserves to be viewed apart from this failure as well as within it. Such a study can reveal both the dimensions of the opportunity Americans faced and the extent of their ability to make use of it.

The "American effort" in rural reconstruction was actually an amalgam of the work of several groups: American Protestant missionaries, their Chinese fellow Christians, other Western-trained

Chinese, foundation personnel, and visiting American experts. As such, the effort reflected the pluralism of the society from which it sprang. What bound these groups together was not only, from time to time, a common enterprise; it was also a shared sense of values —a belief in the individual's ultimate worth, in social service, education, and the democratic process. With the majority there was, to be sure, a shared religious faith; but this was not universal. What united them most of all was evolutionary social activism, whether based on Christ, or on science, Locke, and Jefferson—it made little difference which. They served in China, the conscious bearers of an alien culture, and sought to transform the society as best they could.

The instruments of the effort were as varied as the participants: mission stations, Christian colleges, the National Christian Council, the YMCA, private Chinese institutions, international relief agencies, and a multi-million-dollar foundation. Yet to a notable extent the institutional directorates interlocked. A YMCA official might also serve as a member of the NCC, a trustee of a Christian college, a director of a famine relief commission, a contributor to a Chinese rural experiment, and an adviser to an American foundation.[23]

On the basis of such a definition, it can be said that the American effort in rural reconstruction had its roots in the virtually simultaneous activities of James Yen in mass education and the CIFRC in rural cooperatives. Yen brought to the countryside a consuming zeal for village development through literacy, while the commission first focused attention on socioeconomic aspects of reconstruction. Of the two, Yen's work had the greatest continuing impact. For precisely at the moment, in 1930, when missionaries and officials alike began to look to the countryside, James Yen resolved to broaden his program from its narrow literacy base. At Tinghsien, Yen had grasped two major truths: that no program can teach a man to read without teaching him other things as well; and that a literate man is not a whole man while poverty, sickness, and oppression still wrack his body and mind. And so Yen devised a fourfold reconstruction plan to meet the several needs of the Chinese villager.

No figure dominates the American reconstruction effort more powerfully and continuously than that of the former YMCA secretary and Tinghsien reformer. The writings of the thirties are replete with testimony to his overriding influence: from the neighboring Paotingfu mission community, trying to fashion a Butterfield "community-parish"; from Hugh W. Hubbard and the founders of the infant North China Christian Rural Service Union; from Chang Fu-liang and the NCC delegates to the two Tinghsien Institutes; from William R. Johnson, as he strove to meet the request of Mme. Chiang; from George W. Shepherd, who had lost his hope, and then found it anew at Tinghsien; and from Selskar M. Gunn, who saw in Yen's work the keystone for a new China Program. Even the American journalist who later played Boswell to Mao Tse-tung was stirred by the man behind Tinghsien. "He strikes me," wrote Edgar Snow in late 1933, "as a man of resource and versatility, and events may shape him into a great leader of men. There is a passionate sincerity and conviction behind his words, so that at times he seems more the revolutionary crusader, perhaps, than the evolutionary educator. It does not seem extravagant to say that the movement which he leads may in time become a revolution of far more puissant destiny than any march or counter-march of Chinese troops to which that term has been loosely applied in the past." [24] As George Shepherd later put it, "We all owe a great deal to Jimmy Yen—we caught from him a vision of what could be done." [25]

Yen's position was preeminent, then, in the minds and motivations of American reformers. But there were others as well. Deeply respected, but aloof from the Western community, was Liang Souming with his village work in Shantung. To Christians, of course, the recommendations of Kenyon Butterfield had played a catalytic role. For those who found Yen strong on inspiration but weaker on the institutional aspects of the agrarian problem, the visit and scholarship of R. H. Tawney had a very great impact. And reconstructionists, searching for specifics, found ideas and techniques in the early provincial experiments at Wusih and Hsuchow, and in the limited demonstration centers of various Christian colleges.

To such seminal influences two others of a different nature must be added. The first and lesser of the two was the convulsion of 1931: the combination of natural and man-made disasters that focused attention on the continuing rural crisis as never before. The second, once again, was the Chinese Communists. For by their involuntary but deepening association with the Chinese peasantry, the Communists had underscored and politicized an endemic social problem. In the back of the minds of most reformers, from James Yen through S. M. Gunn, stood the spectre of the Communist alternative. Such were the forces that underlay the American effort. It remains now to evaluate the nature and results of that effort.

*The problem of resources.* The American effort in rural reconstruction evolved in circumstances of grave difficulty. The need for a rural program was most clearly recognized, ironically, at a time when the human, material, and institutional resources for such a program were absent, or at best inadequate.

The first and most obvious deficiency was a lack of people. The total American work force in China—exclusive of government officials and businessmen—never rose above 3,000 during the years 1927–1937; and during the first five years it was probably closer to 2,000. The troubles of 1926–1928, rising criticism of missions at home, Sino-Japanese hostilities, and heavy depression cutbacks— all combined to reduce the number of private citizens at work in China. Such reductions placed a considerable strain on mission stations, hospitals, and educational institutions; there had never been enough people to begin to fill the areas of greatest need—from the empty pulpits of rural parishes to middle-school English classrooms, college science laboratories, and hospital operating rooms —and now there were fewer still. Moreover, the reductions also meant a decrease in the already small number of missionaries with rural training or direct rural experience. Although precise figures are not available, it is probable that the personnel reductions hit mission work in the hinterland most severely of all; for it was rural mission stations—like those of north Fukien—that suffered the worst in the turmoil of the late twenties. Finally, massive cutbacks intensified old problems of denominationalism and station jealousies; Lichuan's troubles over Robin Chen and Hugh Hubbard were a case in point.

The lack of human resources reflected, in part—and was compounded by—a formidable lack of funds. Mission salaries, always low by American standards, were further reduced in the depths of the depression. More important, as old developed projects faced sharp curtailment or even abandonment, virtually no mission funds were available for new departures of any sort. Opportunities for effective work in rural reconstruction were difficult to seize in the face of the personnel shortage; but it was the inevitable need for outside funds that forced Americans and their Chinese associates to look for assistance to wealthy Chinese, foundations, or even the Chinese government.

It might be added at this point that a later era would see the development of a sense of responsibility for reconstruction assistance abroad on the part of the United States government. In the thirties, however, American politicians were just beginning to experiment at home with concepts of broad governmental responsibility for the promotion of social and economic welfare; it would be another 15 years before similar concepts would be applied abroad and foreign aid would become a standard component of the federal budget. Aside from the controversial RFC loan of 1933 and Morgenthau's silver purchase assistance—both designed to aid China's struggle for fiscal stability—direct assistance from the U.S. government was not forthcoming until the outbreak of World War II.

The American effort in the thirties, therefore, remained the work of private citizens, while their government stood by and watched. In China, at least, the watching was done with benevolence and approval, for the American ambassador had a high regard for missionaries and their works. As Nelson Johnson wrote to the secretary of state in early 1933, "The effects of missionary educational, medical, and evangelical work are to be found every place in China today, and it cannot be denied by the severest critic of that work that these effects have gone deeply into the life and thought of the people . . . Whatever happens to Protestant Christian missionary work in China, . . . the effects of that work will not easily be eradicated." [26] Johnson was not only approving of past achievements; he also had suggestions for the future—and they related directly to the rural crisis. In a letter of January 1934 to the noted mission organizer and YMCA leader, John R. Mott, he wrote of a special "job of work which I think the missionary boards can perform out here that is in keeping with the calling of the missionary. I think that a portion of mission funds could be very wisely spent on maintaining in this field a number of experts in rural development work, road building and the like, whose services could be made available to various rural communities throughout China which are awakening to an interest in such matters." [27] Here, in embryonic form, was the concept of bilateral technical assistance programs; but those "mission funds" of which Johnson spoke were simply nonexistent.

The third great deficiency within the American rural effort was an institutional lack: a failing in quantity, quality, and direction. Of the thirteen Christian colleges, only two had full-fledged colleges of agriculture—the University of Nanking, and Lingnan University, near Canton. This fact suggests two drawbacks in mission education: an emphasis, in terms of instruction, on the traditional ingredients of Western learning (the humanities, the natural sciences, and the social sciences); and an emphasis, in terms of production, on college graduates who were overwhelmingly urban-oriented by virtue of their training. The neglect of applied agricultural sciences and the neglect of direct village experience made for a fundamental weakness.

Exceptions there were, of course; and the importance of such institutions was magnified by their rarity. In this respect, Nanking University played a unique role—one unmatched by Lingnan, hampered as the latter was by geographic and political isolation. From the founding of Nanking's College of Agriculture in 1915, in cooperation with Cornell University, this institution pioneered in all phases of farm research, and most especially in agricultural economics. By 1933 the basic land utilization and production studies of J. Lossing Buck had provided invaluable and heretofore nonexistent information not only for Christian reconstructionists but for the Nanking government itself. Indeed, there is some evidence that the studies Buck made during the 1931 floods were a major stimulus to the government's rural efforts under the NEC.[28]

One single agricultural college of up-to-date Western standards was hardly adequate, however, for the needs of the Yangtze Valley; yet Nanking found itself called upon to provide men and recommendations for reconstruction work not only in Kiangsi, but throughout North China as well. Although S. M. Gunn could point with satisfaction to the 90 per cent of Nanking's 300 graduates who pursued careers related to their agricultural training, the labors of 270 specialists could barely scratch the surface of the needs. In sum, the American rural effort was severely handicapped by resource lacks. And the effects of these lacks were quickly apparent, as the reformers attempted to use the opportunities presented to them.

Christian awareness of the need for rural reconstruction stemmed from the National Christian Conference of 1922, if not well before. Yet very little was accomplished—even by way of pilot projects—until Chang Fu-liang became rural secretary of the NCC in 1928. Nor did the Butterfield visit and the two Tinghsien Institutes produce immediate results. By 1933, of course, isolated Christian experiments were under way, in line with the Butterfield recommendations. Yet a vast expenditure of verbiage and enthusiasm —in the Jerusalem meeting of 1928, and in the Hangchow and Sungkiang conferences of 1931 and 1933—had resulted in no solid accomplishment. And one fundamental reason lay, manifestly, in the resource deficiency.

It was within such a context that the government invitation of 1933 burst upon the church. In two of its original versions, the plan would have given the Christian reformers responsibility for all of Kiangsi and even parts of Fukien. In its amended form, it encompassed only five or six hsien. Yet in actuality, the church found itself barely able to establish a project in one *ch'ü,* let alone one hsien. The relentless narrowing of the domain was an indication of total unpreparedness; so, too, was the lengthy delay of the NCC in coming to a decision; and so, as well, was the unending search for adequate personnel. Indeed, the founding and subsequent development of the Lichuan project seem to have confirmed the misgivings of John H. Reisner, who had written, on learning of the government invitation, "how ill-prepared the Church is to face a rural problem of any magnitude." [29] Reisner knew only too well whereof he spoke; for he had been the founder and first dean of Nanking's College of Agriculture. As a result of lacks which Reisner understood, Lichuan was born in a situation of stress and scarcity. It illustrated one aspect of the reconstructionists' failure. Only very late in the decade did the Rockefeller Foundation finally move in to provide one of the missing resources—funds—to obtain the other two: a carefully planned strengthening of the best available institutions to produce the missing personnel.

*The problem of focus.* As a product of pluralistic enterprise, the American effort risked the ultimate danger of the pluralist society:

a diffusion of purpose. On the aim of rural reconstruction there might be little disagreement—the peasant's lot must be improved. But where was the emphasis to lie? What took precedence—his soul, his mind, his body, his economic rights, his freedom of political choice?

James Yen, of course—and others, such as T'ao Hsing-chih—had stressed at first the mind. Literacy was the rural gospel of the twenties, and Protestants first looked to the countryside with mass education as their goal. But Yen was moving ahead of them; and by the time they went to him for literacy aid, he himself had moved on to a fourfold program of education that ranged far beyond training in the skill of reading characters. Even so, the first Tinghsien Institute, and the Christian rural experiments which followed upon it, stressed the Bible-reading peasant as the ultimate goal. Here literacy and religion went hand in hand, for the one was viewed as the key to the other.

Yet even as they undertook their first rural experiments—James Hunter at Tunghsien, near Paotingfu, Frank Price at Shenhuachen near Nanking, and others elsewhere—Christian reformers were operating under a new injunction from Kenyon Butterfield. For Butterfield had warned that "literacy is only a tool," and the objective was a many-sided "rural community parish," with specialists and volunteers for the various needs of the villager. The Butterfield criticism had been directed not only at over-emphasis on mass education; he had seen, as well, a serious fragmentation in the Christian rural approach—"a patchy development, from a lack of coordination of effort." Specialization had already set in: Nanking's College of Agriculture had its own demonstration centers, Nanking Seminary its separate rural parish, Nankai a center for studies of rural economics and local government, Yenching a center for observing social administration, and so forth. The focus depended on the sponsoring department or institution; coordination was nonexistent.

Ironically, one of Lichuan's weaknesses was its attempt to follow the Butterfield recommendations and compensate for such specialization. Its founders chose to produce a rounded project, administering to all the peasant's requirements. In so doing, they opened themselves up to attack from two quarters. On the one hand, Lichuan was condemned by churchmen for its de-emphasis of religion. On the other hand, many found the project ineffective; its program, they said, was "too miscellaneous." [30] Too scattered an effort was especially hazardous in view of the dearth of trained personnel.

Other reformers continued to struggle with the problem of focus. Was it to be literacy or religion? Was it to be specialized or comprehensive? No single answer could be appropriate, given the fragmented nature of the rural reconstruction movement. But in the course of attempting to find an answer, the reformers shared in a fundamental neglect: they gave scant attention to the problem of land tenure.

The reason for neglect of the land tenure problem is difficult to determine with precision. In the early years, overriding concern with the illiterate mind and the non-Christian soul provides something of an explanation. Yet once the mass educationists and rural evangelists were joined by agricultural economists, rural sociologists, and foundation planners, the explanation comes less easily. Awareness of tenancy was certainly widespread; Communist land programs in south central China had dramatized the issue. Nor was there any dearth of advice from the experts; Stampar's recommendations were public information. Indeed, the reconstructionists themselves spoke of the problem in the early thirties—but they mentioned it with lessening frequency as the decade progressed.

In retrospect, four factors seem to have contributed to this neglect. In the first place, there was an inadequate understanding of the problem itself. One result of the work of J. Lossing Buck had been a de-emphasis of the economic implications of tenancy. But Buck's investigations applied primarily to areas north of the Yangtze; and the evils of tenancy were intensified south of the river. Furthermore, data were still scarce on the immense power of landlords. A beginning was made with the completion of Chen Cheng-mo's study of the land tenure in 1933 under sponsorship of the Sun Yat-sen Institute of Culture and Education. But not until the formation of the North China Council was a more thorough socioeconomic study finally undertaken.[31] A second factor seems to have been the receding of the danger: with the collapse of the Kiangsi Soviet, Chinese communism was widely believed to have expired as a force—despite its covert appeal to the urban intelligentsia. In removing the nation's chief proponents of land distribution, the Long March removed the most pressing argument for land reform. As one foundation official was to recall many years later, "In 1935 we weren't thinking at all about the Communists—they were way up in the Northwest, all mixed up with warlords." [32] A third factor, of course, was local opposition from vested interests, namely, landowners and their allies, the local officials. A final factor, inevitably, was the position of the Nanking government on the subject. No reform was possible without Nanking's support, and such support was not forthcoming.

Chiang Kai-shek's views on land reform—obviously central to Nanking's position—had been clearly set forth in his telegram to the executive yuan of January 1934. But underlying his resistance to radical reform was not merely his explicitly stated distaste for the program of the Communists. More fundamental, it seems, was his Confucian notion that economic problems were the result of moral deficiencies rather than the maldistribution of wealth. Chiang's concept of New Life showed a Spartan attitude toward material goods and an emphasis upon moral virtues rather than physical necessities. In a similar vein, Mme. Chiang had remarked in 1935 that there was "plenty of rice" in China, but that "those who do not have it do not understand the dignity of labor." [33] Such views at the top of the Nanking apparatus were complemented by the urban orientation of the government's bureaucrats, many of them Western-trained. As one observer has commented, both Western and Kuomintang education "served to produce an elite unconnected with the life surrounding them and who were not really aware of actual conditions in the country at large." [34] Such an elite chose to channel its talents into the urban professions—banking, engineering, business, and university teaching; as public officials they concentrated on the urban sector. A further key to Nanking's position on land reform was the government's dependence on support from landowning interests: absentee urban landlords and important provincial allies. To tamper with this structure would have undermined the regime itself.

In the circumstances, the question nonetheless remains as to why the reformers did not press harder. In the thirties, George Shepherd sometimes suggested such action to the generalissimo; and Frank Price of Nanking Seminary did likewise in the years of the Chung-king government. [35] As Hugh Hubbard later commented, "The heart of the land tenure problem was not ignorance or neglect but simply that it could not be solved without a) a bitter fight with entrenched interests, and b) strong government backing." [36] But Chiang stood his ground and argued for a "gradual" redistribution that was never put into effect. In Shepherd's view, Communist excesses lay at the root of Chiang's thinking: "I often suspect," said Shepherd, "that he may have had a prejudice against land reform because of his dislike of the entire Communist agrarian movement. There is no question but that the Communists were ruthless, cruel, hard—and Chiang Kai-shek was suspicious of any who advocated such theories." [37] Nor did the generalissimo's views encounter determined and continuing resistance from the American reformers. As one participant has put it, "People were generally comparing the government with the chaos of the Twenties—and were rejoicing in the stability and progress that existed. And considering all things," he adds, "the degree of progress *was* remarkable." [38] As a result of such feelings, pressure for land reform remained minimal throughout the decade. In the process, one potential focus of greatest significance for the prevention of agrarian unrest was absent from the American effort in rural reconstruction. At the same time, it should be noted that some of those who consciously or unconsciously avoided this focus did so because of their fear that the social and political upheaval that might result from tampering with China's old agrarian order would be more destructive than the unrest of the status quo. Only with the advent of Rockefeller funds for a new China Program did ten years of rural experimentation result in agreement on a focus. That focus, however, was institutional in nature; and discussion of it relates to the problem of coordination.

*The problem of coordination.* The greatest institutional failings of both Chinese and foreign-sponsored agencies in the field of rural reconstruction may well have been a lack of coordination of effort. Despite the value of pilot projects, atomization of effort in a period of inadaquate resources meant inefficient use of such resources as were available.[39] By 1934, the degree of fragmentation was extraordinary. In his critical study of "The Rural Movement in China Today," published that year, K'ung Hsüeh-hsiung deplored the fragmentation and pleaded for a long-range national plan and the amalgamation of the disparate efforts. Yet no such plan was ever implemented.[40]

The failure of the government to coordinate its national and provincial programs was more than matched on the part of the private reformers. At least four types of private programs existed: comprehensive village experiments without institutional affiliation (most developed were those of James Yen and Liang Sou-ming); broadgauge interdenominational Rural Service Union experiments (such as Lichuan and the projects of the NCCRSU); specialized demonstration centers for college departments (those of Nanking University in agriculture, Yenching in rural administration, Nankai in economics, and so on); and miscellaneous smaller experiments, undertaken by a single mission station or institution (Shepherd's village work at Yangkow, Nanking Seminary's work at Shenhuachen, and others). Of course, some degree of coordination could not but exist. In most cases, the leading figures were well acquainted with one another; programs were compared, information and advice freely exchanged. Yet the differences in resources and focus limited the value of such contacts. Lichuan's experience serves to illustrate the problem: although Shepherd was able to gather much useful advice, the personnel problem remained acute—Lichuan was simply too backward for Nanking's able and widely coveted graduates, too alien for Tinghsien's education experts, too isolated for PUMC's urban-oriented medical men, too secular for a seminary's pastoral workers. The experts came and went, but few could be prevailed upon to stay; the demand elsewhere was always overwhelming, and "elsewhere" would often as not mean the isolation of an academic position or the embalmment of a government job. Among most Chinese, higher education spelled total alienation from the countryside.

At one point, between 1930 and 1933, it might have been possible for the NCC to assume aspects of the coordinator's role. Its contribution, through the Butterfield visit and the two Tinghsien Institutes, was a substantial one. But three developments prevented the council from exercising further leadership. The first was most crucial: the removal of Chang Fu-liang from the strategic position of rural secretary to government employment in Kiangsi; the rural committee never found itself an effective replacement. A second factor was the NCC's gradual shift into a predominantly promotional role; the shift was an outgrowth of the council's "Five-year Movement" between 1930 and 1935.[41] Finally, the NCC seems to have suffered increasingly from doubts as to its own chief purpose. As Eugene E. Barnett of the YMCA commented in early 1935, the council was "floundering" because of "indecision as to . . . whether the N.C.C. is to be a board of strategy, a council for joint planning, an agency of correlation on the one hand, or a national body undertaking to promote various programs of its own among such groups as it may be able to reach." [42] The council's indecision was graphically illustrated in its fretful relations with the Lichuan project. By late 1936, indeed, when the president of Fukien Christian University urgently requested the summoning of a National Conference of Christian Rural Workers, the NCC was forced to refuse: "Until we have a rural secretary," replied the staff, "it will be difficult or impossible to arrange for a national conference." [43] For the needed coordination in rural reconstruction, it was clearly essential to look elsewhere than to the church authorities.

Coordination, when it finally came, derived from a combination of good sense and good fortune. S. M. Gunn brought to China his own intellect, incisiveness, and imagination; and he brought, as well, the money to put those qualities to work. His China report of 1934 showed both a command of the intricacies of the reconstruction effort and an overriding sense of purpose. On the basis of his investigations, he had emerged with an understanding of the fragmentation of activity and uncertainty of focus that had resulted in a waste of precious resources.

To Gunn, the key to rural reconstruction lay in integrated professional training for rural leadership. Brave as it was, the work of the earlier reformers had been, above all, the work of pragmatic amateurs. Some had had training, to be sure, in one relevant specialty or another; but the absence of integrated instruction in the problems of the villager had made for patchwork solutions. Among the chief reformers, it had been James Yen who first perceived the problem. And it was therefore Tinghsien's evolution that pointed the way for Gunn.

In his pursuit of integrated professional training, Gunn used the human and institutional resources at hand. What the foundation could do, he knew, was not so much to initiate as to coordinate, not to produce models but to train leaders, not to span the nation, but to work where the institutional structure already existed; and not, apparently to change the economic and political conditions of rural life, but to produce leaders who might one day change these conditions. And so, beginning in mid-1935, Rockefeller funds moved in to endow the most promising of China's fragmented institutions—private and government alike—to produce the missing leadership for an attack on rural distress.

By the founding of the North China Council, the Nanking decade was drawing to a close; the Rockefeller effort came too late for a fair evaluation. Through its qualitative example, Gunn had hoped to stimulate a quantitative response on the part of the central government: a growing nationwide program for the training of rural leaders. George Shepherd felt that by 1937 Chiang Kai-shek was preparing to take such action.[44] During that June, a "Plan of Rural Reconstruction" had been approved at the third Plenary session of the Fifth Kuomintang Central Executive and Supervisory Committees and passed on to the executive yuan for execution. This plan would have enlisted "those intellectuals, not suitably employed in the cities, for rural reconstruction work." Special training was to be given to them before their civil service appointment as "directors of agriculture, public health and economics." [45] There is no evidence to indicate that this program would not have gone the way of previous paper schemes. Furthermore, the plan itself seemed to epitomize Nanking's sense of priorities: first claim upon the talents of "intellectuals" was evidently urban work; the villagers could have the leftovers. In any event, with the outbreak of the war this plan remained still-born.

In later years, George Shepherd was to term the Rockefeller program "by far the most enlightened and promising of all the American ventures in rural reconstruction." [46] By the summer of 1937, the North China Council had produced ten master's degree holders in rural administration, 23 new bachelor's degree holders, and 142 undergraduates with a year or more of course preparation. The 175 young men and women marked barely a beginning; but it was an important development where there had previously been only a handful.

More important than training itself, of course, was use of training. And the early evidence from the North China Council was tentatively encouraging: all those who had completed their degree programs were immediately placed with agencies of rural reconstruction. But a more fundamental question would remain unanswered through insufficient evidence: whether the nation's institutional structure for reconstruction would permit full application of the techniques these trainees had learned. All Western-inspired reform efforts assumed, implicitly or explicitly, a government of law—a clear political framework and a stable power structure—in the society in which they worked. But both the political framework and the power structure were at best weak and unreliable in China. Political stability and military control were essential ingredients of an institutional structure which could utilize the reformers. On the basis of a decade of paper plans, bureaucratized inaction and instability, the prospects for effective use of the trainees were hardly encouraging.

The North China Council requires one further speculative comment. In retrospect, it seems to have set the course for the full gradualist alternative not only in rural China, but elsewhere in Asia as well. In village India, 15 years later, rural reconstructionists struggled to find a means for bringing to the countryside both trained personnel and an integrated approach. The resulting plan, India's Community Development Program, was a nationwide application of the principles of James Yen and Selskar Gunn. Backed up by 30 government training centers established with Ford Foundation assistance, 55 village projects were begun, each with roughly 300 villages, occupying 500 square miles, and with a population of approximately 200,000. Each project required a staff of 125 workers—one worker assigned to each three or four villages, assisted by specialists in agriculture, public health and education, and administrative personnel. The figures are suggestive: for 400 community projects (the 1956 target) 30,000 village workers were needed; for the country as a whole, ultimately 100,000. Basic to the whole enterprise of Community Development, however, was not these workers but the underemployed manpower of the Indian village. Through assistance from the experts, the villagers were to be induced to remake their own way of life. And behind them, pressing gradually but relentlessly, was the Indian government's drive for land redistribution throughout the country.[47]

This, then, was the North China Council idea, carried through to its logical development and applied by a government that believed in it. The implications for China in the thirties are imprecise at best. But if India, crisscrossed by communications introduced through decades of colonial rule, required on paper as many as 100,000 trained workers, China would have needed perhaps twice that figure, or more. And what of the results? The Indian case is not encouraging. Although virtually every village in India has now allegedly been brought within the Community Development system, a recent study concludes that early "expectations were grossly overoptimistic," and "in most Indian villages nothing has changed much." [48]

As for the amount of time China might have needed to begin to show results, no estimate is possible; too many factors remain unknown. The gradualist alternative required many things; but above all it required time—the time to train men, the time to apply techniques, the time to produce results. "If we had only had ten more years"—how frequently come these words from the reformers of the Nanking decade. But the ultimate decision about the time available for gradualism in China lay not with the reformers, nor even with the Nanking government, but with Japan.

*The political dilemma.* One further problem confronted the rural reconstructionists in the era of the Nanking government, a problem that related directly to their strengths and weaknesses as private agents of reform, untouched by political association or the stamp of governmental approval. How much traffic were they to have with politics in general, the Kuomintang regime in particular?

Among the reformers, the ramifications of the problem were varied. On the one hand, a few early Chinese experimenters had encountered intense political hostility; their projects, in the first years of the decade, had been closed down, and some leaders, indeed, had met violent death. Others, however, had fared somewhat better. Both Yen and Liang Sou-ming had developed amicable relations with their respective provincial authorities; and both, in time, were permitted some degree of local administrative control. The need for such control was virtually self-evident; without it, hostile hsien officials could thwart all basic reforms. Others still—among them, most of the early mission projects—eschewed politics entirely; it was felt that official connections would only compromise the Christian nature of the effort. Accustomed to frequent change in political rule, they knew well the value of nonalignment.

For the Christian reconstructionists, the problem of political involvement was first posed—in dramatic form—by Mme. Chiang's invitation to the NCC. A government request for church assistance in the rehabilitation of former Communist territory was a request fraught with political implications. It placed the church, informally at least, in a position of collaboration with the government; and the collaboration itself related directly to a continuing if modest civil war. From the beginning, the implications were recognized and discussed by the council's leadership. The concern was not only one of overly close relations with Nanking; it touched as well the problem of undue association with "a particular economic theory" in the Kuomintang's struggle with communism. In the Shanghai deliberations Bishop Ronald Hall had been particularly outspoken on the dangers of close Christian identification with an unjust economic order.

The challenge to Christian rural responsibility, however, required a response; and the Lichuan project was born of a tentative and still vague collaboration between the Christian church and the central government. Although Christians were given complete freedom in the administration of the project, the annual supporting gift from the generalissimo and his wife sustained the church-state relationship.

It was not long, moreover, before the political dilemma recurred in new form. With Governor Hsiung's request that Christians assume political responsibility for the administration of their district, the old doubts flared anew. Yet Kuomintang reconstruction in Kiangsi had resulted in increasingly close ties between the church and the Nanking government. And Chang Fu-liang's appointment as director of the entire NEC program had greatly strengthened those ties. The KCRSU acceded to the governor's demand; Shepherd approved and, indeed, had "no apologies" to offer for the fact that "the Union has gone into politics." Nor was he unclear as to the implications of the decision; for him the die was cast—"We have no use for communism as it exists in China today." [49] In the struggle between the disciples of Christ and Marx, there was little place for scruples in the choice of one's allies.

For Christian reconstructionists, then, Lichuan was a turning point. What had begun as an attempt to steer a middle course, somewhere between the proponents of two rival economic theories, had ended as a solid association with the Kuomintang. Christians who found themselves—in Shepherd's phrase—"riding the tiger" had decided that it would be best to hold on.

By the end of the decade, the Lichuan pattern had been repeated in other reconstruction projects as well. In both Tinghsien and Tsining, the North China Council's project leaders were granted local political authority through having their own personnel appointed *k'o chang*. It was abundantly clear that, although political involvement might be compromising to the reformers, a lack of political control would imperil the whole program. The political dilemma was therefore resolved through collaboration with the authorities. Yet such collaboration took place at an inauspicious time: at a time when these authorities had lost touch with the thinking of major groups within the Chinese population. It is to that development that we must now turn our attention; for it was a development of immediate relevance to the reformers themselves and, indeed, to the gradualist alternative in China.

# Chapter Ten

# The Fate of Gradualism in

# Kuomintang China—II

*Ideological Reform: The Alienated Intelligentsia*

The American effort at rural reconstruction took place not only within a context of government inaction, but also at a time of declining public enthusiasm for the reformist alternative. To a considerable degree, the one development sprang from the other: Nanking's failure to attack the roots of peasant distress diminished the early appeal of rural reconstruction. Gradualism, though never afforded an opportunity to show its full potential, was soon found wanting and was discarded. As disillusionment with the government spread during the first years of instability after 1928, that same disillusionment colored public reaction to the efforts of the reformers. For what neither government nor reformer could or would bring to the Chinese countryside was the transformation of the old order, the rapid change of social revolution. Impatient and despairing, many members of the nation's articulate classes had already begun to look elsewhere for solutions well before the middle of the Nanking decade.

*The legacy of May Fourth.* The phenomenon of withdrawn or receding support under the Nanking government—the desertion of the intellectuals, the alienation of the intelligentsia—has been described in general terms by many students of modern Chinese history.[1] Its roots lay deep in the May Fourth Movement, the first United Front, and the growth of Marxist thought in China. It had important implications for the American effort in rural reconstruction. But its major implications related to the Nanking government's attempt to improvise a viable ideology for the nation; this attempt only widened the gulf between China's political leadership and its intelligentsia. And as the Western reformers became increasingly identified with the ideological effort, they themselves fell victim to the process of polarization.

As carefully analyzed by Chow Tse-tsung, the May Fourth Movement is seen to have marked a unique shift in the history of Chinese thought. For the first time, Chinese intellectuals had "recognized the need for a complete transformation of traditional Chinese civilization." What was demanded was not "half-hearted reform or partial renovation . . . but a vast and fervent attempt to dethrone the very fundamentals of the old stagnant tradition and to replace it with a completely new culture." In addition, Chow notes, the movement also marked "an accelerated awakening of the Chinese intelligentsia to the ideas of individual human rights and national independence." In other ways, as well, May Fourth left its mark: for within the ideological ferment of the years 1917–1921 lay most of the conflicting alternatives that have shaped the development of the world in the period since World War I: liberalism, democracy, science, capitalism, nationalism, socialism, and communism.[2]

From the vantage point of later years, the alienation of the intelligentsia under Kuomintang rule stems from the ominous split within the ranks of the May Fourth leadership in 1919–1920. In the controversies surrounding the visits of John Dewey and Bertrand Russell to China and the founding of societies for the study of Marxism, the nation's leftists, liberals, and followers of Sun Yat-sen became deeply divided over questions of political ideology, economic theory, political activism, and party affiliation. As one section of the leadership moved to form the Chinese Communist Party in 1920–21, while other partisans hotly contested the influx of Marxist thought, the Dewey-oriented liberals persisted in a rejection of political activism as the key to China's future. In so doing, such non-Communist progressives as Hu Shih separated themselves from the mainstream of political activity that was shortly to culminate in the first United Front between Sun's Kuomintang and the Chinese Communists. Such a separation was later to weaken substantially the liberal evolutionary alternative.

The break-up of the May Fourth leadership was compounded, in 1927, with the collapse of the United Front. In cutting itself from its Communist partners, the Kuomintang dispensed with large elements of the intelligentsia who had rallied to the alliance after 1924. And as such support had been based on a shared dedication to the objectives of nationalism, anti-imperialism, and social revolution, the Nanking government's policies soon produced widening dismay. To the first of these objectives—the recovery of national rights—the new government had applied itself with vigor and some success. But the second objective, anti-imperialism, was soon deemphasized in a bid for Shanghai's financial support and recognition from the powers. Furthermore, when the focus of anti-imperialism shifted from Britain to Japan, the Nanking government's five years of dilatory tactics intensified the disillusionment. As for the third objective, social revolution, Kuomintang inaction soon seemed to indicate no great desire to transform the old social order. Indeed, to many intellectuals, by 1932, the Nanking government appeared to be wedded to the suspension of national revolution.

Even more fundamental than such roots of alienation, however, was the Nanking government's continuing condition of weakness. As Chow Tse-tsung has written of the May Fourth Movement, "The most important purpose of the movement was to maintain the existence and independence of the nation." As a result, in the turmoil of the twenties, concern for the emancipation of the individual "was soon balanced by the demand for a well organized society and state and therefore a strong government." [3] This concern with the need for a strong government accounts both for the high hopes that accompanied the overthrow of the northern warlords and the deep disillusionment that set in after 1928. For the continuing civil warfare from 1928–1931, the appeasement of Japan in the years after 1931, and the endless months of anti-Communist campaigns—all combined to dramatize a condition of national weakness that humiliated China's intellectuals. If dismay over the suspension of revolutionary aims embittered the leftist thinkers, dismay over national impotence embittered nonleftists as well. Only in the Yangtze Valley provinces did a sense of progress seem to communicate itself. But China's intellectual capital stood far from Nanking; and so, increasingly, did China's intellectuals.

Disillusion with Nanking in the first years of the thirties was accompanied by a marked shift to the left among the mainstream of Chinese writers. This move had been presaged by the 1925 shift of the Creation Society from romanticism and "art for art's sake" to "revolutionary literature" in the wake of the May 30th Incident. In March 1930, Lu Hsün—"the most powerful figure in modern Chinese letters" [4]—joined with the novelist Mao Tun and some fifty others, many from the old Creation Society, to found the League of Leftist Writers. The participation of such influential figures in an overtly Marxist organization was symptomatic of the alienation from Nanking's policies. Lu Hsün was no Communist; indeed, he had been a supporter of Sun Yat-sen and viewed the Kuomintang as "the legitimate agent of revolution in China, the only hope for reunification of China." [5] But by its neglect of the condition of the masses, its repression of civil liberties, and its weakness in the face of Japanese aggression, the Nanking government had irrevocably lost his support. As one able critic has commented, "Lu Hsün is representative of that group of anguished patriots whom increasing disillusionment with the Kuomintang after 1927 turned to support of the Communist opposition in much the way that the economic debacle of 1929 and the rise of Fascism in Europe turned many Western liberals toward the Communist ideal and Russia in the early thirties." [6] Had he lived "in a society where the social alternatives were not so sharply drawn, where between the Communists on the one hand and the conservatives on the other, there lay a third road to reform," Lu Hsün would presumably have chosen the middle road. [7]

But the polarization of political thought in China had resulted, in part, in the disappearance of the "third road"; and by its attempt at the creation of an ideology, the Nanking government only intensified that polarization.

*The irrelevance of "New Life."* The New Life Movement was inaugurated in early 1934 as an antidote, in part, to the desertion of the intellectuals. More immediately, of course, it was designed to promote upright behavior and social order among the Communist-tainted people of Kiangsi.[8] Yet such ideologues as Tai Chi-t'ao and Ch'en Li-fu were acutely aware of the growing "subversive" tendencies among the intelligentsia; and their attempt to give a neo-Confucian metaphysical base to the generalissimo's code of conduct was a direct outgrowth of this awareness. To be sure, social control was their central objective, and neo-Confucianism suited that objective very well. But Tai Chi-t'ao had been deeply involved in the controversies of the May Fourth Movement, and Ch'en—later Kuomintang minister of Education—fancied himself something of an intellectual; and their aim was clearly to fashion a new orthodoxy which would command the respect if not the allegiance of scholars as well as the masses.[9]

Yet if there was any one essential element common not only to the vast majority of the May Fourth intellectuals, but to the Kuomintang leftists of the first United Front and the Marxist sympathizers as well, it was a fundamental rejection of Confucianism. Such later antagonists as Hu Shih, Ch'en Tu-hsiu, Ts'ai Yüan-p'ei, and Lu Hsün were unanimous in their assault on the Confucian straitjacket which seemed to them the cause of China's centuries of "stagnation." And any attempt to revive Confucianism ran head on into the disciples of "science and democracy" as well as those of Marx and Lenin. With few exceptions, the disagreements that divided the men of May Fourth and their heirs concerned not what should be rejected, but what should be put in its place, and by what means.

Against such a background, the New Life Movement could not but seem both irrelevant and banal to China's intellectuals—professors, students, writers, and college-trained elite. It was irrelevant because of its departure from the mainstream of Chinese thought since World War I and its failure to touch upon the socioeconomic causes of the nation's backwardness. It was banal because of its reversion to the moralistic precepts of a discredited ideology.[10] In its implicit call to selective Westernization on a Confucian base, it also smacked of a return to the fundamental fallacy of the late Ch'ing Self-strengtheners. To be sure, the NLM was more than Confucianism exhumed; its hybrid origins pushed it in several directions, and some indeed saw it as the intended vehicle for the development of fascism in China.[11] Yet, the generalissimo's four virtues remained the theoretical pillars of its structure;

and it seemed such a natural outgrowth of the government-sponsored Confucian revival which had preceded it that it was soon dubbed, even in circles friendly to the Kuomintang, as the "Return-to-the-Old-Life Movement." [12]

From the moment of its inauguration, in any event, the NLM was barely taken seriously among China's writers and academics. Many, in fact, ridiculed or ignored it; of those who reacted, some saw in it an ideological adjunct to the government's suppression of opposition, while the rest severely criticized it for flagrant superficiality. In an age when China's articulate classes were dedicated to antitraditionalism, the traditionalizers were doomed to failure in their quest for intelligentsia support. Coupled with their failure to arouse popular enthusiasm by means of effective rural reconstruction programs, this fact had ominous significance: the Kuomintang was losing contact with two vital sources of power throughout Chinese history—the literati and the peasantry.

### Ideological Uplift: The Entrapment of the Reformers

The curious relationship that developed between the American reformers and the Nanking government in the waning years of the decade was a product of several factors—among them, the growing sense of partnership in rural reconstruction, the Christian affiliations of the generalissimo and his relatives, the recession of the Communist alternative from a position of political power, and tangible signs of modernization in areas of health, communications, education, and political stability. The most widely emphasized vehicle for this gathering relationship, however, was an institutional by-product of some of these factors. The NLM originated in Chiang's effort to change the behavior of the Chinese villager; his concept of its role was strongly affected by the "social cement" of Christianity in the life of Western nations; and the movement stemmed, at least in part, from an attempt to replace the unifying semi-Marxist ideology that had been jettisoned with the collapse of the United Front. In joining forces with the leadership of the NLM, Americans achieved a rapport that had been lacking in their relations with most Chinese governments. At the same time, however, the reformers not only parted company with much of the intelligentsia of the nation (though the closeness of that relationship had been doubtful since the early twenties); they also identified themselves irrevocably with one wing of the Chinese revolution, a wing widely regarded as dedicated to the preservation of the status quo.

*The government's objectives.* In some ways, it is hardly surprising that the generalissimo should have turned to the Westerners—more explicitly to American Protestants and their Chinese Christian colleagues—to buoy up his ideological program. The movement itself resembled nothing quite so much as a Confucian version of the YMCA. The similarity began, of course, with an overlapping in aims: with emphasis on individual improvement and character building—on uprightness, cleanliness, and social service. But it moved on to include a sizable overlapping in personnel—Chinese whose training had originated in service as YMCA secretaries. The link in motivation was clear even to nonbelievers: as the non-Christian Wang Ching-wei announced to a Nanking conference of YMCA officers, "Not until social reconstruction and national regeneration have been achieved can the Young Men's Christian Association in China be said to have completed its task." [13]

Beyond this link in aim and personnel—one that perhaps indicates a link in conception—lay a second obvious reason for Chiang's insistence that the Christian church and its missionary brethren throw their support behind the NLM. In the face of predictable hostility from the intelligentsia, it was essential to obtain backing from groups that had some influence among students and academic faculties. Christians not only produced a high percentage of leaders for the bureaucracy and the nation's professions; they also had a built-in antipathy to communism, or at least to its godlessness. They represented, in short, a potential body of prestigious intellectual, or semi-intellectual, support, a group apparently invulnerable to the attractions of the Far Left.

A final plausible reason belongs to the realm of sheer speculation: cooperation with the church and its predominantly American missionary guides meant avenues of communication with the forces behind those missionaries—American congregations, the American press, and, ultimately, American statesmen. There is little reason to believe that such a motive was present in the first days of the movement. But as the pressure from Japan mounted in the latter half of the decade, the need for foreign support cannot have been far from the generalissimo's thinking. And foreign support, as far as the United States was concerned, would seem to come most readily through the goodwill of those groups with solid foreign ties: Chinese Protestants, graduates of Christian colleges, and returned students from America. Through his wife and her relatives, Chiang had come to know an increasing number of American missionary leaders in the years after 1931; it was perhaps natural that he and Mme. Chiang should intensify their pressure on the Christian community for New Life cooperation on the basis of this acquaintance and in view of the deepening national crisis. The appointment of George Shepherd, coming as it did in the wake of renewed demands from Japan during the autumn of 1935, lends itself to such an interpretation.

The government's side of the relationship, then, is at least explicable—although some aspects of that explanation remain highly speculative. But what can be said of the Christian side of the relationship? What brought the Westerners and their Chinese colleagues into such a close association with the political authorities, and what awareness did they have of the implications of such an association?

*The Christians' motivation.* At the outset, a word of caution is once again necessary. The actions of Christian institutions—Christian parishes and associations, Christian publications, and the National Christian Council—were not the sole indicators of the Christian position on any subject. Many Christians and missionaries there were, of course, who had little or nothing to do with rural reconstruction, whose calling drew them toward other forms of enterprise. Many Christians and missionaries there also were who either ignored or condemned the NLM. Once again, the pluralistic nature of both Protestantism and American society made for a variety of views and activities in China that defies simple generalization.

Once that caveat has been issued, it must be nonetheless asserted that an increasing degree of cooperation did in fact develop between major Christian groups and the Nanking government; and that cooperation took as its focus, by Nanking's continuing demand, the New Life Movement. The relationship that resulted left its mark on the image of Western activity in the Nanking decade: it forced individuals and organizations into close public identity with the Kuomintang regime, and it colored their view of that regime. In the process, the middle ground of nonalignment in a polarizing situation was lost to many Western reformers.

As earlier chapters have shown, the development of Christian cooperation with the NLM was a slow and complex process. Essentially, that process seems to have involved three stages: periods of detached interest, of deepening ambivalence, and of general approval. The first of these dated from the movement's founding in early 1934, the second from the explicit appeals issued to Christian organizations in early 1935, and the third from the encouraging political developments of the autumn of 1936. In general terms, it seems that Christian approval bore a direct relationship not only to mounting insistence from the NLM's leadership but to the fortunes of the Kuomintang as well. As the prestige of the government began to climb, the prestigious implications of the invitation from the government also rose.

It would be an error to underestimate the aspect of flattery that the preceding comment suggests. Many missionaries were above all astonished and pleased to be courted by the Chinese Nationalist government. After years of hostility, years of official obstructionism, here was a government that went to missionaries, that went to the church, and asked their help. Not only that; here was a national leader who confessed his Christian faith openly, who ascribed to it his survival in captivity—and thereby credited it with producing the nation's new unity. The literature of the time is full of such wonder and satisfaction: things were happening, said the leading mission editor, that "would have been unthinkable . . . twenty or so years ago." [14] And George Shepherd spoke quite frankly of the new prestige: the movement, he said, gave the church "a large place in Chinese society, and a standing that has not been previously so frankly acknowledged." [15] As the Fukien missionary lady had written, amazed at the new friendliness and respect accorded her by officials, all this "would have been impossible five years ago." [16] Such official approval—the new status it offered, the new opportunities for service—was extraordinarily difficult to reject.

Some there were, of course—missionaries and Chinese alike—who saw the danger of an overly close association with those in authority. The danger seemed doubly grave in the context of the growing gulf that separated the government from the people, a gulf acutely reflected in the alienation of the intelligentsia. For many were well aware of the gulf and had commented on it during most of the decade.

*Christians and the alienated.* Christians and missionaries who worked among student groups during the years of the Nanking decade were increasingly conscious of two facts: of the steady inroads of Marxist thought on the young people of China, and of their simultaneous alienation from Kuomintang preachments and policies. The gathering alliance between the church and the Nanking regime toward the end of the decade is all the more noteworthy in view of this awareness.

The writings of George Shepherd in the first years of the thirties indicated the flavor of student opinion: the search for a "way out," the desire for strong government, the sharp reservations about Christianity, the doubts about the Nanking government, and—most significantly—the fascination with Marxism and with the Leninist theory of imperialism as a combined explanation and panacea for China's woes. Other missionary reports stressed many of the same points. One such report, from Fukien in 1934, described "the student mind" in the following terms: students waver "between widespread pessimism and the optimism of the Christians. They all seek 'the way out.' Does it lie in Fascism . . . or Communism . . . or militarism? Or is there no way? How can it lie in Christianity? Does that not take a long time? . . . Many talk of favoring a dictator, name often unspecified, on the ground that the latter would bring unity and efficiency, forgetting the unhappy things he might bring along with these; what they seem to want is a dictator pro tem." [17]

Similar reports were sent from many mission stations, YMCA secretaries, and Christian colleges in the early years of the decade. Another, from a YMCA correspondent in Hankow in the summer of 1934, includes the following observation: "Students have been particularly concerned over the rural situation. To many of them it comes very close to home for they are rural born . . . They see no hope in anything but a new order and in most cases the new order is Communism and anti the present government." [18] Even strongly Christian student groups were expressing a similar social protest. The Peiping subsection of the Student Christian Movement approved an appeal in 1934 that noted the failures of world capitalism and the successes of the Soviet Union, then concluded with the following stirring phrases: "Most important of all, we should create a new society, where we can actually practise the Christian ideals of communistic living which shall be a forecast of the social order which should eventually prevail in the entire world—a society of mutual love and service." [19] From Peiping as well, in the same year, came a complaint from one association student secretary that the greatest difficulty he had faced was in "discovering suitable service projects through which the students could give constructive expression to the unselfish impulses which their study of Christianity and their reflections upon the needs of their people have aroused." [20] The same ingredients—dissatisfaction with the old social order and frustration as to how to change it—are recurrent in the reports from all parts of the country half way through the Nanking decade.

The year 1934 marked the expulsion of the Communists from Kiangsi; it also marked the beginning of government-sponsored rural reconstruction in that province and the inauguration of the New Life Movement. In a way, the year was one of hope, a conceivable turning point in the fortunes of those who sought to remake China through gradualism. Late in the autumn, the evangelist Sherwood Eddy, visiting China for his ninth speaking tour, frantically cabled the YMCA in New York to restore its recent cutbacks in personnel as China seemed to him at that moment to present the "World's Greatest Evangelistic Opportunity." [21] Commenting on Eddy's cable, the astute YMCA Secretary E. E. Barnett himself wrote that Chinese youth seemed "let down by communism and other 'isms' by whose slogans they have been captivated during recent years"; they now seemed "with moving wistfulness" to be looking briefly towards Christianity. "One's greatest concern is lest we fail utterly in our response to this opportunity." [22]

In an earlier report of the same year, an international YMCA secretary, commenting on his tour of China, had concluded that "If one were dealing with contemporary religious movements there would be only three great movements to compare: Communism, Nationalism, and Christianity." This secretary saw the essential question for Christians as "the problem of what the Christian ethic has to say about the life of the Chinese village. Communism has a very clear-cut solution for this problem. What is the Christian solution?" The need for Christians was the creation of a church "which elicits from its members a social loyalty comparable to the loyalty demanded of its members by the Communist Party"; to do so, "the Church in the East needs dogma—not the dead dogmatic forms that we have transported from the West, but a living militant dogma born out of the actualities of the Far Eastern Tragedy, and at the same time organically related to the great streams of historic Christian thought. The power of the communists consists in the fact that they have a living doctrine—that is a system of ideas which they believe springs necessarily out of the historic moment in which they live but is at the same time rooted in eternal reality." [23]

Despite such reports, such suggestions, and such stern pleas, there was little indication three years later that the church had made use of the fleeting opportunity of 1934.

In February 1937, in a remarkably frank paper presented to the Christian Council of Higher Education, the YMCA student secretary Kiang Wen-han traced the results of the missed opportunity. Despite nearly a decade of rural reconstruction, and despite both official and private attempts at the construction of a non-Communist ideology, the student classes of China were moving away from both aspects of the gradualist alternative. Kiang's findings related only to the Christian colleges; yet most of the Christian college campuses were conservative by contrast with the national institutions.

Kiang's report dealt with the "secularization" of Christian colleges. As an aspect of this process, he noted the growth of "indifferentism" towards religion: "Religion is on the whole very unattractive" to the students, he wrote, both through lack of leadership, faculty indifference, and confusion through denominational atomization. At the same time, the "busy atmosphere" of heavy schedules, participation in the "National Salvation" movement, and political controversy further decreased the time and inclination for participation in Christian activity. Politics were dominated by a struggle between "leftists" and "fascists," with the former expelled in large numbers for extracurricular activities.[24]

It was in student reading habits, however, that Kiang saw the most obvious signs of the political obsession. More and more, students were concentrating on the social sciences, and here the textbooks were "generally written by leftist writers," Kiang reported, with "dialectical materialism . . . the striking note of all their writing." Furthermore, "recent attempts at 'cultural control' and the recent suppression of fourteen periodicals have given an evident set-back to people's freedom of thought and expression"; yet such attempts only seemed to increase the student appetite for leftist literature.[25]

What of student concerns, about themselves and their country? "The most outstanding perplexity is one of unemployment after graduation," Kiang said; for fully 13 per cent of the college graduates in 1933 and 1934 were still jobless. China's fate also continued to consume undergraduate thought. In recent years there had been deep interest in rural reconstruction in general, the work of James Yen, Liang Sou-ming, and T'ao Hsing-chih in particular. But Kiang then noted a crucially important shift: "We begin to see, however, an increasing feeling of disillusionment about such isolated rural experiments as fundamental solutions of China's problems. The interrelatedness of political and economic problems seems to be too obvious to ignore." Such a shift had produced an intensification of "the social and political-mindedness of the students. They seem to have a deeper understanding of the social situation and a greater yearning for social analysis and are not so easily satisfied with religious principles and generalities." [26] Nor with the formalistic principles and empty generalities of the New Life Movement, Kiang might have added; but he did not, for by 1937—as George Shepherd had noted with dismay—the NLM played no part whatsoever in the thinking of China's youth.

Kiang Wen-han concluded his report with the following terse summary: "The mental trends of the more thoughtful students may rightly be described as radical. (1) The outcry for individual development is now changed to one for a collective struggle. (2) The worship of idealism and liberalism is now changed to sheer realism and authority. (3) The concern for an individual 'way-out' is changed to an actual identification with the masses. (4) The interest in the problem of China is now enriched by a better understanding of the inter-relatedness of the world. (5) The world crisis is no longer interpreted in terms of a recurring cycle but as the end of an era. (6) Solution is sought no longer for minor adjustments but for a fundamental change. These are the underlying points of student thinking today." [27]

Against the background of such shifting tides of opinion, Kiang had warned, the Christian purpose remained obscure. Yet by virtue of the acts of its leadership, the Christian direction by the spring of 1937 seemed increasingly clear: the direction of informal alliance with a government of little popularity, a government that stood firmly in defense of the old social order. Moreover, the alliance itself was based on a movement of little popularity, a movement that seemed all too clearly to be substituting the superficialities of a discredited behavioral code for effective social action. In the contest between the proponents of action to advance the social revolution and those who sought to save the nation through moral uplift, the Christians found themselves aligned with the latter.

And as the Christians fell back on the hope of reconstruction through the agency of a Christian-led government, so did the cause of gradualism itself. By the workings of fate and chance, the leadership of the reformist cause in the Nanking decade had largely resided with the Christian community: with the missionaries, predominantly American, and their Chinese fellow believers. The drift of the reformers into the camp of the Kuomintang was one vital element in the demise of the gradualist alternative. For in a climate of increasing polarization, the middle ground virtually ceased to exist. And forced by later events to a painful choice between one extreme and the other—between the status quo and radical revolution—the Chinese people chose the latter. In the process of this choosing it is ironical that leadership came from the two major groups to whom the American reformers of the Nanking decade had tried in vain to minister—from the peasantry and the intelligentsia. And when the choice was finally made much later—in the years after World War II—the expulsion of the status quo meant, inevitably, the expulsion of its allies: out, with the Kuomintang, went the reformers; and out, with the reformers, went the instruments of the American effort in China.

### Gradualism's Dilemma: The Case of George Shepherd

The dilemma of gradualism, as suggested in the preceding pages, was manifested to different reformers in different ways. No one man's experience was precisely the same as another's. China was too large, its problems too vast, and regional differences too great to permit easy generalization. The progression of George Shepherd's China experience—first as a village missionary, then as a leader in rural reconstruction, then as a leader in ideological reform, and finally as a close confidant of the generalissimo—is not a progression found elsewhere in the careers of Western reformers, although important portions of it were certainly shared by others. George Shepherd's career does illustrate, however, several aspects of gradualism's dilemma: the motivations, the opportunities, the dangers, and the limitations that characterized reform efforts by Americans under the Nanking government.

Shepherd began as the agent of a pluralistic enterprise engaged in a nonpolitical activity, evangelism. His concern for the spiritual welfare of his charges became, inevitably, a concern for their physical welfare as well. A question was therefore raised as to how their physical—their economic and social—plight might most rapidly be improved. But not until the rise of a militant anti-Christian faith proclaiming its own answer did the question become urgent. In the rural reconstruction movement Shepherd found one answer which Christians could wholeheartedly adopt. Highly evolutionary by nature, however, it could succeed only if applied widely by an agency holding political power. Hence Shepherd's elation when the national government moved to support this solution in at least one province. Yet basic to rural reconstruction was a radical reform in land tenure which a private agency had no power to effect and which the government had no will to decree. The only possibility, in the circumstances, was superficial physical improvement coupled with an increasing emphasis on moral uplift. The latter, at least, could be applied on a national scale, with the full force of government support. And it was to the propagation of such moral uplift that Shepherd was ultimately called. In the end the man who had once seen so clearly the need for the reformer to go to the village became himself a withdrawn city bureaucrat and publicist. The free agent of pluralistic reformism was effectively absorbed by a paternalistic and would-be monolithic state unwilling or unable to initiate basic reforms.

The neutralization of the Western reformer suggests three areas for further examination. In each case George Shepherd's experience may shed some light on the paradoxical role of Christian missionaries in revolutionary China. First among these is Shepherd's relationship to the Communist movement in China. Prior to

1927, he seems to have had no direct contact with the problem; one might assume, furthermore, that his limited schooling gave him little or no acquaintance with the theoretical underpinnings of Marxism-Leninism. His first impression of communism, therefore, was direct and personal: it threatened his life, destroyed his property, and drove him out of his parish. All this it did, however, in the name of social justice. And George Shepherd's first-hand knowledge of misery and injustice in rural China was enough to make him pause and consider the aim of the revolutionaries. Shepherd was a hard-headed pragmatist: he judged men by their works; and the Communists did indeed erase the old social order. They moved in with vigor where both state and church had feared to tread. It might be said that the Communists aroused in him a deep sense of shame on behalf of Christian institutions; that they filled him with an awareness of God's judgment upon the mission enterprise; and that they produced in him an intensified desire for atonement through service. It is conceivable, in fact, that Shepherd actually considered cooperation with the Communists; his secret interview with the Red agent in the spring of 1933 was surely a feeler in this direction. For Nanking showed no signs of interest in the welfare of rural Fukien; and the aims of the 19th Route Army were highly unpredictable. All this was changed, however, with the news of the Kuling conferences and the suppression of the Fukien Rebellion. Nanking now emerged as a powerful "convert" to rural reconstruction and, what was more, a convert sympathetic to Christianity. With this development, Shepherd gradually shifted away from his old ambivalence about the Communists. They still posed Christianity's greatest challenge in China; but any thought of collaboration with them was now obviated by the church's new rapport with Chiang and his government.

A second point of interest in George Shepherd's career becomes, with the invitation to Lichuan, his relationship to rural reconstruction. For rural reform was to him and many other Christians the most hopeful instrument of response to the Communist challenge. In effect, Christians now sought to beat the Communists at their own game: to effect social revolution in the village with sufficient speed and thoroughness to undercut the Red appeal. Yet in playing the role of social revolutionaries the Christian missionaries faced an impossible dilemma. As bearers of the gospel of love—

and as heirs to the liberal-democratic tradition—they must eschew violence and bloodshed in changing the social order; yet without some risk of violence and bloodshed, it was virtually impossible to bring about rapid change in the entrenched order of rural China. The Christian reformer was a revolutionary who was barred from using the instruments of revolution. His revolution could be at best only a slow and carefully phased process of evolution; at worst, it actually increased social unrest by revealing new but unattainable possibilities to the villager. To his Communist rival, therefore, he must always be a runner-up: for in both speed and short-term thoroughness the revolution he brought was second best. To be sure, there remained one possible means of extrication from the dilemma. That was the coupling of a Christian social revolution with a political agency intent upon legalized violence: an agency willing to decree and enforce expropriation of lands and equalization of rights in the Chinese countryside, an agency willing to apply thorough tax reforms and create rural credit. Such an institution might have existed in the Nanking government; some reformers, Christian and otherwise, hoped for such a development. It must be remembered that Shepherd himself gave wholehearted approval to Stampar's criticisms of the Kiangsi projects. Yet Nanking balked at alienation of the landlord class; it did little to attack the rural crisis. And the reformers gracefully acceded, still hopeful but not outspokenly critical. Increasingly, their focus shifted from the reconstruction of model villages to the gradual production of trained personnel. Meanwhile, the impact of the gentle revolutionaries on the Chinese countryside remained at best superficial.

Shepherd's activities with the New Life Movement provide a final area for examination. Their result, as we have seen, was the bureaucratization of the reformer and his removal from the field of action. But it would be unfair to conclude that such a result was clearly foreseeable. Undoubtedly the very weaknesses of Kuomintang reform efforts in Kiangsi drove Shepherd to hope for greater personal effectiveness in Nanking. The NLM was feeble and empty; the early enthusiasm which had greeted it was rapidly dissipated, leaving it an object of widespread scorn. Yet Shepherd was convinced of the sincerity of its initiators; revitalized, it might yet infuse the nation with a new spirit of service, self-sacrifice, and idealism. His task was to give the anemic movement fresh, strong rooting in rural reconstruction. Among available foreigners, he was probably well equipped to do so.

But George Shepherd was battling against prohibitive odds. By 1936 gradualism was already well on its way to oblivion as a solution to China's problems. Immediacy was the watchword in all spheres of activity—immediacy in resistance to Japan, in "national salvation," in the granting of political liberties, in the achievement of economic progress. However genuine Chiang Kai-shek's conversion to rural reform, the demands and aspirations of influential sectors of Chinese opinion had already left him far behind. The search for an all-explanatory ideology among intellectuals had produced an increasingly widespread acceptance of the premises of Marxism-Leninism. By early 1937 even Christian institutions were feeling the effects of leftist rejection of liberalism and pragmatism. Earlier enthusiasm for rural reconstruction projects had given way to disillusionment. This was arid soil indeed in which to plant a program that still gave priority to character building through personal hygiene, the destruction of pests, punctuality, and modest attire.

It cannot be said, however, that George Shepherd's illusions were very great. He was endowed with more than a little historical sense. This would-be Borodin felt the tides of history surging about him; the moment for action must be seized, for it would never come again. Borodin himself had been given the chance to shape China's destiny—only to be engulfed in the trough of counterrevolution. And so throughout his career of action Shepherd sensed always that he might be too late; that the moment of opportunity might already be lost; that history had passed by the church in China. And when his banishment came, as it ultimately did, by the forces of Japanese aggression and Kuomintang repression, George Shepherd shed himself of all illusions save one: a lingering faith in the lonely man into whose confidence he had been taken.

### Retrospect and Aftermath

In the summer of 1937, at Marco Polo Bridge, the Nanking decade came to an end. With it passed ten years of efforts at Westernization, modernization, reconstruction, and reform; and in their place came the long harsh struggle of a people for national survival.

Scorched earth, guerilla warfare, and an endless westward trek had become the new preoccupation of all classes of society. On the misty hills of Chungking, a refugee government sought to adjust itself to the newly discovered hinterland and the removal of its urban eastern base.

The later years of the Kuomintang's decline, fall, and exile lie beyond the legitimate confines of this study. It would be all too easy to project forward from the sudden, ill-founded national unity of 1937 and foretell the debilitation and collapse that the war and its aftermath would bring. But it would be an oversimplification as well, for the twelve years from 1937 to 1949 brought new factors to bear on the old ailments of the government, and the war years are a unit unto themselves. The Nanking decade may have nurtured the seeds of destruction, but it cannot be said to have foredoomed the regime to collapse. The very attractiveness of the theory, with its wave-of-history overtones, should caution against its glib acceptance. What can be said, on the basis of the foregoing pages, relates not so much of the future of Nationalist China as to the activities, understanding, and illusions of Americans who dealt with Nationalist China.

There emerges from these pages of exploration—however tentatively—first, a sense of both the grandiose aims and the inadequate instruments possessed by Americans who attempted to influence the development of modern China in the Nanking years. One is struck by the impossibility of the undertaking in normal circumstances: the attempt by a disparate band of 3,000 to transform a civilization of 450 million, or more specifically, to induce among its leaders an activist concern for social welfare. The conditions of the thirties compounded the impossibility. For the Christian Borodins —and for the Christian cadres as well—there existed no monolithic source of directives, no ample foreign funds.

Given such limitations, a second impression emerges: a sense of the reformers' tenaciousness, of their ability to learn and grow, to profit from their errors, and to try anew. Slowly and pragmatically, the pluralistic enterprise groped its way toward understanding, toward policies that met the needs of China. By the end of the decade, the joint efforts of missionaries, foundation agents, and Chinese reformers had begun to show results. They had produced, in time, both an instrument and a program for the transformation of a virtually medieval agrarian society. All that was lacking, it seemed to some, was the necessary score of years.

The very promise of the undertaking and the deepening sense of urgency combined to create a third phenomenon among many of the reformers: an eagerness to join with those who might give them scope for action—who asked for their cooperation, accorded them status, and honored their faith. It mattered little that the offer involved partnership with political authority; indeed, the goodwill of the government seemed itself an element of promise after tumultuous years of antiforeignism. Whatever the lingering doubts, the offer was gratefully accepted.[28]

In some ways it is curious that such a shift should have occurred. For the reformers knew well the government's record of previous years: the promising beginnings, yes; but also the tasks left undone in the forging of a nation, the frustration of the agents of Western liberal gradualism, the deepening alienation from key groups within the country.

By 1937, however, such evidence was blurred by hope and by illusion: by the sudden appearance of a new national unity, by the superficial sharing of the aim of moral uplift, by the hope of gradual progress toward a modernized society. And so the American enterprise, in the last years of the Nanking decade, became increasingly identified with the Chinese Nationalist government.

The involvement of American reformers in the fortunes of the Kuomintang was to give way in later years to a more far-reaching relationship between the two nations. In early 1942 the alliance of reformers and officials was joined by the United States government. With the granting of a first half-billion-dollar loan to the Chungking regime, America's support for Kuomintang China became official, overt, and presumably unlimited. In one sudden stroke, the sympathies of private citizens were transformed into public policy, and Sino-American relations entered a new phase.

To be sure, the shift had been presaged by the outlook of Roosevelt and Morgenthau, and by the diplomats' rising optimism in the wake of the Sian crisis. It was a shift well grounded, too, in years of public compassion toward the oppressed people of China.[29] Nor did the United States have any real alternative once Pearl Harbor exploded upon the nation.

The wartime American commitment to Kuomintang China built

on the hopes and illusions of the reformers' own commitment. It built on a ready willingness to recall only one side of the Nanking record. And it built on a continuing blindness to the polarization of the Chinese revolution. Such a foundation was precarious at best. The polarizing processes, rooted in the split of the twenties and developed in the disillusion of the thirties, were soon to be intensified in the years of the Chungking government. Protracted war, inflation, corruption, and demoralization were all to take their toll on the refugee regime. By 1945, the unsolved problems remained; the unifying threat of Japan had disappeared; and the only alternative to the Kuomintang had burgeoned in power and prestige. So it was that the American commitment to a nation risked becoming a commitment to a faction. And so it was that the American effort in China became tied to the deepening tragedy of the Kuomintang regime.

With the exile of that regime came the end of the American effort and the ouster of the would-be reformers, and with them went the last best chance for the gradualist alternative. The denouement was dramatic; but it was hardly very sudden. Many years before, in the days of the Nanking government, gradualism had already been outstripped by the Chinese revolution.

# Epilogue

During the course of the Kuomintang's decline, the reformers and their colleagues were soon torn by partisanship. In the war and postwar years, the Protestant missionary community became sharply divided—as did American officials and academics—on the question of loyalty to the Kuomintang regime. On the one side stood such indefatigable spokesmen for the Nationalists as Walter H. Judd (formerly of the ABCFM), William R. Johnson (the Nanchang Methodist), George and Geraldine Fitch (of the YMCA), and—for a time—George Shepherd. Ranged against them, with increasing bitterness, were James G. Endicott (the Canadian who had succeeded Shepherd as NLM adviser) and other American missionaries, less outspoken, whose disillusionment with the Nationalists was intense and whose hopes for the Chinese Communists were high on the basis of the Yenan performance.

More dramatic, however, was the split within the Chinese reformer community. While James Yen, Chang Fu-liang, Franklin Ho, and others chose exile in Taiwan or the United States, many Christian leaders from the Nanking decade stayed on the mainland and gave fervent lip service, at least, to the Communist regime. Most outspoken among them were Y. T. Wu (Wu Yao-tsung) and Kiang Wen-han.

Though the actual circumstances of such mainland spokesmen remain unclear, their writings form an interesting postscript to the efforts of the Nanking decade.

In early 1959, Y. T. Wu looked back on the previous year and concluded that "Through socialist education the clergy and the laity of the whole country have had their thinking raised to a new level; the rightists have been decisively defeated; the semi-colonial aspect of the church has been changed; and the Chinese Christian Church is now in process of shaking off the shackles of imperialism, and ready to advance on the road to socialism." [1]

Similar views were expressed in 1959 by Kiang Wen-han in connection with his reflections on service with the Student Christian Movement 30 years before: "This Movement took as its standard, 'Based on the spirit of Jesus, let us create a youth organization, establish strong character, carry out a revolution, and plan for the liberation and development of the livelihood of the people.' That empty dream was entirely in the realm of Reformism [that is, the heresy—from the Communist standpoint—that reform without revolution is possible], and since the Christianity of that day, in both finances and thinking, was under the control of imperialism, so no matter what kind of a 'movement' we tried to initiate, we still remained in the diabolical clutches of imperialism. But now since Liberation, the life of the mass of working people has been revolutionized under the leadership of the Communist party, and has attained that 'liberation and development' that we only talked about." [2]

Eight years earlier, in the summer of 1951, Y. T. Wu had issued a lengthy "Denunciation of American Imperialism," which summarized most cogently the pro-Communist critique of American reformers in the Nanking years. "What is reformism?" asked Wu. "All decorative false fronts, attempts to avoid the class struggle, and methods which oppose the use of revolution to overthrow the old social order."

Wu proceeded to single out John R. Mott and Sherwood Eddy as two of American imperialism's chief "cultural agents in religious garb," who came to China under YMCA auspices "to spread the poison of reformism." The "reformist theories of Eddy and Mott—'National Salvation Through Personal Character' and 'Mind, Spirit, Body, Society'—brought James Y. C. Yen to the fore in the YMCA," a man who "held that China's misfortune was that she was 'poor, ignorant, weak, and selfish'—not that she was oppressed and exploited by imperialism and feudalism." Wu then cited Eddy's belief that " 'the doctrine of Ting Hsien could counter communism' " in order to show that "Yen's Ting Hsien work was basically designed to combat communism, and that this worthless anti-communist churchman was praised by American imperialism as a 'great man.' "

Nor did the Lichuan experiment escape Wu's denunciation: "This Lichuan Rural Service Society functioned in coordination with the unpatriotic 'Communist Annihilation Plan' of Chiang's bandit gang at that time . . . The man in charge of the Lichuan Rural Service Society was Chiang Kai-shek's adviser, George W. Shepherd, an American missionary and secret agent." Finally, Wu excoriated as well the New Life Movement as a vehicle of "reformism . . . for the purpose of deceiving and doping the minds of the people throughout the country." He recalled Chiang Kai-shek's pressure for Christian cooperation with the NLM and concluded that "America and Chiang plotted to use the YMCA and the churches as unpatriotic tools."

What of Y. T. Wu's own involvement in such nefarious enterprises? "In the beginning, my thinking was deeply influenced by Mott and Eddy. I was mentally bemused by their reformism." But in due course he experienced increasing conflict between patriotism, on the one hand, and the "doctrine of brotherly love" on the other; and "in the end, patriotism vanquished the 'brotherly love' which had been propagated by imperialism to cheat the colonial peoples." From 1935 onward, Wu wrote, "I began to comprehend the error of reformism, and embarked upon the path of revolution." And as a further judgment on his reformist sins: "All of us have been the tools of American cultural aggression, perhaps without being wholly conscious of it." [3]

# Notes, Bibliography, Index

## Abbreviations

ABCFM     Archives of the American Board of Commissioners for Foreign Missions (Congregational), 1812–1952, on deposit in the Houghton Library, Harvard University. Three mission regions of the American Board are discussed in the present study: the *North China, Foochow,* and *Shaowu* missions. In each case, the materials referred to are *Letters* or *Reports.*

NCC     Archives of the National Christian Council of China, on deposit in the Missionary Research Library, New York City. Five categories of materials are cited: *Minutes* (of the administrative, executive, and ad-interim committees); *Bulletin* (the council's periodical); *Execom* (special reports and minutes of the executive committee); *Staff* (minutes of the council's staff meetings); and *Biennial Meeting* (proceedings of larger conferences).

YMCA     Correspondence received by the International Committee of the Young Men's Christian Associations of the United States and Canada, 1891–1950, on deposit at the YMCA Historical Library, New York City. In most cases, the abbreviation is followed by *WS,* a file box *number,* and a folder *letter;* these references relate to the "World Service" files prepared in connection with Professor K. S. Latourette's history of the YMCA.

CR     *The Chinese Recorder, Journal of the Christian Movement in China,* Frank Rawlinson, ed., Shanghai.

FR     *Foreign Relations of the United States. Diplomatic Papers,* U.S. Government Printing Office, Washington.

HR     Hugh W. Hubbard, "The Lichwan Service Center," Report of April 20, 1935. NCC, biennial meeting, 1935.

# Notes

*Chapter One. China under the Nanking Government*

1. For an interesting discussion of "the sojourner" as a sociological type, see Paul C. P. Siu, "The Sojourner," *American Journal of Sociology,* 58:34 (July 1952): "The essential characteristic of the sojourner is that he clings to the culture of his own ethnic group as in contrast to the bi-cultural complex of the marginal man . . . It is convenient, therefore, to define the 'sojourner' as a stranger who spends many years of his lifetime in a foreign country without being assimilated by it. The sojourner is par excellence an ethnocentrist."

2. See John K. Fairbank, *Trade and Diplomacy on the China Coast: The Opening of the Treaty Ports, 1842–1854* (Cambridge, Mass., 1953), I, 70.

3. As one American missionary recalls, "I remember writing home in my second year (1909), 'China is a sleeping giant, and it's great fun having a tiny hand in waking her up.'" (Letter from Hugh W. Hubbard to author, April 7, 1964.) See also Paul A. Cohen, *China and Christianity: The Missionary Movement and the Growth of Anti-Foreignism, 1860–1870* (Cambridge, Mass., 1963). Cohen notes not only the hostility of Chinese intellectuals toward the missionaries, but also "counter-hostility" among the Westerners, grounded in inevitable self-consciousness and actual intolerance of Chinese culture.

4. Under extraterritoriality (or "extrality"), foreign nationals in China were subject to the legal jurisdiction of their own governments only, that is, they were exempt from Chinese jurisdiction. Under the unequal treaties, extraterritoriality became a device to protect foreign firms and corporations in the treaty ports from Chinese taxation and, in due course, to preserve the legal immunity of foreign nationals and institutions in the Chinese hinterland.

5. Another factor that increased the status of the foreigners: Chinese receptiveness to Western learning after the Boxer catastrophe. According to Hugh W. Hubbard, "I arrived in Tientsin in 1908 as the first physical

education instructor in four government schools and found students and teachers wide open to western ideas, with no perceptible anti-foreign feeling in the schools. I believe that the introduction of western education was a factor in enhancing the status of the missionary, if not all Westerners." (Letter to author, April 7, 1964.)

6. For some aspects of this continuity, see Paul A. Varg, *Missionaries, Chinese, and Diplomats: The American Protestant Missionary Movement in China, 1890–1952* (Princeton, 1958). However, Varg (p. 71) sees a "turning point between the old stress on snatching the heathen from the jaws of hell and the new view of missions as a humanitarian agency" with the publication in 1897 of James S. Dennis' *Christian Missions and Social Progress: A Sociological Study of Foreign Missions.*

7. See Cohen.

8. Mrs. John E. Williams to Mrs. J. Claude Thomson, April 1927 (quoted in a letter to the author, Oct. 2, 1958). Mrs. Williams' husband, president of the University of Nanking, was shot by Kuomintang soldiers in the Nanking Incident, March 1927.

9. Nelson T. Johnson Papers, Library of Congress: Johnson to Stanley K. Hornbeck, June 1, 1933.

10. For a critical evaluation of the effect of "tutelage," see Carsun Chang, *Third Force in China* (New York, 1952).

11. See Ch'ien Tuan-sheng, *The Government and Politics of China* (Cambridge, Mass., 1950), pp. 152–156.

12. See F. F. Liu, *A Military History of Modern China, 1924–1949* (Princeton, 1956), chap. 12.

13. Ch'ien Tuan-sheng, pp. 101–108.

14. *Ibid.,* p. 99.

15. *Ibid.,* p. 100. See also F. F. Liu, pp. 71–80.

16. Melville T. Kennedy, Jr., "The Kuomintang and Chinese Unification, 1928–1931," (unpub. diss., Harvard University, April 1958), pp. 27 ff.

17. In the absence of a scholarly study of the generalissimo's life and character, see Emily Hahn, *Chiang Kai-shek: An Unauthorized Biography* (New York, 1955).

18. See F. F. Liu, pp. 226–286.

19. Hahn, p. 86. See also Christopher Tang, "Christianity and the New Life Movement in China" (unpub. diss., Department of Church History, San Francisco Theological Seminary, April 1941), pp. 106 ff.

20. The generalissimo's own brief account of this visit is contained in Chiang Chung-cheng (Chiang Kai-shek), *Soviet Russia in China: A Summing-up at Seventy* (New York, 1957), pp. 19–25, or in rev. ed. (New York, 1958), pp. 21–28.

21. Nelson T. Johnson Papers, Library of Congress, Memorandum on "Conversation with G. W. Shepard," Nanking, May 17, 1937.

22. For a summary of the "Rights Recovery Movement," see John K. Fairbank, *The United States and China* (rev. ed., Cambridge, 1958), pp. 181–182.

23. See Meredith P. Gilpatrick, "The Status of Law and Lawmaking Procedure under the Kuomintang," *Far Eastern Quarterly,* 10:38–55 (November 1950).

24. For a comprehensive study of the extraterritoriality problem, see Wesley R. Fishel, *The End of Extraterritoriality in China* (Berkeley, 1952).

25. Fairbank, *The United States and China,* pp. 263–264.

26. *Ibid.,* pp. 206–220.

27. See Chin Fen, "The National Economic Council," in *The Chinese Year Book, 1935–1936,* premier issue (Shanghai, December 1935), pp. 294–347.

28. For a discussion of China's program of technical collaboration with the League, see Dorothy Borg, *The United States and the Far Eastern Crisis of 1933–1938* (Cambridge, Mass., 1964), pp. 56–62.

29. See Chapters 3 and 9 below.

30. T. A. Bisson, *Japan in China* (New York, 1938), p. 50. Bisson attributes Soong's resignation to pressure from Japan; there is other evidence, however, that points to a basic disagreement over the allocation of funds. See Douglas Paauw, "Chinese National Expenditures during the Nanking Period," *Far Eastern Quarterly,* 12:3–26 (November 1952). For a more recent critique of Soong and Kung in office, see Y. C. Wang, *Chinese Intellectuals and the West, 1872–1949* (Chapel Hill, 1966), pp. 422–464.

31. Douglas Paauw, "The Kuomintang and Economic Stagnation, 1928–1937," *Journal of Asian Studies,* 16:213–220 (February 1957). For a more favorable recent judgment of the government's achievements, see John K. Chang, "Industrial Development of China, 1912–1949," *Journal of Economic History,* 28:56–81 (March 1967).

32. Paauw, "The Kuomintang," p. 214; and Paauw, "Chinese National Expenditures," p. 14.

33. Paauw, "The Kuomintang," pp. 218–219.

34. *Ibid.,* pp. 217–218.

35. Fairbank, *The United States and China,* p. 220.

36. Paauw, "The Kuomintang," p. 220.

37. See Mary C. Wright, "From Revolution to Restoration: The Transformation of Kuomintang Ideology," *Far Eastern Quarterly,* 14:515–532 (August 1955).

38. See Harold M. Vinacke, *A History of the Far East in Modern Times* (5th ed., New York, 1950), pp. 540–541.

39. For a useful discussion of the political complexities of this period, see Conrad Brandt, *Stalin's Failure in China* (Cambridge, Mass., 1959).

40. For a study of Communist participation in the Sian episode, see James C. Thomson, Jr., "Communist Policy and the United Front in China, 1935–1936," *Papers on China,* 11:99–148 (Cambridge, Mass., 1957). See also Lyman P. Van Slyke, *Enemies and Friends: The United Front in Chinese Communist History* (Stanford, 1967).

*Chapter Two. Americans and the Nanking Government*

1. Dorothy Borg, *American Policy and the Chinese Revolution, 1925– 1928* (New York, 1947), p. 419. I am greatly indebted to Miss Borg for much of the material cited in this chapter.

2. Secretary of State Stimson, of course, wanted far more but was overruled by President Hoover.

3. Borg, *The United States,* chap. 1.

4. *Ibid.,* see chap. 3.

5. *Ibid.,* see chap. 2. Miss Borg cites a sampling of newspapers which suggests that there was a wide variety of editorial opinion; that the internationalist press would have taken a strong stand where issues of collective security were involved; but that none of these papers would have given the State Department the impression that the country wanted a policy of "bucking" Japan over the issue of China.

6. See John M. Blum, *From the Morgenthau Diaries: Years of Crisis, 1928–1938* (Boston, 1959).

7. Borg, *The United States,* see chap. 4. Also, Allen S. Everest, *Morgenthau, the New Deal, and Silver* (New York, 1950).

8. John Leighton Stuart, *Fifty Years in China* (New York, 1954), pp. 92–93.

9. Roosevelt to Morgenthau, Dec. 6, 1934. (Roosevelt Library, Hyde Park, FDRL, 5–26–53.) I am grateful to Miss Borg for calling this item to my attention.

10. The American air mission to the Nanking government was a shortlived venture. The Chinese government originally approached the State Department for a "mission of aviators to organize and operate an army air school in China" in 1932 but was turned down and referred to the Department of Commerce for assistance on "civilian aviation." As a result, John Hamilton Jouett and ten other aviators who were reserve officers arrived in China in the summer of 1932 to organize the Central Aviation School at Hangchow. The mission achieved substantial success by the time of the aviation show of November 1933. But the U.S. government failed to support Jouett in obtaining a renewal of the contract. In October an Italian Air Mission arrived in China under General Lordi, and six months later Lordi had virtually replaced Colonel Jouett as aviation adviser to the government. (See Borg, *The United States,* p. 74.)

11. Hornbeck to Hull, May 16, 1934. State Dept. files, 711.93/324, cited in Borg, *The United States,* p. 576.

12. Charles F. Remer, *Foreign Investments in China* (New York, 1933), p. 76.

13. East Asian Institute, Columbia University, "Foreign Investment in China and the Chinese Balance of Payments." Research guide, 1944, pp. 72– 73. See also *The China Year Book, 1933,* H. G. W. Woodhead, ed. (Shanghai, 1933), p. 146.

14. Fairbank, *The United States and China*, p. 258.

15. *The China Year Book, 1934*, H. G. W. Woodhead, ed. (Shanghai, 1934), p. 2.

16. Fairbank, *The United States and China*, pp. 258–259.

17. See Shirley Godley, "W. Cameron Forbes and the American Mission to China, 1935," *Papers on China*, 14:87–110 (Harvard University, East Asian Research Center, 1960).

18. Fairbank, *The United States and China*, p. 260.

19. Johnson to Secretary of State, Peiping, Feb. 13, 1933, *FR 1933*, III, 170–174. 893.00/12291.

20. Johnson to Secretary of State, Peiping, Jan. 5, 1934, *FR 1933*, III, 491–493. 893.00/12623.

21. Johnson to Secretary of State, Peiping, July 11, 1934, *FR 1934*, III, 217–220. 893.00/12785.

22. Gauss to Secretary of State, Peiping, Jan. 9, 1935, *FR 1934*, III, 344–348. 893.00/12945.

23. Johnson to Secretary of State, Peiping, July 12, 1935, *FR 1935*, III, 306–309. 893.00/13170.

24. Johnson to Secretary of State, Peiping, Jan. 3, 1936, *FR 1935*, III, 502–507. 893.00/13348.

25. Borg, *The United States*, pp. 197–201. (The Hankow report is File 893.00b/927.) Miss Borg refrains from naming the author, O. Edmund Clubb, who was subjected in the 1950's to repeated loyalty investigations as a result of his long interest in following Chinese Communist developments; it is regrettable that the State Department, which forced Clubb to retire in 1953, made so little use of his thorough, careful, and accurate reporting during the years of his service.

26. Johnson to E. C. Carter, Peiping, May 27, 1933. Johnson Papers, Library of Congress, Box 17.

27. Quoted in Borg, *The United States*, p. 206.

28. *Ibid.* See chap. 7, "Views of American Officials on the Chinese Communists and the Sian Incident."

29. Johnson to Secretary of State, Peiping, July 3, 1936, *FR 1936*, IV, 231–236.

30. See Thomson, pp. 119–120.

31. See C. Y. W. Meng, "The Meaning of the Nation-Wide Celebration of General Chiang's Birthday," *China Weekly Review*, 78:344–345 (Nov. 7, 1936).

32. See Thomson, pp. 134–137.

33. Johnson to Secretary of State, Peiping, Jan. 12, 1937, *FR 1936*, IV, 453–458. 893.00/13989.

34. Johnson to Secretary of State, Nanking, June 10, 1937, *FR 1937*, III, 111–112. 893.00/14145.

35. Address to Harvard University American Far Eastern Policy Studies Meeting, Cambridge, Mass., April 10, 1959.

36. For a collection of useful case studies of American Protestant efforts

in nineteenth- and twentieth-century China, see Kwang-Ching Liu, ed., *American Missionaries in China: Papers from Harvard Seminars* (Cambridge, Mass., 1966).

37. This view is strongly held by Professor M. Searle Bates of Union Theological Seminary, a leading scholar of the mission movement in China.

38. For a description of the vicissitudes of the mission enterprise in the twenties, see Varg, pp. 180–211.

39. *The China Christian Year Book, 1934–1935*, F. W. Rawlinson, ed. (Shanghai, 1935), p. 229. Bates confirms these figures.

40. Kenneth Scott Latourette, *Advance Through Storm*, vol. 7, *A History of the Expansion of Christianity* (London, 1945), p. 346.

41. Address by M. Searle Bates, Harvard University American Far Eastern Policy Studies Meeting, Cambridge, Mass., May 15, 1959.

42. See Varg, chap. 9, "The Crusade Runs into Stumbling Blocks at Home Base, 1919–1931."

43. *Ibid.*, p. 167.

44. ABCFM, North China Reports, 1930–1934, item 113.

45. *Ibid.*, item 116.

46. *Ibid.*, item 125.

47. W. C. Fairfield to E. H. Ballou, April 17, 1933, ABCFM, North China Secretary, 1930–1939, item 18.

48. *The China Christian Year Book*, p. 268.

49. The figures are given in the foundation's "Report of the Committee on Appraisal and Plan," Raymond B. Fosdick, chairman, Dec. 11, 1934. I am indebted to Mr. Fosdick of New York City for permission to see his copy of this report. (See Chapter 6 below.)

50. *Ibid.*, p. 275.

51. *Ibid.*, pp. 275–276 and 279–280.

52. Varg, pp. 195 ff.

53. *Ibid.*, p. 245.

54. Bates address, Cambridge, Mass., May 15, 1959.

55. Lewis S. C. Smythe, "Communism Challenges Christianity," *CR*, 65:359 (June 1934).

56. Jesse B. Yaukey, "Religious Education and Communism," *CR*, 65:353–354 (June 1934).


*Chapter Three. Christians and the Rural Crisis*

1. For a vivid description by a Marxist observer of rural conditions in pre-Communist China, see William Hinton, *Fanshen: A Documentary of Revolution in a Chinese Village* (New York, 1966).

2. Franklin L. Ho, "Rural Economic Reconstruction in China," preliminary paper for 6th Conference of Institute of Pacific Relations, Yosemite, August 1936 (Tientsin, 1936), pp. 1–2.

3. *China Handbook, 1937–1945,* Hollington K. Tong, ed. (rev. ed., New York, 1947), p. 605.

4. Franklin L. Ho, preliminary draft of an economic history of republican China, section on "The Land Tenure System." I am deeply indebted to Professor Ho for allowing me to make use of his important manuscript on the rural economy of Kuomintang China.

5. Franz H. Michael and George E. Taylor, *The Far East in the Modern World* (New York, 1956), p. 409.

6. Ho ms., section on "Agricultural Credit, Marketing, and Taxation."

7. *Ibid.*

8. *Ibid.*

9. Teng Ssu-yü and John K. Fairbank, *China's Response to the West: A Documentary Survey* (Cambridge, Mass., 1954), p. 226.

10. *Ibid.,* p. 228. See Harold Schiffrin, "Sun Yat-sen's Early Land Policy: The Origin and Meaning of 'Equalization of Land Rights,' " *Journal of Asian Studies,* 16:549–564 (August 1957).

11. Ho ms., section on "Agricultural Reconstruction."

12. *Ibid.;* also S. H. Han, *Directory of Rural Reconstruction Work in China* (Shen Mu Hsien, Shensi, 1938). The latter pamphlet is available in the Missionary Research Library, New York City.

13. See China International Famine Relief Commission, *The C.I.F.R.C. Fifteenth Anniversary Book, 1921–1936,* CIFRC series A., no. 47 (Peiping, 1936), pp. 30–34.

14. *Ibid.*

15. Andrew James Nathan, *A History of the China International Famine Relief Commission* (Cambridge, Mass., 1965), p. 71. For a contemporary account of the commission's early years, see Walter H. Mallory, *China: Land of Famine* (New York, 1926).

16. For a contemporary critical study of seven early attempts at rural reconstruction, see K'ung Hsüeh-hsiung, *Chung-kuo chin-jih chih nung-ts'un yün-tung* (The rural movement in China today), preface by Sun K'o (Sun Fo), published by Chung-shan wen-hua chiao-yu kuan (Sun Yat-sen Institute for the Advancement of Culture and Education); rev. ed. Nanking 1934.

K'ung examines (1) Liang Sou-ming's program in Shantung; (2) Yen Yang-ch'u's center at Tinghsien; (3) the work of the Kiangsu Provincial College of Education and the China Vocational Education Association (at Wusih); (4) Peng Yü-t'ing's rural self-government experiment at Chen-p'ing, Honan; (5) the cooperative movement of the CIFRC in Hopei; (6) T'ao Hsing-chih's efforts at Hsiao-chuang; and (7) the self-government project of Shen Hsüan-lu at Tung-hsiang, Chekiang. App. I (pp. 417–422) lists the major Chinese leaders of the rural reconstruction movement in the 1920's and 1930's.

17. *Ibid.* K'ung regards Shen Hsüan-lu's efforts at Tung-hsiang as the "most progressive" of the early experiments in that it stressed radical reform in economics, including land reform, as well as politics. He severely

criticizes the KMT's members for failing to "follow the ideas of Shen Hsüan-lu" in the wake of the Northern Expedition (pp. 411–412).

On Peng Yü-t'ing, Shen Hsüan-lu, and T'ao Hsing-chih, see also Robert Lee, "The Rural Reconstruction Movement," *Papers on China,* 4:160–198 (Cambridge, Mass., 1950); also, Ho ms.

18. T'ao was able to relocate his experiment at Shanghai and Pao-shan, Chekiang, under the auspices of his "Kung-hsüeh t'uan" (labor-science union). See K'ung Hsüeh-hsiung, chap. 7.

19. Quoted in Lyman P. Van Slyke, "Liang Sou-ming and the Rural Reconstruction Movement," *Journal of Asian Studies,* 18:457 (August 1959). The rest of this paragraph draws heavily on Van Slyke's careful study. See also Chow Tse-tsung, *The May Fourth Movement: Intellectual Revolution in Modern China* (Cambridge, Mass., 1960), pp. 329–332.

20. K'ung Hsüeh-hsiung particularly admired the "cooperative spirit" of the Tsouping project—its achievement of good understanding between rural workers and the rural community (K'ung Hsüeh-hsiung, chap. 2 and 9).

21. Yen held a B.A. from Yale (1918), an M.A. from Princeton (1921). The Sino-American Joint Commission on Rural Reconstruction, established in 1948 with Yen's participation, applied his techniques first in South China, then on Taiwan with considerable success. Yen himself was invited by the Philippine government to do similar work there after the fall of the Mainland. In 1951–1952 the government of India undertook a nationwide community development program directly influenced by Yen's experience. For an early account of the latter, see Chester Bowles, *Ambassador's Report* (New York, 1954), pp. 196–198.

22. Y. C. James Yen, *The Ting Hsien Experiment in 1934* (Peiping, n.d.), pp. 2–3. For a sociological analysis of the Tinghsien district, see Sidney D. Gamble, *Ting Hsien: A North China Rural Community* (New York, 1954).

23. Yen, *The Ting Hsien Experiment in 1934,* p. 5.

24. *Ibid.,* pp. 10–11.

25. Y. C. James Yen, *The Ting Hsien Experiment, 1930–1931* (Ting Hsien, 1931), p. 2.

26. *Ibid.,* pp. 28–30.

27. *Ibid.,* p. 37.

28. William A. Brown, "The Protestant Rural Movement in China, 1920–1937," *Papers on China,* 9:177–178 (Cambridge, Mass., 1955). Reprinted in Kwang-Ching Liu, ed., *American Missionaries in China* (Cambridge, Mass., 1966). The quotation is found in Frank Rawlinson, ed., *The Chinese Church as Revealed in the National Christian Conference* (Shanghai, 1922), pp. 323–324.

29. *Ibid.,* p. 178.

30. One late exception was the pioneer work begun by the ABCFM missionary James A. Hunter at Tunghsien, near Peking, in 1926. His Tunghsien Rural Service Center, with four or five Chinese specialists, organized rural

fairs and Farmers' Winter Schools (patterned after Danish Folk Schools). Hunter's work became the nucleus of the later North China Christian Rural Service Union. (Letter from Hugh W. Hubbard to author, April 7, 1964.)

31. NCC, *Report of the Conference on Christianizing Economic Relations,* held under the auspices of the National Christian Council of China, Shanghai, Aug. 18–28, 1927. Pamphlet in Missionary Research Library, New York City.

32. Brown, p. 179.

33. See Jerusalem Meeting, International Missionary Council, VI: *The Christian Mission in Relation to Rural Problems* (New York, 1928), 5–27, 225–228, and 245–255.

34. NCC, Minutes of the Administrative, Executive, and Ad-Interim Committees, May 1929–May 1933: Administrative, Oct. 3–5, 1929.

35. Chang Fu-liang, born in 1899 in Shanghai, attended St. John's University, Yale, and the University of Georgia. His wife's two sisters were married to James Yen and to the Reverend Y. Y. Tsu (of the NCC).

36. See Hugh W. Hubbard, "A Church Experiment in Mass Education," *Bulletin of the National Christian Council of China* no. 35:1–6 (April 1930). Regarding cooperation with Yen, Hubbard wrote: "Sometimes we dream that the Christian churches of China, united and determined, might, by means of some such methods as these, lead not only in the reconstruction of a new China, but also lay the foundation stone for the Kingdom of God" (p. 6).

37. Yen's connections with the North China missionaries were apparently far closer than Yen cared to indicate in a time of rising nationalism in China and secularism in the United States. Hugh Hubbard recalls his first meeting with Yen, on a train in the winter of 1923–1924: "He had just severed his connection with the YMCA and had come to Peking to organize the National Association of the MEM. Up to that time his campaigns had all been in cities. He must have been somewhat conscious of rural needs, since he had already invited Dr. Paul C. Fugh, fresh from Cornell, to be his rural secretary. I told Jimmy of our village classes and secured a promise from him to visit them with Fugh . . . This they did and spent three days touring the countryside and then two days at a Thousand Character Institute, to which I brought in my 40-odd rural workers . . . In 1926 Jimmy decided to move to the country and told me, to my great satisfaction, that he would like to select some place on our Paoting field, where we had already conducted some 750 classes. Various considerations led him to choose Tinghsien. He asked me to release our head evangelist for that district, as we had just completed a successful season of these classes. This we did for a time." (Letter from Hubbard to author, Apr. 7, 1964.)

38. Yen, *The Ting Hsien Experiment, 1930–1931,* p. 9.

39. *Ibid.,* p. 11. See also, "The Tinghsien Literacy Institute," *NCC Bulletin,* no. 36:9–10 (July 1930): "It would be a strange delegate who could go away without a quickened enthusiasm for and belief in the urgency of such work."

40. "General Secretary's Address Report," Nov. 15, 1930, NCC Minutes, May 1929–May 1933.

41. Kenyon L. Butterfield, "The Christian Church in Rural China," *CR,* 62:344 (June 1931).

42. Kenyon L. Butterfield, "Rural Community Parishes," *NCC Bulletin,* no. 37:13–15 (June 1931).

43. *NCC Bulletin,* no. 37:10 (June 1931).

44. NCC Minutes, May 1929–May 1933: Ad-Interim, May 18, 1931. According to Hugh Hubbard and James Hunter, no such "branch committee" ever functioned in Hopei. (Hubbard letter to the author, April 7, 1964.)

45. Circular Letter from Frank J. Rawlinson, Aug. 20, 1931, ABCFM, North China Letters, 1930–1939: 1931, item 156.

46. See NCC Minutes, May 1929–May 1933: Executive, pp. 11–14, October 1931: "Bishop Roots said that the situation caused by the Flood, by Communism, and by the Manchurian question was calling us back to fundamentals. We have what alone can meet the situation, belief in God."

47. Ho ms.

48. General News Letter of Frank J. Rawlinson, Dec. 29, 1931, ABCFM, North China Letters, 1930–1939: 1931, item 166.

49. "Report of Rural Secretary," Nov. 1, 1932, NCC, Executive Committee, Reports and Minutes, May and November 1932.

50. "Five Year Movement Report," May 4, 1932, *Ibid.,* May and November 1932. See also, *NCC Bulletin,* no. 33:8–9 (July 1929), for original objectives of Five-year Movement.

51. NCC Minutes, May 1929–May 1933: Ad-Interim, Sept. 19, 1932. See also "Report of Rural Secretary," Nov. 1, 1932, NCC Executive Committee, May and November 1932.

52. Besides James A. Hunter, an agricultural missionary at Tunghsien, Hopei, who had founded a Rural Service Center in 1926, the North China Christian Rural Service Union's chief driving force was Hugh W. Hubbard. James Yen worked closely with Hubbard in planning a program of rural cooperative societies, survey projects, and literacy training. As a coordinating instrument, however, the Union was severely handicapped by a lack of personnel and funds.

53. "A Brief Resume of the Biennial Meeting of the National Christian Council of China, Sungkiang, May 3–11, 1933," NCC, biennial meeting, 1933.

54. See "Report on the Tinghsien Institute on Rural Reconstruction to the Biennial Meeting of the NCC of China," by Hugh W. Hubbard (received Sept. 23, 1933), ABCFM, North China Reports, 1930–1934, item 103.

55. *Ibid.*

56. Margaret H. Brown, "Christian Communism at the Ting Hsien Institute," in *The Church and Rural Reconstruction: A Symposium on the Ting Hsien Rural Institute of 1933* (Shanghai, 1933).

57. "The NCC Rural Work Report," May 3, 1933, NCC, biennial meeting, 1933.

58. "Daily Minutes" of biennial meeting for May 9, 1933, NCC Minutes, May 1929–May 1933.

59. The Nankai University economist Franklin L. Ho (Ho Lien) gives special credit to Tawney for deepening public understanding of China's agrarian problems. Tawney visited Nankai, Tinghsien, and the University of Nanking in 1930. His book was translated into Chinese and serialized in the press. (Letter from F. L. Ho to author, Dec. 8, 1961.)

60. See the favorable editorial comment on this formula in the *North China Herald,* no. 186:3413 (Jan. 4, 1933), and no. 187:3435 (June 7, 1933). In the later issue: "General Chiang Kai-shek has made economic rehabilitation a necessary feature of his campaign. First there is to be the clearance of the former Red area; then occupation followed by a rough and ready resettlement of the country under the guidance of specially selected economic experts." (pp. 363–364).

61. *North China Herald,* no. 187:3435:383 (June 7, 1933).

62. William Richard Johnson, born Cornell, Illinois, 1878; B.S. Northwestern University, 1905; appointed to China under Methodist Board, 1906; retired Sept. 30, 1945. He died in 1967.

63. W. R. Johnson to Bishop Herbert Welch of Shanghai, June 9, 1933. (Copy for the Mission Corresponding Secretaries, preserved on microfilm, Methodist Mission Board, New York City.)

64. *Ibid.*

65. *Ibid.*

66. *Ibid.*

67. *Ibid.*

68. *Ibid.*

69. W. P. Mills, "Memorandum of Discussions Regarding Rural Reconstruction Work in Kiangsi Province, Kuling, Aug. 19–20, 1933. Confidential." A copy of this document is enclosed, with a letter from G. W. Shepherd to W. C. Fairfield, in ABCFM, Shaowu Letters, 1930–1934, item 244. Mills, a Southern Presbyterian missionary in Nanking and a former YMCA official, served as recording secretary for these sessions.

70. *Ibid.* The sub-committee that met on the 18th included, among others, Lewis S. C. Smythe, Nanking University sociologist, and Frank W. Price of Nanking Theological Seminary. The seminar meetings of 1933 had been held at the Kuling home of Lewis Smythe.

71. *Ibid.* In addition to Bishop Roots, the meeting of the 19th with Mme. Chiang included Smythe and Mills.

72. *Ibid.* Significantly, the vital question of land tenure was raised at this meeting. Madame Chiang agreed to request that President Y. G. Chen (Ch'en Yu-kuang) of Nanking University loan the noted agriculturalist J. Lossing Buck for a survey of land tenure in Kiangsi; there is no evidence that this loan was ever negotiated.

73. *Ibid.* This time the participants included Johnson and Price as well as Roots, Smythe, and Mills.

74. William R. Johnson, "A Suggested Plan for Rural Reconstruction

Work under Christian Auspices in Kiangsi Province, China," Kuling, Sept. 14, 1933 (abridged and revised), mimeographed pamphlet on file in Missionary Research Library, New York City.

75. *Ibid.*, pp. 6–7. For an account of the Kiangsu experiment, see R. S. Yu, "Introducing a New Educational Experiment," *China Weekly Review,* 64:262–263, 274 (April 15, 1933).

76. William R. Johnson, pp. 3–5, and 9–13.

77. *Ibid.*, p. 2.

78. *Ibid.*, p. 19.

79. W. P. Mills.

80. NCC Minutes, May 1933–May 1937: Members of the Executive Committee and Staff, Shanghai, Aug. 26, 1933. Those present were R. Y. Lo (presiding), L. T. Chen, A. J. Fisher, Miss M. A. Frame, T. H. Lee, and L. H. Roots of the executive committee; C. L. Boynton, L. D. Cio, E. C. Lobenstine, and T. H. Sun of the staff. Also present, by invitation, was G. Findlay Andrew.

81. *Ibid.*

82. NCC, Staff, January 1932–June 1934: Aug. 28, 1933.

83. NCC Staff, January 1932–June 1934: Sept. 18, 1933.

84. *Ibid.*

85. NCC Minutes, May 1933–May 1937: Ad-Interim, Sept. 19, 1933.

86. *Ibid.;* the sub-committee included E. E. Barnett of the YMCA, Bishop Welch of the Methodist Mission, NCC Chairman R. Y. Lo, and Miss Gertrude Shao.

87. NCC Minutes, May 1933–May 1937: Sub-committee of Ad-Interim, Sept. 26, 1933.

88. *Ibid.*

89. NCC Minutes, May 1933–May 1937: Ad-Interim, Sept. 28, 1933.

90. Lobenstine to Shepherd, Aug. 28, 1933, ABCFM, Shaowu Letters, 1930–1934, item 242.

91. NCC Minutes, May 1933–May 1937: Executive, Nov. 8–9, 1933.

92. Chang Fu-liang, "The Christian Rural Reconstruction Project in Restored Communist Areas," Nov. 7, 1933, NCC Executive Committee, November 1933, April and November 1934.

93. *Ibid.*

94. Shepherd to Fairfield, Nov. 5, 1933, ABCFM, Shaowu Letters, 1930–1934, item 250.

95. Chang Fu-liang Report, NCC Executive Committee, November 1933, April and November 1934.

96. NCC Minutes, May 1933–May 1937: Executive, Nov. 8–9, 1933. In his letter to Fairfield of Nov. 5, (see n. 94 above), Shepherd had written: "I am to give them part of a morning on Communism and Christianity. When I get through with that they may all change their minds."

97. NCC Staff, January 1932–June 1934: Nov. 15, 1933.

98. *Ibid.*, Nov. 29, 1933.

99. *Ibid.*, Dec. 6, 1933.

100. *Ibid.,* Jan. 10, 1934.

101. *Ibid.:* Staff Retreat, Jan. 22, 1934.

102. Chang Fu-liang Christmas letter, Nov. 23, 1933. NCC, Mimeographed Materials, May 1933–January 1934, vol. 3, item 71.

103. NCC Staff, January 1932–June 1934: Staff Retreat, April 7, 1934.


*Chapter Four. The Missionary as Rural Reformer*

1. "Chiang's Missionary Aide," *Newsweek,* 13:33 (April 3, 1939).

2. "For China," *Time,* 33:40 (April 17, 1939).

3. ABCFM, Papers of Accepted Candidates, 1925–1928, S (vol. 5).

4. *Ibid.* Shepherd adds, however, "Our relations with the Christian Mission in Many Lands [i.e., Plymouth Brethren] have been most cordial and still are."

5. *Ibid.*

6. ABCFM, Shaowu Reports, 1930–1939, item 10.

7. *CR,* 62:145–149 (March 1931).

8. *Ibid.,* pp. 146–147.

9. G. W. Shepherd, "Facing Some Facts," *CR* 62:712 (November 1931). Shepherd notes the general collapse of the rural parish over the past fifteen years: "Thousands who united with the church from all manner of motives, have suddenly discovered that as a life long insurance agency the organization has failed them."

10. Shepherd to Fairfield, July 14, 1931, ABCFM, Shaowu Letters, 1930–1934, item 38.

11. "Shaowu Annual Letter," July 31, 1931, by G. W. Shepherd, ABCFM, Shaowu Reports, 1930–1939, item 11.

12. Shepherd to Fairfield, July 14, 1931, ABCFM, Shaowu Letters, 1930–1934.

13. "Shaowu Annual Letter," July 31, 1931, ABCFM, Shaowu Reports, 1930–1939, item 11.

14. "Foochow Annual Letter, 1931–1932," Sept. 1, 1932, by G. W. Shepherd, ABCFM, Shaowu Reports, 1930–1939, item 17.

15. Shepherd to Fairfield, Oct. 12, 1932, ABCFM, Shaowu Letters, 1930–1934, item 146.

16. Shepherd to Fairfield, Oct. 27, 1932, *ibid.,* item 148.

17. Shepherd to Fairfield, Oct. 29, 1932, *ibid.,* item 149.

18. Shepherd to Fairfield, Nov. 26, 1932, *ibid.,* item 152.

19. Shepherd to Fairfield, Aug. 30, 1932, *ibid.,* item 144.

20. Shepherd to Fairfield and Mrs. Lee, Dec. 26, 1932, *ibid.,* item 155.

21. Shepherd to Fairfield, Feb. 14, 1933, *ibid.,* item 220.

22. Shepherd to Fairfield, Jan. 31, 1933, *ibid.,* item 218.

23. Shepherd to Fairfield, March 8, 1933, *ibid.,* item 222.

24. Mimeographed enclosure "Shaowu News," Feb. 25, 1933, *ibid.*

25. See also item 225, Shepherd to Fairfield, March 22, 1933, *ibid.*

26. Shepherd to Fairfield, May 19, 1933, *ibid.,* item 226.

27. George W. Shepherd, "Tinghsien's Challenge to the Church of Today," *CR,* 64:391–392 (June 1933).

28. Shepherd to Fairfield, May 26, 1933, ABCFM, Shaowu Letters, 1930–1934, item 229.

29. *Ibid.*

30. *Ibid.*

31. Shepherd to Fairfield, May 19, 1933, *ibid.,* item 226.

32. Fairfield to Shepherd, Aug. 3, 1933, *ibid.,* item 238.

33. Shepherd to Fairfield, June 3, 1933, *ibid.,* item 230.

34. Shepherd to Fairfield, June 16, 1933, *ibid.,* item 232.

35. NCC Staff, January 1932–June 1934: Staff Retreat, Jan. 22, 1934. Shepherd gave the NCC staff his evaluation of the 19th Route Army program and attributed its failure to its alleged "alliance" with the Chinese Communists. It should be noted that the Communists in fact rejected the overtures from the 19th Army leaders.

36. Shepherd to Fairfield, June 16, 1933, ABCFM, Shaowu Letters, 1930–1934, item 232.

37. Shepherd to Fairfield, June 23, 1933, *ibid.,* item 237.

38. Shepherd to Fairfield, May 30, 1933, *ibid.,* item 229.

39. Shepherd to Fairfield, Sept. 1, 1933, *ibid.,* item 239.

40. Shepherd to Fairfield, Sept. 19, 1933, *ibid.,* item 241.

41. Shepherd to Lobenstine, Sept. 19, 1933, *ibid.,* item 245.

42. Lobenstine to Shepherd, Aug. 28, 1933, *ibid.,* item 242.

43. Lobenstine to Shepherd, Sept. 30, 1933, *ibid.,* item 252. Shepherd left Foochow on October 12.

44. Shepherd to Fairfield, Nov. 5, 1933, *ibid.,* item 250.

45. *Ibid.;* see also, NCC staff, January 1932–June 1934: Sept. 18, 1933. Commissioner Ch'eng Shih-kuei, a graduate of Tokyo Normal College (1915), held an M.A. from Columbia (1925); he had served as Commissioner of Education in Fukien, 1928–1932, and moved to the Kiangsi post in 1933.

46. *Ibid.*

47. *Ibid.*

48. *Ibid.*

49. Lobenstine to Johnson, Dec. 7, 1933, ABCFM, Shaowu Letters, 1930–1934, item 253. "It is quite clear that the reason why both Mr. Shepherd and his mission are so keenly interested in the proposed Kiangsi project and are prepared to participate in it is their hope that this will prepare the way for the reopening of their Shaowu work."

50. Shepherd to Fairfield, Nov. 5, 1933, *ibid.,* item 250.

51. *Ibid.*

52. Shepherd to Fairfield, enclosure, "Rural Reconstruction in the Communist Devastated Areas of Kiangsi and Fukien," n.d., received Dec. 2, 1933, *ibid.,* item 251.

53. *Ibid.*

54. *Ibid.*

55. "The Christian Rural Project in Kiangsi," April 16, 1934 (marginal note in Shepherd's handwriting: "Chang Fu-liang's report to NCC Executive Committee"), ABCFM, Shaowu Reports, 1930–1939, item 23. See also Shepherd to Fairfield, Nov. 22, 1933, ABCFM, Shaowu Letters, 1930–1934, item 255.

56. The precise nature of the Fukien Rebellion remains something of a mystery. At the time, the Chinese Communists rejected Foochow's request for an alliance. This decision was later condemned by Communist ideologues as an example of Left opportunism, however, and both Li Chi-shen and Ts'ai T'ing-k'ai eventually joined the "coalition government" of Mao Tse-tung as non-Communist associates after 1949.

57. Shepherd to Fairfield, Nov. 22, 1933, ABCFM, Shaowu Letters, 1930–1934, item 255.

58. See Chapter 2 above, n. 10.

59. ABCFM, Shaowu Reports, 1930–1939, item 20. This is a longhand mimeographed news-sheet entitled "Foochow News," Jan. 8, 1934, prepared by Shepherd.

60. Shepherd to Fairfield, Jan. 25, 1934, ABCFM, Shaowu Letters, 1930–1934, item 280.

61. *Ibid.*

62. Rawlinson to Fairfield, Jan. 24, 1934, ABCFM, North China Letters, 1930–1939: 1934, item 236.

63. "The Christian Rural Project in Kiangsi," by Chang Fu-liang, April 17, 1934, NCC Executive Committee, November 1933, April and November 1934.

64. Shepherd to Fairfield, March 17, 1934, ABCFM, Shaowu Letters, 1930–1934, item 283. In a letter of March 16 (item 32), Mrs. Shepherd had written the mission secretaries of her husband's activities: "The movement is as it were in its birth pangs still. The plans are all in the making and, if you will excuse me as a wife for saying so, I felt that they all felt, for the present, George is the key man. He has the confidence of all. The job challenges him. As it developes it ought to give opportunities for the fulfillment of dreams for our part of China that have been interrupted again and again by circumstances." Mme. Chiang had invited Mrs. Shepherd to her home to tell her "how very pleased they were that George had been allocated for the work for they felt that with his experience, knowledge and love for the people added to his easy language facilities he was just the man for the project."

65. See Chapter 5 below, n. 15.

66. Shepherd to Fairfield, March 17, 1934, ABCFM, Shaowu Letters, 1930–1934, item 283.

67. Shepherd to Fairfield, April 2, 1934, *ibid.*, item 284.

68. *Ibid.*, item 283.

69. Shepherd to Fairfield, April 14, 1934, *ibid.*, item 286.

70. *Ibid.*, item 284.

71. Shepherd to "Bob," April 27, 1934, *ibid.,* item 292.

72. *Ibid.*

73. NCC Staff, September 1934–June 1936: Staff Retreat, Sept. 10, 1935.

74. For a full account of the NEC programs, see *The Chinese Year Book, 1935–1936,* Kwei Chung-shu, ed., premier issue (Shanghai, 1935). The NEC effort was stimulated by the League of Nations and financed, in part, through the RFC loan of 1933.

75. Shepherd to Fairfield, April 17, 1934, ABCFM, Shaowu Letters, 1930–1934, item 286.

76. "The Christian Rural Project in Kiangsi," NCC Execom, November 1933, April and November 1934.

77. NCC Minutes, May 1933–May 1937: Executive Committee, April 17–18, 1934.

78. *Ibid.*

79. Shepherd to Chang Fu-liang, April 27, 1934, ABCFM, Shaowu Letters, 1930–1934, item 294.

80. Shepherd to Fairfield, May 6, 1934, *ibid.*

81. Shepherd to Judd, May 5, 1934, *ibid.* Walter Judd was later to become an indefatigable publicist for the Kuomintang government and a 10-term Republican Congressman from the 5th district of Minnesota, 1943–1962.

82. *Ibid.*

*Chapter Five. The Church on Trial*

1. Ho, "Rural Economic Reconstruction in China," p. 18.

2. For full accounts of these three National Conferences of Rural Reconstruction Workers, see Chang Yüan-shan and Hsü Shih-lien, eds., *Hsiangts'un chien-she shih-yen* (Experiments in rural reconstruction); vol. 1, Shanghai, 1936; vols. 2 and 3, Canton.

The 1933 meeting was organized by Chang and Hsü; the former was secretary general of the CIFRC, the latter a professor of sociology at Yenching University. Major roles were played in the second and third meetings by Chang Wen-yu (of the Chung Hua Vocational Education Association) and by Liang Sou-ming.

3. For data on the population-land ratio as a spur to rural reconstruction, see Ho, "Rural Economic Reconstruction in China," pp. 1–2.

4. *Ibid.,* pp. 3–4.

5. See Chapter 3 above, n. 13.

6. For an account of the work of Nanking University, see Brown.

7. Shepherd to Fairfield, May 14, 1934, ABCFM, Shaowu Letters, 1930–1934, item 296.

8. HR.

9. This drawback was emphasized by a leading Christian reconstructionist, Frank W. Price, in an interview with the author, New York City, July 16, 1959.

10. HR.

11. George W. Shepherd, "Reconstruction in Kiangsi," *International Review of Missions,* 26:167–176 (April 1937).

12. See G. E. Taylor, "Reconstruction after Revolution: Kiangsi Province and the Chinese Nation," *Pacific Affairs,* 8:302–311 (September 1935).

13. Shepherd to Fairfield, May 22, 1934, ABCFM, Shaowu Letters, 1930–1934, item 297.

14. *Ibid.*

15. *Ibid.*

16. Shepherd to Fairfield, June 18, 1934. *ibid.,* item 302. Shepherd's affliction was an attack of pyelitis, a kidney infection.

17. Report of E. H. Ballou, "A Spring Excursion by the Mission Secretary," July 1934, ABCFM, North China Reports, 1930–1934, item 133.

18. Methodist Episcopal Church, 17th Annual Session, Kiangsi Annual Conference, Nanchang (Conference Minutes, Kiangsi, 1927–1936, V. 2). This material is available in the library of the Methodist Board of Missions, New York City.

19. *Ibid.*

20. Fairfield to Shepherd, May 22, 1934, ABCFM, Shaowu Letters, 1930–1934, item 300.

21. See NCC Staff, September 1934–June 1936: Oct. 23 and 30, 1934.

22. See "An Experiment in Christian Rural Reconstruction at Fanchiachuang, Paotingfu: Report from Nov. 1, 1933 to June 30, 1934," ABCFM, North China Reports, 1930–1934, item 124. See also, Varg, pp. 276–279. For a full account of the Hubbard enterprise at Fanchiachuang, see Mabel Ellis Hubbard, "An Experiment in Teaching the Christian Religion by Life Situations in Fan Village, China" (M.A. thesis; Oberlin College, 1938).

23. "Report of the Associate General Secretaries to the Biennial Meeting of NCC," April 25–May 2, 1935, NCC, mimeographed material: reports, June 1926–May 1935. The release of Shepherd and Hubbard by the ABCFM was termed "a fine illustration of a type of cooperation which will need to become increasingly common if the Christian forces in the country are to take full advantage of the new opportunities for service opening up before them, at a time of serious financial stringency."

24. Extracts of letter from Hugh W. Hubbard to Elmer Galt, Oct. 28, 1934, ABCFM, North China Letters, 1930–1939: 1934, item 92. Hubbard quotes pleas he has received from E. A. Turner as well as from Shepherd and Chang.

25. See Chapter 3 above, p. 83.

26. Hubbard to Galt, Oct. 28, 1934, ABCFM, North China Letters, 1930–1939.

27. Fairfield to Galt, Dec. 7, 1934, ABCFM, North China Letters, 1930–1939: 1934, item 41. The text of the cable is given here.

28. P. C. Hsu, "Lessons from the Lichwan Experiment," *CR,* 68:678 (November 1937). At Yenching Hsu had been deeply interested in problems of rural reconstruction. He attended the Second National Conference of

Rural Reconstruction Workers at Tinghsien, October 1934, and was especially affected by Liang Sou-ming's plea for the "creation of a new culture, with the rural community as its center of gravity." See Chang Yüan-shan and Hsü Shih-lien, II, 490–494.

29. HR.

30. P. C. Hsu, p. 678.

31. "Survey, Kiangsi Conference of the Methodist Episcopal Church in China," mid-year 1935; report on file in the library of the Methodist Board of Missions, New York City.

32. William R. Johnson, "The Christian Rural Program at Lichwan, China," typescript on file at the library of the Methodist Board of Missions, New York City (enclosure with letter to W. W. Reed, New York, Dec. 26, 1940).

33. See HR.

34. HR. Hubbard was later to stress his doubts about the "excessive publicity" given to the village projects. "The stream of visitors to Lichuan, and Tinghsien even more, could not be neglected as they represented the public, if not the supporters. They disrupted the program, took an inordinate amount of time of the top leaders, caused the best subjects for display to be constantly shown off and thus often spoiled . . . It was like pulling up a plant to see if it was growing." (Hubbard letter to author, April 7, 1964.)

35. HR. Hubbard recalls that the search for a Chinese general secretary led first to Dean Y. P. Mei of Yenching, who declined, then to P. C. Hsu of the Yenching School of Religion, who eventually accepted despite "grave misgivings"; second priority was given to recruiting "mature, experienced Christian rural specialists"; third priority: "a tentative program of work. I found the lively young group getting restless under inactivity, splitting into factions (Nanking and Peking) and about three couples pairing and having lovely times two by two." (Hubbard letter to author, April 7, 1964.)

36. "Recommendations of the Rural Group," May 1, 1935, NCC, biennial meeting, 1935.

37. "Report of the Associate General Secretaries to the Biennial Meeting of NCC," April 25–May 2, 1935. NCC, mimeographed material, Reports on Council's Work, June 1926–May 1935.

38. NCC Staff, December 1934–June 1936: May 28, 1935.

39. Mrs. G. W. Shepherd to Fairfield, March 15, 1935, ABCFM, Shaowu Letters, 1935–1939, item 28. "Of course," she added, "it is the advertising that connection with the Lichuan Project will give them that brought it."

40. Shepherd to Fairfield, July 17, 1935, ibid., item 26. This "movement" had been launched by Chiang Kai-shek on April 1 as an adjunct to the New Life Movement.

41. Ibid.

42. Minutes of the KCRSU, June 30, 1935, ABCFM, Shaowu Reports, 1930–1939, item 27.

43. Minutes of the KCRSU, Board of Directors Retreat, Oct. 16–19, 1935, ibid., item 29.

44. *Ibid.*

45. Shepherd to Fairfield, Dec. 4, 1935. ABCFM, Shaowu Letters, 1935–1939, item 33.

46. *Ibid.*

47. Minutes of the KCRSU, Dec. 18, 1935, ABCFM, Shaowu Reports, 1930–1939, item 30.

48. Shepherd to Fairfield, Jan. 18, 1936, ABCFM, Shaowu Letters, 1935–1939, item 38.

49. Minutes of KCRSU, March 7, 1936, ABCFM, Shaowu Reports, 1930–1939, item 34.

50. Shepherd, "Reconstruction in Kiangsi," p. 173.

51. NCC Staff, September 1934–June 1936: May 20, 1935.

52. *Ibid.:* Sept. 3, 1935.

53. *Ibid.:* Staff Retreat, Sept. 10–11, 1935.

54. *Ibid.*

55. *Ibid.*

56. Kiangsi Conference Letter, May 1934, from Ruth N. Daniels, Gertrude M. Cone, Myra L. McDade; in library of Methodist Board of Missions, New York City.

57. Interview with Franklin L. Ho, New York City, July 17, 1959.

58. Taylor, pp. 309–311.

59. Hugh Hubbard recalls this survey. As for his reaction at the time, "We felt that this was a good time to devise some better system of land distribution, and this was suggested to Chiang. He was reported to have said, 'If we are going to take the land away from the landlords, why are we driving out the Communists?' Without government support, little could be done, but at the time I was there we were discussing the possibility of reclaiming unused land, much of it covered with red, sandy soil, and settling the poorer farmers on it. I never heard whether this was attempted." (Hubbard letter to author, April 7, 1964.)

60. Shepherd, "Reconstruction in Kiangsi," p. 172.

61. See "New Life Centers in Rural Kiangsi," special bulletin no. 2, Head Office of Kiangsi Rural Welfare Centers (Nanchang, 1936). The preface was by Chang Fu-liang, and it is conceivable that he was the author of the pamphlet itself. "Some friends of China feel that the reconstruction attempts in China in general and in Kiangsi in particular are not thorough because the authorities have not tackled the problem of land tenure"; yet the costliness of an aerial survey precluded any such action because "unless this fundamental work is complete, the problem of land tenure cannot be scientifically studied and a wise solution thereof suggested" (p. 26).

62. Andrija Stampar, "Report on Rural Welfare Activities in Kiangsi," mimeographed document dated February 1936. (This report is item 41 in the Shaowu Reports for 1930–1939.) Stampar, a physician, had been Director of Health of Yugoslavia; see his "Observations of a Rural Health Worker," *The New England Journal of Medicine,* 218:991–997 (June 1938).

63. *Ibid.*

64. *Ibid.*

65. *Ibid.* Shepherd's comments constituted an attachment to the Stampar report as forwarded to the mission board in Boston. His comments are dated March 1936.

66. *Ibid.*

67. William R. Johnson, "The Christian Rural Program at Lichwan."

68. HR.

69. Shepherd comment on Stampar report, see n. 65.

70. Shepherd to Fairfield, Dec. 4, 1935, ABCFM, Shaowu Letters, 1935–1939, item 33.

71. NCC Staff, September 1934–June 1936: June 2, 1936.

72. P. C. Hsu, pp. 678–679. As an example of personnel friction, Frank W. Price recalls that George Wei of Nanking University went to Lichuan with equipment for a paper mill but was unable to work with P. C. Hsu and soon departed from Kiangsi. (Price interview, July 16, 1959.)

73. Shepherd, "Reconstruction in Kiangsi," p. 168.

74. NCC Minutes, May 1933–May 1937: Ad-Interim, Feb. 16, 1937.

75. P. C. Hsu, p. 678.

76. Shepherd, "Reconstruction in Kiangsi," p. 171.

77. P.C. Hsu, p. 680.

78. *Ibid.,* p. 679.

79. Shepherd, "Reconstruction in Kiangsi," p. 175.

80. P. C. Hsu, p. 679.

81. NCC Staff, September 1934–June 1936: June 2, 1936.

82. *Ibid.* It was reported that Shepherd and Chang both desired a change in the location of the center, greater coordination of the staff work, and an increase in the average term of staff service.

83. NCC Minutes, May 1933–May 1937: Ad-Interim, June 16, 1936.

84. *Ibid.:* Executive, Nov. 4–6, 1936.

85. NCC Staff, July 1936–May 1939: Conference, Nov. 21, 1936.

86. *Ibid.: Conference,* Dec. 21, 1936.

87. NCC Minutes, May 1933–May 1937: Ad-Interim, Jan. 19, 1937.

88. *Ibid.:* Ad-Interim, Feb. 16, 1937.

89. Interview with Frank W. Price, New York City, July 16, 1959. Price visited Lichuan on three occasions, twice before World War II and once during the war.

*Chapter Six. The Rockefeller Effort*

1. Leonard S. Hsu (Hsü Shih-lien), "Rural Reconstruction in China," *Pacific Affairs,* 10:249–265 (September 1937).

2. The First National Conference of Rural Reconstruction Workers in July 1933 established informal inter-project study groups, which created a

continuing dialogue between the annual meetings. See Chang Yüan-shan and Hsü Shih-lien, vol. 1.

3. Ho, "Rural Economic Reconstruction in China."

4. *Ibid.,* pp. 53–56.

5. *Ibid.,* p. 56.

6. See Paauw, "Chinese National Expenditures"; and Paauw, "The Kuomintang."

7. See Chapter 3 above; Johnson to Bishop Herbert Welch, June 9, 1933. Correspondence of W. R. Johnson (microfilm), Board of Methodist Missions, New York City.

8. Selskar Michael Gunn (1883–1944) was "an Irishman by ancestry, an Englishman by birth, an American by adoption, a European by principal residence, and a thorough cosmopolitan in training and outlook." (Rockefeller Foundation, *Annual Report,* 1944, xiii.) Gunn received a B.S. from MIT in 1905 and a certificate in public health from Harvard in 1917. He taught public health at MIT prior to joining the foundation in 1917.

9. Photostat copy of S. M. Gunn itinerary, 1931 China trip, obtained from the secretary of the Rockefeller Foundation, New York City.

10. Interview with Franklin L. Ho, New York City, July 17, 1959.

11. S. M. Gunn to Max Mason, Sept. 8, 1931, Letter of Transmittal accompanying "Report on Visit to China, June 9th to July 30th, 1931," by Selskar M. Gunn. I am deeply indebted to Mrs. Selskar M. Gunn, of Santa Barbara, California, for giving me access to her personal copies of Mr. Gunn's several reports to the foundation. The originals, on file at the Rockefeller Foundation in New York, are closed to researchers.

12. See Chapter 2 above, pp. 38–39.

13. Raymond B. Fosdick, *The Story of the Rockefeller Foundation* (New York, 1952), p. 183.

14. Selskar M. Gunn, "Report on Visit to China, June 9th to July 30th, 1931," p. 21.

15. *Ibid.,* p. 7.

16. *Ibid.,* pp. 5–6.

17. *Ibid.,* p. 4.

18. *Ibid.,* p. 5.

19. *Ibid.,* p. 1.

20. *Ibid.,* p. 17.

21. *Ibid.,* p. 85.

22. *Ibid.,* p. 86.

23. *Ibid.,* p. 97.

24. Gunn to Mason, Jan. 23, 1934, Letter of Transmittal accompanying "China and the Rockefeller Foundation," Report to the Trustees, Shanghai, Jan. 23, 1934. Copy in the possession of Mrs. S. M. Gunn, Santa Barbara, California. In this letter Gunn noted that it was Mason's "broad conception of the whole question which made it easy for me to accept your proposal and give up my splendid position in the European office to undertake the new assignment."

25. Gunn's quickness to understand the deficiencies of the rural effort to date is confirmed by F. L. Ho, who talked with Gunn at great length during the latter's visit of 1932–1933. (Interview with Ho, New York City, July 17, 1959.)

26. Gunn to Mason, Jan. 23, 1934, China Reports for the Rockefeller Foundation.

27. Selskar M. Gunn, "China and the Rockefeller Foundation," Report to the Trustees, Shanghai, Jan. 23, 1934, China Reports for the Rockefeller Foundation, p. 2.

28. *Ibid.*, pp. 1–2.

29. *Ibid.*, pp. 4–5.

30. *Ibid.*, p. 6.

31. *Ibid.*, pp. 8–11.

32. *Ibid.*, pp. 12–15. The foundation's investment to date in the natural sciences totalled $2,192,138, of which $1.8 million had gone directly to 13 institutions, with the balance spent on development, research, and fellowships; ten of the thirteen were mission colleges, two were national universities, and one (Nankai) a private Chinese university.

33. *Ibid.*, p. 19.

34. *Ibid.*, pp. 25–26.

35. *Ibid.*, p. 31. Gunn's critique of the returned-students finds support and elaboration in Y. C. Wang, *Chinese Intellectuals and the West, 1872–1949* (Chapel Hill, 1966).

36. Gunn, China Reports for the Rockefeller Foundation, Jan. 23, 1934, p. 34.

37. *Ibid.*, pp. 36–37.

38. *Ibid.*, p. 40.

39. *Ibid.*, p. 42.

40. *Ibid.*, pp. 42–43.

41. *Ibid.*, pp. 45–46.

42. *Ibid.*, pp. 60–61. The US$300,000 figure derived, in part, from a breakdown of the foundation's previous rate of expenditure in China: of the US$38.2 million allocated through 1933, US$31.5 million had gone to the China Medical Board and PUMC; the remaining US$6.7 million, spent over the 18-year period, averaged out to US$373,109 per year.

43. *Ibid.*, pp. 47–48.

44. Fosdick, Report, pp. 105–106. The Gunn proposals are discussed in Section VII: "Mr. Gunn's Program for China."

45. *Ibid.*, pp. 106–107.

46. *Ibid.*, p. 107.

47. Rockefeller Foundation, *Annual Report, 1935* (New York, 1936), p. 321.

48. Interview with Raymond B. Fosdick, New York City, Sept. 23, 1959.

49. Rockefeller Foundation, *Annual Report, 1935,* pp. 323 ff.

50. *Ibid.*, pp. 327–328.

51. *Ibid.,* p. 329.

52. *Ibid.,* pp. 321–323.

53. NCC, mimeographed material, Reports on Council's Work, June 1926–May 1935: "Report of the Associate General Secretaries to the Biennial Meeting of the NCC," April 25–May 2, 1935.

54. S. M. Gunn, "China Program Progress Report," April 1936 (mimeographed copy in possession of Mrs. S. M. Gunn, Santa Barbara, Calif.), p. 20.

55. *Ibid.,* p. 2.

56. Rockefeller Foundation, *Annual Report, 1936* (New York, 1937), pp. 313–314.

57. *Ibid.,* p. 314.

58. *Ibid.,* p. 315.

59. *Ibid.,* pp. 312–313.

60. *Ibid.*

61. *Ibid.*

62. Rockefeller Foundation, *A Review for 1936,* by Raymond B. Fosdick, President (New York, 1937), pp. 48–49.

63. Rockefeller Foundation, *Annual Report, 1937* (New York, 1938), pp. 357 ff.

64. *Ibid.,* pp. 363–364.

65. *Ibid.,* p. 361.

66. Selskar M. Gunn, "China Program Progress Report for the Period July 1, 1935–Feb. 15, 1937" (mimeographed copy in possession of Mrs. S. M. Gunn, Santa Barbara, Calif.), pp. 4–5.

67. *Ibid.,* p. 20.

68. Mayling Soong Chiang to S. M. Gunn, Feb. 5, 1937, in *The Rockefeller Foundation Confidential Monthly Report, April 1937.* I am grateful to Miss Flora M. Rhind of the Rockefeller Foundation for sending me excerpts from several of these reports.

69. Gunn, "China Program Progress Report," (July 1935–Feb. 1937), p. 7.

70. *Ibid.,* p. 20.

71. Rockefeller Foundation, *A Review for 1937,* by Raymond B. Fosdick, President (New York, 1938), p. 53.

72. Rockefeller Foundation, *A Review for 1938,* by Raymond B. Fosdick, President (New York, 1939), pp. 58–61.

73. Rockefeller Foundation, *A Review for 1939,* by Raymond B. Fosdick, President (New York, 1940), pp. 59–61. See also the Presidential *Reviews* for 1940 (pp. 59–60), 1941 (pp. 47–48), and 1942 (pp. 48–49).

74. See *Review* for 1942, pp. 48–49.

75. Fosdick, *The Story of the Rockefeller Foundation,* p. 184.

76. Gunn, "China Program Progress Report," (July 1935–February 1937), p. 19.

*Chapter Seven. The New Life Movement*

1. For some useful comments on Liang's place in this tradition, see Van Slyke, "Liang Sou-ming and the Rural Reconstruction Movement." The concern with thought versus action was shared, of course, by both Sun Yat-sen and Chiang Kai-shek.

2. Mary C. Wright, "From Revolution to Restoration."

3. I am indebted to Professor Benjamin I. Schwartz, of Harvard University, for some stimulating insights into the generalissimo's ideological legacy. In the absence of a definitive biographical study, all conclusions on this subject are necessarily tentative.

4. Note especially the generalissimo's famous textbook, *China's Destiny,* in either the Wang Chung-hui translation (New York, 1947) or the edition by Philip Jaffe (New York, 1947); the latter edition's companion text, *Chinese Economic Theory,* is also illustrative of the point.

5. "Excerpts from an address by Chiang Kai-shek," Ginling College, June 24, 1934, ABCFM, North China Reports, 1930–1934, item 136. The next item in the series, 137, is "My Religion," by Mme. Chiang, reprinted in *The English Loose-Leaf Selections for Chinese Students* from the *Shanghai Evening Post and Mercury,* May 14, 1934; she discusses the Kiangsi reoccupied territories as a challenge to her own Christianity.

6. Interview with Frank W. Price, New York City, July 16, 1959. Dr. Price, of Nanking Seminary, first met the generalissimo when asked to conduct such a service shortly after the Mukden Incident in 1931. He became one of the missionaries most frequently asked to serve in this capacity and was later (in World War II) an informal adviser to both Chiang and his wife.

7. For a useful Chinese source on the New Life Movement, see Pei Ching-hua, ed., *Hsin-sheng-huo lun-ts'ung* (Essays on the New Life Movement; Shanghai, 1936). This volume includes fourteen essays by the movement's promoters (including Chiang Kai-shek and Wang Ching-wei), as well as twelve articles by Chinese intellectuals of the May 4th era on the general concept of "New Life." The latter group has nothing to do with the movement itself.

8. Colonel Huang Jen-lin (J. L. "Fatty" Huang) was a large, jovial, gregarious man who served as a valuable KMT link with Americans. During World War II he was director of the War Area Service Corps, the organization that housed American forces in China. In the 1960's he was Nationalist China's ambassador to Nicaragua.

9. Kenneth Scott Latourette, *World Service, A History of the Foreign Work and World Service of the Young Men's Christian Associations of the United States and Canada* (New York, 1957), p. 285.

10. See Chapter 3, pp. 60–61 and note 65. The arrangement was made between Huang and W. R. Johnson.

11. See Chapter 3 above, p. 54 and note 48.

12. Samuel C. Chu, *The New Life Movement, 1934–1937* (Researches

in the Social Sciences on China, Columbia University, East Asian Institute; New York, 1957), p. 3.

13. *North China Herald,* no. 190:3476:438 (March 21, 1934). The first report is dated Nanking, March 14.

14. *Ibid.,* p. 438.

15. *Ibid.,* p. 447.

16. Christopher Tang, "Christianity and the New Life Movement in China." Unpub. diss., San Francisco Theological Seminary, April 1941, p. 106. Available in the Missionary Research Library, New York City, this highly eulogistic account contains a comprehensive bibliography of Chinese pamphlets on the NLM.

17. Robert Berkov, *Strong Man of China* (Boston, 1938), p. 177. Ch'en Li-fu, one of the Kuomintang's chief ideologues, held an M.A. degee from the University of Pittsburgh; he served in the 1930's and 1940's in a number of high posts, most notably as minister of Education. Ch'en's philosophy, an elusive eclectic potpourri sometimes termed "vitalism," is elaborated in his *Philosophy of Life* (New York, 1948).

18. "New Life Movement and Other Developments on China's Political Stage," *China Weekly Review,* 68:126 (March 24, 1934).

19. Chiang Kai-shek, *Outline of the New Life Movement,* tr. Mme. Chiang (Nanchang, 1934?), pp. 2–3.

20. *Ibid.,* p. 13.

21. Samuel C. Chu, p. 3.

22. Chiang Kai-shek, *Outline,* pp. 12–13.

23. Taylor, p. 303. (See Chapter 5 above.)

24. *Ibid.,* pp. 302–311.

25. Berkov, p. 177.

26. See C. Y. W. Meng, "People's Economic Reconstruction Movement Launched at Nanking," *China Weekly Review,* 77:206–207 (July 11, 1936). The committee set up to direct this movement had 554 members; Meng enthusiastically notes that "possibly, this is the largest committee we have ever seen since the adoption of the committee system in China."

27. Samuel C. Chu, p. 9.

28. *A Brief Historical Sketch of the New Life Movement,* series 2 (Nanking, May 1937), p. 10.

29. Samuel C. Chu, p. 13.

30. "Annual Administrative Report of Raymond S. Hall," Nanking, May 26, 1933, YMCA, WS 98, China Annual Reports 1933.

31. "Administrative Report of Lennig Sweet," Peiping, June 10, 1933, YMCA, WS 26d, China 1933.

32. "Annual Administrative Report of Lyman Hoover," Peiping, June 1933, YMCA, WS 26d, China 1933.

33. "Administrative Report of Eugene E. Barnett," Shanghai, May 15, 1933, YMCA, WS 26d, China 1933.

34. Kiang Wen-han, "Student Situation in China," *CR,* 64:304–306 (May 1933).

35. Y. T. Wu, "Make Christianity Socially Dynamic," *CR*, 65:9–11 (January 1934). After 1949, both Y. T. Wu and Kiang Wen-han (above) became major Christian advocates of close collaboration with the Chinese Communists and outspoken critics of "American imperialism"; see Epilogue.

36. See E. E. Barnett report for 1933, above; also, Earle H. Ballou, *Dangerous Opportunity: The Christian Mission in China Today* (New York, 1940).

37. *North China Herald,* no. 190:3476:447 (March 21, 1934).

38. YMCA, WS 98c, Secretary's Minutes: "Minutes of the Autumn Setting-up Conference of the National Headquarters and Regional Special Staff," Shanghai, Aug. 31–Sept. 1, 1934. Of Nanchang: "This city has risen to a position of preëminent importance due to the presence in the city of General Chiang Kai-shek and his headquarters. The YMCA has been drafted for considerable help in connection with the New Life Movement program."

39. Shepherd to Fairfield, March 17, 1934, ABCFM, Shaowu Letters, 1930–1934, item 283.

40. NCC Minutes, May 1933–May 1937: Executive, April 17–18, 1934.

41. "The 'New Life Movement,' " *CR*, 65:277–278 (May 1934). Although unsigned, this editorial and its sequel were undoubtedly the product of the *Recorder's* activist editor, Frank Rawlinson.

42. "China's Revival Movement," *CR*, 65:610 (October 1934).

43. According to Shepherd, Paul Yen had become "quite political-minded, a Chang Hsüeh-liang man" as a result of his Mukden service with the YMCA; hence his replacement. (Interview with Shepherd, Middleboro, Mass., Dec. 7, 1959.)

44. List of YMCA former secretaries "now occupying important positions of great influence," 1935, YMCA, WS 27a, China 1935.

45. Memo from F. V. Slack to J. M. Clinton, March 6, 1935, YMCA, WS 27a, China 1935.

46. Copy of "China Mail File No. 146," Jan. 8, 1935, YMCA, WS 27a, China 1935. This document takes the form of an Associated Press draft release.

47. *Ibid.*

48. "Conference of General Secretaries of the Big Cities," Hangchow, pp. 13–17, June 1934, YMCA, WS 98d, Secretary's Minutes.

49. *Ibid.*

50. "Administrative Report of Eugene E. Barnett," Shanghai, July 14, 1934, 26e, China 1934.

51. *Ibid.* It should be noted that the YMCA was able to do far more rural work in India than in China, particularly in the development of credit cooperatives.

52. *Ibid.*

53. E. E. Barnett to F. S. Harmon, March 16, 1935, YMCA, WS 27a, China 1935.

54. The same folder contains a conference report of May 29, 1935, on

the possibilities of YMCA expansion into rural work. The major obstacles continued to be a lack of staff, a lack of rural experience, and a lack of trained experts. It was pointed out that several former YMCA secretaries were already active in the Tinghsien program; but James Yen was said to be "not desirous of promoting the YMCA, church or any other organization." The discussions were inconclusive.

55. "Annual Report for 1933–1934," by Roderick Scott, Foochow, n.d., ABCFM, Foochow Reports, 1930–1939, item 96.

56. "Report for 1933–1934," by Lyda S. Houston, Diongloh, July 25, 1934, *ibid.,* item 94. "The Year 1934 with the Diongloh Churches," by Laura D. Ward (item 100), includes the statement, "The New Life Movement gives us excellent lines for co-operation with non-Christian leaders."

57. Lin and Topping to Fairfield and Wilson, Dec. 1, 1934, ABCFM, Foochow Secretary, 1930–1939, item 154. The annual meeting cited took place on Nov. 10–13, 1934.

58. Administrative Report of W. R. Stewart, Kaifeng, n.d., YMCA, WS 98b, China Annual Reports 1934–1935.

59. "China's Present Attitude to Christianity," *CR,* 65:674 (November 1934).

60. Kimber H. K. Den, "New Life Movement and Christian Church," *CR,* 66:99 (February 1935).

61. "Missionaries and the New Life Movement," *CR,* 66:61–62 (January 1935).

62. NCC Staff, September 1934–June 1936: Jan. 15, 1935. It was suggested that the theme's subtitle should be the passage from John 10:10: "I am come that they might have life, and that they might have it more abundantly." See also minutes for Jan. 8, 1935.

63. *Ibid.:* Feb. 12, 1935.

64. *Ibid.:* Feb. 26, 1935.

65. NCC Minutes, May 1933–May 1937: Ad-Interim, March 25, 1935.

66. NCC Staff, September 1934–June 1936: Subcommittee, April 5, 1935; also April 11, 1935.

67. "Report-Letter," Eugene A. Turner, Nanchang, Feb. 25, 1935, YMCA, WS 98a, China, January–May 1935.

68. "Report-Letter," Eugene A. Turner, Tryon, North Carolina, Sept. 20, 1935, YMCA, WS 98b, China Annual Reports 1934–1935.

69. Turner to F. S. Harmon, Jan. 29, 1936, YMCA, WS 97e, China, January–March 1936.

70. "Ten-Year Policy of the National Committee YMCA's of China," YMCA of China, 1935 (booklet on file in YMCA Historical Library, New York City, with covering letter from S. C. Leung to F. S. Harmon, April 26, 1935).

71. F. S. Harmon to Henry S. Young, June 7, 1935, YMCA, WS 27a, China 1935.

Chapter Eight. The Gathering Entente

1. Shepherd to Fairfield, Dec. 4, 1935, ABCFM, Shaowu Letters, 1935–1939, item 33.

2. *Ibid.*

3. G. W. Shepherd, "The Chinese Communists," *China Christian Year Book, 1934–1935* (Shanghai, 1935), pp. 89–96.

4. Shepherd to Fairfield, Dec. 13, 1935, ABCFM, Shaowu Letters, 1935–1939, item 34.

5. Shepherd to Fairfield, March 7, 1936. *Ibid.,* item 43.

6. *Ibid.*

7. *Ibid.*

8. Rawlinson to Fairfield, March 7, 1936, ABCFM, North China Letters, 1930–1939: 1936, item 150.

9. Fairfield to Rawlinson, April 2, 1936. *Ibid.:* 1936, item 146.

10. Minutes of KCRSU, April 9, 1936, ABCFM, Shaowu Reports, 1930–1939, item 35.

11. For a discussion of the background to these demonstrations, see John Israel, *Student Nationalism in China, 1927–1937* (Stanford, 1966).

12. C. Y. W. Meng, "The 'New Life Movement' in Full Swing in China," *China Weekly Review,* 75:450–451 (Feb. 29, 1936).

13. *Ibid.*

14. "New Life Movement Revamped," *CR,* 67:311 (May 1936).

15. Shepherd to Fairfield, March 16, 1936, ABCFM, Shaowu Letters, 1935–1939, item 45.

16. *Ibid.*

17. Interview with G. W. Shepherd, Middleboro, Mass., Dec. 7, 1959.

18. *Ibid.*

19. *Ibid.*

20. NCC Staff, September 1934–June 1936: Nov. 19, 1935.

21. "Notes of Informal Conference of International Committee Secretaries," Shanghai, April 16, 1936, YMCA, WS 27b, China 1936. On the subject of the generalissimo's attitude it should also be noted, however, that a request in November 1936 for a renewal of his annual pledge produced "a telegram back immediately that he will give $5000 this year. This is an unsolicited increase of $2000 and brings us very gratifying assurance of the Generalissimo's continued confidence." (H. A. Wilbur to E. E. Barnett, Nov. 27, 1936, YMCA, WS 27b, China 1936.)

22. *Ibid.*

23. "New Life Movement and the Churches," *CR* 67:661 (October 1936).

24. See Chapter 2 above, pp. 32–33. For some further background to the shift of 1936, see Thomson.

25. T. S. Young, "The Chinese Have Found Their Leader," *China Weekly Review,* 78:452 (Nov. 28, 1936).

26. See reports in *China Weekly Review,* 79:153–155 (Jan. 2, 1937).

27. Nelson Trusler Johnson Papers, Library of Congress, Washington, D.C.: Memorandum on "Conversation with G. W. Shepard," Nanking, May 17, 1937. The "General Teng" remains unidentified although some evidence points to Teng Hsi-hou. It is interesting that Generals Teng Hsi-hou and Ho Ying-ch'in were both members of the Oxford Group (Moral Re-armament); another Buchmanite was Ch'en Li-fu, the NLM's chief theoretician. The relationship between the NLM and MRA is a potential subject for further research.

28. *Ibid.*

29. Among many others, Frank W. Price vividly recalls the unanimity of rejoicing in the foreign and Chinese community when the generalissimo's release was announced: "I will never forget his return from Sian—the tremendous shout that went up from the immense crowd that had gathered when he alighted from the plane at the Nanking airport. That was the high water mark of the Nanking years." (Interview with F. W. Price, New York City, July 16, 1959.)

30. See Mayling Soong Chiang, *Sian: A Coup d'État* (Shanghai, 1937).

31. "General Chiang's Christian Message," *CR,* 68:267–268 (May 1937).

32. "China's Attitude To Religion," *CR,* 68:269 (May 1937).

33. "The New Life Movement," *CR,* 68:269–271 (May 1937).

34. George W. Shepherd, "Church and the New Life Movement," *CR,* 68:281–282 (May 1937).

35. George W. Shepherd, "Cooperation with New Life Movement," *CR,* 68:286–288 (May 1937).

36. R. Y. Lo, "Christians! Support the New Life Movement," *CR,* 68:285 (May 1937).

37. Mme. Chiang Kai-shek, "Christians and the New Life Movement," *CR,* 68:279–280 (May 1937).

38. C. Kuangson Young, "The New Life Movement," *The China Press Weekly Supplement,* 3:32 (April 18, 1937).

39. Symposium, "What Can Christian Cooperation Add to the New Life Movement?" *CR,* 68:293 (May 1937).

40. "NCC, International Missionary Conference, Sub-Committee on Studies," April 10, 1937, NCC, Mimeographed Material III, January–May 1937, item 724. See also, NCC Staff, July 1936–May 1939: April 13, 1937.

41. NCC Staff, July 1936–May 1939: April 27, 1937.

42. "Report of a Memo on the New Life Movement," April 30, 1937, NCC, mimeographed material III, January–May 1937, item 754.

43. *Ibid.*

44. *Ibid.*

45. *Ibid.*

46. *Ibid.,* item 768, address of general secretary at 11th biennial meeting, May 5, 1937.

47. NCC pamphlet, "Christian Cooperation in China, as illustrated by the biennial meeting, Shanghai, May 5–11, 1937" (Missionary Research Library,

New York City). One account of the change in missionary attitude is contained in Ballou: "Christian leaders had at first been of two minds regarding the Movement . . . there was a fear lest the Movement become a political tool, through its intimate connection with the heads of the government. Yet as time went on this fear was dissipated. Assurances of its non-political nature were given, and it was recognized as something to be furthered as a spontaneous movement of and among the people of China." p. 109.

48. NCC Staff, July 1936–May 1939: May 25, 1937.

49. "Annual Report," George A. Fitch, Nanking, May 1, 1937, YMCA, WS 27c, China 1937.

50. *Ibid.,* printed newsletter from George A. Fitch, Nanking, July 10, 1937.

51. I am indebted to Professor M. Searle Bates of Union Theological Seminary (formerly of the University of Nanking) for stressing the skepticism in the Christian and missionary community. In Bates' view, the criticisms of the NLM expressed in the Rawlinson memorandum (p. 190) were characteristic of widespread Christian attitudes; at the same time, such critics were willing to support gestures of cooperation with the only government that was capable of creating national unity in the crises of 1936–37. A backdrop to this willingness was the growing threat from Japan. (Letter to author from Bates, April 21, 1962.)

52. See Fox Butterfield, "A Missionary View of the Chinese Communists, 1936–1939", in Kwang-Ching Liu, ed., *American Missionaries in China: Papers from Harvard Seminars* (Cambridge, 1966), pp. 249–301. Butterfield views 1936 as a transitional year in relations between Communists and American Congregationalist (ABCFM) missionaries in North China. He describes the development of a tacit "alliance" between the two groups in 1937–1939, after the renewal of Sino-Japanese hostilities, an alliance based on a common dedication to the overthrow of "poverty" and "tyranny." One of the first missionaries to study the Communists at close hand in this era was Hugh W. Hubbard who was briefly captured by guerrillas near Paotingfu in November 1937 (p. 270).

53. Shepherd to Fairfield, March 7, 1936, ABCFM, Shaowu Letters, 1935–1939: item 43.

54. Shepherd to Fairfield, March 16, 1936. *Ibid.,* item 45.

55. Fairfield to Wilson P. Minton, Feb. 12, 1945, ABCFM, Shaowu Letters, 1940–1952: item 355.

56. Johnson Papers, Library of Congress: Memorandum on "Conversation with G. W. Shepard," Nanking, May 17, 1937.

57. *Ibid.*

58. Fairfield to Shepherd and Mrs. Shepherd, May 28, 1941, ABCFM, Shaowu Letters, 1940–1952, item 300.

59. James G. Endicott, "A Report from China" (pamphlet, n.d., in Missionary Research Library, New York City). After Endicott had parted with Chiang in 1942, the generalissimo asked Frank W. Price of Nanking Seminary to become his confidential adviser. Price declined the offer, how-

ever, in view of the Shepherd and Endicott experience. In 1944, after a furlough in America, Price returned to Chungking to become a key liaison figure between the U.S. Army and the foreign affairs bureau of the Military Affairs Council. As such he maintained a uniquely close relationship with Generalissimo and Mme. Chiang. (Interview with Price, New York City, July 16, 1959.)

60. See Shepherd Pamphlet collection, in Missionary Research Library, New York City. These include articles, booklets, press releases, and radio broadcast transcripts.

61. Interview with G. W. Shepherd, Middleboro, Mass., Dec. 7, 1959.

62. Wilson P. Minton (State Superintendent of Conference of Congregational and Christian Churches of Pennsylvania) to Fairfield, Nov. 29, 1944, ABCFM, Shaowu Letters, 1940–1952: item 352.

63. Shepherd to Fairfield, June 5, 1943, *Ibid.:* item 326. By this time Shepherd placed his hope in T. V. Soong as a potential successor to Chiang under the impending constitution.

64. *Ibid.*

*Chapter Nine. Gradualism in Kuomintang China*

1. See Michael and Taylor, pp. 389–410.

2. In 1931, for instance, the Nanking government listed as its American advisers the following: Henry Ford (honorary), Owen D. Young, Charles R. Crane, Thomas F. Millard, and Paul M. Linebarger, all in the field of government administration; Arthur N. Young, F. B. Lynch, B. B. Wallace, O. C. Lockhart, and William Watson, advisers to the Ministry of Finance; G. F. Shecklen in the Ministry of Communications; John Earl Baker and R. S. Norman in railroad development; B. G. Young in industry development; H. H. Arnold and A. M. Shaw on the National Reconstruction Commission, and G. G. Stroebe on the Yangtze River Board. By 1934, Linebarger, Arthur Young, Norman Shaw, and Stroebe had remained and had been joined by H. H. Love in the Ministry of Industries and R. E. Lewis in Foreign Affairs. In 1936, the official list included Linebarger, Young, Love, Norman, Shaw, and Stroebe.

Recent scholarly by-products of this advisory tradition have been the writings of Arthur N. Young: *China and the Helping Hand, 1937–1945* (Cambridge, Mass., 1963) and *China's Wartime Finance and Inflation, 1937–1945* (Cambridge, Mass., 1965). Mr. Young is now completing a study of the Nanking decade, 1928–1937.

3. *China Handbook, 1937–1945,* Hollington K. Tong, ed. (rev. ed., New York, 1947), p. 605. See Chapter 3 above.

4. See Ho ms., section on "The Land Tenure System."

5. Interview with Franklin L. Ho, New York City, July 17, 1959. Dr. Ho collaborated with the League agricultural experts, Andrija Stampar, Sir Arthur Salter, and Briand Clausen, on their study of Chekiang province, the

one region where the rent reduction was actually enforced in 1929–1930. Landlord demands that all contested rentals be settled in court soon ended the experiment, for tenants were unable to afford legal fees. It should be noted that a 37.5 per cent rent ceiling was also attempted elsewhere by the KMT prior to 1930—in Kwangtung, Hupei, and Kiangsu in 1927, and in Hunan in 1928. In no case was significant success achieved.

6. See Chapter 5 above, n. 63.

7. See Chapter 5 above, n. 58.

8. Mention should be made of the solid study of land tenure undertaken by the Sun Yat-sen Institute of Culture and Education at Nanking in 1933 under the direction of Chen Cheng-mo. Another study was simultaneously attempted by the Rural Rehabilitation Commission of the executive yuan. Likewise, even the KMT's Central Political Institute established an "Institute of Land." The problem, therefore, was recognized; what was lacking was the *political will* to treat the problem.

9. K'ung Hsüeh-hsiung, pp. 411–412. K'ung's admiration for Shen Hsüan-lu's abortive rural experiment in Chen-p'ing, Honan, stemmed from the priority Shen gave to land reform. Yet Shen, like other progressives, mistakenly viewed a land survey as the prerequisite, and funds for such a survey were never available.

10. The full text of Chiang's telegram is found in: League of Nations Council, Committee of Technical Collaboration with China, *Report to the Council of its Technical Delegate on his Mission in China from Date of Appointment until April 1, 1934* (Nanking, April 1934), pp. 21–23. The message is dated only January 1934 and is a reply to Wang Ching-wei's telegram of the 17th.

11. *Ibid.*, pp. 21–22.

12. *Ibid.*, pp. 22–23.

13. *Ibid.*, p. 23.

14. *Ibid.* The source of this estimate is not given.

15. Ho ms., section on "Agricultural Credit, Marketing, and Taxation."

16. *Ibid.*, section on "Towards Agricultural Reconstruction."

17. *Ibid.*, "Agricultural Credit, Marketing, and Taxation."

18. See *Chinese Year Book, 1935–1936*, pp. 313–316.

19. See C. F. Strickland, "China's Cooperative Movement," *China Christian Year Book, 1934–1935*, pp. 296–305.

20. On the Kincheng role, see Y. C. James Yen, *The Ting Hsien Experiment in 1934.*

21. Ho ms., section on "Towards Agricultural Reconstruction." For a discussion of Nanking's failure to provide agricultural credit, see Y. C. Wang, pp. 490–492.

22. Ho interview, July 17, 1959.

23. A large percentage of the CIFRC's founders and directors, for instance, were foreign and Chinese YMCA officials. The wide-ranging activities of YMCA personnel left a substantial mark on Sino-foreign relations in the first half of the present century. To cite only one additional example, the

era's foremost research organization on the problems of modern China, the Institute of Pacific Relations, owed its founding to a YMCA conference in the 1920's.

24. Edgar Snow, "How Rural China is Being Re-made," *China Weekly Review,* 67:98–101; and 67:202–203 (Dec. 16 and 30, 1933).

25. Interview with George W. Shepherd, Dec. 7, 1959.

26. Johnson to Secretary of State, on "American Missionary Enterprise in China as Affected by Conditions since 1926," March 28, 1933. Johnson Papers, 19: report no. 2021.

27. Johnson to John R. Mott, Jan. 6, 1934. Johnson Papers, 20. The ambassador's comments to Albert L. Scott, chairman of the Laymen's Inquiry Commission, are also of interest: "I might almost say that I am the product, in so far as my early religious training was concerned, of missionary enterprise. I have always had a feeling of deep interest and sympathy for the missionary and his work." Johnson adds a comment on the future of Protestant missions in China: "The Protestant missionary is peculiarly colored by the nationalism of the country of his origin. I feel that this is an inevitable situation, for after all the Protestant church is the twin of nationalism, born at the same time when church and people separated themselves from the control of the old church during the Reformation. This is a weakness which it is difficult for the Protestant missionary to overcome, and until it is overcome it seems to me that the Protestant missionary is going to have a difficult time of it in the rather supercharged nationalistic atmosphere that seems to be growing here in the East." (Johnson to Scott, June 5, 1933.)

28. Interview with Frank W. Price, New York City, July 16, 1959.

29. See Chapter 3 above, n. 98.

30. Ho interview, July 17, 1959.

31. *Ibid.* Chen Cheng-mo's study was published by the Commercial Press, Shanghai, in 1936.

32. Interview with Raymond B. Fosdick, New York City, Sept. 23, 1959. The reference is to his trip with Gunn in 1935.

33. See Chapter 7 above, n. 61.

34. Y. C. Wang, p. 374.

35. Price interview, July 16, 1959.

36. Hugh W. Hubbard letter to author, April 7, 1964.

37. Shepherd interview, Dec. 7, 1959.

38. Price interview, July 16, 1959.

39. Hugh W. Hubbard would question this judgement. He writes: "While we may deplore the lack of coordination among the various scattered rural reconstruction projects at this period, I think there is something to be said for the small, experimental, pilot project as a type. It should be encouraged, and valuable lessons may be learned from it; from its errors more serious mistakes may be avoided in larger undertakings, and from its successes valid principles can be laid down for wider application. No project I was ever engaged in taught me so much in so short a time as the Fan Chia Chuang experiment." (Hubbard letter to author, April 7, 1964.)

40. K'ung Hsüeh-hsiung, Introduction. Such a plan constituted K'ung's third condition for the success of the rural reconstruction movement. The other two: the training of rural leadership, especially among intellectuals who had left the villages for the cities; and the awakening of the rural masses through reform of the economic conditions of their existence.

41. See Ronald Rees, "The National Christian Council of China," *China Christian Year Book, 1934–1935,* pp. 192 ff.

42. E. E. Barnett to John R. Mott and Francis S. Harmon, Jan. 28, 1935, YMCA, WS 27a, China 1935.

43. NCC Staff, July 1936–May 1939: Dec. 14, 1936.

44. Shepherd interview, Dec. 7, 1959.

45. *China Weekly Review,* 81:262 (July 17, 1937). Interestingly enough, the aims of this plan included: reconstruction of the interior; distribution of the educated people in the interior; and "suppression of the latent social and political danger."

46. Shepherd interview, Dec. 7, 1959.

47. See Bowles, pp. 202–203.

48. Gunnar Myrdal, *Asian Drama, An Inquiry Into the Poverty of Nations* (New York, 1968), II, 870. For a fuller discussion, see also II, 1339–1346.

49. See Chapter 5 above, n. 46.


*Chapter Ten. The Fate of Gradualism*

1. See Michael and Taylor, pp. 406–409 and 432–436; Fairbank, *The United States and China,* pp. 190–205; Ch'ien Tuan-sheng.

2. Chow Tse-tsung, pp. 13–15.

3. *Ibid.,* p. 360.

4. Harriet C. Mills, "Lu Hsün and the Communist Party," *The China Quarterly,* 1:17 (October–December 1960). On the "changing intelligentsia" of the period, see Y. C. Wang, pp. 378–421.

5. Mills, p. 18.

6. *Ibid.,* p. 17.

7. *Ibid.,* p. 26.

8. It should be noted, in passing, that the concept of "New Life" was resurrected in somewhat analogous circumstances thirty years later in South Vietnam: in 1964–1965 the South Vietnamese government's rural pacification effort was redesigned to focus on the creation of "New Life Hamlets."

9. Some insight into the KMT's defensiveness—and ambivalence— vis-à-vis the May 4th intellectuals can be gained from Pei Ching-hua. Part One of this volume presents 14 pro-NLM articles by the generalissimo and his KMT associates, and Part Two is a collection of 12 articles on "New Life" in general by Ts'ai Yüan-p'ei, Hu Shih, and other May 4th figures. Although the latter essays antedate the movement itself, the volume's apparent pur-

pose is to give the movement intellectual respectability through association with the May 4th luminaries.

10. *Ibid.* For KMT attempts to answer the movement's intellectual critics, see especially essays by Ho Chung-han (35–45) and Yü Wen-wei (69–80). Ho, who was director of the Political Department of the Military Affairs Council, is particularly severe in his denunciation of Hu Shih and Ch'en Tu-hsiu. He accuses Hu of undermining China's national strength through the introduction of liberalism; and he accuses Ch'en of shattering China's social stability by introducing the concept of class struggle. "The sole purpose of the New Life Movement is to transform the destructive measures of the May Fourth New Culture Movement into a constructive Movement."

11. "Chiang Kai-shek Developing Fascism à la Chine," *China Weekly Review,* 68:387 (May 5, 1934).

12. See Paul K. Whang, "Let Marshal Feng Yu-hsiang Lead the New Life Movement," *China Weekly Review,* 68:172 (Mar. 31, 1934); C. Y. W. Meng, "The Revival of Confucianism," *ibid.,* 70:16–17 (Sept. 1, 1934); and Paul K. Whang, "The Revival of Confucianism," *ibid.,* 70:51 (Sept. 8, 1934).

13. E. E. Barnett, "Notes on the Evolution of the Young Men's Christian Association in China," p. 7, YMCA, WS 27a, China 1935.

14. "General Chiang's Christian Message," *CR,* 68:267–268 (May 1937).

15. George W. Shepherd, "Church and the New Life Movement," pp. 281–282.

16. "Report for 1933–1934," by Lyda S. Houston, Diongloh, July 25, 1934, ABCFM, Foochow Reports, 1930–1939, item 94.

17. "States of Mind," report by Roderick Scott for 1933–1934, ABCFM, Foochow Reports, 1930–1939, item 96.

18. Annual Report of Hankow YMCA, by Lawrence Todnem, Aug. 25, 1934, YMCA, WS 98b, China Annual Reports, 1934–1935.

19. P. C. Hsu, "The Student Christian Movement," *China Christian Year Book, 1934–1935* (Shanghai, 1935), p. 79.

20. "Administrative Report for the Year 1933–1934," by Lyman Hoover, Student Department, Peiping, n.d., YMCA, WS 26e, China 1934.

21. Quoted in E. E. Barnett, to F. S. Harmon, Shanghai, Dec. 8, 1934, YMCA, WS, 26e, China 1934.

22. *Ibid.*

23. "The Position of Protestant Christianity in Japan and China as Seen From the Universities," by Francis P. Miller, March 12, 1934, ABCFM, North China Reports, 1930–1934, item 138.

24. Kiang Wen-han, "Secularization of Christian Colleges in China," *CR,* 68:302–305 (May 1937).

25. *Ibid.,* p. 304.

26. *Ibid.,* p. 305.

27. *Ibid.*

28. In those regions where effective Chinese "political authority" was largely the rural authority exercised by Chinese Communist guerrillas,

rather than Nanking, some Americans had entered a highly informal partnership with the Communists in 1937–1939. Hugh W. Hubbard was one of the first to have direct contacts with the guerrillas when he was captured—and courteously treated—near Paotingfu in November 1937. See Fox Butterfield.

29. For a major contribution to the documentation of this sympathy, see Harold R. Isaacs, *Scratches on Our Minds: American Images of China and India* (New York, 1958).

*Epilogue*

1. Quoted in *China Bulletin of the Far East Office,* 9:13 (June 22, 1959).
2. Quoted in *ibid.,* 9:12 (June 8, 1959).
3. From *Soviet Press Translations,* Far Eastern and Russian Institute, University of Washington, 6:527–531 (October 1, 1951).

# Bibliography

ABCFM: American Board of Commissioners for Foreign Missions, Archives for the years 1812–1952, on deposit in the Houghton Library, Harvard University.

Abend, Hallett. *My Life in China, 1926–1941*. New York, 1943.

American-Far Eastern Policy Studies, Harvard University, "Discussion Reports" of addresses by O. Edmund Clubb, Stanley K. Hornbeck, C. E. Christopherson, and M. S. Bates. Cambridge, 1958–1959.

Ballou, Earle H. *Dangerous Opportunity: The Christian Mission in China Today*. New York, 1940.

Barnett, Eugene E. "As I Look Back: Recollections of Growing Up in America's Southland and of Twenty-six Years in Pre-Communist China." Mimeographed memoir, n.d., loaned by the author.

Berkov, Robert. *Strong Man of China*. Boston, 1938.

Bisson, T. A. "Ten Years of the Kuomintang: Revolution versus Reaction." *Foreign Policy Reports*, 8:25 (Feb. 15, 1933).

———— *Japan in China*. New York, 1938.

———— *American Policy in the Far East, 1931–1941*. Rev. ed. New York, 1941.

Blum, John M. *From the Morgenthau Diaries: Years of Crisis, 1928–1938*. Boston, 1959.

Borg, Dorothy. *American Policy and the Chinese Revolution, 1925–1928*. New York, 1947.

———— *The United States and the Far Eastern Crisis of 1933–1938*. Cambridge, Mass., 1964.

Bowles, Chester. *Ambassador's Report*. New York, 1954.

Brandt, Conrad. *Stalin's Failure in China*. Cambridge, Mass., 1959.

*Brief Historical Sketch of the New Life Movement*. Ser. 2. Nanking, 1937.

Brière, O. *Fifty Years of Chinese Philosophy, 1898–1950*. London, 1956.

Brown, William A. "The Protestant Rural Movement in China, 1920–1937." *Papers on China*, 9:173–202. Harvard University, East Asian Research Center, 1955. Reprinted in Kwang-Ching Liu, ed., *American Missionaries in China*, pp. 217–248. Cambridge, Mass., 1966.

Buck, Pearl S. *Tell The People: Talks with James Yen about the Mass Education Movement.* New York, 1945.

*Bulletin of the National Christian Council of China.* Shanghai, 1928–1937.

Butterfield, Fox. "A Missionary View of the Chinese Communists, 1936–1939." *Papers on China,* 15:147–199. Harvard University, East Asian Research Center, 1961. Reprinted in Kwang-Ching Liu, ed., *American Missionaries in China,* pp. 249–301. Cambridge, Mass., 1966.

Butterfield, Kenyon L. "The Christian Church and Rural Life in China." *International Review of Missions,* 12:182–190 (April 1923).

———— "The Christian Church in Rural China." *Chinese Recorder,* 62:344 (June 1931).

———— "Rural Community Parishes." *NCC Bulletin,* 37:13–15 (June 1931).

Callahan, Paul E. "Christianity and Revolution as Seen in the National Christian Council of China." *Papers on China,* 5:75–106. Harvard University, East Asian Research Center, 1950.

Chang, Carsun (Chang Chun-mai). *Third Force in China.* New York, 1952.

Chang, John K. "Industrial Development of China, 1912–1949." *Journal of Economic History,* 28:56–81 (March 1967).

Chang Yüan-shan 章元善 and Hsü Shih-lien 許仕廉, eds. *Hsiang-ts'un chien-she shih-yen* 鄉村建設實驗 (Experiments in rural reconstruction). 3 vols. Shanghai and Canton, 1936.

Chen Fu-sheng, "Can Restoration of Old Order Save China?" *China Weekly Review,* 70:98 (Sept. 15, 1934).

Chen Li-fu. *Philosophy of Life.* New York, 1948.

*Chiang Chieh-shih hsien-sheng chia-yen lei-ch'ao* 蔣介石先生嘉言類鈔 (Classified choice quotations from Chiang Kai-shek). Shanghai, 1937.

*Chiang Chieh-shih hsien-sheng yen-shuo-chi* 蔣介石先生演説集 (Speeches of Chiang Kai-shek). 2 vols. Canton, 1927.

Chiang Chung-cheng (Chiang Kai-shek). *Soviet Russia in China: A Summing-up at Seventy.* Rev. ed. New York, 1958.

Chiang Kai-shek. *Outline of the New Life Movement,* tr. Mme. Chiang. Nanchang, 1934. [?]

———— *Resisting External Aggression and Regenerating the Chinese Nation.* Hankow, 1938. [?]

———— *A Philosophy of Action or What I Mean by Action.* Chungking, 1940.

———— *China's Destiny,* tr. Wang Chung-hui. New York, 1947.

———— *China's Destiny and Chinese Economic Theory,* ed. with notes and commentary by Philip Jaffe. New York, 1947.

———— *Selected Speeches on Religion by President and Mrs. Chiang Kai-shek.* Taipei, 1952.

Chiang Kai-shek, Mme., "Christians and the New Life Movement." *Chinese Recorder,* 68:279–280 (May 1937).

———— (Chiang, Mayling Soong). *Sian: A Coup d'État.* Shanghai, 1937.

Ch'ien Tuan-sheng. *The Government and Politics of China.* Cambridge, Mass., 1950.

*China Bulletin of the Far East Office.* Division of Foreign Missions, NCCC/USA. New York, 1950–.

*China Christian Year Book,* ed. F. W. Rawlinson. Shanghai, 1933–1937.

*China Handbook: 1937–1945, A Comprehensive Survey of Major Developments in China in Eight Years of War,* ed. Hollington K. Tong. Rev. ed. New York, 1947.

China International Famine Relief Commission. *The C.I.F.R.C. Fifteenth Anniversary Book, 1921–1936.* CIFRC ser. A, no. 47. Peiping, 1936.

China International Famine Relief Commission. *Annual Reports.* Peiping, 1928–1937.

*China Weekly Review,* ed. J. B. Powell. Shanghai, 1928–1937.

*China Year Book,* ed. H. G. W. Woodhead. Shanghai, 1932–1936.

*Chinese Recorder, Journal of the Christian Movement in China,* ed. Frank Rawlinson. Shanghai, 1928–1937.

*Chinese Year Book, 1935–1936,* ed. Kwei Chung-shu. Premier issue. Shanghai, 1935.

Chow Tse-tsung. *The May Fourth Movement: Intellectual Revolution in Modern China.* Cambridge, Mass., 1960.

Chu, Clayton H. *American Missionaries in China: Books, Articles and Pamphlets Extracted from the Subject Catalogue of the Missionary Research Library.* Cambridge, 1960.

Chu, Samuel C. *The New Life Movement, 1934–1937.* Researches in the Social Sciences on China, Columbia University, East Asian Institute. New York, 1957.

Clubb, O. Edmund. *Twentieth Century China.* New York, 1964.

Cohen, Paul A. *China and Christianity: The Missionary Movement and the Growth of Chinese Antiforeignism, 1860–1870.* Cambridge, Mass., 1963.

*CR:* see Chinese Recorder


Den, Kimber H. K. "New Life Movement and Christian Church," *Chinese Recorder,* 66:97–100 (February 1935).

Dulles, F. R. *China and America: The Story of Their Relations since 1784*. Princeton, 1946.

East Asian Institute, Columbia University, "Foreign Investment in China and the Chinese Balance of Payments." Research Guide. New York, 1944.
Endicott, James G. *A Report from China*. Chungking, n.d.
Everest, Allen S. *Morgenthau, the New Deal, and Silver*. New York, 1950.

Fairbank, John King. *Trade and Diplomacy on the China Coast: The Opening of the Treaty Ports, 1842–1854*. 2 vols. Cambridge, Mass., 1953.
———— *The United States and China*. Rev. ed. Cambridge, Mass., 1958.
Fairbank, John K., Edwin O. Reischauer, and Albert M. Craig. *East Asia: The Modern Transformation*. Boston, 1965.
Fishel, Wesley R. *The End of Extraterritoriality in China*. Berkeley, 1952.
Fong, H. D. "Cooperative Literature in China." *Nankai Social and Economic Quarterly,* 8:130–155 (April 1935).
———— "Bibliography on the Land Problems of China." *Nankai Social and Economic Quarterly,* 8:325–384 (July 1935).
Fosdick, Raymond B., Chairman, "Report of the Committee on Appraisal and Plan of the Rockefeller Foundation, Dec. 11, 1934." Loaned by Mr. Fosdick, New York City.
———— *The Story of the Rockefeller Foundation*. New York, 1952.
*FR:* U.S. Department of State. *Foreign Relations of the United States. Diplomatic Papers, 1931–1937*. Volumes on the Far East. Washington, D.C., 1948–1953.

Gamble, Sidney D. *Ting Hsien: A North China Rural Community*. New York, 1954.
Gilpatrick, Meredith P. "The Status of Law and Lawmaking Procedure under the Kuomintang." *Far Eastern Quarterly,* 10:38–55 (November 1950).
Godley, Shirley. "W. Cameron Forbes and the American Mission to China, 1935." *Papers on China,* 14:87–110. Harvard University, East Asian Research Center, 1960.
Gould, Randall. "Cleaning up after Communism." *Asia,* 35:337–341 (June 1935).
———— *China in the Sun*. Garden City, 1946.
Grant, John B. "Philosophy of Rural Reconstruction in China." *Journal of the Royal Asiatic Society of Bengal. Letters,* 6:119–138 (1940).

Gregg, Alice H. *China and Educational Autonomy, The Changing Role of the Protestant Educational Missionary in China, 1807–1937.* Syracuse, 1946.

Griswold, A. Whitney. *The Far Eastern Policy of the United States.* New York, 1938.

Gunn, Selskar M. "China Reports for the Rockefeller Foundation, 1931–1937." Loaned by Mrs. S. M. Gunn, of Santa Barbara, Calif.


Hahn, Emily. *Chiang Kai-shek: An Unauthorized Biography.* New York, 1955.

Han, S. H. *Directory of Rural Reconstruction Work in China.* Shen Mu hsien, Shensi, 1938.

Heinrichs, Waldo H., Jr. *American Ambassador: Joseph C. Grew and the Development of the United States Diplomatic Tradition.* Boston, 1966.

Hinton, William. *Fanshen: A Documentary of Revolution in a Chinese Village.* New York, 1966.

Ho, Franklin L. "Rural Economic Reconstruction in China." Preliminary paper for 6th Conference of Institute of Pacific Relations, Yosemite. Tientsin, 1936.

———— Manuscript in preparation for publication on the economic history of Republican China. Loaned by the author, New York City.

HR: Hubbard, Hugh W. "The Lichwan Service Center," Report of April 20, 1935. NCC, biennial meeting, 1935.

Hu Shih. *The Chinese Renaissance.* Chicago, 1934.

Hubbard, Hugh W. "The Lichwan Service Center," see *HR*.

———— "A Christian Approach to the Chinese Village." *International Review of Missions,* 28:240–245 (April 1939).

Hubbard, Mabel Ellis. "An Experiment in Teaching the Christian Religion by Life Situations in Fan Village, China." M.A. thesis. Oberlin College, 1938.

Hsu, Leonard S. (Hsü Shih-lien). "Rural Reconstruction in China." *Pacific Affairs,* 10:249–265 (September 1937).

Hsu, P. C. "The Student Christian Movement." *China Christian Year Book, 1934–1935.* Shanghai, 1935.

———— "Lessons from the Lichwan Experiment." *Chinese Recorder,* 68:677–680 (November 1937).


Irick, Robert L., Ying-shih Yü, and Kwang-Ching Liu. *American-Chinese Relations, 1784–1941: A Survey of Chinese Materials at Harvard.* Cambridge, Mass., 1960.

Iriye, Akira. *After Imperialism: The Search for a New Order in the Far East, 1921–1931*. Cambridge, Mass., 1965.

———— *Across the Pacific: An Inner History of American-East Asian Relations*. New York, 1967.

Isaacs, Harold R. *Scratches on Our Minds: American Images of China and India*. New York, 1958.

Israel, John. *Student Nationalism in China, 1927–1937*. Stanford, 1966.

Jerusalem Meeting, International Missionary Council. Vol. 6, *The Christian Mission in Relation to Rural Problems*. 7 vols. New York, 1928.

Johnson, Nelson Trusler (1887–1954). Papers, 1916–1950, on deposit in the Manuscript Division, Library of Congress, Washington, D.C. Personal letters and memoranda of conversations, 1931–1937.

Johnson, William R. "A Suggested Plan for Rural Reconstruction Work under Christian Auspices in Kiangsi Province, China." Kuling, Sept. 14, 1933. Mimeographed report, abridged and revised, on file in Missionary Research Library, New York City.

———— "The Christian Rural Program at Lichwan, China." Typescript on file in the library of the Methodist Board of Missions, New York City.

Kiang Wen-han. "Student Situation in China." *Chinese Recorder,* 64:304–306 (May 1933).

———— "Secularization of Christian Colleges in China." *Chinese Recorder,* 68:302–305 (May 1937).

———— *The Chinese Student Movement*. New York, 1948.

Kiangsi Rural Welfare Centers. "Rural Reconstruction in Kiangsi." No. 1. Nanking, 1935.

———— "New Life Centers in Rural Kiangsi." No. 2. Nanchang, 1936.

Kennedy, Melville T., Jr. "The Kuomintang and Chinese Unification, 1928–1931." Unpub. diss., Harvard University, 1958.

K'ung Hsüeh-hsiung 孔雲雄 . *Chung-kuo chin-jih chih nung-ts'un yün-tung* 中國今日之農村運動 (The rural movement in China today). Rev. ed. Nanking, 1934.

Latourette, Kenneth Scott. *Advance Through Storm*. Vol. 7, *A History of the Expansion of Christianity*. 7 vols. London, 1945.

———— *World Service: A History of the Foreign Work and World Service of the Young Men's Christian Associations of the United States and Canada*. New York, 1957.

League of Nations Council, Committee on Technical Collaboration with

China. *Report to the Council of Its Technical Delegate on His Mission in China from Date of Appointment until April 1, 1934.* Nanking, 1934. (Also, with a slight title variation, Geneva, 1934.)

Lee, Robert. "The Rural Reconstruction Movement." *Papers on China,* 4:160–198. Harvard University, East Asian Research Center, 1950.

Liu Kwang-Ching, ed. *Americans and Chinese: A Historical Essay and a Bibliography.* Cambridge, Mass., 1963.

———— ed. *American Missionaries in China: Papers from Harvard Seminars.* Cambridge, Mass., 1966.

Liu, F. F. *A Military History of Modern China, 1924–1949.* Princeton, 1956.

Linebarger, Paul M. A. *The China of Chiang Kai-shek.* Boston, 1941.

Mallory, Walter H. *China: Land of Famine.* New York, 1926.

Meng, C. Y. W. "The Revival of Confucianism." *China Weekly Review,* 70:16–17 (Sept. 1, 1934).

———— "The 'New Life Movement' in Full Swing in China." *China Weekly Review,* 75:450–451 (Feb. 29, 1936).

———— "People's Economic Reconstruction Movement Launched at Nanking." *China Weekly Review,* 77:206–207 (July 11, 1936).

———— "The Meaning of the Nation-Wide Celebration of General Chiang's Birthday." *China Weekly Review,* 78:344–345 (Nov. 7, 1936).

Methodist Episcopal Church, Kiangsi Conference, Materials on file in the library of the Board of Missions of the Methodist Church, New York City. Letters from Kiangsi missionaries, 1932–1937.

Michael, Franz H., and George E. Taylor. *The Far East in the Modern World.* New York, 1956.

Mills, Harriet C. "Lu Hsün and the Communist Party." *The China Quarterly,* 1.4:17–27 (October–December 1960).

Myrdal, Gunnar. *Asian Drama: An Inquiry into the Poverty of Nations.* 3 vols. New York, 1968.

Nathan, Andrew James. *A History of the China International Famine Relief Commission.* Cambridge, Mass., 1965.

NCC: National Christian Council of China Archives, 1922–1949. Bound in volumes as the "Charles Luther Boynton Collection of Christian Life and Work in China." Missionary Research Library, New York City. Minutes, reports, and other materials relating to the work of the Council, 1927–1937.

Minutes of the Administrative, Executive and Ad-Interim Committees.

*Bulletin.*

Execom (Special reports and minutes of the executive committee).

Staff (Minutes of the council's staff meetings).

Biennial Meeting.

Mimeographed materials (miscellaneous).

———— *Report of the Conference on Christianizing Economic Relations.* Held under the auspices of the National Christian Council of China, Shanghai, August 18–28, 1927. Pamphlet in Missionary Research Library, New York City.

———— *Christian Cooperation in China as Illustrated by the Biennial Meeting.* Shanghai, May 5–11, 1937. Shanghai, 1937.

———— *The Church and Rural Reconstruction: A Symposium on the Ting Hsien Rural Institute of 1933.*

National Economic Council. *Annual Reports.* Nanking, 1934–1936.

"New Life Movement in China." *Missionary Review,* 57:323–325 (July 1934).

"New Life Movement and Other Developments on China's Political Stage." *China Weekly Review,* 68:126 (March 24, 1934).

North, Robert C., with Ithiel de Sola Pool. *Kuomintang and Chinese Communist Elites.* Stanford, 1952.

*North China Herald and Supreme Court and Consular Gazette.* Shanghai, 1933–1937.

Paauw, Douglas S. "Chinese National Expenditures during the Nanking Period." *Far Eastern Quarterly,* 12:3–26 (November 1952).

———— "The Kuomintang and Economic Stagnation, 1928–1937." *Journal of Asian Studies,* 16:213–220 (February 1957).

Pei, Ching-hua 貝警華 , ed. *Hsin-sheng-huo lun-ts'ung* 新生活論叢 (Essays on the New Life Movement). Shanghai, 1936.

Powell, John B. *My Twenty-five Years in China.* New York, 1945.

Remer, Charles F. *Foreign Investments in China.* New York, 1933.

Rockefeller Foundation. *Annual Report, 1935,* et. seq. New York, 1936–1944.

———— *A Review for 1936.* et. seq. By Raymond B. Fosdick, president. New York, 1937–1943.

Rostow, W. W., *et al. The Prospects for Communist China.* Cambridge and New York, 1954.

Rosinger, L. K. *China's Wartime Politics, 1937–1944.* Princeton, 1945.

Salter, Sir Arthur. *China and the Depression: Impressions of a Three Months Visit.* Nanking, 1934.

Schiffrin, Harold. "Sun Yat-sen's Early Land Policy: The Origin and Meaning of 'Equalization of Land Rights.'" *Journal of Asian Studies,* 16:549–564 (August 1957).

Schwartz, Benjamin I. *Chinese Communism and the Rise of Mao.* Cambridge, Mass., 1951.

————— *In Search of Wealth and Power: Yen Fu and the West.* Cambridge, Mass., 1964.

Selle, Earl A. *Donald of China.* New York, 1948.

Sharmon, Lyon. *Sun Yat-sen: His Life and Its Meaning.* New York, 1934.

Shepherd, George W. "Facing Some Facts." *Chinese Recorder,* 62:712 (November 1931).

————— "Tinghsien's Challenge to the Church of Today." *Chinese Recorder,* 64:391–392 (June 1933).

————— "The Chinese Communists." *China Christian Year Book, 1934–1935* (Shanghai 1935), pp. 89–96.

————— "Reconstruction in Kiangsi." *International Review of Missions,* 26:167–176 (April 1937).

————— "Church and the New Life Movement." *Chinese Recorder,* 68:281–282 (May 1937).

————— "Cooperation with New Life Movement." *Chinese Recorder,* 68:286–288 (May 1937).

————— Miscellaneous Papers on Kiangsi Rural Reconstruction Work, 1935–1942. Missionary Research Library, New York City.

Smythe, Lewis S. C. "Communism Challenges Christianity." *Chinese Recorder,* 65:359 (June 1934).

Snow, Edgar. "How Rural China is Being Re-Made." *China Weekly Review,* 67:98–101 and 67:202–203 (Dec. 16 and 30, 1933).

————— *Random Notes on Red China, 1936–1945.* Cambridge, Mass., 1957.

————— *Journey to the Beginning.* New York, 1958.

Stampar, Andrija. "Observations of a Rural Health Worker." *The New England Journal of Medicine,* 218:991–997 (June 1938).

Stuart, John Leighton. *Fifty Years in China.* New York, 1954.

Tang, Christopher. "Christianity and the New Life Movement in China." Unpub. diss., San Francisco Theological Seminary, 1941.

Tawney, R. H. *Land and Labour in China.* New York, 1932.

Taylor, G. E. "Reconstruction after Revolution: Kiangsi Province and the Chinese Nation." *Pacific Affairs,* 8:302–311 (September 1935).

Teng Ssu-yü and John King Fairbank. *China's Response to the West: A Documentary Survey, 1839–1923.* Cambridge, Mass., 1954.

Thomson, James C., Jr. "Communist Policy and the United Front in

China, 1935–1936." *Papers on China*, 11:99–148. Harvard University, East Asian Research Center, 1957.

Tong, Hollington K. *Chiang Kai-shek, Soldier and Statesman*. 2 vols. Shanghai, 1937.

Tsou Tang. *America's Failure in China, 1941–1950*. Chicago, 1963.

U.S. Department of State. *Foreign Relations of the United States*, see *FR*.

Van Slyke, Lyman P. "Liang Sou-ming and the Rural Reconstruction Movement." *Journal of Asian Studies*, 18:457–474 (August 1959).

———— *Enemies and Friends: The United Front in Chinese Communist History*. Stanford, 1967.

Varg, Paul A. *Missionaries, Chinese, and Diplomats: The American Protestant Missionary Movement in China, 1890–1952*. Princeton, 1958.

Vinacke, Harold M. *A History of the Far East in Modern Times*. 5th ed. New York, 1950.

Wang Ching-wei. "Two Years of National Reconstruction." *China Weekly Review*, 68:25–27 (March 3, 1934).

Wang, Y. C. *Chinese Intellectuals and the West, 1872–1949*. Chapel Hill, 1966.

Whang, Paul K. "The Revival of Confucianism." *China Weekly Review*, 70:51 (Sept. 8, 1934).

White, Theodore H., and Annalee Jacoby. *Thunder out of China*. New York, 1946.

Wright, Mary C. "From Revolution to Restoration: The Transformation of Kuomintang Ideology." *Far Eastern Quarterly*, 14:515–532 (August 1955).

———— *The Last Stand of Chinese Conservatism: The T'ung-Chih Restoration, 1862–1874*. Stanford, 1957.

Wu, Y. T. "Make Christianity Socially Dynamic." *Chinese Recorder*, 65:9–11 (January 1934).

———— "Denunciation of American Imperialism for Its Use of Reformism in the YMCA to Practice Aggression against China." *Ta Kung Pao* (Shanghai, July 30, 1951). From *Soviet Press Translations*, Far Eastern and Russian Institute, University of Washington, 6:527–531 (Oct. 1, 1951).

Yaukey, Jesse B. "Religious Education and Communism." *Chinese Recorder*, 65:353–354 (June 1934).

Yen, Y. C. James. *The Ting Hsien Experiment, 1930–1931.* Ting Hsien, 1931.

——— *The Ting Hsien Experiment in 1934.* Peiping, n.d.

Yen, Y. C. James, and J. P. McEvoy. *Freedom from Ignorance: A Practical Manual for Mass Education.* New York, 1943.

Young, Arthur N. *China and the Helping Hand, 1937–1945.* Cambridge, Mass., 1963.

——— *China's Wartime Finance and Inflation, 1937–1945.* Cambridge, Mass., 1965.

——— Manuscript in preparation for publication on the financial policies of the Nanking government. Loaned by the author, East Asian Research Center, Harvard University.

Young, C. Kuangson. "The New Life Movement." *The China Press Weekly Supplement,* 3:32 (April 18, 1937).

Young Men's Christian Association of China. *Ten-Year Policy of the National Committee, YMCA's of China.* Shanghai, 1935.

Young Men's Christian Associations of the United States and Canada. Correspondence received by the International Committee, 1891–1950. Deposited at the Historical Library, National Council of the Young Men's Christian Associations, New York City. Letters from China secretaries, 1927–1937.

Young, T. S. "The Chinese Have Found Their Leader." *China Weekly Review,* 78:452 (Nov. 28, 1936).

Yu, R. S. "Introducing a New Educational Experiment." *China Weekly Review,* 64:262–263, 274 (April 15, 1963).

# Index

# Harvard East Asian Series

# BRAIN
# TRUST

**ALSO BY GARTH SUNDEM**

*The Geeks' Guide to World Domination*

*Brain Candy*

# 93 Top Scientists
**Reveal Lab-Tested Secrets to**
**Surfing, Dating, Dieting, Gambling,**
**Growing Man-Eating Plants,**
**and More!**

# BRAIN TRUST

**GARTH SUNDEM**

THREE RIVERS PRESS
NEW YORK

Published in the United States by Three Rivers Press, an imprint of the
Crown Publishing Group, a division of Random House, Inc., New York.
www.crownpublishing.com

Three Rivers Press and the Tugboat design are registered trademarks of
Random House, Inc.

Library of Congress Cataloging-in-Publication Data

Sundem, Garth
Brain trust : 93 top scientists reveal lab-tested secrets to surfing, dating,
dieting, gambling, growing man-eating plants, and more! / Garth Sundem.
p. cm.
Summary: "Based entirely on original interviews with Nobel laureates,
MacArthur geniuses, National Science Medal winners, and other leading
scientists, *Brain Trust* delivers more than 100 proven, scientifically valid
tips guaranteed to make you more awesome"—Provided by publisher.
1. Science—Miscellanea. I. Title.
Q173.S947 2012
500—dc23
2011022036

ISBN 978-0-307-88613-2
eISBN 978-0-307-88614-9

Printed in the United States of America

Book design: Maria Elias
Illustrations: Garth Sundem
Cover design: Kyle Kolker
Cover photographs: (shirt) © Brand X Pictures;
(scientists) Lambert/Archive Photos/Getty Images

1  3  5  7  9  10  8  6  4  2

First Edition

To the 130-ish brilliant scientists who took time
from teaching, research, and their otherwise busy lives
to tutor me in how to best live mine.

# CONTENTS

# INTRODUCTION

**When you open the passenger-side door of my car,**
one of the following things tends to fall out: a kid's shoe, a water
bottle, or a once-coveted stick, pinecone, acorn, large leaf, pill
bug, or rock. On special occasions it'll be an In-N-Out french
fry. Once it was a favorite running sock I'd been missing for
months.

I had ample opportunity to note these ejaculations every morning as I jumped into the passenger seat with my laptop and cell
phone to do the interviews for this book.

You see, the car's messy, but the garage is also the quietest
place in my house. In the background of the first interviews I
did, before stumbling onto the soundproof powers of Subaru, you
can hear my "extremely fierce" Labrador protecting the house
from things like early-rising birds and people in hats jogging past
(joggers with bare heads are fine—who can know the mind of a
Labrador?). Or you can hear me saying to my four-year-old, "Hey,
good morning, buddy! Go jump in bed with Mom." I've put some
of the recordings online at garthsundem.com—they're worth a
chuckle.

I can't tell if talking to Nobel Laureates, MacArthur geniuses,
National Medal of Science winners, and the like while hiding
in the garage is empowering, embarrassing, or just odd in the

manner of the proverbial mom with her hair in rollers pretending to be a nymph while talking dirty for a 1-900 service.

Anyway.

This book is what happens when science hits life. It gets messy.

And when you get off the script that some of these top-notch scientists have perfected over years of keynotes, classes, invited lectures, and interviews with people sitting at actual desks, you find that scientists are messy too. You hear the story of psychologist Stephen Greenspan's initiation into the science of gullibility when his mother duped him into marrying his then girlfriend. Or about mathematician Ian Stewart's wife trying to use rotational mechanics to teach their malfunctioning cat to land on its feet. You get to listen to statistician Wayne Winston yelling at USA basketball while on the phone because his model predicted a wider point spread. You hear about how MIT prosthetics researcher Hugh Herr replaced his lost legs with DIY feet to climb some of the most difficult rock faces in the world, or how physicist Charles Edmondson used the geometry of roadways to chase down a turbo Porsche with a lowly Dodge Neon.

It turns out that the root of today's best science is the passenger seat of scientists' messy cars. In other words, the science in this book comes from the very real experiences and problems of scientists' own lives.

And rather than ice-eyed intellectuals perched in ivory towers (as their precisely worded papers might imply), it turns out that scientists are passionate, excited, and bubbly about their specialties to the point of schoolgirls with Justin Bieber infatuations. (You should hear the utterly awesome Steve Strogatz talk about crickets, bridges, and his high school calculus teacher.) Get a scientist talking about her search for discovery and it starts to sound like a page-turning adventure book, which is exactly what I hope this book has turned out to be.

That said, don't let the glib delivery lull you into thinking this is puff pastry. This book is supposed to be fun and practical, but it's also one of the most info-dense entities in the known universe ($I = mc^2$).

OK, maybe that's a tiny bit of an exaggeration. But if you slow down, maybe hang your head out the window like the aforementioned Labrador, you'll find that the one hundred–some bite-sized bugs of how-to science stuck in your teeth in fact represent whole fields of cutting-edge research.

I loved writing this book—who gets to wear boxer shorts and drink Sumatra blend in the passenger seat of a parked Outback while chatting with Steven Pinker about how to bribe a cop? But the truth is, talking to sometimes three or four Nobel, MacArthur, and National Medal of Science winners in a morning nearly drove me batty.

You see, in addition to being overwhelmingly brilliant and passionate, it's a fair stereotype to note that each scientific field tends to either attract or create people with its own brand of quirks. For example, computer science professors respond to e-mails immediately or not at all. Physicists almost always have a serious side interest in basketball or race cars or sailing or card tricks or the like. (Thank you, Richard Feynman?) Social psychologists are happy to talk off the cuff, but are very concerned about being misquoted. Mathematicians tended to seem a bit surprised I would get in touch, were likely to tentatively dip a toe into the conversation, but then if I understood anything at all in the first five minutes, would ramble happily and fascinatingly for hours. Economists were sure to point out that their theoretical work is borne out in the real world, and biologists and anthropologists were sure to point out that their field observations are replicable in the lab.

Amid 130-ish interviews, it was hard to avoid jumping on the quirk train myself. For example, after a week spent mining a particularly deep vein of behavioral economists and applied mathematicians, I found myself charting my car's passenger-door ejections from one day to the next, hoping to glean some sort of great statistically predictive insight. When might the great oracle my family has affectionately nicknamed Zippy the Wonder Tank return my other running sock?

In fact, with my brain now addled by ricocheting thoughts born of that special leading edge where science meets fiction, I can't seem to stop mishmashing together my messy life with the work of these scientists.

I wonder about the pigeons that splinter off from the flock that circles the street by my house every night at sunset. I wonder if Cliff Lee should still throw heat to a batter who specializes in hitting fastballs. I wonder how I should best list ride-on-top toys on eBay to encourage rabid bidding. I wonder why the Ping-Pong balls my kids race in gutters on rainy days tend to stick together like Cheerios in a bowl. I start charting the detritus that falls out of my car. . . .

Yes, this book will teach you how to improve your life with science. You'll learn tricks for dieting better, dating better, driving better, and betting better. You'll learn how to get better odds from the lottery, you'll learn how to learn, and avoid car theft, and win poker, and get away with crimes in broad daylight. But I hope by the end, rather than having all your questions answered, you find yourself wandering around as totally wonder-struck as I am: With a bike and a bus pass, what's the most efficient way to visit every bakery in this city? Am I more likely to get hit with pigeon poop or find a twenty-dollar bill? Should I wait or circle to find a parking spot in this busy lot? What in the small space between my Labrador's ears makes him distrust people in hats?

Life is messy, and starting to pick it apart with science shows you just how brilliant and wild and interconnected and fascinating it is.

It's a good messy.

# BRAIN
# TRUST

# TRANSFORM A RELATIONSHIP WITH LANGUAGE

**Steven Pinker** COGNITIVE SCIENCE, HARVARD UNIVERSITY

"Imagine you've been pulled over by a police officer," says Steven Pinker, Harvard psychologist, prolific author, and one of Britannica's *100 Most Influential Scientists of All Time*. In this case, you'd like to know if the relationship is adversarial or conspiratorial: In other words, you'd like to know if you can bribe the cop. But you can't just come out and say it. "Instead, you start by talking about the weather," says Pinker, "and then you mention that it must be difficult to get by on an officer's salary." You start with extremely indirect speech and with every step become slightly more direct. "And after each step, the police officer has the opportunity to accept or rebuff the overture," says Pinker. If the police officer isn't open to being bribed, he or she should cut you off at the weather, before you've incriminated yourself.

Pinker explains this in terms of game theory, with payoffs shown here:

|  | Dishonest Cop | Honest Cop |
|---|---|---|
| **NO Bribe** | Ticket | Ticket |
| **Yes Bribe** | Free | Arrest |
| **Indirect Bribe** | Free | Ticket |

It's like trying to sleep with a coworker.

"The mistake of Clarence Thomas was to jump steps in this continuum," says Pinker. Thomas brought up the subject of porn videos when he should've prepped that level of directness, perhaps by "asking Anita Hill to call him by his first name, or by adopting a less formal style of speech." Thomas went straight to the equivalent of handing the cop a fifty-dollar bill, dooming himself to a scandal and the closest Senate confirmation in a century.

So language must match the relationship. "This is what we call 'tact,'" says Pinker. And when it doesn't, it creates uncomfortable friction—it's what drives the awkward comedy in a sketch posted to YouTube in which Irish comedian Dave Allen uses the terms "buddy," "chum," "friend," and "mate" with strangers and thus comes off as tactlessly aggressive. This would be like me trying to speak Cockney rhyming slang in a London pub, or walking into a group of local surfers and saying, "Yo brahs—where you shreddin' the swell today?" Language that oversteps the bounds of a relationship is in every way the equivalent of trying to hold hands with a stranger on the subway.

But what's even cooler is this: "Not only does language reflect a relationship, but it can serve to create or change it," says Pinker. And so if you can avoid overstepping in your slow evolution of indirect to direct language with a police officer or attractive coworker, not only can you discover the nature of the relationship, but you can pull the relationship along with it.

So make a script. Start with nearly innocuous comments that are almost certain to be taken as such ("It was nice to see you in the meeting today"). Then move ever so slowly toward the midground ("Wow, that's a sexy haircut!"). Then move glacially toward the thinly veiled overture you're trying to make (Pinker writes, "Would you like to come over sometime and see my etchings?"). Done tactfully and without overstepping, this language of closeness can create closeness.

Note that this entry doesn't necessarily recommend bribing cops or sleeping with coworkers, mirroring a common ethical dilemma in science: just because you can doesn't mean you should.

### EAT FOR EIGHT HOURS, LOSE WEIGHT

Satchidananda Panda REGULATORY BIOLOGY, SALK INSTITUTE

"If you overlay the CDC diabetes map with the NASA nighttime satellite map, there's an almost perfect match," says Satchin Panda, regulatory biology specialist at the Salk Institute. The more light in a region at night, the higher the incidence of diabetes. According to Panda, this is because your liver needs sleep. Actually, it's not the sleep per se that your liver needs, but a defined period of fasting each day, which throughout humanity's evolutionary history was the hours of darkness when you couldn't really do much but snooze.

"We started out as diurnal," says Panda, "but learning to control fire allowed us to get away from diurnal needs and into nocturnal space." All of a sudden, we could spend all day hunting and still

cook and eat the catch once the sun went down. Then with electricity and the industrial revolution, we went a step further—why make widgets during only twelve hours of daylight when you can flip on the lights and run the assembly line for twenty-four hours a day? Thus was shift work born.

"People who work at night have a 150 percent higher rate of metabolic disease," says Panda. And with people in the United States now averaging more than 160 hours of TV viewing per month, "we have 100 to 120 million people who are social shift workers," says Panda. Did you think the twinkling lights on the NASA nighttime map that align so evenly with the diabetes map were due to factory lights? Nope. They're due in large part to the throbbing screens that stay on in American households long after dark. Led by the TV's silver tongue, Americans have made the social decision to act like shift workers. "And this population is more at risk for every type of metabolic disease," says Panda.

The first reason for this is obvious: If you're awake more, you eat more. Panda points out that Americans consume 30 percent of their daily calories after eight o'clock at night. If there were a way to create a nighttime auditory map, you'd hear the roar of a great, collective munching in those same regions you see the light of TV screens.

But the effects of this nighttime munching go a step further than simply packing on extra pounds.

Let's take a closer look at your liver. Among its many functions is storing excess calories as glycogen and then, when you're starving, converting this glycogen into usable glucose. Actually, it's the liver's little autonomous mitochondria that do this, and like any population of millions of single-celled organisms, they're constantly dying and dividing, which in the case of your liver generally maintains a constant population. And, generally, it's at night, when their food processing duties are (or should be) decreased, that these mitochondria do their dividing.

"Our circadian clock separates functions throughout the day so that our organs stay healthy," says Panda. Mitochondria don't multitask well—if they work when they're dividing, they're much more prone to making faulty copies of their DNA. Over time, mutations creep in, and down that path lies all sorts of metabolic badness.

And the clock in your liver isn't a sundial—it doesn't simply monitor lightness and darkness and click through its organ functions based on time of day. Instead, "it gets information about time by when we eat," says Panda. Your liver needs to know when you've taken your last bite of the evening so that it can tell mitochondria it's safe to divide. "And if you eat all the time, the clock gets the clue too many times, it tries to adjust too many times, and it never knows when it's breakfast," says Panda.

Many millions of years precede electricity, and it's this great chunk of time for which our bodies are optimized. Simply, evolution hasn't had enough time to prepare us for nighttime work— our clock isn't nearly nimble enough to flip its schedule to allow efficient night sleeping on the weekend, following day sleeping during the workweek (and instantly back again).

Panda explored this with mice. Mice who are given the ability to eat for only eight hours a day quickly adjust their habits to consume the same number of calories as mice that are allowed to eat for sixteen hours per day. So given an equal calorie count, you might not expect any health differences between eight-hour and sixteen-hour feeding mice. But eight-hour mice live longer. And everyone knows that mice given a high-fat diet gain weight, right? But Panda's new work shows they don't—not if they consume this high-fat diet in an eight-hour window.

"Look at one-hundred-year-olds around the world, across all

different diets, and across all different professions, and you find one common denominator," says Panda. "They always stick to a scheduled feeding pattern, and they always have an early dinner followed by a defined fasting time."

So if you want to live long and prosper, don't eat at night. If you want to lose weight on your current high-fat diet, eat your calories in an eight-hour window.

## What's the basis of our biological clock?

Panda found that it's cells in our eyes that express the photopigment melanopsin, which allows us to measure the intensity of ambient light. The more light, the more melanopsin is expressed, and the more awake our biological clock allows us to feel. An older person who has difficulty falling asleep at night may have perfect sight, but blindness to light intensity due to faulty production of melanopsin. Likewise, if you're wide awake after a flight from Los Angeles to New York, you soon might be able to take a pill that shuts down melanopsin, allowing you to sleep when you get in.

## A Swedish study of identical twins separated

at birth found that lifestyle trumps genetics in determining how long people live. Writing about the study in the *New York Times*, Jane Brody describes the secrets of a long life as "the Three 'R's' of resolution, resourcefulness, and resilience." Extroversion, optimism, self-esteem, and strong ties to community help too.

# HOW TO BUILD TINY, FLYING CYBORG BEETLES

**Michel Maharbiz** ELECTRICAL ENGINEERING, UNIVERSITY OF CALIFORNIA–BERKELEY

"Humans can't build tiny things that fly autonomously," says Michel Maharbiz, electrical engineering and computer science guru at Berkeley. "As you scale things down a couple problems come up." One is airflow: "Turbulence and optimal wing structure are different for a tiny flier than they are for an airplane. Small things fly more like a two-armed chopper, horizontally sweeping," says Maharbiz, who's extremely entertaining to chat with because he says things like "Mike Dickinson at Caltech is one smart mo-fo!" or "My entertainment in life is to build cool shit."

And then there's the power problem. "You can't miniaturize the combustion engine enough," says Maharbiz, "and lithium-ion batteries are ten to forty times less efficient than burning hydrocarbons." To power a tiny flier, the power provided has to be worth the engine weight. Currently, it's not.

Finally, we can't build the actuator part of it, "the little muscles and skeletal components," says Maharbiz. Again, at least not efficiently enough for its power to justify its weight.

So there you go. The answer to, Can we build tiny, flying spy-bots? is No, not yet.

But nature can.

"There's tons of these things flying around," says Maharbiz. "They eat for energy, and they're great at miniaturizing flight systems."

We call them bugs. And while we can't build tiny flying robots, we're getting better at collaborating with nature on tiny flying cyborgs.

Cyborg green June beetles, to be precise. (Which, as you'll note, is pretty frickin' sweet.) Guys like Maharbiz favor these beetles because the bugs are big enough to carry some gadgetry and small enough to do things like deploy as a swarm into a collapsed building to search for the biosignatures of survivors, or fly through combat areas gathering information without being blasted.

Here's how it works.

First, Maharbiz implants a thin silver wire just behind the beetle's eye into the flight control center of its brain. To it, he attaches a tiny battery repurposed from a cochlear implant. An electric pulse of about -1.5 V starts the beetle's wings, and the same positive pulse stops them. (One can only imagine that a stronger pulse would transform a beetle into a firefly.)

Then the trick is steering.

"You can either pack a muscle full of force fibers or tubes that suck up energy," says Maharbiz, "so muscles can either be strong or fast, not both." So to get the (fast) rate of wing strokes at the (strong) power needed to fly, evolution's equipped beetles with a sweet little oscillator that allows them to pump their wing muscles once—hard!—and count on rebounding musculature to keep the wings pumping for another four beats. It's like the rebound of a stick off a drumhead—one stroke for five beats, repeat as necessary for flight and/or the opening of the iconic 20th Century Fox fanfare.

What this means is that a beetle's wings can only buzz at one speed—the oscillator rebounds at a fixed rate, so you can't simply drive beetle wings faster or slower for increased or decreased thrust. Still, Maharbiz found that wires delivering pulses to these resonators could control the amplitude of wing beats. Both wires pulsing 10 Hz at ten beats per second for three seconds increases wing amplitude and makes the beetle gain altitude. The same pulse in only the right wing makes the beetle turn left—like paddling harder with the right oar of a rowboat. By uniformly throttling down the wing amplitude, you can land the beetle.

The cool part is that precision piloting isn't needed here. "We don't try to fly the beetle—we try to *guide* the beetle," says

Maharbiz. Nature remains the pilot, used for leveling to the horizon, powering the system, and all the other intricacies of flight currently lost to human engineers.

A quick online search returns video of the cyborg beetle in action as well as a pdf with the full specs for creating your own. Seriously.

**Maharbiz writes, "When I dream of the** future, I see machines built from what we would now call 'living things': tables that are derived from plant cell lines, which breathe your office air and use ambient light for energy to fix themselves or grow new parts; houses whose walls are alive and whose infrastructure hosts an ecology of organisms who perform tasks both microscopic and macroscopic; computational elements whose interfaces completely blur the line between cell and chip."

## HOW TO LEARN

**Robert Bjork** PSYCHOLOGY, UNIVERSITY OF CALIFORNIA–LOS ANGELES

The one hundred-ish skills in this book can help make you awesome. But your ability to put them to use is bound by one thing: your ability to learn. The more you can learn, the more awesome you can become. So consider this a keystone entry.

First, think about how you attack a pile of study material. "People tend to try to learn in blocks," says Robert Bjork, Distinguished Professor of Psychology at UCLA, "mastering one thing before moving on to the next." But instead he recommends interleaving, a strategy in which, for example, instead of spending an hour working on your tennis serve, you mix in a range of skills like backhands, volleys, overhead smashes, and footwork. "This creates a sense of difficulty," says Bjork, "and people tend not to notice the immediate effects of learning." Instead of making an appreciable leap forward with your serving ability after a session of focused practice, interleaving forces you to make nearly imperceptible steps forward with many skills. But over time, the sum of these small steps is much greater than the sum of the leaps you would have taken if you'd spent the same amount of time mastering each skill in its turn.

Bjork explains that successful interleaving allows you to "seat" each skill among the others: "If information is studied so that it can be interpreted in relation to other things in memory, learning is much more powerful," he says.

There's one caveat: Make sure the miniskills you interleave are related in some higher-order way. If you're trying to learn tennis, you'd want to interleave serves, backhands, volleys, smashes, and footwork—not serves, synchronized swimming, European capitals, and programming in Java.

Similarly, studying in only one location is great as long as you'll only be required to recall the information in the same location. If you want information to be accessible outside your dorm room, or office, or nook on the second floor of the library, Bjork recommends varying your study location.

And again, these tips generalize. Interleaving and varying your study location will help whether you're mastering math skills, learning French, or trying to become a better ballroom dancer.

So too will a somewhat related phenomenon, the spacing effect, first described by Hermann Ebbinghaus in 1885. "If you study and then you wait, tests show that the longer you wait, the more you will have forgotten," says Bjork. That's obvious—over time, you forget. But here's the cool part: If you study, wait, and then study again, the longer the wait, the more you'll have learned after this second study session. Bjork explains it this way: "When we access things from our memory, we do more than reveal it's there. It's not like a playback. What we retrieve becomes more retrievable in the future. Provided the retrieval succeeds, the more difficult and involved the retrieval, the more beneficial it is." Note that there's a trick implied by "provided the retrieval succeeds": You should space your study sessions so that the information you learned in the first session remains just barely retrievable. Then, the more you have to work to pull it from the soup of your mind, the more this second study session will reinforce your learning. If you study again too soon, it's too easy.

Along these lines, Bjork also recommends taking notes just after class, rather than during—forcing yourself to recall a lecture's information is more effective than simply copying it from a blackboard. "Get out of court stenographer mode," says Bjork. You have to work for it. The more you work, the more you learn, and the more you learn, the more awesome you can become.

## "Forget about forgetting," says Robert Bjork.

"People tend to think that learning is building up something in your memory and that forgetting is losing the things you built. But in some respects the opposite is true." See, once you learn something, you never actually forget it. Do you remember your childhood best friend's phone number? No? Well, Dr. Bjork showed that if you were reminded, you would retain it much more quickly and strongly than if you were asked to memorize a fresh seven-digit number. So this old phone number is not forgotten—it lives somewhere in you—only, recall can be a bit tricky.

And while we count forgetting as the sworn enemy of learning, in some ways that's wrong too. Bjork showed that the two live in a kind of symbiosis in which forgetting actually aids recall. "Because humans have unlimited storage capacity, having total recall would be a mess," says Bjork. "Imagine you remembered all the phone numbers of all the houses you had ever lived in. When someone asks you your current phone number, you would have to sort it from this long list." Instead, we forget the old phone numbers, or at least bury them far beneath the ease of recall we give to our current number. What you thought were sworn enemies are more like distant collaborators.

**Forget just learning.** University of California–Davis psychologist Dean Keith Simonton knows how you can become a genius. First, pick the definition of "genius" you're aiming for—superior IQ, prodigious talent, or exceptional achievement. OK, let's be realistic: You've either got Marilyn vos Savant's 228 IQ or you don't, and if you had prodigious talent, you'd already know it.

But the "genius at" category can be trained. Anyone can be Michelangelo at something. "Sometimes it just takes more than the usual amount of time to find your thing," says Simonton. If you haven't got it yet, keep searching. Once you find it—be it topiary, competitive Rubik's cube-ing, folding proteins, or painting creation scenes on inverted domes—"it takes about a decade of hard work to develop domain-specific skills," says Simonton.

Get aggressive in your far-and-wide search for your talent. Then retreat to that cave high in the Himalayas, where you can spend ten years perfecting it. When you emerge—BAM!—you'll be a genius.

## THE BODY LANGUAGE OF DOMINANCE AND LOVE

**David Givens** ANTHROPOLOGY, CENTER FOR NONVERBAL STUDIES

Who hasn't needed to bluff? In business, sports, and romantic pursuit, it's often useful to seem more powerful—or more vulnerable—than you really are. Sure, you can try flashing a smile or a frown or a come-hither, but "we've learned to control our faces," says David Givens, director of the Center for Nonverbal Studies, in Spokane, Washington. And so people have learned to be wary of them. If you want to bluff convincingly—and figure out what others are really thinking—you'll need to focus on another body part.

"Our shoulders are much less tutored," says Givens.

For instance, the shrug is reflexive, and because it's unfiltered by the scheming brain, it's telling.

This is because the shrug comes from your inner lizard. And this lizard part of the brain knows how to show subordination—it crouches. Specifically, lizards duck their heads while rotating their lower arms outward, thus lowering their bodies. Mammals do it too—witness my yellow Lab in the second after I've caught him neck-deep in the Thanksgiving turkey. We call this cowering. In humans, it's the knee-jerk response to "Look out!" and also the who knows? gesture that shows subservience and uncertainty in classrooms and boardrooms around the world.

Opposite the cringe is what Givens calls "the antigravity sign." This is humans' palm-down speaking gesture or the high-stand display of a dominant lizard. "People in the military or business try to mimic this gesture by augmenting the shoulders and squaring them with uniforms and suits," says Givens. Again, witness my yellow Lab, whose shoulder hackles flare threateningly when he's confronted with intense danger in the form of squirrels on the porch or (for some reason) pumpkins. Make your shoulders bigger, and you'll look badder.

And once you're done being big and bad, perhaps you'll take a second to reconnect with your softer side. Just as there are evolutionarily programmed signals for dominance and subservience, there are hardwired signals of love (admit it—these signals are why you're still reading this entry). You know about the neck-revealing hair adjustment and the one-eyebrow-raised smoldering smile. But did you know about pigeon toes? Givens points to it as a sure sign of attraction. Toes in means "come hither" and toes out—reminiscent of a soldier at rest—means "not today, maybe not ever." Also on a spectrum from inviting to denying is head angle: Forehead down, eyes up should make you recall Lauren Bacall's famous come-hither to Humphrey Bogart. And on the flip side, chin up with eyes looking down is bad, bad news—a sure sign of disdain.

If you're seeing pigeon toes and downward forehead along with the vulnerable lizard shrug, your evening is looking up. All together, you know what it looks like? Well, it looks exactly like Betty Boop. That naughty minx.

Givens is quick to point out that not only can you learn to recognize these signs in their natural habitat and thus know things you might otherwise not, but you can learn to control them for your own evil purposes (my words, not his). These collected signals not only function as subconscious conduits of information, but they can create reciprocity, too.

You want a better chance with that special someone you glimpsed across the bar? Get your pigeon-toed, forehead-tilting, shoulder-shrugging groove on. You might want to practice in the mirror first.

**David Givens's books include *Love Signals***
and *Your Body at Work*. His nonverbal dictionary is online at www
.center-for-nonverbal-studies.org.

**Body language isn't solely the domain of the** living. Cynthia Breazeal of MIT's Media Lab creates robots that rock nonverbal communication. "We've seen that if doctor-patient or teacher-student nonverbal behavior is compatible, health and learning outcomes are improved," says Breazeal, and she's seen the same with her 'bots—her robots that guide users' weight loss or education are most successful when their choices to remind, persuade, cajole, or bully their humans gels with users' personalities. Going a step further, she says, "We're experimenting with robots that have a version of mirror neurons," referring to the cells in the human brain that allow us to internally imitate others' behavior, thus inferring their feelings and intentions. Similarly, Breazeal's robots now learn to imitate the gestures and interaction patterns of their users, making themselves both more liked and more persuasive.

## HOW AND WHEN TO OVERRULE CHOICE

**Sheena Iyengar** SOCIAL PSYCHOLOGY, COLUMBIA BUSINESS SCHOOL

In American culture, "Choice is more than a decision," says Sheena Iyengar, social psychologist at the Columbia Business School. The desire for choice is so strong in our culture that the word's become an adjective describing something good—as in a choice chicken breast.

"At the most basic level, we're born with the desire for choice," says Iyengar. "But we're not born knowing how to make a choice." Instead, culture teaches us how to choose.

To make a broad comparison, American culture teaches people to make choices as individuals, whereas Asian cultures teach people to make choices in consultation with a group. "We can decide what we're going to be, whom we're going to marry, what we're going to eat. But if you go to Japan, what you're going to wear or whom you're going to marry is seen as such an important choice that it's made in consultation with important others," says Iyengar.

In a TED talk (www.Ted.com), Iyengar illustrates this point with the following story. In Japan, Iyengar ordered green tea with sugar. No, the waiter informed her, one does not take sugar with green tea. Iyengar persisted in her desire for sweetened tea and eventually pushed her request up the food chain (as it were) to the restaurant's manager, who informed her that, unfortunately, the kitchen was out of sugar. In that case, Iyengar asked for a cup of coffee instead. The coffee arrived on a saucer with a small pitcher of cream . . . and two packets of sugar.

In this case and in this culture, the decision to embarrass herself with the improper addition of sugar to tea was not Iyengar's alone—it was the group's responsibility to ensure she made what was so certainly (unbeknownst to Iyengar) the best choice.

This was one of the original roles of religion, says Iyengar—to help us inform our decisions with input from our significant prefrontal cortexes, rather than depending on some willy-nilly demand for sugar from our id. In order to conquer this classic self-control problem, we gave God the right to make our choices for us about killing, coveting, watching football on Sunday, and how we prepare and eat many of our foods.

The problem is that we American neo-heathens have the tendency to let our ids run wild, unbound by the wise words of elders or the dictates of proscriptive religion. For example, Iyengar was *this close* to taking sugar in her green tea, and certainly would have if it weren't for the swift and decisive intervention of the restaurant staff. That's a trivial example, but the implications are real. All by your lonesome, without similar wise oversight or religious dictates, how can you be assured of doing the right thing?

One way is to make your own commandments. "We can make

our own rules—look at Confucius," says Iyengar. These may include "I will not have cake in the house," or "If I fail to exercise three times in the course of a week, I will donate twenty dollars to the most egregious cause I can find," or "I will not date my friends' exes, no matter how attractive and charming they may seem." These rules can overrule choice and used enough, they become habit.

This reminds me of eminent physicist and jokester Richard Feynman, who wrote in his autobiography (which remains one of my all-time favorite books) about his decision while studying at MIT to always, from that point forward, eat chocolate ice cream for dessert. In his opinion, this rule eliminated an unwanted nightly choice—what to have for dessert—and left him free to focus on more important matters, like how to pick locks and convince his colleagues that he spoke every possible language.

So ask yourself, Does a choice lead to beneficial/delectable variety, or does it include a clear winner in competition with attractive but detrimental alternatives? If it's the first, keep the choice as a choice. But if it's the second, delegate/relegate it to your rulebook. In a world in which choice knows no cultural or religious bounds, the best rules to live by may be your own.

## Iyengar explored the proverb "Success is

getting what you want, but happiness is wanting what you get," with college seniors entering the job market. Seniors who were maximizers completed exhaustive searches and took jobs paying on average 20 percent more than satisficers, who spent much less time searching and took lower-paying jobs. But satisficers were measurably more satisfied with the jobs they landed—perhaps because maximizers relied more on external than internal measures of success in job seeking, and were more aware of the opportunities that didn't pan out.

## THE COOLEST CARD TRICK EVER

**Ian Stewart** MATHEMATICS, UNIVERSITY OF WARWICK

Ian Stewart, mathematician, prolific puzzle author, and very fun person to chat math with, explains the following best card trick I've ever seen, invented by mathemagician Art Benjamin at Harvey Mudd College.

First, prepare a stack of sixteen cards so that cards 1, 6, 11, and 16 are the four aces. Now deal them facedown in four rows of four. Turn up cards 3, 8, 9, and 14 to make the arrangement shown on page 20.

OK, you're done with the setup and ready to start the trick proper. Ask your dupe to imagine the grid as a sheet of paper and to "fold" it along any straight horizontal or vertical line between cards (as shown on page 21).

Continue "folding" along any lines until you've restacked the cards into one pack of sixteeen. Done right, twelve cards should be facedown and four should be faceup (or vice versa). Of course, the trick seems destined to return the original four faceup cards. And that would be neat. But what's even neater is that no matter

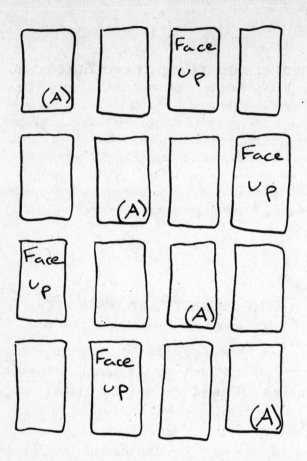

how you fold the grid of sixteen, the four cards that face opposite the others are—wait for it . . . wait for it—the FOUR ACES!

I had to do this trick three times to believe that it actually works. (It does.) Alternatively, I could have listened more closely to Stewart's explanation.

"The number two is very important," he says. Odd and even is a fundamental property of mathematics, and in this trick means that if you flip a card an even number of times, it ends with its original up side facing up. If you flip it an odd number of times, the side that was down faces up. Now imagine arranging this trick's sixteen cards in the pattern of a chessboard, as shown on page 22.

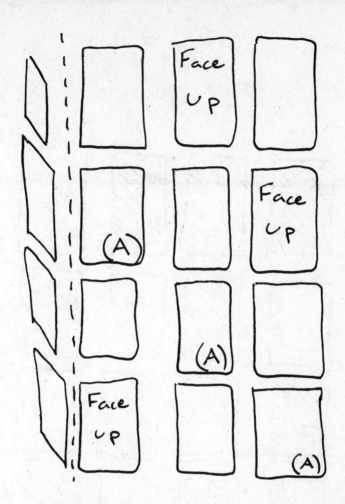

However you fold a chessboard, all the white spaces undergo exactly one more or one fewer flip than the black spaces—one is odd and one is even—and so no matter how you fold chessboard-patterned cards, they will eventually turn into a pile of sixteen cards all facing the same way. Try it. But in this trick, you didn't arrange the cards like a chessboard, did you? No. Exactly four cards in this trick's setup differ from the chessboard pattern. And so these same four cards will point the wrong way in your folded stack.

Of course, these cards are the four aces.

## Ian Stewart studies animal gaits and knows

why a cat always lands on its feet. It's a surprisingly interesting question: A nonrotating, upside-down cat that becomes a nonrotating right-side-up cat seems to break the laws of mechanics. Where does this phantom rotation come from?

"Our first cat couldn't do it," says Stewart, "and my wife tried to train him by holding him upside down above a cushion." Presumably this was for the cat's safety and not purely for entertainment. (Yes, after reviewing a draft of this entry, Stewart confirmed safety was indeed the motive.) What cats other than Stewart's rotationally challenged feline do is use the physics of merry-go-rounds. They twist their back legs in one direction and counterbalance by twisting their front legs in the other direction. Great: equal and opposite.

But here's the trick: The cat pulls in its front legs and extends its back legs, so that its front undergoes more rotation (just like the body-in/body-out speed trick of merry-go-rounds . . . that is, before they were banned from American playgrounds for reasons of safety and pediatric wussification). Then the cat repeats and reverses the operation, extending its front legs, which act as a rotational anchor allowing the constricted back legs to catch up.

Voilà! Without turning Newton in his grave, the cat has turned itself butter-side up! It's a neat trick; you can see it happening in slow motion at *National Geographic*'s website by video searching "cat's nine lives."

## Puzzle #1: Math Is Too Sexy

As you know, math is extremely stylish. Use well-known physics equations to transform "mat = hematic" into "G = uccci."

## HOW TO BET SPORTS

**Wayne Winston** DECISION SCIENCE, INDIANA UNIVERSITY–BLOOMINGTON

Betting seems like you versus the odds, but in fact it's a mano a mano competition between you and a bookie. And unfortunately, the game's rigged: The standard bookie payout is 10/11, meaning that a win pays ten dollars but you pay eleven dollars for a loss. So bookies don't gamble: They set a statistically fair line so that (theoretically) half the money is bet one way and half the money is bet the other. Each loser pays for a winner, and the bookie cleans up on transaction fees.

It's exactly like roulette: Over time, the losers pay the winners and the 2/34 times the ball lands on green, the casino gets paid.

OK, sports betting isn't exactly like roulette. In sports betting, humans set the opening line. For example, bookies predicted the Lakers and Celtics would score a combined 187 total points in Game 7 of the 2010 NBA Finals. You could've bet over or under this total. Or bookies had the Colts winning by 5 points over the Saints in the 2010 Super Bowl. You could've taken Colts -5 or Saints +5.

With the bookies' rake (much different than the sports fundraiser rookies' bake), you have to beat the line more than 52.4 percent of the time to make money. And it comes down to this: Who's got the best kung fu, you or the Wookiees—er . . . bookies?

Wayne Winston, decision science professor at Indiana University, Mark Cuban's former stats guru for the Dallas Mavericks, and author of the book *Mathletics* has especially strong kung fu. (His website, www.WayneWinston.com, is a cornucopia of statistical awesomeness for all things sports.)

One of his nicer attempts at a Shaolin throw down was trying to beat the NBA over/under by including referees' influence on total score. Basically, a ref who calls more fouls creates a higher final score—free throws are easy points and players in foul trouble can't defend as aggressively. This is what former NBA referee (and convicted felon) Tim Donaghy did—he called more fouls or allowed teams to play in order to manipulate the total points scored. But other referees are naturally permissive or restrictive. For example, from 2003 to 2008, when the referee Jim Clark officiated, teams went over the predicted total 221 times and under the predicted total 155 times (more ref data at Covers .com). Bingo! It looks like you can make money! Just bet the over whenever Jim Clark's on the ticket!

But it's not that easy. First, there are three refs on any NBA ticket. Averaging their predicted over/under makes any single ref less powerfully predictive. And you're also counting on the idea that past performance is going to equal future prediction. This is a problem with most mathematical modeling: You look into the past and hope like heck the future's going to be similar. But what if Jim Clark realized he'd been calling games too tight and decided to ref a little differently this year? You'd be out of luck.

As was Wayne Winston, who found refs could help him beat the NBA total over/under more than 50 percent of the time, but not more than the 52.4 percent he needed in order to make money. Unfortunately, he says, bookies in the big three sports—football, baseball, and basketball—are very sophisticated and tend to set very good opening lines—you're as likely to win on one side of the line as you are on the other.

But what happens after a bookie sets a line? Well, it moves based on how people bet. If a basketball over/under started at 187 points and for whatever reason more people bet over, the line might jump to 190 points to encourage equal money on either side. Remember, bookies don't want risk and to avoid it, the over has to match the under.

So when an opening line is released into the wild, it goes from being a statistical system to being a human system. And human systems are beholden to irrationality. For example, take Roger Federer versus Rafael Nadal. You'd have a tough time beating the line in Vegas, but what about in Zurich or in Madrid? People like to bet their home team, and so after a statistically accurate opening line hits the streets in Switzerland, Swiss bookies are likely to see more money bet on Federer. To avoid risk, the line would adjust to encourage bets on Nadal. If Vegas thought Federer/Nadal was an even match, a bet might pay 1:1, but a bookie in Geneva might give people 1:1.2 odds to encourage the otherwise-inclined Swiss to bet Nadal.

When you find inequalities between bookies, what's the best thing to do? Well, one option is arbitrage: You can bet both. Imagine putting $100 on Federer with a Spanish bookie paying 1:1.2, and $100 on Nadal with a Swiss bookie paying 1.2:1. No matter who wins, you lose $100 and win $120. But, Winston points out, differences in bookies are likely to be very small and so only big-money bets earn anything appreciable in arbitrage. And throwing big money at a Swiss bookie might change the line. For example, $100,000 on Nadal in Geneva might balance all the hometown fans betting Federer, swinging the payout back to 1:1. And arbitrage websites are likely to rake a little more than the standard 10/11 of Vegas bookies. That said, it's worth keeping your eyes on rivalries, says Winston. "It's probably a crime to bet Serbia in the World Cup if you're living in Croatia."

Here's another tip that Winston recommends (via an article by the economist Steven Levitt): People like to bet NFL favorites. Bookies discovered this, and if the point spread in a certain game should statistically have been +9, bookies found they could set the line at +10 and people would still bet the favorite. Adjusting the line created slightly more losing bets and thus slightly more money for the bookies. Combine this with a hometown favorite and you have a powerful engine of irrationality—emotion leads fans to overbet hometown favorites, and so you can sometimes find unreasonably good odds if you're willing to bet the opposite: Go for visiting-team underdogs, which are statistically likely to cover the inflated point spread.

But if you're looking for consistent money in sports betting, there's one easy rule: Stay away from data. "Where there's not good information, there's inefficiency. And where there's inefficiency, there's money to be made," says Winston. Like the stock market, there are enough people running enough numbers and placing enough bets on football, basketball, and baseball that it's extremely difficult to find something that no one's thought of. Unless you can find and act on information no one else has (insider trading), you're unlikely to beat the opening line 52.4 percent of the time in the big three sports. (Try cricket, says Winston, because the information and the people evaluating it aren't yet supersaturated.)

## Puzzle #2: **Dr. Stat Cricket Prop**

Dr. Stat (as in, "Get me 1,000 cc of espresso, stat!") specializes in betting on a specific cricket bowler. Bookies know that each time the bowler throws, he has a 1/46 chance of knocking the wickets. So betting that any single throw takes a wicket pays forty-six times your wager for a win (for simplicity's sake we'll assume no bookies' rake). What makes this a special prop is the fact that Dr. Stat (and only Dr. Stat) knows this bowler is a cold-weather specialist. When it's below 15°C this bowler adds 1 percent to every throw's chance of taking the wicket. And so Dr. Stat follows this bowler and follows the weather and bets accordingly. If he lays $1,000 per wager over one hundred cold-weather bets, how much money should he expect to win?

# The Chevalier de Méré was a seventeenth-

century French writer who liked to gamble. Or was he a seventeenth-century French gambler who liked to write? Either way, dupes caught on that de Méré's meat-and-potatoes bet—that he could roll any prenamed number in four tries with a six-sided dice—was stacked against them. And so de Méré went a step further, betting he could roll boxcars (double sixes) in twenty-four tries with two dice. That makes sense: The first seems like 4-in-6 odds and the second seems the same only dressed up to look trickier at 24-in-36 odds.

Only it's not nearly that simple. Over time the bet just didn't seem to pay off. But why? In his book *What's Luck Got to Do with It*, Marlboro College mathematician Joseph Mazur explains the odds. Let's look at the first bet, first.

Rolling one six-sided die four times yields $6^4$, or 1,296, possible patterns—you could roll 2, 2, 2, 2 or 3, 5, 4, 6 or 1, 5, 6, 2 etc. through all 1,296 possible combinations. But in $5^4$ of these, you lose—these are all the ones without the number you want—625 ways to lose in all. But check this out: This means there are $1,296 - 625 = 671$ ways you can win! Trying to roll a specific number with a six-sided die thrown four times, you win more than you lose, and so it's a good bet for the roller. In fact, the bet has a $671 \div 1,296 = 0.52$ probability of paying off.

Now let's look at de Méré's second bet: boxcars in twenty-four tries. There are thirty-six different combinations you can get by rolling two six-sided dice. So if you roll these two dice twenty-four times, you can come up with $36^{24}$ possible combinations; $35^{24}$ of these combinations lose. These are really, really big numbers that you most certainly don't want to see printed here, but take Mazur's word for it, there are slightly more ways to lose than to win—there's only a 0.49 probability of winning the bet. As de Méré ascertained by his dwindling bankroll, that's bad.

But just one more throw tips the probability over 0.50. So there's another bet you can win: boxcars in twenty-five, not twenty-four, tries.

If you insist on betting big sports, Winston recommends prop bets. These are the strange, in-the-moment conjectures that have become all the rage in Vegas. At the 2010 Super Bowl, the line was 5.5 on how many times the Who's Pete Townshend would do his windmill move. And the line was 2.5 on how many times CBS would cut to Kim Kardashian in the stands.

In the case of prop bets, bookie kung fu may not be very strong. If you can specialize in a certain kind of prop, you may be able to outmaneuver the underpowered bookie underling setting the line. Maybe you can ferret out information or design a more accurate model that allows you to know a bookie's line is a little high or a little low on something like the number of times a certain lineman will be shown firing snot rockets, or how many players in a given season will be fined for comments posted to Twitter.

Or you can run your own prop.

Find something interesting that you think you've got a good line on (see above). And then prop it with odds that only you know are slightly off. Bet to win. Can you prop bet the office pool?

## AVOID CONSUMPTION QUICKSAND

**Niro Sivanathan** ORGANIZATIONAL BEHAVIOR,
LONDON BUSINESS SCHOOL

Luxury is a status symbol. You tote a $37,000 Hermès Birkin handbag or drive a million-dollar McLaren F1 to show that you have the wealth to do so. It's a signal that you belong in society—some would say a signal of genetic quality and mate desirability.

At least that's the popular theory.

Niro Sivanathan, professor of organizational behavior at the London Business School, took the theory into the lab to kick the tires. Specifically, he gathered 150 subjects and made them feel bad about themselves. With self-worth thus threatened, subjects said they'd pay more for luxury cars and watches than did subjects allowed to retain their self-worth. Interestingly, though, devalued people's valuation of ordinary goods—ones that had no relation to status—was unaffected.

In Sivanathan's words, "Subjects with low self-esteem sought to heal ego threat with consumption of status goods." If you feel your inherent worth is lacking, you seek to buy your way back to a full self.

So don't shop when you feel crappy about yourself. You'll overspend.

But that's just the start.

In a follow-up study, Sivanathan measured the natural self-esteem of a cross section of American consumers. Then he had subjects read about and suggest a price for a luxury car. As you might guess, people below the average income of $50,233 had significantly lower self-esteem. And these people said they would pay more for the car. "People of low socioeconomic status naturally experience higher levels of threat to self and can be prone to overconsumption of costly, showy goods," says Sivanathan.

This was especially true when credit was involved, which offers less sense of something of yours being transferred to someone else (see this book's entry with Brian Knutson).

And these are the components of what Sivanathan calls "consumption quicksand." "Low self-esteem leads to more consumption on credit, which leads to debt and lower self-esteem, which leads to more consumption," he says. "It's a dangerous positive feedback loop."

Does this quicksand look familiar? If so, you need to break the loop. And Sivanathan knows how.

In a follow-up study, before presenting devalued subjects the chance to splurge on luxury, he encouraged them to reflect on meaningful things—family, health, well-being. Thus recentered, subjects were less likely to overprice luxury goods.

"One reason people consume is to protect the ego," says Sivanathan. But there are other ways to feel good about yourself, including spending time thinking about what's important to you. So in addition to not shopping when you're down, before you walk through a mall-entrance department store, or before you stroll through a car lot on the hunt for a minivan though tempted by a Porsche, take a minute to reflect on your priorities. You'll shield yourself against the mistaken idea that you can buy the missing chunk of your self-esteem.

## Niro Sivanathan also explored corporate

promotion tournaments, which are competitions with rules and contestants that are commonly used to fill open executive positions. "Just like Barry Bonds used steroids to hit more home runs, organizational actors sabotage, bribe, and assume high risk to get ahead," says Sivanathan. As on the show *Survivor*, competitors in these tournaments also start by eliminating the weakest links, but switch strategy at the midpoint to eliminate the strongest competition. "In this way companies can ensure they instate the best manipulator as CEO and not the best businessperson," says Sivanathan.

## HOW TO HANG TEN

**Paul Doherty** PHYSICS, THE EXPLORATORIUM

As a former SoCal transplant, I went surfing thrice in three years, all when gung-ho friends visited with the idea of catching a wave, snapping a pic, and posting something to Facebook that would make friends in the rainy Northwest or icy Northeast feel even worse about their environs than they did already. And after each of these three sessions, I was completely flabbergasted by something I may otherwise never have had the opportunity to notice: how much salt water the human sinus cavities can hold. Really, days later I'd be leaning over to tie my shoes and a stream of water would leak from my nose. I imagined that when the same happened to my friends, now back in some office in Seattle or New York, they used the salt water as a welcome conversation starter about the gnarly waves they shredded off the SoCal coast. Does this kind of thing win dates in the lands of rain and snow, or does leakage from one's sinuses remain repulsive no matter what?

Anyway, the roundabout point is that there are many steps before hanging ten. The first is catching a wave. (Actually, the first is finding the right point in the right wave, but that's another long hydrologic story.) It seems easy: The wave pushes, your board moves, and you stand up. But, "catching a wave is actually an amazingly complex computation," says Paul Doherty, who earned a PhD in physics from MIT and taught at Oakland University before founding the Center for Teaching and Learning at San Francisco's Exploratorium. Beginning surfers paddle and kick furiously. Experienced surfers "know the wave and know their bodies, and can match the wave's speed in a couple strokes," says Doherty. If you're too slow, the wave pushes right past you. Too fast and you're out ahead—and when you slow down from fatigue or to let the wave catch up, you're too slow and it blows right past you.

So watch from the shore as sets roll in—how much paddle power do the best surfers need to match the waves' speed? And try chasing a couple waves after they've rolled past to get a feeling for how hard you have to paddle to keep up with them.

Then there's the matter of where to stand on the board—the genesis of most of the salt water in my sinus cavities.

"Every surfboard has a center of buoyancy," explains Doherty.

This is the point where, if the board was floating in the water, you could push down with your fist and the entire board would sink equally. And a surfer has a center of gravity—the point over which your mass pushes directly down. "If the center of gravity is behind the center of buoyancy, the tail of the surfboard sinks and the nose comes up," says Doherty. This causes the board to decelerate and pull back through the wave. The opposite is my nemesis: As a surfer's center of gravity moves ahead of the board's center of buoyancy, the board's nose digs beneath on-rushing water, sending the would-be surfer tumbling, and compacting salt water deep, deep into the sinus cavities.

But imagine if you get the speed and the centers of mass/buoyancy right. Finally you're standing! You're really standing! "You're on a strange sliding board riding down an up escalator, which also happens to be moving forward laterally," says Doherty. After sliding straight down the wave's face, if you somehow avoid digging the nose of your board into the trough at the wave's base, your momentum takes you far ahead of the wave . . . at which point you decelerate, start to sink, and are flattened by the wave as it catches you, prone and quivering.

This is why you need to turn across the wave. Turn now. Turn before it's too late. The best surfers seem to catch waves having already started their cut across its face. Intermediate or big-wave surfers make a turn near the wave's base and cut back into it. Beginning surfers become intimate with salt water.

But in addition to staying afloat, there's another neat thing about the turn: It allows you to accelerate to faster than wave speed (if you're into that sort of thing). At the bottom of a turn, you push not only against the force of gravity, but against the centripetal force of the turn itself (see this book's entry describing how to take a corner). If you're crouching down at the bottom of the turn and then stand while turning, the energy of your legs pushes against this centripetal force like a skateboarder on a half-pipe, pumping energy into the system, which, in this case, makes you go faster.

And now, rocketing around the wave in arcs and slashes, you have but one task left: hanging ten, or intentionally shifting your center of gravity as far forward as the board allows in order to hang your toes off its front edge in a move that is just as awesome as it is suicidal. Surely holding this position defies the laws of physics?

Doherty points out that the key to hanging ten is not what happens at the (suicidal) front of the board, but what happens at the back. If a surfer is hanging ten, you can be sure the board's tail is no longer buoyant on the surface of the wave. Instead, it's shoved back into the breaking wave like a pry bar under a heavy object, counterbalancing the weight of the surfer up front. This is one reason hanging ten is a move reserved for longboarders—you need a lengthy pry bar for leverage.

Read. Visualize. Learn. As for me, I moved to Colorado.

## A quick search for Paul Doherty finds his

Exploratorium homepage, where he describes about 250 very cool hands-on science experiments, including how to make a lava lamp and how to ollie a skateboard.

**I would maybe have surfed more if it weren't**
for a 2010 article in the *Santa Barbara Independent* describing a
kayaker in the Channel whose boat was mouthed by a great white
shark. But what if my board could protect me from sharks? A
surfboard patent application by inventor Guerry Grune describes its
included locator device and alarm, alerting the user to "large aquatic
animals" as well as a "signal generator configured for transmitting
interference signals to disrupt the electrosensory perception system
of the aquatic animals." That, truly, is awesome.

## HOW TO SELL FOR BIG BUCKS ON EBAY

**Gillian Ku** ORGANIZATIONAL BEHAVIOR, LONDON BUSINESS
SCHOOL

Using an idea imported from Switzerland (where
else?), Chicago and New York invited local artists to decorate fi-
berglass cows. For a set display period, these cows graced city
public areas, after which the bovine couture was auctioned, with
the proceeds going to charity. Toronto did moose. Boston did cod.
St. Paul did Snoopys.

In addition to stuffing cash in city coffers and (presumably) providing mad backyard kitsch for winning bidders, the Cow Parade
program created huge amounts of auction data. How do you sell
a painted version of a city's iconic animal for the biggest possible bucks? You put bidders in a live setting, ratchet up the time
pressure, and create competition. The more emotional arousal
you can create in bidders, the higher the eventual selling price.
Simply, when people lose their heads, they reach for their wallets.

Gillian Ku, assistant professor of organizational behavior at the

London Business School, wondered if the same would be true on eBay. She got data from (where else?) cows. Specifically, from an eBay seller with the screen name Browncow, who was selling Tommy Bahama shirts. "He was manipulating whether shirts had straightforward descriptions or puffed descriptions," says Ku—you know, descriptions that promise the most amazing shirt ever that hot strangers will want to rip from your body!!!! That's puffery. And it helped sell Tommy Bahama shirts.

But only if a couple other things were true too. One of these factors was starting price. And here's where it starts to get interesting.

Gillian Ku found that eBay starting prices throw conventional economics on its ear. "It should be all about anchoring," she says—meaning that a high starting price should signal an item's worth and lead to a higher selling price. This is what Steve Jobs did when he anchored the price of an iPhone at $599, making the on-sale price of $299 look like a steal. "But what we found on eBay is that low starting prices, not high prices, led to a higher selling price."

But (again), only if a couple other things were true too.

If an auction was misspelled, a higher starting price provided the anchor that economics expects—higher starting price equals higher ending price. And having a reserve price nixed the effect of a low start.

And by this time, Ku started to see a pattern: "It's all about traffic," she says. A low starting price decreases barriers to entry. Having more entrants increases the chances of hooking a serious one. And even bidders who didn't mean to be serious can get sucked into an escalation of commitment by investing time in bidding and rebidding while the price is still low. And finally, high auction traffic in the form of page views and number of bids is another way to signal value—certainly it has high worth because, well, look at all the people who've been here! (It's like evaluating a book's worth based on its number of online reviews—hint, hint.)

Let's be clear: With little traffic, it's best to anchor expectations to a high starting price and list the item in an accurate, business-like way. If you're going to doom yourself to pitiful traffic by misspelling your item, you'd better hope someone clicks BUY IT NOW. Same if you're listing an item that's so niche, it's inconceivable that many people would give it a look. But if you've got a shot at an auction with more widespread appeal, create traffic with a low starting price, no reserve, and high puffery. This is the competitive arousal model. In cities it created spotted-cow fever, and on eBay it means higher selling prices.

## Ku and co found the opposite to be true of

negotiations: A high starting price for a firm up for acquisition, salary negotiation, or asking price of a used car leads to a higher final agreement price. The essential difference is the number of possible bidders—in a negotiation, you're only going to have a few buyers, so your best bet is to anchor expectations to a high opening price.

### SHOULD YOU MULTITASK?
**David Strayer** COGNITIVE SCIENCE, UNIVERSITY OF UTAH

I don't multitask. Or, I do it so badly that it quickly devolves into a massive cluster of tangled badness with me standing baffled at its center. This frustrates my wife to no end. She can balance on a beach ball while writing things in her calendar, listening to Radio Lab, text-messaging, and juggling chain saws (it's a neat trick—and also kind of hot). I hold that monotasking allows me to get a string of things done right, one at a time. Kristi thinks that multitasking is a prerequisite for inclusion in post–Stone Age society and that monotaskers should be rounded up and reprogrammed at underground government facilities.

The question is, Should I strive for less inept sessions of multitasking, or should I just give it up completely?

David Strayer, director of the applied cognition lab at the University of Utah, studies multitasking in the fertile realm of distracted driving and found that, "ninety-eight percent of people can't multitask—they don't do either task as well." But here's the interesting part: 2 percent of people can juggle without dropping a ball or, indeed, without any ball even sailing less high—they show no ill effects from multitasking. Strayer calls these people supertaskers. "The question we had," says Strayer, "is, Who are these people?"

To find out, he put supertaskers through a battery of tests, including neuroimaging and genetic evaluation. And he found that, sure enough, the very structure of the supertasker brain looks different than those of 98 percent of us. "These brain regions that differentiate supertaskers from the rest of the population are the same regions that are most different between humans and nonhuman primates," says Strayer. In other words, the brains of supertaskers are just that much further away from those of apes, "the leading edge of evolution," says Strayer. Specifically, "Certain parts of the frontal cortex are recruited in an interesting way," says Strayer. In fact, these areas show less activity when multitasking than do the same areas in normal, human, mammalian, nonalien-overlord brains like mine.

And it's distinct—you either efficiently recruit this region or you don't. You're either a supertasker or you're not. You're either human like me, or a supertasking, blood-drinking, shape-shifting, reptilian alien like my wife.

If you're a supertasker, you know it. Please feel free to continue reading this book while you drive one-handed and one-eyed down the freeway. But if you're not a supertasker, the overwhelming message of science is this: Just give it up already! By multitasking, you do everything less well. Instead, if you want to get the most done right, design your life to monotask. Your brain will thank you for it.

## "Writers from Muir to Abbey have talked

about the benefits of getting into nature," says Strayer, "but we haven't studied it at a neuroscience level until now."

This is attention restoration theory, based partly on the idea that refraining from multitasking in a text-rich environment might detox, rest, and restore fried neurons in the frontal lobe. While Strayer is quick to say that more research is needed, he points out that from a large pool of anecdotal evidence, "After three days, you start to experience radically different thoughts." (For an example, video search "double rainbow.")

And so there may be hope for me, and by extension all of humanity, yet. If you find your frontal lobe freaking out, head for the hills as quickly as possible. You'll meet me on the way. And if you do, please be alert because I'm likely texting and may swerve dangerously.

## Puzzle #3: **Multitasking Mix and Match**

You have 20 minutes before you need to leave for work, and nine things to accomplish before you go, each of which takes the specified amount of time: brush your teeth (2 min), get dressed (5 min), drink coffee (5 min), make breakfast (5 min), eat breakfast (8 min), check headlines (2 min), read things you were supposed to read for work (5 min), clean (4 min), and fret aimlessly (4 min). Obviously you'll need to multitask. But there are some things that don't go well together—for example, you can't drink coffee or eat breakfast while brushing your teeth. Likewise, you can't eat breakfast until you make it, and can't do either (nor can you brush your teeth) while getting dressed, and aimless fretting can take place only while getting dressed or brushing your teeth. Imagining you can only do a maximum of two things at once, in what order should you complete these six tasks?

### TEACH YOUR TODDLER PERFECT PITCH

**Diana Deutsch** AUDITORY PSYCHOLOGY, UNIVERSITY OF CALIFORNIA–SAN DIEGO

Being a music prodigy would be totally awesome because it would nix the need to converse, cook, flirt, provide, smolder, or otherwise prove your sexiness—you could simply strum your way into your mate's heart.

While studies have shown that becoming a virtuoso is similar to learning a trade—ten years including ten thousand hours of practice seems to do the trick—there's a shortcut to musical maestrosity, allowing you to spend the saved time snogging: Simply be born with perfect pitch, the seemingly innate ability to hear a note and name it. Once you truly hear music, externalizing it through an instrument is as simple as learning to type (mostly . . .).

But if you had perfect pitch, you'd know it, if for no other reason than people whistling in the airport would sound physically, painfully, out of tune. (This according to my friend Ariel, who was an orchestral recorder prodigy before switching to heavy-metal guitar in college and environmental architecture after.) And until recently, experts thought that that was it—at birth, you can hold a note in your mind's ear or you can't. If you're born without the gift, the theory went, your only hope is the consolation prize of painstakingly training relative pitch. For example, learning that the "way up high" leap in "Over the Rainbow" is the interval of a major sixth, as is the iconic leap in the Miles Davis tune "All Blues." Likewise, the first interval in "Twinkle, Twinkle, Little Star" is a perfect fifth. And based on learning these leaps, you can learn to deduce any note on the keyboard given a starting point. In university music programs around the world, a teacher plunks a note, names it, then plunks another note, and students who have successfully trained their relative pitch can name the second note.

But what about naming the first note? What about perfect pitch? What about that shortcut to limitless snogging?

Diana Deutsch, UCSD prof and president of the Society for Music Perception and Cognition, thinks perfect pitch can be trained—but only if you start early.

In part, she bases this opinion on an illusion.

In music, a tritone describes the interval that splits an octave exactly in half. For example, C and F# form the interval of a tritone, and so do the notes D and G#. The interval was banned during the Inquisition as the *diabolus in musica* (the devil in music). Today it starts *The Simpsons* and makes Danny Elfman scores of Tim Burton movies immediately recognizable. Now imagine alternating C and F#, like the siren on a British ambulance. Really, you wouldn't know if the pattern is ascending (C-F#, repeat) or descending (F#-C, repeat).

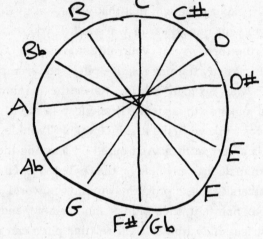

**Chromatic Scale w/ tritones**

But here's the thing: You do know. Every note has a companion that's exactly half an octave away, and depending on which tritone is played, you perceive the interval as either descending or ascending. And you don't ever switch. It's fixed. Deutsch discovered this tritone paradox and calls it "an implicit form of perfect pitch." Somehow, some way, we all fix notes and hold them in our minds.

So why doesn't the universal ability to hold abstract pitches allow us all to know note names when we hear them? Why—dammit—can't we all be prodigies!

Deutsch found that fixed pitch does, in fact, allow perfect pitch . . . but only in certain cultures.

Sure, an individual American's perception of the tritone paradox is fixed—maybe you hear C-F#-C-F# as an ascending pattern—

but as a culture, Americans may each hear tritones differently. Your friend Barb may hear C-F#-C-F# as a descending pattern. But here's the interesting bit: In Vietnam, the vast majority of the population hears tritone paradoxes in the same way—they're fixed not only on an individual, but on a cultural level.

Blame it on language, says Deutsch. In Vietnamese and other tonal languages, a high "ma" can mean something very different than a low "ma," and so infants learn very early to pair fixed tones with fixed meanings. Later, it's easy to use this same brain mechanism to pair tones with note names like A, B, and C. Deutsch explored data from the Singapore Conservatory and other Asian music schools, and found that—sure enough—the incidence of perfect pitch is much higher in speakers of tonal languages.

Deutsch thinks it might be possible to create a similar mechanism in English speakers. "If your son or daughter has a keyboard at home, use stickers to label the notes with whatever symbols they understand first." If your child recognizes barnyard animals or pictures of family members or colors before he or she recognizes letters, label the keyboard with animal, family, or color stickers. (All G's get a cow, all F's get a pig, etc.) This encourages your budding Beethoven to pair tone with meaning—any meaning works!—which you can then switch to note names once your child knows his or her letters.

It's too late for you—"It seems as if the window for creating this pairing is closed by about age four," says Deutsch—but perhaps early action can allow your progeny to be prodigy.

**You can hear examples of the tritone paradox**
and more cool auditory illusions at Diana Deutsch's faculty
homepage: deutsch.ucsd.edu.

**You know how to pull a song out of your music**
library that rocks or soothes. And you know about services like the
Internet radio station Pandora or the iTunes "Genius" feature that
similarly recommend new music. But what about Zeppelin's "Stairway
to Heaven," or other songs that first soothe and then rock, or vice
versa, or ping-pong moods from verse to chorus? Drexel University's
Youngmoo Kim created an online game, MoodSwings, (music.ece
.drexel.edu/mssp) to gather real-time data about songs. As you listen
to a song, you move your cursor around quadrants labeled with
emotions and for the time your cursor overlaps the areas most chosen
by previous users, you rack up points. "Imagine you feel like crap but
want to be uplifted," says Kim. With your help, MoodSwings will soon
know which songs fit the desired mood trajectory.

## HOW TO AGREE
## (AND WHY NEGOTIATIONS FAIL)

**George Loewenstein** BEHAVIORAL ECONOMICS,
CARNEGIE MELLON UNIVERSITY

Why do people have such a hard time reaching a compromise?
Blame fairness.

That's the message of behavioral economist George Loewenstein
of Carnegie Mellon University. In many types of negotiations, he
says, "People aren't trying to get the maximum payoff, they're

just trying to get what they see as fair." And if there's wiggle room in what's fair, parties on opposing sides are likely to wiggle toward opinions of fairness that are personally beneficial, eventually entrenching like four-hundred-pound sumo wrestlers staring each other down across the ring.

Loewenstein offers the following example: Imagine you and I are splitting twenty poker chips. When all's said and done, each chip you're holding will be worth five dollars and each chip I'm holding will be worth twenty dollars (ha!). Now we have to negotiate how to split the twenty chips.

What do you think is fair? Maybe you propose keeping sixteen chips and giving me four. That way, we each get eighty dollars. That's fair.

But wait—the chips are worth more to me than they are to you! What are you going to do with a measly eighty dollars? If I keep all the chips I'll have four hundred dollars. Now that's worth something. Certainly you can see it's better to squeeze the most out of the system, even if you don't happen to be the beneficiary this time, right?

This is an example of a self-serving bias—your idea of fairness is influenced by what's best for you. But there's still hope for agreement. If the top range of my fairness overlaps the bottom range of your fairness, there's shared territory for a deal. But if I'm only willing to give eight chips max, and you're only willing to accept twelve chips min, then we're at loggerheads. In this case, Loewenstein explains, "People are frequently willing to incur a loss rather than take what they see as an unfair payoff."

In other words, we'd rather burn money than share with a cheater. No deal.

To see if self-serving bias jumps the confines of abstract poker chip games, Loewenstein and his colleague Linda Babcock sent letters to all the school board presidents (on one side) and heads of teachers' unions (on the other) in Pennsylvania. The letters asked the boards or unions to make a fair list of the nearby towns that are comparable to their own—like valuing a house, salaries in comparable districts help negotiators set teacher salaries in a target district. Loewenstein and Babcock found that the school board heads consistently listed towns with low teacher salaries, while the heads of teachers' unions consistently listed towns with high teacher salaries.

Which towns were fairly comparable? Well, whichever ones allowed school board presidents to propose lower salaries or union heads to propose higher ones. And generating lists with little overlap was a strong predictor of an eventual strike.

So if you believe you're on the fair side of the fence and I believe I'm on the other fair side of the fence, and between these fences is a gaping demilitarized zone, what's the negotiation solution? "Well," says Loewenstein, "we did a lot of research trying to debias it." How can you remove this pesky self-serving bias? Nix writing an essay about the other side's point of view. It didn't work. Having both sides list the holes in their own case helped a bit.

But check this out: Rather than trying to diffuse self-serving bias, Loewenstein recommends using it to create a solution—the stronger the bias, the better. That's because a strong bias can blind combatants to the idea that a third party could see it any way but their own.

It's not just that I would like at least eight poker chips, but that I believe the abstract idea of fairness is certain to award me at least these eight chips. And you're equally certain you'll get at least the twelve chips at the bottom end of your fairness scale. So we're both happy to let a fair third party make the call, both blithely confident that the outcome will be the one we want. Self-serving bias makes us both likely to agree to arbitration.

When you notice a demilitarized zone between the two fences of entrenched parties, rather than trying to nudge these fences closer together—toward the shared space of agreement—let them stand apart. And pick an arbitrator to split the difference. We're likely to be equally surprised when this impartial third party awards us ten chips each, but you gotta admit it's fair.

## George Loewenstein explored the difference

between how much people want something and then how much they like it once they get it. With drugs, people almost universally want them more than they end up liking them. With sex, it can be the other way around: People can end up liking sex more than they initially wanted it, especially as both men and women get older, and with more time in a relationship.

### WIN THE LOTTERY

**Skip Garibaldi** MATHEMATICS, EMORY UNIVERSITY

One second you're standing at the 7-Eleven checkout counter with a Slim Jim and a Styrofoam cup of syrupy hazelnut espresso and the next second—BAM!—you're a gazillionaire! Hello château on the French Riviera!

That's the lottery.

The lottery's also a stack of one-dollar slips of toilet paper, which eventually leave you unable to afford Slim Jims and gas station coffee.

Assuming drawings actually are random, science can't help you pick the winning numbers. But, that said, some fiendishly simple stats can make the dollar you put down likely to win back that dollar and more. Here's how.

"Find a drawing in which the jackpot is unusually large and

the number of tickets is unusually low," says Emory mathematician Skip Garibaldi. The March 6, 2007, Mega Millions drawing reached a record $390 million; 212 million tickets were sold. Elaine and Barry Messner, of New Jersey, split the pot with truck driver Eddie Nabors, of Dalton, Georgia, who, when asked what he would do with the money famously said, "I'm going to fish."

But it was a bad bet.

Despite the massive prize, the huge number of tickets sold meant that a dollar spent on this lottery returned only $0.74 (versus $0.95 for roulette). In fact, Mega Millions and Powerball have never once been a good bet: Extreme jackpots generate extreme ticket sales, increasing the chance of a split pot—the average return on a one-dollar Mega Millions ticket is only about $0.55.

"But state lotteries don't get the same kind of press," says Skip. In rare cases, a state lottery jackpot will roll over a couple times without jacking ticket sales.

Here's the formula for finding a good lottery bet: Look for an after-tax, cash value of the jackpot that exceeds 0.8 times the odds against you, and in which the number of tickets sold remains less than one-fifth this jackpot. If this makes absolutely no sense or if you happen to be away from your spreadsheets, here's how to approximate the formula: Look for a jackpot that's rolled over at least five times and that remains below $40 million. It's a good bet that it's a good bet. And by a good bet, I mean a positive expected rate of return—over time, a dollar invested returns more than a dollar. To wit: a $1.00 ticket for the March 7, 2007, Lotto Texas drawing had an expected rate of return of $1.30. That rocks.

Take a minute to scroll through online lottery listings till you find one that meets the criteria for a good bet.

OK, OK, so you finally found one—what now?

Pick the most unpopular numbers, that's what. By playing unpopular numbers you won't win any more or less often, but you'll less often split the pot with other winners.

Don't pick the number one. It's on about 15 percent of all tickets. Similarly, avoid lucky numbers 7, 13, 23, 32, 42, and 48. Better are 26, 34, 44, 45, and especially overlooked number 46. Avoid any recognizable pattern, but give slight preference to numbers at the edge of the ticket, which are underused. In mathematical terms, picking a unique ticket makes the jackpot look bigger.

If players in a 1995 UK National Lottery drawing had played unpopular numbers, they might've avoided splitting a £16 million pot 133 ways. That's right—133 people picked the numbers 7, 17, 23, 32, 38, 42, and 48, all straight down the ticket's central column. Each got £120,000. Play smart over enough drawings, and eventually you'll win more than you spend. That is, if you don't run out of money first.

## If you want to get deeper into the lottery
thing, Garibaldi has accessible and not-so-accessible versions of the paper linked from his faculty bio.

## Once you win the lottery, you'll certainly
have more time to look deep into your conversation partner's eyes and know her true feelings, right? Wrong. In a series of studies at the University of California–San Francisco researchers found that people of low socioeconomic status were better than wealthier subjects at recognizing and interpreting others' emotions, including being better at predicting emotion from snapshots of eyes.

# IMAGINE EATING TO EAT LESS

**Carey Morewedge** DECISION SCIENCE,
CARNEGIE MELLON UNIVERSITY

Imagine M&M's. There's the crinkle of the bag, the tinkling sound of hard shells shifting inside; when you pop one in your mouth, a brief hint of sweetness as the shell starts to dissolve, followed by the meaty burst of chocolate. Do you let the shell melt slowly or do you crunch immediately into the center?

I bet your mouth is watering (mine is . . .). I bet you'd really like an M&M right about now (I do). And according to Carey Morewedge, decision science professor at Carnegie Mellon University, you should. "There's a long history of research showing that cues of desired stimulants—the smell or the thought of steak or cigarettes—sensitizes you to the stimulus," he says. A whiff or a remembrance makes you want it more.

Sure enough, when Morewedge had subjects imagine moving M&M's from one bowl to another, they then ate more M&M's from a bowl he gave them to snack on. They were sensitized—primed and ready to munch.

But when Morewedge had subjects imagine actually eating the M&M's, they then ate fewer when given the chance. The more candy subjects imagined eating, the less they actually ate. The same was true of cheddar cheese squares—subjects who imagined eating more actually ate fewer.

The lesson here is obvious. If you imagine consuming any specific food, you can inoculate yourself against gorging on it in real life.

Try imagining eating potato chips before sitting down with a bag to watch football. Or imagine eating Cherry Garcia before touring the Ben & Jerry's factory. Or chocolate chip cookies while baking them for your kids. In all cases, you'll be likely to eat less once temptation is at hand.

Is this because imagining eating makes you feel full?

To test this, Morewedge had subjects imagine eating either M&M's or cheese, and then offered them a cheese bowl. Only the subjects who imagined eating cheese ate fewer squares. So it's not a phantom feeling of fullness that keeps you from overindulging, it's that—as opposed to just cuing the food, which sensitizes you to it—imagining eating a food habituates you to it. One piece of cake is great, two is good, three is OK, but four is bad. And imagining you've already had a couple slices means that when you actually start eating, you're further into the downward trajectory of enjoyment.

"But the effect is undone when you're exposed to a different stimulus," says Morewedge. So if you're going to be tempted by potato chips you have to imagine chips. If it's ice-cream-and-movie night, you have to specifically imagine eating ice cream. If you go down the list of goodies at an upcoming Thanksgiving meal, when you imagine eating yams, you will overwrite the inoculation of having previously imagined eating stuffing.

But if you can predict a tempting food, imagine eating it—the more the better. Then when it's there in front of you, you'll eat less.

## Speaking of the health benefits of the mind,

a study at Harvard Medical School found that even when patients were explicitly told the drugs they were taking were placebos, devoid of active ingredients (in fact, the pill bottles were labeled PLACEBO), their health improvements far outstripped peers given no sugar pills. While more research is needed, the study's authors suggest that the "medical ritual" of taking pills—any pills—might be to blame.

## USE RUBBER BANDS TO BE A RADICAL ROCK CLIMBER

**Hugh Herr** BIOMECHATRONICS, MASSACHUSETTS INSTITUTE OF TECHNOLOGY

Believe it or not, Hugh Herr is this book's lone representative of the Sports Hall of Fame. A prodigy rock climber, Herr lost both lower legs to frostbite, the result of three nights in -20°F temps stranded in a blizzard on Mt. Washington. After rehab, Herr built prosthetic feet and hopped back on the rock, not in an I-still-want-to-climb-even-though-I-really-can't kind of way, but with the intent of picking up where he left off—on a tear through the country's hardest climbs. He showed up at the steep granite cliffs of Index, Washington, with tiny wedges of rubber-covered steel attached to metal tubing, which he planned to use as "feet" on the notorious overhanging crack City Park, which despite a bevy of able-bodied suitors had previously seen only one ascent.

Three days later, Herr styled it. And he did so partly because his prosthetic feet let him do something that ordinary climbers couldn't—wedge his "toes" into the viciously thin crack in order to take weight off his arms.

Not only had his prosthetics allowed him to perform as well as other humans, they made him superhuman. And it's this lack of human-as-end-goal approach that Herr brings to his work at MIT. "About half the work we do is augmentative," says Herr, meaning that while he's designed some of the world's best replacement legs and feet, he also designs mechanics to be worn on healthy humans. These are the exoskeletons that futurists and sci-fi buffs have imagined at least since 1963 when the character Iron Man debuted in *Tales of Suspense #39*. Imagine being able to run for miles with a hundred-pound backpack or jump from a two-story building. Herr's exoskeletons will make both possible.

But even more awesome is a project that brings Herr's interests full circle. "We're in the process of building a spider suit that augments the human ability to climb," says Herr. Basically, the suit will be a soft and flexible second skin jacket, with strong latex webs at the joints. These webs hold the suit and thus the arms, hands, and fingers in a fully flexed position—as at the apex of a pull-up. "It's cool 'cause there's no power source," says Herr. Instead, the suit makes use of muscle power that's generally unused while climbing—your pushing muscles. To extend your arms above your head, you push to stretch these latex webs, and when you pull down, the bands contract to pull with you. "The bicycle was invented, and now we have the sport of cycling," says Herr, "and just like that, someday we'll have a new sport of power climbing or augmented running. Augmentative technology will allow humans to do things we haven't even imagined yet."

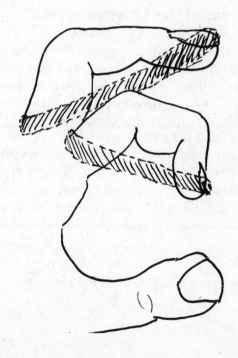

If you want a preview, as I most certainly did, try the following: Connect short lengths of surgical tubing from both shoulders to both hands so that you can only raise your arms with effort. Then stretch strong rubber bands from each fingernail to the base of each finger, as shown on page 53. The tricky part is keeping the bands in place, which I did with the liberal application of Super Glue (in the name of science!). Though only a rough prototype and admittedly pretty cumbersome, the bands made me immediately able to chuck mad dynos (translation: pull from hold to hold, not lob angry diplodocuses) at the climbing gym.

I'm sure that at least the gathered muscle-bound, knuckle-dragging college students thought it was pretty awesome.

## On display at the Museum of Natural History

is a 4' × 11' swatch of 96-thread-count spider silk cloth—as strong as steel and much tougher. It represents the contribution of more than one million female golden orb spiders, which were milked by hand in Madagascar. That's the problem with spider silk—spiders don't spin cocoons and they eat only live food, and so farming them for silk is nearly impossible. Which is why it's especially exciting that scientists from Notre Dame and the University of Wyoming have inserted spider genes into silkworms. Already the worms are producing stronger, softer fabric than any previous silkworms. In addition to textile applications (including bulletproof vests), researchers hope their new hybrid silk will someday replace cadaver-derived artificial tendons.

## DECOUPLING "COMFORT" AND "FOOD"

**Mark Wilson** PSYCHOBIOLOGY, YERKES NATIONAL
PRIMATE RESEARCH CENTER

"It's like you need X amount of good feeling in the course of existence and you can get it in different ways," says Mark Wilson, psychobiologist at Emory University and Yerkes National Primate Research Center. One way monkeys in his lab get this good feeling is through dominance in the social hierarchy. It feels good to be top rhesus.

But there's another way.

Wilson gave his monkeys banana-flavored pellets, much richer in sugars than their normal diet. As you'd expect, all monkeys liked the banana pellets—I mean, who wouldn't? But check this out: Monkeys at the top of the social hierarchy regulated banana pellets to keep their caloric intake roughly similar to that of their standard diet.

Subordinate monkeys didn't. They binged.

Specifically, while the dominant monkeys might opportunistically snack on pellets during the day, subordinate monkeys stayed up late into the night, stuffing their faces with sugary goodness. (Midnight ice cream, anyone?)

The explanation Wilson favors is that a sugary diet excites dopamine pathways in the brain. Dominant monkeys already get their dopamine fix from social interactions, while subordinate monkeys get none. So we're back to "X amount of a good feeling"—subordinate monkeys eat their way to the dopamine release that dominant monkeys get naturally.

Going human, Wilson posits that, "If you're much less than X, you're much more prone to addictions of all sorts—food, exercise, shopping, gambling, psychostimulants."

It's easy to see how this applies to something like diet. "It's the notion my grandmother talked to me about," says Wilson, "comfort food." The trick in losing weight is to find comfort another way—without the food. Simply, if you make your life happier, you'll be less driven to overeat.

## A survey of 30,816 Europeans found that

Danes are happiest and Bulgarians the least happy. Factors most responsible for happiness were younger age, satisfaction with household income, being employed, high community trust, and religious conviction. However, an unrelated study found that while short-term happiness rises and falls with a country's economy, long-term happiness has nothing to do with your country's wealth.

## WRING AN EXTRA $20 OUT OF A USED CAR

**Devin Pope** BEHAVIORAL SCIENCE, UNIVERSITY OF CHICAGO BOOTH SCHOOL OF BUSINESS

Ted Williams entered the final two games of the 1941 season batting .39955. If he'd sat them out, the average would've been rounded up to .400, making him the first (and still the only) MLB player to bat the milestone. Manager Joe Cronin told Williams the decision to play and risk it or simply sit on the record was up to Williams, who famously said, "If I can't hit .400 all the way, I don't deserve it." He went six for eight in the season-ending double-header and finished with a .406 batting average.

"But many players make the other choice," says Devin Pope, behavioral scientist at the University of Chicago's Booth School of Business. Though no one's yet had the good fortune to confront the decision while camped at .400, many players have entered their last at bat with a .300 average. "More than 30 percent of those batters send in a pinch hitter," says Pope. On the flip side of the .300 fence, Pope explains that batters at .299 never send in pinch hitters—and they never walk. For better or for worse, players who go into their final at-bat with a .299 average swing, trying to get the hit that puts them over the .300 hump.

The same is true of the diamond market. "You can't find any .99-carat diamonds," says Pope. Dealers know their customers will pay significantly more for a 1-carat diamond than they would for a .99-carat one, and so cut the stones accordingly.

So too with SAT scores. If a student scores xx90—like 1,590 or 1,690—they're about 20 percent more likely to retake the test than someone who scored lower in the last two digits. Next time—certainly—they'll hit that next hundred-point marker!

Thanks to our irrational human brains, we value these milestones—a .300 hitter, a 1-carat diamond, an 1,800 SAT score—disproportionately more than if they were just a tick lower. This means that batters have incentive to ride the pine at .300 or swing for a single at .299, trying to get to the high side of a value fence and thus likely earn a higher salary after the next contract negotiation. Conversely, advertisers exploit the low side of the value fence, pricing a gallon of milk at $3.99 and a car at $19,995. To our brains, the savings looks much larger than it actually is.

This also means that every time your car's odometer gains a digit in the hundreds spot, it loses twenty dollars in resale value. Devin Pope showed that a car with 50,799 miles is worth twenty dollars more than a car with 50,800 miles. That's an expensive mile. But a car with 50,899 miles is still worth as much as it was at 50,800. In respect to miles, your car doesn't lose value smoothly—it ratchets downward with the hundreds digit.

The effect is a little stronger when you tick a thousand miles. That'll cost you $250. But, "while all the 10,000-mile marks were huge," says Pope, "it seemed like people caught on to the

100,000-mile game." Even with the human mind's inability to see $3.99 milk as $4.00, with used cars, it's too obvious that a seller is trying to unload a car just before it charts 100,000 miles, so the price starts dropping at about 99,900.

So if you're buying a car, your best deals will be just after it's hit a round number—following 50,000 or 100,000 is ideal. And if you're selling, make sure you do it before the car reaches those milestones that make it seem old. If that looming milestone is the big 100,000, sell it before 99,900.

Or at least before the odometer's last two digits roll from 99 to 100. It'll bring an extra twenty dollars.

## University of Washington accounting

researcher Dave Burgstahler found that businesses act very much like baseball players—if a company's camped just below the yearly break-even point, or an influential analyst's earnings prediction, or last year's profits, it'll swing for that fence. Unfortunately, this tendency also creates an incentive to indulge in "creative" accounting, similar to a ballplayer's morally questionable decision to send in a pinch hitter when batting .300.

## HAPPINESS, WHY LAWYERS DON'T VOLUNTEER, AND HOW TO FUND A NONPROFIT

**Sanford DeVoe** ORGANIZATIONAL BEHAVIOR, UNIVERSITY OF TORONTO ROTMAN SCHOOL OF MANAGEMENT

Is happiness having the time to listen to milkmaids yodeling, smell the much-honored roses, and watch kittens doing whatever they do that everyone finds so ungodly cute on YouTube? Or is it cold, hard cash that lights your happiness lamp?

It depends on whether you're paid a salary or by the hour.

Sanford DeVoe, professor of organizational behavior at Rotman School of Management in Toronto, found that "people who think of time as money are more likely to rely on how much they earn when evaluating what it means to be happy." But this doesn't mean that the salaried are necessarily happier. Being paid handsomely by the hour makes you happier than if you'd earned the same amount from a salaried position. But if you're paid peanuts, it's better not to have your nose rubbed in the butter by highlighting a paltry hourly pay—you'd be better off salaried.

If you're a business owner, there's application here: Because time is money to those paid hourly, DeVoe found that hourly workers are much more likely to give up free time to earn more money. On the other hand, salaried workers take their vacations.

But here's a cool twist: Because hourly versus salaried pay affects how much you value your time, it also affects how you choose to spend your time. "Even outside lawyer jokes, this explains why lawyers don't volunteer," says DeVoe. He asked seniors at Stanford Law how many hours a week they volunteered, and then followed these greenhorn lawyers as they left school and got jobs in which they were either salaried or billed by the hour. After six months, he found their behaviors had changed—while both groups volunteered a bit less (presumably they were busier . . . or across the board more cynical), those who billed by the hour cut their volunteer hours more drastically than those who were salaried. Across professions and income, people paid hourly are 36 percent less likely to volunteer than those who are salaried.

In a follow-up, DeVoe asked the now battle-tested lawyers if they'd be more likely to volunteer an hour of their time at a charity of their choice, or if they'd rather write a check to the same charity for the money they made working for one hour. You guessed it: The salaried lawyers volunteered time, while the bill-by-the-hour lawyers wrote checks.

"There's a lot of personal utility you get from volunteering," says DeVoe, "but making lawyers aware of their hourly rate made them see volunteering as a purely economic decision, outside any personal utility factors."

Here's the obvious significance to your small community non-profit: If you can guess how your prospective donors are paid, you can decide what to ask for. Should you ask for volunteer hours or should you ask for cash?

If you're hoping for the cash, take another tip from DeVoe. He had salaried people calculate their hourly rate before exploring their willingness to give money or hours. Sure enough—even the previously time-giving can be tricked into coughing up the cash by bringing time-is-money to the forefront of their minds.

So if your nonprofit needs cash (not volunteer hours), consider a donation flyer with a chart showing how common salaries convert to dollars-per-hour. Putting hourly wage at the top of donors' minds should help make them cough up the cash.

## DeVoe and collaborator Chen-Bo Zhong
showed that even subconscious exposure to fast-food symbols made people read faster and reduced their willingness to save money for a rainy day. In short, priming with fast-food symbols makes people impatient.

**A Gallup survey of 153 countries found that a** country's overall happiness was a better predictor of its population's charitable giving than was wealth. In overall giving, the United States ranks sixth, behind (in order) Australia, New Zealand, Ireland, Canada, and Switzerland. Interestingly, while people in poorer countries were less likely to give money, they were more likely than people in most richer nations to help strangers, with Liberians being the world's most stranger-friendly. In the United States, 60 percent of people had given money in the past month, 39 percent had donated time, and 65 percent had helped a stranger.

## THE SCIENCE OF SPEED DATING

**Paul Eastwick and Eli Finkel** SOCIAL PSYCHOLOGY, TEXAS A&M UNIVERSITY, NORTHWESTERN UNIVERSITY

Social networking sites keep you connected with people you swapped sandwiches with in the third grade. Online forums let you argue about DIY lightsaber design with people on the other side of the world. And online dating sites offer the immediate ability to meet hundreds of local singles, some of whom are allowed to live near elementary schools.

But is it just me, or has it gotten much, much harder to meet people in the real world? Earbuds block even the nicety of "Hey, can I get a spot?" at the gym. iPhone Scrabble keeps people from accidentally meeting gazes across a crowded restaurant. And it's become impossible to tell the schizophrenic from those simply chatting on their cell via hidden mike.

Thank God for speed dating.

True, it's three minutes of resume-forward romance, but at least it's face-to-face, right? And being face-to-face suddenly changes speed dating from a cold comparison of data to a situation beholden to interpersonal psychology. Simply, there are things you can do in person to land a mate that are far beyond the reach of your Internet profile. Here's how.

First, "there's a lot to be said for being a liker—if you treat people agreeably, they treat you likewise," says Paul Eastwick, psychologist at Texas A&M University. "But there's a wrinkle when it comes to initial romantic attraction," says Eli Finkel of Northwestern University, Eastwick's coauthor. It turns out that speed daters who rate everyone highly are liked less in return. Finkel explains that unlike in platonic situations of work, play, and friendship, "In dating, liking everyone can come off as desperate."

The duo's research shows that rather than liking everyone, what predicts being liked in return is the difference between your baseline "like" and how much you like a specific person. When sitting across from your dream date, you want to show a "like spike." Unfortunately it has to be honest. "One thing that's fascinating is that people can tell so fast—whether the flavor of the liking is unique versus general," says Finkel. You can't fake unique attraction, but neither should you try to tamp it down when it wallops you. Showing someone they're special makes them like you.

A second cool trick comes from the world of embodied cognition, which is a much-studied form of subconscious crossover between actions and thoughts. For example, people excluded from a social group in a lab setting report the lab itself feels colder. Finkel and Eastwick also point to a study of the "attractiveness" of Chinese characters—subjects found characters more attractive when they pulled them toward themselves than they found the same characters when they pushed them away.

In the world of speed dating, embodied cognition means that you want to sit instead of rotate—you tend to like things you approach. Sure enough, Finkel and Eastwick showed that while women are overall pickier than men, if men stay put while women rotate, it shortens the pickiness gap. (Think about this in terms of gender stereotypes, in which men pursue and women are pursued.) So in addition to letting your "like spike" (as it were) show, find a speed dating situation that allows your sex to sit—dates will approach you and so will like you more.

## Mining dating data—try saying that ten times

fast. Now bask in the glory that is a truly massive data set, generated by millions and millions of online dating profiles and their click rates. First, men get more responses to their messages if they don't smile in their profile pictures. And $20,000 in salary compensates for an inch in height. (Online daters lie, adding an average of two inches and 20 percent to their true heights and salaries.) And there are good and bad words to use in messages. Netspeak like "ur" for "your" hurts message response, as do physical compliments including the words "sexy," "hot," and "beautiful." Instead use words that show interest that runs more than skin-deep like "awesome" and "fascinating."

# Puzzle #4: Matchmaker

You're the benevolent facilitator of a speed dating session. John, Jake, Jeremy, and Justin arrive to meet Emma, Ella, Eliza, and Eva. As per regulations, they all chat and then they all score each other—er, evaluate each other. If the chart below shows these scores (girls' evaluation of guys on the left, and guys' evaluation of girls on the right—the higher score the better), how should you pair these love-struck contestants in order to create the most overall happiness?

|  | Emma | | Ella | | Eliza | | Eva | |
|---|---|---|---|---|---|---|---|---|
| John | 3 | 9 | 7 | 7 | 2 | 6 | 4 | 7 |
| Jake | 9 | 9 | 1 | 5 | 1 | 6 | 9 | 3 |
| Jeremy | 2 | 9 | 6 | 6 | 5 | 8 | 4 | 2 |
| Justin | 5 | 7 | 3 | 4 | 4 | 5 | 3 | 2 |

## HOW TO BE A BALLER

**John Fontanella** PHYSICS, UNITED STATES NAVAL ACADEMY

In the immortal words of rapper Skee-Lo, do you wish you were a little bit taller? Wish you were a baller? Wish you had a girl who looked good and you would call her? Wish you had a rabbit in a hat and a bat and a '64 Impala?

It's a lengthy list.

John Fontanella, physicist at the US Naval Academy, can help you with the second—being a baller, that is. He wrote the book on basketball, or at least on *The Physics of Basketball*, which you can use to light up the scoreboard regardless of height and/or possession of said Impala.

First, the basics. In homage to the Naval Academy, think about basketball as ballistics. You're blasting a projectile that travels up and then down, while also traveling horizontally, describing a parabola from your hand to the hoop (ideally). In basketball's case, the higher the arc, the more straight down the projectile travels as it nears the hoop, and thus the bigger the target looks (you already knew this). But the shortest distance between two points is a straight line and so the higher the arc, the longer the shot's total distance and thus the more precise it has to be leaving your hand (error is magnified over distance).

So there's an optimal angle of release—one that balances the desire to drop straight down at the hoop with the desire for a short, overall path. What's the balance? Another physicist, Peter Brancazio of Brooklyn College, used some nifty trig to show that due to the size of the ball and the surface area of the hoop, any angle shallower than 32 degrees hits the back of the rim. The angle that gives the most margin for error is 45 degrees plus half the angle from the top of the player's hand to the rim.

Imagine this angle: You're hanging in the air, hand extended—draw a line from your fingers to the rim. Now scoot this frozen-in-time jump shot closer to the rim. As the hand gets closer, the angle gets steeper, and as you move the hand out past the three-point line, the angle of the line connecting fingers to rim gets shallower. This makes the ideal angle of a shot from just beneath the rim almost straight up and a long-range jumper almost exactly 45 degrees. It also means that a shot released above the rim can be shallower still, subtracting half the angle between fingers and rim from the balance point of 45 degrees.

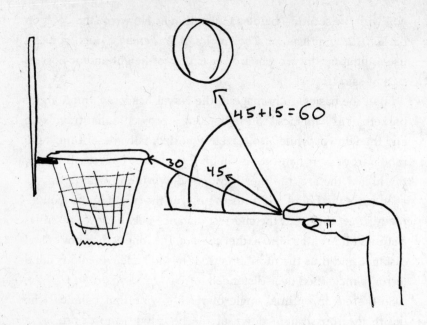

Practice it from different distances—a shallower shot from farther out, but assuming you're releasing from below the rim, never less than 45 degrees.

Another problem that Fontanella points to with a high-arc shot is that of approach speed. "A good shooter minimizes the ball speed at the basket," he says. "That's a soft touch." On the off chance that your perfectly angled shot catches metal, you want it to grab like a golf ball catching the green, bouncing around in the small, defined cylinder above the basket where it has the greatest chance of rolling in. And like golf, a big piece of a soft touch is backspin. Simply, it takes speed off the ball and keeps it in the cylinder.

Finally, with about 359 degrees around you where the ball won't go in the hoop and only about one degree where it will, randomness isn't in your favor. And any aspect of your shot that increases randomness is an aspect that hurts the chance of success. "The really good shooters do it the same every time," says

Fontanella. Good shooters land in the same place they took off, and they release the ball at the jump's apex, meaning they're traveling neither side to side nor up and down at the instant the ball leaves their hand. It's a perfectly still moment in time, with no random movement that creates drift. To see randomness in action without a jump, look at a Shaquille O'Neal free throw. The arm never travels the same path twice.

On the other end of the spectrum, if your memory can't call up a snapshot of Reggie Miller hanging in the air like a plumb bob with his shooting arm extended at 50 degrees, find a vid online.

That's how to be a baller.

## Puzzle #5: Tramp Trouble

And with that geometric refresher, imagine the following dilemma: It's Christmas Eve day and the trampoline your in-laws shipped to you—which you'd meant as the holiday gift centerpiece—is too big for your condo's porch. But if it weren't for that darn support pole in the middle of your garage, the trampoline would fit in there easily. Hey, maybe it will still fit! Can you possibly, possibly somehow stuff a trampoline with a 12-foot diameter into the two-car garage shown on the next page, thus saving Christmas?

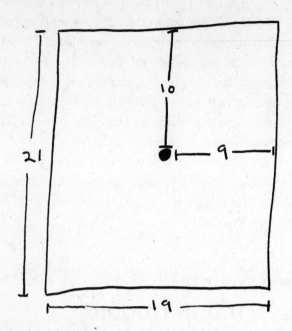

## HOW TO PANHANDLE
**Lee Alan Dugatkin** BIOLOGY, UNIVERSITY OF LOUISVILLE

Why do bees give away meat or defend other bees at cost to themselves? Doesn't this behavior decrease the likelihood of Mr. Care-and-share bee passing on its let's-all-hold-hands-and-sing-"Kumbaya" genes? Doesn't evolution prune these pinko hippie bees from the genetic tree of life? "Altruism drove Darwin crazy," says Lee Alan Dugatkin, biologist at the University of Louisville and author of *The Altruism Equation*, "but the answer is deceptively simple."

Whether or not you help someone in need comes down to three factors: (1) how much it costs you to help; (2) how much the person gains by your help; and (3) your genetic relatedness to the person in need.

This is the altruism equation: $r \times b > c$. If relatedness times benefit outweighs cost, then you help. You'd throw yourself in front of a train to save two of your siblings or eight of your cousins, but not one of your sibs or seven of your cousins. This is because, on some level, you recognize that a sibling has half of your genes—saving two brothers passes on the equivalent of your genetic material. Same with eight cousins. Similar might be true of an airplane full of people of your ethnicity, or a cruise ship full of people from all over the world. Altruism makes sense "if you can somehow make up for the cost of being altruistic by increasing the chances that your genetic relatives survive and reproduce," says Dugatkin.

Anthropologist Napoleon Chagnon famously studied this relationship of altruism and kinship among the Yanomami of Venezuela. From the mid-1960s to late 1990s, when Chagnon lived with the Yanomami, they were into all sorts of nifty things like periodically banding together in ever-changing alliances to cut off heads, shrink them, eat people, etc. Chagnon almost lost his noggin more than once, but survived to compile extensive genealogies of the Yanomami, showing interrelatedness among the many widely dispersed tribal groups. And what he found is a clean (inverse) correlation between relatedness and the likelihood you'll chop off and shrink someone's head and/or eat them. Even without prior knowledge of kinship, the Yanomami somehow knew not to eat family.

"I think the human psyche has been designed to pick up clues that come from gene expression," says Dugatkin. Certainly, studies have shown that we're very, very good at recognizing people we're related to, even without having met them before. What cues this recognition? Is it genetic? "Even the evolutionary biologists are trying to develop models of culture in which the gene is not the central player," says Dugatkin, "but this thing called a meme that represents information is the unit that selection operates on."

So, the theory goes, when we instantly recognize a long-lost relative in a lineup, it's not that we somehow intuit this relative's genetic makeup—it's that we similarly intuit memes, or the many signals not only of genetics but of cultural similarity, including Aunt Joan's clipped "T's," Great Uncle Wilbur's habit of winking as punctuation, and Grandpa Gary's bad sense of humor that makes one pepper terrible puns throughout a book of scientific tips.

This reliance on memes rather than genes to determine relatedness bodes well for your ability to fool others into being altruistic toward you—to, for instance, make them give you money—for while it's rather cumbersome to change your genetic structure to be more similar to that of a person you're hitting up, changing your memetic structure—the ways you signal genetic similarity—is totally doable. "There are ways to create the illusion of genetic relatedness among people," says Dugatkin. "Look at the military or religious organizations referring to people as brothers." This language creates false kinship . . . and people in these organizations help one another.

Further evidence for the power of kinship language comes from another sort of evolution. How many lines do you think a panhandler tries in a career of begging? And why do you think some lines become more used than others? Because they work, that's why—the others are selected against. And what's the stereotypical, clichéd panhandling line? It's "Brother, can you spare a dime?" By implying relatedness, the panhandler thumbs the scale of the altruism equation and makes it in your genetic interest to give (remember: Relatedness times benefit must outweigh cost).

And if you're going to try to get money or other aid out of a population, you'd do well to walk like them and talk like them too. "We use similarity as a proxy for kinship," says Dugatkin, "and the slightest indication of relatedness can stimulate altruistic behavior." If you want money from your uncle, be sure to use Aunt Joan's clipped "T's" when making your request.

So you can influence the perception of relatedness.

Next let's look at cost (again, not to beat it over the head or anything, remember: r × b > c).

You know the saying "It's better to give than to receive." While this is so obviously parent-speak for "For God's sake just give your little sister the My Little Pony Tea Set!" it contains at least an element of truthiness. That element is the fact that we can gain by giving. A person might not gain money by giving you a dime (or they might, in the long run, due to reciprocity, but that's another long scientific story), but instead they might gain the admiration of a date, or giving a dime might allow your target to feel like a swell fellow. Or hold a sign that gives a laugh in return, like NINJAS KILLED MY FAMILY. NEED MONEY FOR KUNG FU LESSONS! Or think of the broader meaning of "cost." To a well-dressed woman in a business suit, a dollar may have the same "cost" as a dime to you and (especially) me.

Or think about the perceived worth of money: A quarter seems useful, while a dime is the first denomination that, for whatever reason, seems worth less than its face value. In other words, it seems like it costs $0.35 to give a quarter, while it only costs about $0.07 to give a dime. We're back to the logic of "Brother, won't you spare a dime?"

Finally, it also matters how much this dime would benefit you. Imply that it will save your life or at least provide the tipping point into something tangible like a sandwich or a bed or a beer, and you're more likely to get what you need.

So if you're asking for anything—your boss for a raise, your parents for a car, or a stranger for a handout—imply relatedness, decrease the cost of giving, and promise massive personal benefit to tip the scale of altruism in your favor.

**In his book *Mr. Jefferson and the Giant Moose***
(surprisingly, not a children's title), Dugatkin tells the story of the
French notion that the fledgling United States was populated by
underevolved, inferior, weakling species. To counter this ethnocentric
arrogance, Thomas Jefferson had the skeleton of a seven-foot-tall
moose shipped first-class from New Hampshire to Paris.

**Researchers at Washington State University**
found that across a number of studies, instead of applauding people
who contributed more than their fair share to a group while taking
little in return, other group members wanted to kick the do-gooders
out entirely. Reasons include making others look bad, setting an
example that others would rather not have to follow, and simply
acting contrary to established social norms. So if you're a natural
angel, find a little devil to express or risk being shunned.

## HOW TO TAKE A CORNER

**Charles Edmondson** PHYSICS,
UNITED STATES NAVAL ACADEMY

At the end of the day racing comes down to what
you've got under your hood, right? Not necessarily. When I chatted with Charles Edmondson, physicist at the US Naval Academy
and author of the book *Fast Car Physics*, he was fresh back from
the track. The truck with his fast car on it hadn't started, so
he'd been forced to borrow a friend's Neon. Edmondson, who's
also an instructor for road-legal racing, said, "Even with this
tiny little four-banger econo-car, I was able to run down all the

students in the intermediate group, including a guy in a turbo Porsche."

This is because straightaway speed isn't the crux of racing. It's how you take a corner that counts.

"Friction's a finite resource," says Edmondson. It's this friction of rubber meeting the road that keeps your car connected to and thus turning around a corner. And using any of this limited friction to brake takes away from the friction available to turn. "Experts do 80 to 90 percent of their braking before they hit the corner," says Edmondson. Allotting all possible friction to turning instead of braking allows a higher max speed before skidding.

And tires are a neat little physics problem—sure they're spinning, but as each little panel of the tread hits and grips the road, it becomes momentarily static in regard to the pavement. Because this static friction (the grip something has while sitting still) is so much greater than tires' kinetic friction (the grip something has when it's already sliding), the consequence of a small slip tends to be pretty spectacular—a tiny skid slashes a car's friction limit from static (high) to kinetic (low) and the slide is off to the races, as it were. Commence catastrophic failure and general fiery badness.

But braking early isn't the end of the story. Next you want to take a racing line. Imagine you can hug the tight inside of a curve or you can go high, riding the curve's outside arc. Which is best? It turns out it's nearly a wash—on the inside arc, you're forced to go slower but the arc is shorter overall; on the outside arc you can go faster but you also have to go further. Either way, you get to the end of the curve at pretty much the same time. So instead of taking the radius your lane gives you, "open up the radius of the turn as much as possible," says Edmondson. This means starting the turn high, tagging the low point of the inside corner, and then exiting the turn high.

It's the same in baseball. Frank Morgan, a math professor at

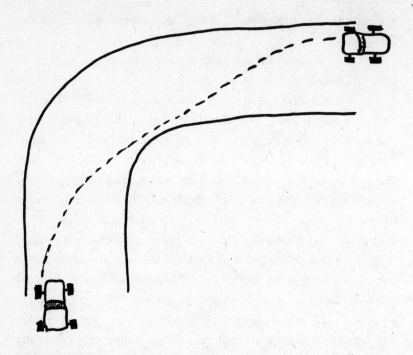

Williams College, showed that if you know you're going for second, you should immediately widen your path to first to the right of the baseline, allowing you to open up the radius of your turn around the base.

For a single turn, that's it: Brake before the turn and draw a kind arc.

But now imagine you're in an S turn (or any set of multiple turns). Exiting the first turn high brings you into the second turn low. That's bad. And if you're at your friction limit in the first and late recognizing the danger of a sharper turn in the second, braking only eats up that last little bit of friction, sending you over the static/kinetic threshold and into the wall. That's really bad.

So the best you can do among multiple turns is to prioritize the tightest turns—set up high coming into tight turns by taking non-optimal lines on the wider turns.

That is, unless you have a straightaway coming up after the last

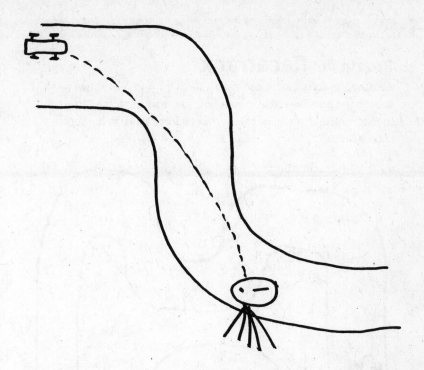

turn in a set. Because you want to travel as fast as possible over the longest distance possible, you should prioritize this last turn in the set so that the impact of your higher exit speed is magnified across the entire length of the following straightaway.

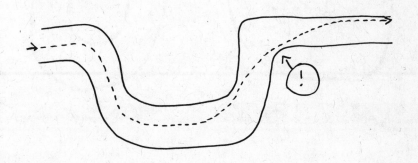

# Puzzle #6: **Racetrack**

Because the equation for centripetal force is $F = mv^2 \div r$, drawing the longest possible radius means your car feels less force. Draw the racing line that minimizes centripetal force through the course shown below.

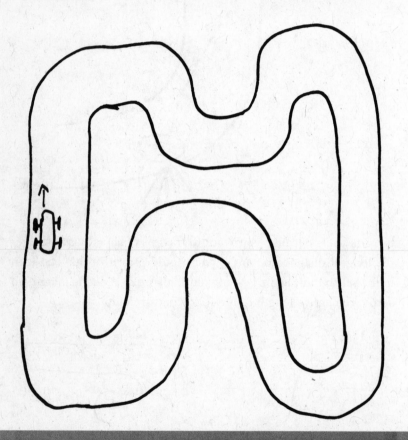

## DESTROY STUFF WITH AWESOME SUPERVILLAIN POWERS

**Steve Strogatz** MATHEMATICS, CORNELL UNIVERSITY

Is Superman cool? No. He's a do-goody Boy Scout in tights and a codpiece. You know who's cool? General Zod, that's who.

And you can be too.

The easiest thing to destroy with your bare hands is a bridge: They swing.

Like London's Millennium Bridge, which, under the weight of six hundred people on opening day, June 10, 2000, started to boogie aggressively. There was no wind. And the people weren't marching in lockstep . . . at least not at first.

Then, as you can see in the Internet video, "People spread their feet wide and started walking in this hilarious Ministry of Silly Walks kind of way," says Cornell mathematician Steve Strogatz. Imagine standing in a rowboat. It starts rocking. What do you do? You spread your feet and go with the flow. "And they actually got in step with the vibrations in a way that pumped energy into the bridge," says Strogatz. This is a positive feedback loop: Strogatz showed that even a slight wobble causes people to synchronize in a way that creates an ever-increasing wobble (causing more people to synchronize, etc.).

And soon synchronicity of disastrous proportions arose spontaneously from randomness, with six hundred people pumping the Millennium Bridge like a swing, while the queen watched in horror.

But what created the first wobble? There are a couple theories, but Steve Strogatz chalks it up to chance: Of the 600 people on the bridge, at some point 301 people put their left foot down as only 299 put down their right. From there, positive feedback was off and running.

You can be that 301st person.

## Good ol' Galloping Gertie, the Tacoma

Narrows Bridge, ripped herself to shreds in 1940 due to aeroelastic flutter: She flapped in the breeze. But unless you were born on Krypton, you simply don't have the wind power for that kind of thing. Likewise, the Angers Bridge collapsed in 1850 when almost 500 French soldiers marching across the bridge accidentally matched its vertical resonant frequency. But engineers wised up and no modern bridge grooves to the vertical beat of human feet. If you want to crash a bridge, you'll have to swing it.

## CREATE A CULTLIKE POSSE OF WORSHIPFUL AUTOMATONS

**Eli Berman** ECONOMICS, UNIVERSITY OF CALIFORNIA–SAN DIEGO

Once you have supervillain powers, you'll need an army of henchmen. Don't have one? Don't worry! Science can make one for you.

All you have to do is solve the problem of loyalty.

All organizations struggle to keep people: You help an employee cut her teeth in the business, but the second a more attractive offer comes along, she blows town. Businesses control defection with counteroffers and promotions. But admit it—you're too cheap to buy a posse. The Mafia has ways of dealing with defection too. But you need the trunk of your car for groceries.

And so the best way for you to keep a posse is with the tried-and-true method of Hamas, Hezbollah, the Taliban, and al-Qaeda: "All of today's successful terrorist organizations require a signal of commitment," says University of California–San Diego economist Eli Berman.

This up-front signal of commitment must outweigh the potential gains of later defection. For example, the initiation rite for the Hells Angels includes being peed on by the rest of the gang and then wearing your soaked leathers for a month. Once you've spent a month wearing the urine of large, hairy men, the cost you've paid to enter the club is higher than any potential gain you could earn by later defecting from it.

Cool: cost of initiation must outweigh potential gains of betrayal.

But what about recruiting your posse in the first place? There's another thing these top four terrorist organizations—Hamas, Hezbollah, al-Qaeda, and the T-ban—have in common: "They all started as mutual aid societies," says Berman. They provided services in communities that lacked them. And with limited resources, clubs had to learn how to be exclusive—they developed and tested initiation rites as signals of commitment, and wove club membership deeply into communities, families, and the fabric of culture.

Contrast this with the would-be terrorists known as the Toronto 18. They played soccer together—oh, and plotted the beheading of the Canadian prime minister. Word leaked and soon the group accepted a new member, Mubin Shaikh—a police plant who hung out until gathering enough evidence to arrest the lot of them.

Their downfall? They didn't require a signal of commitment, and their connection to each other was topical, rather than growing from mutual support ingrained in culture.

What this means for your posse is this: first, make yourself indispensable in a benign way, creating an exclusive club with membership benefits. Then require a stout initiation rite.

Only then will you have snitch-proof henchman capable of carrying out your supervillainy.

## Can you guess how Eli Berman recommends

squishing terrorist organizations? "Competent governments must provide social services," he says, thus removing the need for independent aid societies—the societies that can so successfully turn violent. Eli Berman is the research director for international security studies at the Institute for Global Conflict and Cooperation, and author of the extremely cool book *Radical, Religious, and Violent*.

## Do you want to find a friend of a friend who

plays cricket, World of Warcraft, and speaks Cantonese? Ask V. S. Subrahmanian of the University of Maryland, who created an algorithm that mines online social networks like Facebook. Or maybe you want an entrée into a terrorist network? Dutch researchers defined the mathematical signatures of likely terrorists within large, online social networks, and Subrahmanian now knows how to find them.

## BUILD A CYBERNETIC THIRD ARM

**Yoky Matsuoka** BIOROBOTICS, UNIVERSITY OF WASHINGTON

If you want a smart third arm for diapering or dueling or gourmet cooking, MacArthur genius and University of Washington biorobotics expert Yoky Matsuoka can attach one directly to your brain.

"We go anywhere from skin contact to something that goes on the surface of muscles to brain surface interface to opening up the skull, peeling off the skin, and sticking needles into the brain itself," Matsuoka says.

That's very cool: Robotic prosthetics can now attach directly to and be controlled by neurons. If you're down an arm, you can strap a replacement to the neurons that would naturally control the missing limb. Or if you're still in possession of a full set and just looking for that "wow" factor, you can hook a prosthetic to a random, excitable neuron and train the neuron to control the arm. Check out online footage of monkeys at the University of Pittsburgh MotorLab: after using a brain-connected prosthesis to eat an apple, one monkey brings the hand close so he can lick his "fingers."

The question is, how much autonomy do you allow in your third arm? "We're going to have to warm up to the idea of letting the robot do more," says Matsuoka. That's because brain control is still a bit crude. And so instead of an arm that you instruct to pick up a Stratocaster and push each fret at exactly the right millisecond, it's easier to leave some "smartness" or degree of control in the prosthetic: Your brain may initiate "play guitar solo from Danish glam band White Lion's 'When the Children Cry,'" but then it's simpler to let the limb do it independently than it is to leave your brain in control.

Is that a bad thing? OK, in the preceding example it probably is—with or without a third arm, there's no excuse for wanting to play the guitar solo from "When the Children Cry." But in terms of robotic autonomy versus human control, ceding volition to robot overlords isn't a new thing. We already allow robot autonomy in devices like dishwashers, garage door openers, and Little League pitching machines—once we give the command, they automatically do the work. Would it be so wrong or even so different to "hijack a couple neurons," as Matsuoka puts it, and attach these machines to our brains rather than pushing buttons with our hands?

# Puzzle #7: Dismembered Zombies

Oh no! The zombies below have become inconveniently dismembered! But even a zombie missing one limb is viable. How can you combine the pieces below to create the most viable zombies? Assume right and left limbs are not interchangeable, you can't double up limbs, bodies, or heads, and you have no access to a chainsaw, axe, or other tool of further dismemberment.

"Here's the story of the only truly awesome play I've ever made," says understated Jason Katz-Brown, former US #1-ranked Scrabble player, and cocreator with John O'Laughlin of the gold-standard Scrabble site Quackle (www .quackle.org). "There were two tiles left in the bag and I was down by, like, a hundred points, holding E-G-I-N-S-Y-Blank." There are a lot of bingos he could've played from this bunch—words that use all seven tiles and thus score an additional fifty bonus points. "But it wouldn't have mattered," he says, "because next turn my opponent could've scored more points," and Katz-Brown would've been stuck playing catch-up again, with only the two tiles he drew from the bag as ammunition. He computed or intuited the odds—exactly which, he's not sure—and realized that his best play was to pass and ditch his E in hope of getting a higher-value letter that would allow him to bingo out. He drew a P, for G-I-N-P-S-Y-Blank. His opponent played and drew the only remaining tile, a J. Playing off a G on the board, Katz-Brown bingoed out with "gypsying," which my spell check doesn't like, but which is most certainly included in the *Official Scrabble Players Dictionary*. Not only did he bingo out big, but his opponent had to eat the J, swinging the score by another sixteen points. "I won by, like, a few points," says Katz-Brown. Lucky as it may seem, the thing is he foresaw this as his only chance.

I'm a casual Scrabble player, usually on my phone in bed at night, and I reciprocated with the very exciting story of my best play—the word "prejudice" off an existing "re" while playing against the computer a couple months ago. Katz-Brown was kind enough to pretend to be impressed.

This is to say that there are many levels at which Scrabble can be played. But according to Katz-Brown, the two basic tenets of good play are as applicable to me as they are to him: (1) know your words; and (2) be aware of the likely value of letters you leave in your rack. This is how Quackle computes word score—points plus leave value—and Katz-Brown says that when he sets Quackle to play only according to these two parameters, it can beat all but the best human players.

First, the words. After his freshman year at MIT, Katz-Brown took a summer internship in Japan (where he now works for Google). "And instead of taking advantage of, you know, Japan," he says, "I'd go back to my room and spend all night learning words." That summer, he learned all the words in *The Official Scrabble Players Dictionary*.

Let's imagine you're not going to do the same. Is there a way to get better at Scrabble with minutes—rather than months—of memorization? If you only wanted to spend time learning a handful of words, which should they be?

To find out, Katz-Brown and O'Laughlin had Quackle play itself thousands of times and looked for the best words. But these aren't simply the highest-scoring words; rather, they're the ones that allow the most advantage over other words you'd play with the same rack if you didn't know the big kahuna. For example, with an opening rack of E-H-O-P-Q-R-T, the best word is "qoph" (valued by Quackle at 46.6) and the second best word is "thorpe" (at 24.8). There's a big difference for knowing "qoph," and so it has high "playability."

In order of playability, the top forty words you absolutely must know are: qi, qat, xi, ox, za, ex, qis, ax, zo, jo, ja, xu, qadi, qaid, of, oo, if, oe, io, qua, yo, oi, euoi, oy, ow, wo, yu, fy, ee, joe, aw, we, zee, oxo, exo, axe, ye, fa, ou, ef. The first bingo on the list is "etaerio." You can find the full list with a quick search for "O'Laughlin playability."

Now to leave values, which are a bit more esoteric. Sure, it's nice to score points. But it's also nice to set yourself up to score points next time. This is what you do when you play tiles that leave compatible letters in your rack. Again, Katz-Brown and O'Laughlin engineered massive Quackle-on-Quackle action to discover the combinations that predict success on the next turn. If you're going to keep only one tile, best keep the blank (notated "?"), followed by S, Z, X, R, and H. Many of the same suspects show up in two-tile leaves, with the best being ?-?, ?-S, ?-R, ?-Z and the first without a blank being S-Z. If you're leaving three tiles, none of them blank, oh please let them be E-R-S! Other great three-tile leaves are E-S-T, E-S-Z, R-S-T, and E-R-Z. And it's likely worth ditching one letter if you can leave A-C-E-H-R-S, E-I-P-R-S-T, or E-G-I-N-R-S. You can find full lists by searching for "O'Laughlin maximal leaves."

To demonstrate the power of leave values, Katz-Brown suggests imagining an opening rack of A-E-P-P-Q-R-S. "There's no bingo, and there's no obviously exciting play that scores a lot," he says. So what should you do? Despite Q's high points and what Katz-Brown describes as most players' "animal fear of having two of the same letter in your rack," the best play is to exchange the Q. With A-E-P-P-R-S, drawing any vowel will allow you to bingo next turn.

Data generation to solve specific questions? While Katz-Brown is the only person in this book without a PhD, knowledge creation through experimentation sounds suspiciously like science to me. There you have it: Scrabble solved with science.

## "I can only define the two-letter words," says

Katz-Brown, which puts him two letters ahead of most players in the world's top Scrabble country, Thailand, where players generally memorize acceptable and unacceptable letter patterns without connecting these patterns to words or meanings. At the yearly bigwig tournament in Thailand, Katz-Brown describes being mobbed by groupies for pictures and autographs. This, he implies, is somewhat different than the way top Scrabble players are treated in the United States.

## Puzzle #8: Bingo! (Scrabble)

What five bingos can you make with the letters E-A-S-T-E-R-L?

## GET YOUR SPOUSE TO DO MORE HOUSEWORK

**George Akerlof** ECONOMICS, UNIVERSITY
OF CALIFORNIA-BERKELEY

In a 2000 paper that Google Scholar shows cited 1,683 times and counting, Nobel Laureate and Berkeley economist George Akerlof writes that in married couples, "When men do all the outside work, they contribute on average about 10 percent of housework. But as their share of outside work falls, their share of housework rises to no more than 37 percent." In other words, even when the wife is the primary breadwinner, she's likely to also do more of the housework.

But why? Assuming spouses have equal bargaining power, they should settle on equal "personal utilities"—when utilities are out of whack, bad feelings ensue and to heal this rancor, fairness must be restored. So why do relationships in which the wife works more reach equilibrium when she also does most of the housework?

"Actually, it's simple," says Akerlof. "The idea is that in any situation, people have a notion as to who they are and how they should behave. And if you don't behave according to your identity, you pay a cost."

In this model, the red-blooded American male takes a hit to his identity when his wife earns more money than he does, and a further hit when he does housework (the size of the hit commensurate with how much he's internalized the identity of "red-blooded American male"). To bring the "utilities" of husband and wife back into balance, she does more housework.

Similarly, if you adopt the identity of "host," you maximize your utility by serving drinks, and if you adopt the identity of "life of the party," you maximize your utility by consuming them. And within us are many, many identities—maybe you hold within you the identities of father, husband, rock climber, professional speaker, Grateful Dead fan, and author, each to varying degrees and thus with different bonuses and penalties to identity and personal utility for acting certain ways in certain situations. (At a speaking gig, I'm unlikely to pick an audience member to fence with a foam sword, but in my capacity as father . . . well, you get the point.)

Identity bonuses and penalties also explain why soldiers charge machine gun nests, while wussified authors of pop-science books can't imagine making the same decision in identical circumstances. Simply, the Army builds in recruits the identity of "soldier" and then the decision whether to charge is a balance with the chance of death sitting on one side and identity sitting firmly on the other. What's the greater penalty: the chance of death for charging or the identity loss for cringing? If the Army's done its job well, identity expectations of "soldier" overrule risk.

The same is true of schools and businesses. Organizations that help members adopt the identity of "student" or of "employee" create behaviors that would otherwise be illogical: Students learn; employees work. Akerlof also points to marketers of Marlboro or Virginia Slims cigarettes, who imply that to earn the identity bonus of "real man" or "sophisticated woman" you should set fire to and inhale their products.

Again, we act according to the social expectations of our identities or we pay a very real, tangible cost in personal utility. "The point is that you can socially engineer these things," says Akerlof. Witness the Army, a good school, a good business, or good cigarette marketers.

If you want your spouse to do more housework, you too will learn to socially engineer these things. There are exactly two ways to do it. First, you can encourage your spouse to modify his or her identity. Social scientists have known for years that identity is influenced by surroundings. In fact, Akerlof points to this sculpting power of culture as one of the (many) reasons poverty persists—by trying to transcend existing identity, a motivated teenager at a tough school forces identity penalties on all his or her peers. And so instead of applauding the motivated teen, peers tend to maximize the utility of their own identities by teasing away unwanted deviance. The use to you is this: Jumping directly into yoga class might be a stretch—no pun intended—but instead of nagging or cajoling or straight talk aimed at changing your spouse's identity, find situations—friends, classes, TV shows, magazines, etc.—in which culture will do the work for you. People who cheer with the team become more cheerleader-like. Your challenge is to find the right team.

Or you can frame the desired behavior so that it aligns with the existing identity. For example, if you're a wife trying to get your husband to put dirty clothes in the hamper rather than strewn around the floor near the hamper, how can you align this behavior with the identity of a real man? Is hitting the hamper like making the winning three-pointer? Is doing housework sexy? Does efficiently loading the dishwasher require manly spatial skills that only he can provide? Thus framed in terms of manliness, he can clean without paying an identity cost for it.

If you're a husband trying to get your wife to do more housework . . . well, shame on you. (That said, these techniques should work equally well.)

Akerlof is best known for his paper "The Market for 'Lemons': Quality Uncertainty and the Market Mechanism," for which he won the Nobel Prize in Economic Sciences. The paper addresses not fruit but used cars, and shows that because a buyer can never be certain of a used car's quality, it's more advantageous for sellers to put lemons than cherries on the market because prices converge toward an assumed low point. His newest book (with Rachel Kranton), which occupies brave new territory between the previous encampments of economics and sociology, is *Identity Economics: How Our Identities Shape Our Work, Wages, and Well-Being.*

## MAKE THE MOST OF THE GENES YOU GOT

**Joseph Ecker** GENETICS, SALK INSTITUTE

You know how it works. There are birds and bees. Daddy birds get together with mommy bees and they unzip their . . . chromosomes, throwing exactly half their genetic material into a pot. The stork, who's an old-school synthetic biologist, stirs the pot with his long beak, and out flaps the pair's unholy love child, feathers, stinger, and all.

Or something like that.

The point is this: Your child gets half its chromosomes from you and half from your mate. These form a tidy bundle known as a genome, and every cell in your child's body gets a copy. If you get a good genome, you'll be smart, beautiful, and happy. If you get a bad genome, you're doomed to a life of loveless and tormented bell ringing at the nearest cathedral.

Or something like that.

And in the wiggle room implied by "something like that" lies extremely cool and extremely new science. It turns out that while your genome is fixed, the expression of this genome is not. The software that controls this expression is the epigenome, and you can rewrite it.

On a basic level, "that's why we have eye cells and ear cells and every other kind of cell, despite the same genes in each," says Joseph Ecker, geneticist at the Salk Institute. It's said that a cook's only as good as his ingredients, but I'll tell you what: With flour, butter, eggs, milk, and caramelized bacon, the epigenome of Anthony Bourdain creates a very different meal than does the epigenome of Garth Sundem (which expresses only pork-flavored, unleavened pancakes).

So if you want to be smart, beautiful, happy, and cancer-free, the trick becomes not only reaching back in time to select super-parents and thus the right ingredients in your genome, but also convincing your epigenome to make the most of the ingredients it's got—to cook your genome like Bourdain.

Teaching your epigenome to cook depends on something called methylation. (Very) basically, attaching a methyl group silences part of a gene—in a cell that becomes eye tissue, all the other tissue types get the ball gag of a little methyl attachment, leaving only eye tissue to be expressed. When your eye cell copies itself to make more eye cells, it copies this methylation, too.

But over time, your DNA accumulates junk—viruses may insert snippets of Trojan code—and every time a cell duplicates itself, mutations may occur. So over time your genes generally get a bit messy. To avoid expressing the mess, you methylate everything you'd rather stayed quiet. It's like living in Maoist China, where you constantly jail potential dissidents.

And if you fail to silence the proletariat, your cells may rise up against you. We call this cancer. A mismethylated cell is unbound by its history, has no direction in life, and can and very well may party like it's 1999, leaving its directionless, cancerous progeny strewn about your body in places you wish it would not.

There are many drugs in the pipes to promote healthy methylation, troubleshoot mismethylation, and seek and destroy cells with the profiles of bad methylation. In fact, some of these are extremely promising alternatives to traditional chemotherapy. But until then, "there are bottles of folic acid on the shelves of Whole Foods," says Ecker.

The body's methyl comes from folic acid. Spread your folic acid too thin, and your epigenome doesn't have enough ball gags to silence the junk. That's why pregnant women take folic acid supplements—cells are duplicating at an abnormal pace and so need additional folic acid to keep pace with the epigenome's massive methylation. The same overtime cell duplication is true if you get a bad sunburn or otherwise cause tissue damage that needs big-time repair—your cells go into copying mode, and you need enough folic acid to ensure correct methylation of these copies. You know that sunburn causes skin cancer, and now you know why: increased chances for bad methylation.

But on the flip side, Ecker points out that taking too much folic acid may aid cancers in replicating out of control. In fact, some of the first cancer drugs were "antifolates" that stopped methylation and thus cancer cells' ability to reproduce.

So there are two things you can do right now, today, to ensure a happy epigenome: Please refrain from destroying your tissue and, barring that, take just enough folic acid to rebuild it properly. When you get a burn, pop a supplement but don't make it a habit.

## Joseph Ecker and other extremely cutting-

edge scientists are writing another chapter to the story of epigenomic effects. It turns out that in addition to rewriting your own epigenome and thus genetic expression through the way you live, you can pass elements of this rewritten epigenome to your children. For example, if you smoke before puberty, your grandchildren have a greater chance of reaching puberty early. And not only did Dutch mothers forced to near starvation during World War II have small babies, but their grandchildren were smaller too. Smoking and starving didn't affect genes, but it affected how the epigenome expressed them.

So to the age-old question of nature or nurture is added another player that splits the difference—keeping the epigenome happy through nurture affects the very nature of your children and grandchildren. So don't smoke, and eat right. Do it for the children. It's true we make a better day, just you and me.

## Why be content to fiddle benignly with the

epigenome when you can alter the very building blocks of life itself? Jim Collins, MacArthur genius and synthetic biologist at Boston University and Howard Hughes Medical Institute, inserted toggle switches into cells' DNA that "allows cells to flip on and fluoresce in the presence of certain chemicals or heavy metals," says Collins. These engineered cell mats are the new canaries in the coal mine. Then Collins inserted similar switches into yeast DNA, forcing the yeast to "commit cellular hara-kiri," says Collins, after counting seven days. Naturally—for example in beer—yeast can clump together before dying, but Collins's switches preempt this clumping and so can do away with the foul-tasting sediment in homebrew.

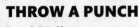

## THROW A PUNCH

**Jearl Walker** PHYSICS, CLEVELAND STATE UNIVERSITY

"When I studied tae kwon do as a teenager, my master always told me to aim a forward punch inside my opponent's body," says Jearl Walker, Cleveland State professor and author of the classic book *Flying Circus Physics*. And when he got the professor gig, he decided to investigate why. First, he filmed himself throwing forward punches and then measured the distance his hand traveled each frame to discover where the punch reached maximum velocity. Sure enough, a punching hand is fastest at 80 percent of arm extension. After that, it's already slowing down to retract. Imagining a punch detonating behind the target's surface helps to ensure maximum speed on impact.

But max speed is only one of three factors that make the perfect punch. Imagine the superfast flick of your finger—it's annoying behind the ear, but it's unlikely to cause real damage. "What you want is maximum pressure," says Walker. This is high momentum applied over a small surface area, and it's why many martial arts teach striking with the side of the hand or the four pointy knuckles of your bent fingers—decreased surface area is like whacking a person with a stiletto heel instead of the sole of a sneaker. Ideally you'd punch with the fingertip of death, but unless you've trained for decades at a Shaolin temple, your one pointed finger is likely to crumple between your opponent's sternum and your onrushing arm.

In addition to speed and outside of adjusting your fist size, the best factor to focus on when throwing a punch is the third piece of pressure—mass. One reason a punch from a heavyweight does more damage than a flyweight's punch of the same speed is simple arm weight. A big wrecking ball does more damage than a little wrecking ball. "But an effective punch uses more than just the fist," says Walker. You've heard the phrase "Put your body behind it" and in punching that's exactly right.

"Rocky Marciano was an extremely effective fighter, partly because he was short," says Walker. Being shorter than his opponents allowed Marciano to punch upward, using his legs to add to the force of the punch—rather than bracing his punch against his weight alone. Speaking of bracing a punch against your weight, the wider your stance, the more horizontal force you can create. Likewise with a forward lean of your body—it's all about bracing your punch against the floor. For this reason, "what you see a lot of in movie martial arts—jumping up into the air—costs a lot of force," says Walker. By jumping you might gain the force that gravity exerts on your dropping body, but you lose the much greater force you could generate by pushing against the floor.

In fact, if you want to see the perfect punch in action, watch videos of Olympic shot-putters: a low crouch, a forward-leaning upper body, and a rotating torso, all with the aim of creating max force through one extended hand. A one-punch knockout comes from the legs.

**Another punch researcher, psychologist John** Pierce, at Philadelphia University, used sensors embedded in the gloves of professional boxers to measure punch force during matches. What he found is that while a one-punch knockout is certainly possible, much more common is knockout by accumulated force. "Once neck muscles fatigue, they can't absorb as much force, and so while later punches aren't necessarily thrown any harder, their force on the victim is much increased," says Pierce. He calls this point of neck muscle fatigue "the tipping point."

## MAKE PEOPLE LAUGH

**Robert Provine** NEUROSCIENCE, UNIVERSITY OF
MARYLAND-BALTIMORE COUNTY

Robert Provine played baritone sax with the Delbert McClinton band. He's also a neuroscientist at the University of Maryland-Baltimore County and wrote the book *Laughter: A Scientific Investigation*. From one to the other isn't the leap you might expect. "Good jazz and laughter are both products of listening to and responding to social signals," says Provine.

For example, take the opening of my recorded call with Provine—why do I laugh after saying, "Do you mind if I click RECORD? Because I'm thinking about podcasting quotes later . . . ha, ha, ha!" It's because I'm trying to signal that I'm no threat— to assure him that I won't stitch the quotes together into a Mel Gibson diatribe that I can then submit to celebrity gossip sites or otherwise use these recorded words against him.

Similarly, throughout the call, I chuckle to indicate understanding as in, "ha, ha, that's right!" And I laugh to indicate uncertainty, as in "I wonder if anyone's ever thought about that . . . ha, ha, ha?" Provine's spent thousands of hours cataloging similar uses of laughter, from campus gathering places to high school cafeterias to mall food courts. His findings include the facts that speakers are about 46 percent more likely to laugh than listeners, laughter is thirty times more likely in social situations than when alone, laughter frequently takes the place of periods or commas, and only 10–15 percent of prelaugh comments are even remotely funny.

"Actually," Provine says, "laughter is more about relationships than jokes." Human laughter evolved from the grunts and snorts of playing apes, who use these vocalizations to signal social inclusion. Sure, you may overlay the trigger of a punch line or a wry aside or a pun or a surprising observation, but if you want to bring the funny, you have to first become part of the pack. That's why so many jokes start with "There I was, standing in line at the grocery store," or "Don't you just hate airplane seats?," or other descriptions meant to create the bond of shared experience between joker and jokee.

"We don't laugh at Jay Leno because he's funny," says Provine. "We laugh because we empathize with Jay Leno."

So if you want to make people laugh, instead of practicing your punch lines, practice your empathy and listening skills.

## Chris Ballinger of Magic Geek

(www.magicgeek.com) points out that just like humor, magic depends as much on connecting with people as it does on trick mechanics. "Even when you buy a trick that's self-working, you need a story to make it magical," says Ballinger. He counts as his best trick a simple sleight of hand in which sponge rabbits multiply, saying, "the audience can be part of the story of these rabbits both physically and emotionally." Like humor, Ballinger says the crux of magic is "about being able to connect with the audience and fool them at the same time."

### SEE UNHOLY COLORS

**Jay Neitz** OPHTHALMOLOGY, UNIVERSITY OF WASHINGTON

At your local Baskin-Robbins you might order a waffle cone dipped in chocolate with sprinkles, but cones in your eyes come in only three set flavors: S, M, and L. Each flavor of photoreceptive cone fires in the presence of a certain wavelength of light, and while there's some color crossover, effectively one recognizes red, another green, and another blue.

So your eye is like an RGB computer screen, with all the other colors of the rainbow a mixed twinkle of SLM cones firing in varying combinations.

That is, unless you're color-blind. Common red-green color blindness is caused by defective genes on the X chromosome, which code for whacked green cones—the wavelength these cones recognize is squeezed toward red, leaving green undetected. And because these bad genes are on an X chromosome, dudes without a backup X are especially susceptible—red-green color blindness affects 6 percent of males.

Jay Neitz hopes to change that. Neitz is an experimental ophthalmologist and head of the Color Vision Lab at the University of Washington, and he injected viruses into the eyes of color-blind monkeys.

Here's what a virus does: It attaches to a cell like a mosquito and injects genetic material. Commonly, viruses inject genes that appropriate the cell's machinery to create more viruses, which eventually rupture forth like battle orcs to continue the great cycle of viral life. But Neitz engineered his viruses to inject another kind of genetic material—genes that use a cell's machinery to make missing color pigments. (This, in a nutshell, is gene therapy. It's like downloading a software update.)

And—voilà!—these monkeys, once color-blind, now could see! One can only imagine their increased skill at discovering which guavas are ripe, and at driving amid traffic signals. Human application is in the pipes.

But why stop at bringing a deficit up to normal? (See this book's entry with Hugh Herr.) Why not keep a foot on the accelerator and blow right past the puny abilities evolution hath wrought?

"It's not a question of could," says Neitz. "It's a question of should." For example, he says, what about putting a light detector in your fingertip? Or creating a brain-linked array that would sense radiation or allow you to see heat? "It's hard to know what energies are out there we're not exploiting," says Neitz.

But even within the realm of existing senses, there's room for some good-natured, unholy augmentative technology reminiscent of creating a human-snake-meerkat chimera. For example, "What would a fourth type of photoreceptor be?" wonders Neitz.

Again, humans lacking the pigment needed to see green might mislabel yellow as orange or call a dark green car black. But what if we're all incapable of distinguishing, say, purple-quack from purple-not-quack, due to lack of a gene that codes for the quack pigment? What if instead of RGB we could see in RGBQ?

Personally, I'll take *Predator* vision, but seeing an inhuman color would be pretty awesome too.

## While at the University of Wisconsin, Neitz

consulted on a project that asked WDDS? After answering the question What do deer see?, it was a short step to creating more effective camouflage for human hunters. Interestingly, evolutionary biologists propose that the common red-green color blindness may actually help humans see through some types of jungle leaf patterns, making this color blindness an evolutionary advantage, especially for male hunters.

## Speaking of supersight, neurobiologist Mark

Changizi, formerly of Rensselaer Polytechnic Institute and now director of human cognition at 2AI Labs, has telepathy and X-ray vision. In fact, you do too. "We have an extra cone in our eyes that dogs don't have," says Changizi, and this cone is specifically calibrated to sense the minute color changes in skin due to hemoglobin oxygenation. "Human vision has not evolved to find ripe fruit in the forest," says Changizi, "but to sense emotions in others."

And about X-ray vision: "For a hundred years, they thought forward-facing eyes had something to do with stereovision," says Changizi, maybe allowing you better depth perception for jumping from branch to branch, grabbing fruit, and later chucking spears at passing mammoths and hitting balls of twine-wrapped cork. But there's a fairly glaring problem with that theory: Most animals that jump and catch have sideways-facing eyes. Instead, Changizi thinks forward-facing eyes are born of the forest. "Hold your finger in front of your eyes and you can see right through it," he says, pointing out that large forest animals with forward-facing eyes are equipped to see 6.5 times more stuff than forest animals with sideways eyes.

## DRINK MORE TO EAT LESS
**Brenda Davy**  NUTRITION, VIRGINIA POLYTECHNIC INSTITUTE

"The average American consumes two hundred calories of sugar-sweetened beverages every day," says Brenda Davy, health and nutrition researcher at Virginia Tech. Using the widely accepted (translation: debatable and vastly over-simplified) conversion of thirty-five hundred calories per pound of fat, this means that if you changed Pepsi into water, all else equal you would lose almost two pounds a month.

But Pepsi isn't the only thing you can replace with water. Water replaces food, too. And you don't even have to own enough willpower to consciously reach for a glass instead of a bite. Dr. Davy showed this by prescribing two cups of water before a meal. In the course of a twelve-week study, subjects who drank water before a low-calorie meal lost an average of five pounds more than subjects who simply ate the low-calorie meal.

In a yearlong follow-up to this study, Davy found that even with the removal of the low-calorie diet, people who drank water before meals were able to keep the weight off while people who went back to their lives as usual tended to gain some, most, or all of the weight back.

As an addendum to the first study, Davy had subjects rate their feelings of fullness and found that, sure enough, subjects who drank water felt more full. It's that simple: Drinking water takes space in your stomach you would otherwise fill with food. Interestingly, this means that the effect is weaker for younger people—gastric emptying rates are faster for the young, and so in a further test, by the time the meal was served twenty minutes after drinking water, not enough water remained in young stomachs to produce the effect. (If you're under thirty, consider chugging your two cups as you sit down to the table.)

But in addition to making subjects feel fuller, Davy thinks it's likely that drinking water before a meal functions as a psychological check-in with your weight-loss goals (see this book's entry on commitment devices with Katherine Milkman). The ritual of water before a meal is a gentle reminder to respect feelings of fullness.

## HOW TO AVOID CAR THEFT

**Ben Vollaard** CRIMINOLOGY, TILBURG UNIVERSITY

"Car thieves are just like you and me," says Ben Vollaard, criminologist at Tilburg University in the Netherlands. "They seek to maximize gain and minimize loss." In other words, they're rational animals. Vollaard showed this by looking at car theft data before and after 1998—the year the Netherlands required that all new cars be equipped with an engine immobilizer, making hot-wiring nearly impossible.

Not surprisingly, with hot-wiring nixed, the rate of car theft plummeted. But the key fact here is that the immobilizers don't make stealing a car impossible. "You can still get a tow truck or download a program from the Internet that takes over a car's computer, but if you make it more difficult, crime goes down. It's an opportunistic behavior," says Vollaard. In this view, the thief walks down the street looking for a target whose value exceeds the risk and when he finds a car with the right balance, he looks up and down the block and jimmies the lock. And with engine immobilizers in place, risk went way up, making car theft less frequently a rational choice.

So if not a car, maybe a house? Not after the Netherlands wrote into their building code the requirement for burglary-proof doors and windows—houses built after the 1999 regulation are 25 percent less likely to be burgled.

What about a bike? In the case of cars and houses, the Netherlands employed a technique known as target hardening—making something more difficult to steal increases a would-be thief's risk and thus decreases the chance it will be stolen. In the case of bikes, they're trying something else: distorting the market to decrease a hot bike's value. New bikes in the Netherlands come with chips, and police have scanners. So with a wave of the magic wand, police can tell which bikes in the area are stolen. Who's going to buy a guaranteed police magnet? Instead of increasing risk by target hardening, putting a chip in a bike decreases the value of the stolen item, making theft similarly irrational.

Back to cars. The United States is one of the few countries in the developed world that hasn't yet required the engine immobilizer. (Don't tread on Detroit.) So you're still at risk. That is, unless you paint your car pink. Cyclists have done something similar for a long time—it's why the first thing you do with a sweet commuter bike is to paint it bland, scratch it up, and plaster it with stickers. Bikers call this "urban camouflage." Painting a car pink (or "distressing" a new bike) is like fitting it with a Dutch chip: It decreases its value—who's going to buy a pink car or a distressed bike?

Vollaard's DMV data shows that black cars are at highest risk for theft, perhaps because black looks the most luxurious. What was the theft risk for pink cars? Zero. Of the 109 pink cars in the study, not one was stolen.

If you want to keep your ride, paint it pink.

# Now that you've avoided car theft, there are

two more things you'll want to avoid: traffic jams and stoplights. Morris Flynn, mathematician at the University of Alberta, showed that at a certain overcapacity of cars on the road, following drivers don't have time to react to brake lights ahead, and so stomp their brakes harder than warranted, "and the information travels like a detonation wave through all the cars downstream of the braking," says Flynn—until everyone's stopped cold. Flynn calls these phantom jams "jamitons" and also showed that in these conditions, your best action—instead of stopping and starting with the flow of traffic—is to go at a uniform slow speed. You'll help the jamiton eventually clear itself, get to your destination just as fast, save gas, and decrease the chance of a crash-caused jam—one that can really put the kibosh on your timeliness.

As for stoplights, check out the video linked from computer scientist Peter Stone's faculty bio at the University of Texas–Austin of cars zipping through intersections, controlled not by lights and human drivers but by onboard computers. In Stone's autonomous intersections, car-mounted computers call ahead to an intersection "reservations manager" to reserve the milliseconds the car needs to pass through the intersection without becoming a twisted ball of plastic and metal. Then the onboard computer takes over to ensure the car drives through the intersection in its reserved time. "Technologically, it's feasible to do this right now," says Stone. "The barriers are the legal and insurance industries." A quick peek at the online video shows why—it's terrifying—but it does away with stoplight wait times almost entirely.

## TO KNOW OTHERS, KNOW THYSELF

**Julian Keenan** NEUROSCIENCE, MONTCLAIR STATE UNIVERSITY

She says she's just a happy-go-lucky girl who likes loud music, a cold beer, and a guy in a cowboy hat.

He says what he'd really like to do is settle down and have a family.

What do you think the chances are that either's telling the truth? How good are you at spotting deception in the opposite sex? No matter your current skill, Julian Keenan, director of the Cognitive Neuroimaging Lab at Montclair State University, can make you better.

He knows because his lab stuck a host of female undergrads in front of videos showing guys being honest, guys playing good, and guys playing bad, and then looked at the personality and demographic characteristics of girls who were good at sniffing out naughty rats.

First, Keenan found that people who are more self-aware are better at spotting deception in others. (Note: this does not necessarily mean that by becoming more self-aware, you would increase your lie-detection skills. Beware the jabberwocky of correlation and causation.)

But check this out: Keenan also found that single women are much better than women in committed relationships at detecting male deception. While this may be a news flash, it makes sense from an evolutionary perspective: If you're in a long-term relationship, you no longer need to be as edgy around guys who could very well be talking a big game about love and family and commitment in hopes of winning a one-night stand. You're not only out of practice but also lack the proper motivation, and have accordingly lost your edge.

So if you're in a relationship and want to spot deception, ask a single, female (unbiased!) friend to help spot it for you. And if you're single but generally oblivious, pick your most self-aware friend for a second opinion. Evolutionary need has put these all-knowing tigresses atop the deception-detection food chain—they can help you ferret out a rat as opposed to being the tempting rat to a hungry ferret (unless you're into that sort of thing).

**Put a hand on your widow's peak.** About an inch below your fingertips in your medial prefrontal cortex is the home of your sense of self. Julian Keenan did a nifty trick: He used what is effectively an electric Ping-Pong paddle to zap this region in healthy subjects, overexciting every neuron within range, and thus for about a fifth of a second, knocking that one-cubic-centimeter area of the brain off the grid.

And while he did this, he flashed pictures of faces. Blasted subjects retained the ability to recognize faces of loved ones or even learned strangers, but for this fifth of a second, they failed to recognize themselves.

Interestingly, there's one type of person who retains sense of self even with the medial prefrontal cortex blasted: narcissists. Keenan explains that, "in narcissists, more brain areas are dedicated to self-deception." So when a narcissist's medial prefrontal cortex is taken offline, backup generators are in place to maintain that overblown sense of self.

It's a stark enough difference that soon there may be a neuroimaging diagnosis of narcissism. Does your sense of self sit in the medial prefrontal cortex box designed for it, or does it creep out to colonize other areas of your brain?

## HOW TO SPOT A LIAR

**Paul Ekman** PSYCHOLOGY, UNIVERSITY OF CALIFORNIA–SAN FRANCISCO

Sure there are skin conductivity tests, pupil dilation tests, and now the burgeoning field of neuroimaging to test the truth of words. But unless you're packing a mobile lab, none of those do you a whole heck of a lotta good when asking your co-worker whether he dinged your door in the parking lot yesterday, a student if he plagiarized that essay, or your four-year-old if he knows anything about the toothpaste lining every tile crease in your bathroom. In those cases, you'll have to rely on lie detection the old-fashioned way: by the tingling of your own spidey senses.

Luckily these spidey senses can be trained.

"First, there's a simple rule to catching liars," says Paul Ekman, professor emeritus at University of California–San Francisco: "Things don't fit together. The voice doesn't fit with the content of words, the words don't fit with the look on the face, or the face doesn't fit with the words." This is the person who says "no" while nodding their head "yes," and simply knowing to watch for these incongruities can help you catch unpracticed liars.

But from there it gets trickier. "The second, more specific step is microexpressions," says Ekman. Rather than lasting two or three seconds, these expressions last about one twenty-fifth of a second and "almost always show emotions the person is trying to conceal," says Ekman. That is, if you can spot them. To these ends, Ekman's created a nifty online tool that trains your ability to recognize these microexpressions (www.paulekman.com, trial version free). In addition to being a nice training tool, it's fascinating to watch people flashing emotions that they almost instantaneously mask with more situationally appropriate expressions.

"But just because you detect a microexpression doesn't mean someone is lying," says Ekman. Imagine the police asked if you killed your spouse. You might flash a microexpression of anger at being questioned that has nothing to do with the truthfulness of your answers. Or if the police asked you about the quality of your marriage to the deceased spouse, you might flash sadness before going on to describe a happy marriage.

"When you see a microexpression, it's a cue to probe further," says Ekman.

Still, "there are about 5 percent of people we can't catch with this," says Ekman. He describes these 5 percent as natural performers. How can you learn the flip side of catching liars—how can you learn to be a liar yourself? Despite many requests for help in seeming more credible (mostly by politicians, both domestic and international), Ekman refuses to teach the strategies of good lying. "I only run a school for lie catchers, not liars," he says.

## Paul Ekman has written books, including

*Telling Lies*, is a frequent police trainer, and is scientific advisor to the show *Lie to Me*. His current research hopes to predict violent assaults ten to twenty seconds before they occur. He thinks he's about two-thirds of the way to an answer. "It'll at least allow you to duck," he says.

## GROW HUGE CARNIVOROUS PLANTS

**Louie Yang**  ECOLOGY, UNIVERSITY OF CALIFORNIA–DAVIS

You've seen the sign: BEWARE OF DOG! Yeah, that's badass and all. But imagine a yard full of giant humanivorous plants. That'd be totally boss!

And if homicidal plants are your game, then the person to talk to is Louie Yang, ecologist at the University of California–Davis. "There's a specific recipe for carnivorous plants," Yang says. "You need ample sunlight, ample water, but a lack of nutrients." This happens in rain forests, where the massive plant biomass sucks every last speck of nitrogen from the soil. And it happens in the high fens of the Sierra Mountains, where the boggy, sunbaked soil is nearly sterile.

In these nutrient-starved places, plants turn to the flesh of the living for food. Take, for example, the *Nepenthes rajah*, a pitcher plant common to the Borneo highlands. The *N. rajah* has sun and water aplenty, but its growth is limited by the nutrient-poor soil, and so it's evolved two foot-long traps with up to a gallon of digestive fluid, capable of trapping and eating creatures as large as mice.

A plant that eats small mammals rocks. But why stop there? Check this out:

When a pitcher plant catches a fly, it enlarges its fly-catching machinery. That makes evolutionary sense: Focus on what works. But when a plant starts focusing its resources on the creation of grabbing tools, its overall growth stalls—meaning it'll never get big enough to consume, say, your prying next-door neighbor. Or even her cat.

So, once you've got a budding Audrey II, resist your urge to keep feeding her flies. Instead, now's the time to start fertilizing her roots.

Yang caught wind of this trick when he noticed that the largest in a population of carnivorous plants was the one growing next to a pile of deer poop. Again, plants focus on what works: Nutrients entering through the roots signal the usefulness of a more extensive root system. More roots support a bigger plant. As long as the poop holds out the sucker will grow wide, strong, and large.

And this is cool: As a carnivorous plant starts to run out of nutrients, it'll shift resources back to fly catching.

So once you've fertilized your floral army to appropriately monstrous size, starve it to reprioritize growth of its prey-grabbing mechanisms. A hungry plant is a dangerous plant.

## When I visited Louie Yang's lab at UC–Davis,

he was contemplating a refrigerator that held ten thousand cigar-shaped insect traps and wondering how he might most efficiently go about slitting them open and examining the contents under a microscope to see what egg or larval goodies they held. I asked if maybe there were grad students or other proverbial "people for that"—leaving Yang and his oversized brain free to more efficiently design and manage investigations. But Yang echoed many scientists I talked with, saying that having his fingers in the grunt work of data collection is the way he gets ideas—he needs to slit insect traps to generate questions.

## CHOOSE PEOPLE WHOSE COLLABORATION WILL BE GREATER THAN THE SUM OF THEIR PARTS

**Brian Sauser** SYSTEMS MANAGEMENT,
STEVENS INSTITUTE OF TECHNOLOGY

"Look at cell phone cameras," says Brian Sauser, complex systems expert at Stevens Institute of Technology. "Originally they were designed to take pictures of your family. Now everyone's a reporter." From a somewhat mundane design purpose came a use that's fundamentally changed culture and society.

This is emergence: a behavior that arises spontaneously from a system. But just because any specific emergent behavior can only be reverse engineered and not forward engineered (you can tell how it came about, but couldn't have predicted it), systems designers remain able to put in place elements that maximize the likelihood of emergence.

In fact, according to Sauser, this idea of emergent purpose has become one of the central forces in twenty-first-century systems design. "It's been about control," he says, "but now we have to learn to build something and take our hands off the control." Look at the evolving use of micromessaging sites like Twitter. Or at the system of fiber-optic lines that carries the data of the Internet itself. From a flexible infrastructure come crowdsourced uses a designer may never imagine. Build it, open it up, and functionality will come—and in this brave new world, emergent functionality may far outstrip the usefulness of a designer's limited vision.

So how do you design a system with emergence in mind, be it a multicomponent technological marvel or simply a group of people working together on a project? How can you go about intentionally creating a system whose product exceeds your intention?

Sauser thinks of system design from the bottom up—as a combination of the basic building blocks of autonomy, belonging, connectivity, diversity, "and the interaction of the first four gives you emergence."

Unfortunately, there's frequently a trade-off, says Sauser. For example, systems of people tend to trade diversity for belonging (think of Salt Lake City). A similar trade-off can be true of connectivity and autonomy—once you streamline communication (connectivity) the temptation exists to use it for micromanagement, thus dooming autonomy.

But now imagine New York City. "At one level, it's extremely diverse," says Sauser. "You have Chinatown, Little Italy, etc." But on another level it's inclusive: "People came because by being different, they were normal." Sauser points to New York City as a rare example of a system with both high belonging and high diversity. Despite the individualistic spirit commonly held as essential to the New York mentality, "people walking down the street don't believe they're isolated," says Sauser. Instead, "People believe they're part of something bigger." Likewise, New Yorkers' high connectivity detracts little from their autonomy.

Certainly people in New York City could be more diverse, autonomous, connected, or belonging, but somehow this system has managed to push all four factors fairly high simultaneously. And this is why, according to Sauser, so much culture, innovation, and vision emerge from the city—outcomes for which you could never specifically design.

The same combination characterizes the best teams. To maximize the chance for emergence from a hypothetical group of people, "Think about the first four characteristics as win/win or win/lose," says Sauser. Try to increase each of these four factors without your group composition and protocols creating decreases elsewhere. For example, if you've brought diverse people together, you may need to train belonging. Or in a group with high autonomy, you may need to work to increase connectivity. Or in a team with massive belonging, you might need to ensure that team members remain able to work autonomously. You get the point.

You won't ever reach 100 percent in any factor, but by edging each higher without ceding the others, you can maximize the chance that the system you design will create emergent products that neither you nor any individual member could imagine.

**Does diversity have inherent value?** This may be the twenty-first century's most important question. Think ecosystems, think countries and immigration policies, think financial markets. Scott Page, professor of complex systems and political science at the University of Michigan–Ann Arbor and author of the book *Diversity and Complexity*, explored the question in the realm of problem solving. First, he and collaborator Lu Hong gathered a group of college students and tested them on a range of puzzles. Then they wondered: How would a team randomly chosen from this pool perform against a team of the top problem solvers? What they found is surprising—diverse teams outperformed homogenous teams of all-stars—but only if three conditions existed: (1) a baseline level of competence in all puzzlers (no total duds); (2) a wide enough range of puzzle types to nix the power of specialization (a complex system); and (3) a wide enough puzzler pool to ensure diversity is present.

Imagine a basketball team. "One power forward is great and two power forwards is good, but three is ridiculous," says Page. At a certain density of power forwards, you'll get every rebound but your homogeneity makes you susceptible to counter by one specific strategy: the full-court press. A team of power forwards would never get the ball up the floor.

In complex systems like basketball teams, "the hope is you create this interesting, innovative, pulsing, growing system," says Page. If your team does something noncomplex, like picking apples, you'd want a team of strong apple pickers. If your team's going to compete with Apple, Page shows that diversity for diversity's sake, as long as everyone reaches baseline competence, has value.

# Do you concentrate best under pressure?

Do you contemplate best when melancholic? Are you most analytic when angry? A pair of studies shows it's best when mood matches the problem. Specifically, researchers at Northwestern University found that when they showed subjects a short comedy routine, amused subjects were then better at solving word puzzles with sudden insight. On the flip side, Dutch researchers showed that teams better solved analytic tasks when a certain degree of animosity existed in the room.

## GET A JOB!

**Roger Bohn** MANAGEMENT, UNIVERSITY OF CALIFORNIA-SAN DIEGO

If you're a laid-off bum looking for work while living in a van down by the river, wouldn't it be great to know which field is poised for the kind of leap your skills could help create—aka, who'll hand over the $$ for work you're naturally inclined to do?

You've heard about evolution in industry—how today's techniques are built on yesterday's innovations—and it turns out there's a common progression of this evolution that allows you to predict, surf, and potentially profit from what's next in any field. "From semiconductor manufacturing to agriculture to aeronautics to firearms to professional services like architecture, all industries seem to fit a developmental model of six stages," says Roger Bohn, director of the Global Information Industry Center at the University of California–San Diego.

An industry starts as a craft, which you learn through experience or apprenticeship. "It's the 'lone gunman' or 'intrepid flier' stage," says Bohn. Picture a gent in a leather helmet and goggles peering over a precipice with a stick-and-skin glider strapped to his back.

Some of these people survive, and enter what Bohn calls "the rules-and-instruments stage." The effort becomes collaborative as the (lucky) intrepid flier adopts and installs others' innovations that allow him to fly in a more structured way. The Wright brothers took to the sky in 1903, but it was Paul Kollsman who added the accurate altimeter in 1928 and Jimmy Doolittle who showed pilots how to use the artificial horizon in 1932. As you'll note, both when you're going to hit the ground and at what angle you're likely to hit it are good things to know. "Before the artificial horizon, if you flew into a cloud, you were probably gonna die," says Bohn. This applied even to expert pilots—we use our inner ear to tell us which way is up, and in an airplane it doesn't work right.

The next stage, procedures, formalizes how you use all these multifarious gadgets. Aeronautics took this great leap forward in 1935 when the US Army Air Corps invented the preflight checklist. Today, before starting the engine on a tiny Cessna 140 you're required to check the tail wheel, flaps, fuel, seat belts, etc.

Next is automation—in aeronautics, this is the autopilot, or in the 1980 FAA training film *Airplane*, the copilot blow-up doll phonetically named Otto. In this stage, action takes place autonomously but with human supervision.

But in the final stage, computer integration, the human is pruned from the functioning system entirely. Machines are the overseers and humans are relegated to the job of technicians, troubleshooting any glitches that arise.

What creates industry evolution? Darwin would be happy to know it's natural selection, in this case taking the form of market pressure. It's bad for business when planes crash and it's also bad for business when you have to pay humans to do work that machines could do better (for the most part . . .). So generation II is necessarily more cost-efficient than generation I, and this drives all industries along the righteous sixfold path.

Some industries don't experience or are immune to these pressures and therefore fail to evolve. "Education hasn't made it far along the continuum," says Bohn. "Not enough economic pressure. [Or] take health care. What's happening today is that standard procedure is just fighting its way in."

If you need a job, your trick is this: First define the industry stage that matches your strengths. Are you an intrepid flier? A tinkering tweaker of existing systems? Are you a rule-maker at heart, salivating over the prospect of a seat-of-the-pants industry ripe for systematizing? Do you automate? Or are you a technician glitch-fixer?

Now find an industry that's in the stage that matches your specialty. For example, until the tech bubble popped in 2001, the Internet as a whole was the realm of intrepid fliers—now it's consolidating the best ideas.

Picking an industry that fits your fancy may be your best shot at getting out of the van down by the river.

**In his book in progress, *From Art to Science in***
*Manufacturing*, Roger Bohn writes about the two hundred years in which the Italian gun manufacturer Beretta went from individual craftsmanship to automated production lines, during which period craftsmen expertise was written into production protocol.

# KNOW IF PEOPLE ARE OUT TO GET YOU

**Jennifer Whitson** MANAGEMENT, UNIVERSITY OF TEXAS

MCCOMBS SCHOOL OF BUSINESS

A study, famous in circles in which this kind of thing is famous, showed pictures of pure static to falling skydivers (imagine the logistics). While plunging rapidly toward the unforgiving earth, skydivers were more likely than subjects sitting in the plane to see phantom pictures in the static.

Another study found that in periods of economic uncertainty, more books on astrology are published.

And another found that nursing-home patients who care for plants in their rooms have lower mortality rates than patients whose staff care for the plants.

What do these three findings have in common? Not yet! Keep reading.

Jennifer Whitson, professor of management at the University of Texas's McCombs School of Business, showed subjects a series of symbols and asked them to predict the next shape. Whitson then made half the subjects feel correct—revealing the shape they predicted—and made half the subjects feel incorrect, showing them an unrelated symbol (actually, there was no pattern, but that's beside the point). Then she showed subjects twenty-four images blurred by a snowstorm. The wrong-shape subjects found pictures in the snow, even when none existed.

Finally the punch line: it's all about control. Do you have it, do you lack it, and what will you do to get it. "Lacking control is a very aversive state," says Whitson. "People like it so little we'll do almost anything to take control." Like spotting patterns where none exist. Or reading astrology books.

Here's an example closer to home. Whitson presented subjects with the following story: You work in an office, monitoring and troubleshooting e-mail communications. You're up for a promotion. Suddenly you see a sharp rise in e-mail traffic between your boss and the person in the cube next to you. Then you don't get the promotion. Whitson asked, Are these two events connected? Subjects Whitson had primed to feel in control were likely to see a coincidence. Subjects whom Whitson had asked, prior to the story, to imagine a time in their lives in which they lacked control saw a conspiracy.

The person in the next-door cube is out to get you.

Or is he?

It's a tough call. And it's a call you shouldn't be making if you're out of control.

Whitson tells the following illustrative (and possibly apocryphal) story: Deep in winter, a group of Swedish soldiers goes on a military exercise. It starts snowing, and they get lost. Soon they start to panic—until one of the soldiers yells, "Wait, wait, I found a map!" which they follow back to base camp. When they get there, a superior looks at the map and says, "This is a map of a different mountain range!"

Every day, when trapped in your equivalent of a Swedish snowstorm (you'll know it when you see it), finding control—be it real or illusion!—can help you reclaim rationality in decision making. It's as if by retaking control of your mental space, you can be objective about the world at large. You can, as the saying goes, change the things you can change, and accept the things you can't—and you can know the difference between the two.

When the niggling worm of conspiracy whispers in your ear, Whitson recommends a quick mental check-in with an area of your life in which you do have control. Maybe keep pictures of your family on your desk. Or an assortment of flies from your last fishing trip. Not only can the feeling of control help you avoid the trap of the half-baked conspiracy theory, but, like Swedes in a snowstorm, confidence can lead to success.

## When my kids were babies, I would lie in bed

listening to the hum of a noise machine that I swear spoke to me. In my defense, it was on some sort of soundtrack loop so that "jungle" or "waterfall" or "summer night" settings did actually have audible patterns. I would start with a blank mind, eventually zero in on a layer of the innocuous pattern, it would suggest words, and the more I listened the more distinct the repeating words would become. I talked about this with my wife, a psychologist, which for reasons that should be obvious was a rather egregious mistake. I wonder: If I'd been able to take control of my sleep, my work, or my play at that point, would I have continued hearing words in the sound machine?

## Whitson and collaborators explored the

speech styles of young, dressed-down experts versus established, suited experts and found that experts are both more liked and more influential when their formal/informal speech style matches their appearance. If you're a young hotshot, speechifying just sounds pompous—even if you know your stuff. If you're a venerable lion or lioness, some degree of informality is fine, but can quickly be seen as crossing the line into inappropriateness.

# DESIGN A POLL TO GET THE RESULTS YOU WANT

**Charles Franklin** POLITICAL SCIENCE,
UNIVERSITY OF WISCONSIN-MADISON

Your condo's front door faces the pool. In the summer months the irritation of noisy people splashing is balanced by the fact that you can so easily stroll across the walkway to join them. But this winter the condo association board has proposed a major pool renovation: months of jackhammering followed by the smell of sealant seeping into your living room and piles of construction materials outside your door.

Needless to say, you'd rather the pool renovation didn't go ahead as planned. Maybe if you can show that other owners are against it, you could stop it before it starts.

"Almost universally among real pollsters, there's no reason to bias the results," says Charles Franklin, poli-sci professor at the University of Wisconsin-Madison and codeveloper of pollster .com. This is because polls with fringe results receive fringe respect. But you're not a real pollster, and your results aren't likely to be set next to results from a half dozen other firms—you don't have to hit a sweet spot to be taken seriously. And luckily for you, there are many ways to sneakily insert poll bias, allowing you to fake a groundswell against pool renovations while continuing to appear impartial.

Franklin points first and most obviously to language. In the world of politics, Democrats may word an issue differently than Republicans (think "tax relief") and depending on the level of language bias, you see a similar bias in poll results. In your campaign against pool renovation, use the language of the faction that opposes it—listen to how your neighbors talk about the work and repurpose their language for your poll. Do detractors wonder about the wisdom of "ripping up the pool"?

The sequence of questions also matters. "Suppose a poll opens with a series of questions about the slow rate of change in unemployment, follows with the handling of the Gulf oil spill, then asks about Obama's job approval," says Franklin. The approval rate will rank lower than if the poll had opened with questions on issues that painted Obama in a more favorable light. At your condo, have there been memorable renovation fiascos? If so, highlight these fiascos in the way you ask about the pool.

Question sequence can also encourage poll respondents to frame issues in certain ways. If a political poll opens with questions about the economy, respondents are likely to evaluate later questions in terms of their economic impact, more so than if the poll had opened with questions about the environment. You can do the same: Ask how people feel about recent increases in condo dues before asking how they feel about pool renovations.

Still another way polls drift is the way they push for answers. "When you ask people factual information, women tend to score lower on knowledge than men, but it's largely due to answering 'don't know,'" says Franklin. "But if you push people to guess, it turns out that women are just as accurate." Men are simply more willing to guess up front. And so polls that push for answers tend to include in the mix a more accurate representation of the female vote. Is there a gender gap in pool opinion? If so, push or don't push for answers in order to exploit it.

Also, how deeply does a poll ask you to think about a question before responding? One theory of how we answer survey questions holds that we each carry one, true opinion—but it may take considerable digging to find it. And while digging we must pass and discard many opinions that are good enough. If a poll encourages you to satisfice, your quick answer can be much more beholden to poll mechanics, pop opinion, and the twelve-hour news cycle. So after inserting bias in your pool poll, asking for quick answers will dial up the effectiveness of this bias.

In fact, all this adds up to extreme difficulty for real pollsters to design a poll that doesn't do any of these things. For you, it means the pool renovation proposal days are numbered—as is any issue that provokes your shiny, new, deliciously nasty skills for showing that public opinion is on your side.

## Early in the lead-up to the 2008 Iowa caucus,

the American Research Group was the only firm in the state polling likely Democratic voters. Their polls showed John Edwards leading with Barack Obama far behind. Then, as things started to heat up in November and December, new pollsters arrived asking new questions, which showed very new results—suddenly Obama was polling much closer!

Was Obama really the beneficiary of a new popular groundswell, or did the change in polling methods more accurately describe the support that Obama had had all along? No matter, the media storyline read OBAMA GAINING SPEED IN IOWA! And this hopeful story line paved the way for Obama's sweep through later primaries and then the general election.

## HOW TO BEAT SUCKERS AT POKER

**Jonathan Schaeffer** COMPUTER SCIENCE,
UNIVERSITY OF ALBERTA

Mathematician and computer games expert Jonathan Schaeffer at the University of Alberta solved checkers. After using up to two hundred computers running simultaneously for ten years to consider $10^{14}$ possible board states, his program, Chinook, eventually discovered a path of optimal play that never loses. And after solving checkers, Schaeffer turned his cerebral and computational firepower to another game—poker—specifically, two-player, limit Texas Hold 'Em.

In limit poker, you can only bet so much and so the game becomes a fairly mathematical exercise—based on your hole cards and the community cards, what's the chance of winning? (If this makes no sense, you can familiarize yourself with Texas Hold 'Em rules online.) Generally, if you have a more than 50 percent chance of winning, you bet.

But even this simple version of poker is tricky to study because "you can get lucky and unlucky and bad luck can last for a very long time," says Schaeffer. Bad luck can make even the best players look like rookies, so in a study it's hard to disentangle good play from good luck. Schaeffer and his research team found an interesting solution: They played two human-versus-computer pairs, each pair playing the same cards, but with the hands reversed. This way both sides get lucky or unlucky to the same degree. By comparing win/loss rates, Schaeffer and his collaborators discovered what strategies won over time.

"The best way to play against a computer is mathematically," says Schaeffer. Aggression or conservatism are trends that a computer will recognize and exploit.

"But playing against a human, aggression is correlated with success," says Schaeffer. "Pushing a lot of money into the pot forces your opponents to make many tricky decisions," and especially against weak opponents, these decisions are likely to result in mistakes.

When playing suckers, push chips.

## In a surprisingly fun and interesting paper

subtitled "Human Perfection at Checkers," Schaeffer tells the story of his program Chinook's 1994 battle against the human checkers champion, Marion Tinsley. In thirty-nine games, there were thirty-three draws, four wins for Tinsley, and two for Chinook. This was a great triumph for Chinook, considering that Tinsley only lost five other games between 1950 and his death in 1995 (paper linked from Schaeffer's faculty bio). What made Tinsley so great? According to Schaeffer, it was Tinsley's uncanny memory that even toward the end of his life allowed him to quote move sequences from games dating back to 1947, and a sixth sense born of experience. Yes, when playing checkers Tinsley "just knew" the best move—but, according to Schaeffer, it was because Tinsley had painstakingly added these moves to his mental Rolodex over many thousands of hours of play and study.

## There are 43,252,003,274,489,856,000

possible states for a Rubik's Cube. Researchers at Kent State opened up a can of supercomputing whoopass on these states, showing that the max number of moves needed to solve the cube at any time is twenty. This task would've taken a desktop computer thirty-five years, but took supercomputers at Google about a week.

# DISAPPOINTED OR PLEASANTLY SURPRISED? ADJUST YOUR EXPECTATIONS

**Gordon Dahl** ECONOMICS, UNIVERSITY OF CALIFORNIA–SAN DIEGO

What happens when you get a decent meal at a great restaurant? Or pay fourteen dollars to see an Oscar-winning film that turns out to be so-so? Or get a 3 percent raise when you expected 5 percent? You're disappointed, that's what. You expected greatness, you got mediocrity, and you're pissed. But look at it another way: Dude, you got a raise! That's awesome.

This is what economists call gain/loss reference dependence—human happiness really isn't about the amount of liquid in the glass, it's about that old half-full, half-empty thing. Or, more precisely, it's about how much liquid you expect to be in the glass. More than you expect and you're chuffed; less and you're disappointed.

How strong is the effect? It's hard to tell because it's extremely tricky to create emotionally charged expectations in the lab—a prerequisite to smashing these expectations and seeing how mad people get (or exceeding these expectations and looking for happiness).

So instead, Gordon Dahl, economist at the University of California–San Diego, turned to football. Before a game starts, there exists a very definite measure of expectations in the form of Vegas odds. You know who's supposed to win and by how much. And you know how emotionally charged a game is—is the team in playoff contention? Is the game against a traditional rival? Finally, there's an unfortunate but telling measure of how people are affected by football outcomes.

"We find that upset losses lead to a 10 percent increase in

domestic violence in the losing team's home city," says Dahl. If the losing team has an unusually high number of sacks and turnovers, make that a 15 percent spike. And if the upset loss is against a traditional rival, domestic violence in the team's home city increases by 20 percent. You can see it in police reports: As an upset starts to look likely in the game's final hour, domestic violence starts to climb, peaking just after the game, and returning to normal about two hours after the final whistle.

But it's not the loss that does it. If a team is expected to lose and then does . . . there's no spike. It's only when a team favored by four or more points chokes that football fans form fists. "The more salient the emotional shock is to you, the worse it is for your spouse," says Dahl.

And the rosy side isn't nearly as true. A home team's upset win does little to lower domestic violence. Or in other terms—sure, getting an unexpected great meal at a questionable restaurant makes you happy, but it doesn't nearly balance the unhappiness of a great restaurant missing. It's as if a happy surprise is (for example) +3 while a disappointment is -8. Over time, betting on restaurants is a losing proposition—this is likely one reason we get stuck in safe ruts, eating at the same decent place every time we go out. "But if we learned to manage our expectations, we'd all be better off," says Dahl.

You can't really adjust your surprise happiness/unhappiness payouts of +3/-8, but imagine lowering your expectations so that you're happily surprised at more than two-thirds of the new restaurants you visit. Now, in the long run, you're better off exploring.

Restaurants aren't the only medium in which expecting less allows life to frequently exceed your expectations. I grew up a Seattle sports fan and reflecting on how I now watch sports, even when the Mariners or Seahawks are ahead, I've ingrained the fatalistic attitude of "well, they'll probably blow it in the end."

My expectations stay low and so I'm happily surprised more than I'm disappointed (OK, with Seattle sports this barely allows me to break even).

The trick is to do this without becoming Eeyore. First, remember that your goal is to adjust your expectations without blunting your payoff. You can still root like heck, just imagine chopping a touchdown or three runs off Vegas's prediction for your team. And keep your lowered expectations to yourself—you don't want expecting less to lead to getting less.

## Gordon Dahl also explored how violent

blockbuster films affect violence in the neighborhoods surrounding theaters. Do violent films create violence? "Surprisingly," says Dahl, "during the movie, violent crime goes down." Dahl attributes this to temporary, voluntary incarceration: For the film's duration, violent people are off the streets. And the rate stays down for a couple hours after the film because after three hours in a theater, these violent people are sober.

## GDP, per capita income, unemployment,

educational performance: these are the measures of national well-being. But the United Kingdom hopes to add one more—a national happiness index. What's cool is that the prime minister imagines its use in driving and evaluating policy decisions. Just as an increase in GDP might be a reason for reform or an indication of an initiative's success or failure, so too could change in the happiness index drive decisions in government.

# HOW TO CHANGE YOUR EVIL WAYS

**B. J. Fogg** PERSUASIVE TECHNOLOGY, STANFORD UNIVERSITY

"I eat a lot of popcorn," says B. J. Fogg, experimental psychologist and founder of the Persuasive Technology Lab at Stanford. "I cook it in oil and I eat it at night. It's a kind of addiction." But Fogg broke this addiction by announcing to his social network that for the rest of the month, he would become a popcorn teetotaler. This is self-manipulation—by putting his social reputation on the line, Fogg forced himself to change his snacking habits. And he makes a career out of designing technology that does the same to you.

"Can we be manipulated by robots and code into doing things we don't want to do? The answer is clearly yes," says Fogg. "But you can't just grab techniques from Alcoholics Anonymous and apply them to getting people to sign up for Flickr."

Instead, Fogg's Behavior Model (behaviormodel.org) lists three things that need to be true to change behavior: high motivation, high ability, and a trigger. Think about the person who bought this book. He/she must have wanted to buy it, had the ability to do so—money in the pocket, an Amazon.com account, etc.—and then something happened that actually made this person reach for his or her wallet. But exactly how to create these three things depends greatly on what kind of behavior you want to change.

Fogg's chart of fifteen types of behavior change (behaviorgrid .org) crosses five types—do a new behavior, do a familiar behavior, increase an existing behavior, decrease an existing behavior, and stop an existing behavior—with three durations: once, for a duration, and from now on. Fogg applies codes to each of the fifteen types of behavior change, like "BlueDot," which is performing a familiar behavior one time—for example, buying a book on Amazon.com. The type of change coded "BlackSpan" is stopping an existing behavior for a period of time—not eating popcorn for a month. "PurplePath" describes increasing a behavior from now on, like exercising more.

Fogg's Behavior Wizard (behaviorwizard.org) asks questions that help you define the code of the behavior you'd like to change, and then lands you in the appropriate resource guide. Simply click through the wizard for concrete, usable strategies.

For example, let's take a look at getting yourself or others to do a familiar behavior one time—a BlueDot behavior. If it ain't happening right now, ability, motivation, or trigger must be too low (or some combination thereof). Fogg recommends attacking triggers first—they're the easiest to manipulate and could be a quick fix. For example, if you want to make sure you go for a run this afternoon, schedule a text message for after work saying "Go for a run now!" If you want employees to do the ergonomic wrist stretches they've been taught, you can have a manager walk around and encourage an immediate two-minute time-out or send a quick e-mail memo.

If triggers don't do the trick, Fogg's next step is to adjust ability, which he divides into the categories time, money, physical effort, mental effort, social deviance (is the behavior unexpected?), and nonroutine (is it out of the ordinary?). For example, if customers are still not ordering movies online even after being bombarded by your e-mail spam campaign (in a benevolent way), perhaps you need to streamline the ordering process and thereby decrease the time or mental effort needed to make a purchase. Or perhaps even with a trigger to go running, you're stymied by the inability to find a matching pair of running socks. In this case, increase ability by sorting that pile of clean clothes.

Finally, and only finally, does Fogg recommend working with motivation. (To Fogg, going here first is the sure sign of an inexperienced designer.) This is because motivation's tricky to measure and tricky to adjust in a uniform way. For Fogg, putting his social network reputation on the line increased his motivation to abstain from popcorn. And maybe for you, imagining toned calf muscles would increase your motivation to run. But others might not care about their calves or mind backsliding on Facebook and may be more motivated to run by the thought of a healthier heart. So it's tricky. Fogg suggests thinking about motivation in terms of sensation (pleasure/pain), anticipation (hope/fear), and belonging (acceptance/rejection).

Fifteen types of behavior, three factors to create it, each with subclasses—Fogg boils it down to nine words, which he calls his mantra for behavior change: "Put hot triggers in the path of motivated people." Again, let BehaviorWizard.org be your guide. It will lead you sheeplike to a better tomorrow.

## STOP YOUR BODY FROM DISSOLVING ITSELF

**Gerald Weissmann**   MEDICINE, NYU SCHOOL OF MEDICINE

"The function of evolution is not to make it possible to drink martinis at my age. It's to get us to child-producing age," says Gerald Weissmann, professor emeritus at the NYU School of Medicine. A major way your body does this is by responding immediately and aggressively to infection.

"When microbes invade our tissue, throat, or gut, our cells produce hydrogen peroxide in defense," explains Weissmann. It's like the body's chemotherapy, killing the microbes, but at the cost of collateral damage in the surrounding tissue. This collateral damage is nothing compared to the havoc the microbes could otherwise wreak, and if you died at age forty as Nature intended, you wouldn't even notice it. But the degenerative effect of all this hydrogen peroxide adds up. Especially in those genetically predisposed, this tissue damage can result in arthritis and other autoimmune diseases.

But even when not fighting infection, the body produces hydrogen peroxide.

Your cells take in more oxygen than they really need. This makes sense—the body errs on the side of caution, and it's certainly better to have too much rather than too little oxygen. But excess has to be disposed of, which your cells do by combining excess oxygen with water to form $H_2O_2$.

Where does this hydrogen peroxide go? Over time, it accumulates in hair follicles, eventually poisoning away their ability to produce the coloring pigment melanin. This is why your hair goes gray. But, again, this should happen after you've reproduced, so evolutionarily speaking, who cares?

So the conclusion is obvious. If you want to avoid arthritis and gray hair, stop oxygen at its source: Don't breathe. But, as Weissmann points out, "This wouldn't work so well." Instead, you can try eating things that soak up this extra oxygen before it can become the corrosive fourth atom hooked onto a benevolent water molecule.

While, Weissmann says, it's extremely difficult to measure possible benefits of antioxidation from dietary supplements (how can you disentangle diet from all the other environmental and genetic factors?), he sees the most potential benefit in polyphenols such as those in most fruits (especially berries), most vegetables (especially ones you can imagine British people cooking, like cabbage), honey, and green tea. Weissmann specifically recommends resveratrol, which you might recognize as the wonder drug in red wine, and which Weissmann calls "my polyphenol of choice."

**You've heard it before: red wine is good for**
your body. But did you know that it improves cognitive function,
too? A seven-year study of 5,033 Norwegians found that moderate
consumption of red wine (but not beer or spirits) improved
cognitive function in both men and women.

## SCAM-PROOF YOURSELF
**Stephen Greenspan** PSYCHOLOGY,
UNIVERSITY OF CONNECTICUT

I AM MARIAM ABACHA, WIDOW OF THE LATE NIGERIAN HEAD
OF STATE, GEN. SANI ABACHA. How many words did it take—two?
three?—before you knew this was spam? But once you get past
desperately lame e-mails and people in trench coats selling "designer" watches, scams can get a little trickier, a little more bor-
derline, and a little more appealing. Just ask Bernie Madoff's
investors.

Or look at Vegas. Just after getting hitched, my wife and I found
ourselves passing through Sin City as the cheapest way to visit
West Coast schools, where she was looking at PhD programs.
Being nearly indigent, we thought it'd be great to jump on a time-
share tour, collect the free show tickets and meal vouchers, and
use them to paint the town.

Fitting the classic profile of rubes, we were bussed out to a
brand-spanking-new time-share high-rise, planted atop what was
recently desert and would otherwise have been a strip mall. After
an agent showed us around, we were placed in a holding tank and
required to meet with a salesperson before we would be given
our swag. Great—we were five minutes from show tickets and a
free meal.

The salesperson asked us to estimate how many days we travel every year, and how much we spend on hotels while traveling, and explained that we could trade our weeks in Vegas for accommodations at any of their properties worldwide. Wow! It would take only twenty-five years to pay back our initial $80,000 investment, which, of course, would be doing nothing but gaining equity during this time. When we regretfully declined, the price went down to $40,000, and then eventually to $20,000.

And the thing is, it started to seem like a pretty good deal. Could we sleep on it? No. The offer was on the table—we had to decide now or never, and if "now," we could proceed directly to their financing center.

We chose "never." But it was much, much closer than it should've been. And I remember on the van ride back to the Strip, couples talked about how they'd done. The old hands had beat the system out of hundreds of dollars in casino chips in addition to the show and meal vouchers. And the few couples who'd become proud owners of a time-share in Vegas were just then realizing they'd been duped.

How, oh how, could they possibly have been so stupid?

"Think of gullibility as a threshold," says Stephen Greenspan, professor emeritus of psychology at the University of Connecticut and author of the book *The Annals of Gullibility*. Below this threshold you realize that with each "owner" paying $20,000 for ten days a year, that's a combined $730,000 for two rooms of slapdash construction in the desert. (Not to mention the fine print of astronomically high dues, blackout days, etc.) And above this threshold, well . . . you become an "owner." Greenspan lists four factors that push you toward this threshold: situation, cognition, personality, and affect. Ratchet them all high enough and anyone will tip into the abyss of foolishness. Learn to dial them down, and you can proof yourself against gullibility.

First, situation. This is a believable scam, or a "situation so compelling few people could resist," says Greenspan—like a time-share that takes only five years to pay for itself in reduced travel costs, which you can trade for travel anywhere in the world, and which you can sell at any time for more than you paid. That's believable, right? (OK, OK, I was young and foolish and in love!)

But if you have cognition—that is, background information and the mental firepower to use it—you still have hope of smelling the rat. I wish I could say that's how my wife and I snubbed the time-share scammers. However, I'm afraid I have to admit that we were just slightly out of their target demographic, having lied about our income to get the proffered free stuff. If we'd had the money, I'm not sure our cognition could have fended off the time-share. Certainly that was the case for many, many young couples that looked not so different from us.

Thirdly, woe be unto ye who are predisposed by personality to be unusually trusting. According to Greenspan, a trusting person-ality was a major factor in the success of a California scam target-ing Mormons. The scammers, themselves posing as Mormons, promised to triple investors' money if they would contribute to a legal fund pushing for the sale of gold bullion from Israel to the Middle East. And these California Mormons were taken in, "in part due to their tendency to be trusting, especially of people in their religious community," explains Greenspan.

Finally, your affect matters. This is the in-the-moment version of personality and it's why there's free wine at art auctions. It's also why my wife and I weren't allowed to sleep on the rock-bottom offer of $20,000 for a Vegas time-share. "Gullibility hap-pens under pressure, when you don't have time to think about things," says Greenspan, "and it helps explain why smart people do dumb things."

With the stamp of legal legitimacy, the Vegas time-share system had evolved to become nearly the perfect scam. You've got a be-lievable situation, assault on cognition in the form of seemingly airtight logic to buy, the perfect rube personality in the demographics of the people they stick on the bus in the first place, and heightened affect through the pressure to buy it now or never.

But you, dear reader, are now armed with the tools to avoid the fate of so many rubes. You can't do much about the situation (that's up to the scammers), and it's tricky to alter your trusting personality, so focus on cognition and affect when making yourself scam-proof. First, you can be almost assured that any offer that's on the table now-or-never is something you'll wake up regretting. If you find yourself pressured to make a decision in the heat of the moment, always ask to sleep on it. Any legit offer will be there in the morning.

This also buys time to increase cognition. Try the phone-a-friend option. Outside the framework of the scammers' believable situation, does a trusted friend think it sounds like a good deal? And do your research—all it takes is a quick online search for "Vegas time-share scam" to return enough chatter to make even the most wide-eyed rube think twice.

So just chill out. Think. Do your homework. And you'll realize that the widow of the late Nigerian head of state is unlikely to transfer $20 million to your bank account, if only you pay the legal costs.

## After I admitted to him how close I came to

buying a sucker time-share, Greenspan told me the following story.

"When I was dating my now ex-wife, my mom called up and said that my aunt Ruby was selling her jewelry and she could get me a great deal on an engagement ring. I said I wasn't ready, but my mom pressed, and finally said she'd already bought the ring for me. My fatal mistake was saying 'Yeah, OK, fine,' and the next thing I knew I was getting congratulated on being engaged."

Greenspan's mother had duped him into marriage.

First, she created a believable situation—Aunt Ruby's jewelry— which Greenspan hadn't the cognitive background information or tenacity to fend off. And his personality was predisposed to trust his mother. And then his mom did something especially slick—when she said she'd already bought the ring, she ratcheted Greenspan's affect, requiring an immediate decision.

Greenspan cracked. And so would you.

## AVOID BUYING STUFF YOU DON'T NEED

**Brian Knutson** NEUROSCIENCE, STANFORD UNIVERSITY

"On an airplane, you pick up SkyMall and you think Ooh, that's cool!" says Stanford neuroscientist Brian Knutson. "And then you look at the price and say No way!" In a nutshell, this is the theory of oh-wow/oh-yikes shopping (my words). Knutson can see it in the brain.

He had undergrads evaluate items in a catalog and, "Sure enough, when people saw products they liked, a reward area in their brain lit up," says Knutson. "Independently, a prefrontal area that monitors price lit up." Whichever of these two ignitions was the most powerful—"oh wow!" or "oh yikes!"—won the shopping battle.

The application on the marketing side is obvious: You could use fMRI imaging to perfectly price a product so that the reward for the target market is ever so slightly greater than the cost. People would buy and you'd make the max on each sale.

On the personal side, Knutson knows how to change these activation patterns. For example, beware the lure of bargains, which light your brain's reward pathways irrespective of whether the bargain price is actually low, allowing the reward area of your brain an extra bargaining chip to use against your stodgy prefrontal. But most important, Knutson found that paying with credit lit the nay-saying prefrontal less than paying the same amount with cash—"anesthetizing the money loss," he says.

If you want to dampen your shopping impulse, pay cash, not credit. And when you hit a bargain, allow your brain that extra second (or day) to think twice—reason overruling impulse—do you really need that battery-operated tie rack, even if it is 50 percent off?

## Steve Schlozman, codirector of the Harvard

Medical School psychiatry program says, "The balance between the frontal lobe's executive function and the amygdala's base instincts is what makes us human." And he offers imbalance as the cause of zombiism. In his decidedly tongue-in-cheek scenario, a decayed frontal lobe would leave no check for the anger and lust of the zombie amygdala. Schlozman also points out that the National Institutes of Health's definition of cerebellar degeneration describes a "wide-base, unsteady, lurching walk, often accompanied by a back and forth tremor in the trunk of the body." And degeneration of the hypothalamus can result in an insatiable hunger. In Schlozman's opinion, exactly this damage could be caused by a mutated influenza, which would be especially transmittable, say, by bite. The zombie tide is real, baby. And it's coming to get you. (For more science-of-the-undead fun, Google "Schlozman zombie podcast.")

## Puzzle #9: Boomerang v. Zombie

Our hero throws a boomerang in the attempt to decapitate a zombie standing 30 yards away. But two seconds after he releases the 'rang, the zombie charges. The boomerang tracks a perfect circle at 30 mph, and the zombie instantly lurches to a surprisingly speedy 15 mph (no "Romero" zombie is this, apparently). Here's the question: Should our hero stand his ground and await the return of his weapon, or one second after the zombie charges, should he run at 10 mph toward a tree 8 yards directly behind him that would take him 2 seconds to climb to the height of safety?

## CONTROL GOSSIP

**Tim Hallett** SOCIAL PSYCHOLOGY,

INDIANA UNIVERSITY–BLOOMINGTON

Gossip's bad, right? According to Tim Hallett, social psychologist at Indiana University, it depends on your point of view. "Gossip is a weapon of the weak," says Hallett. "Like the French Revolution, it's a way the powerless band together to retake power from authority."

In his study, the proletariat was composed of middle school teachers, and playing the part of a soon-to-be-noggin-challenged French noble was a new principal with an authoritarian administrative style and awkward social skills. Hallett videotaped these teachers as they went about their business—in conversations, in the teachers' lounge, and especially in teacher-led formal meetings—generating more than four hundred pages of single-spaced transcripts.

He coded the language of these transcripts and explored the data for insights into the inner workings of gossip.

One thing Hallett found is that "Gossip is a ubiquitous part of everyday life—it's unrealistic to ban it formally." If you're on the monarchy side of the revolution and thus have the goal of squishing gossip, banning it simply makes it more covert and potentially more insidious. Instead, providing a clear channel to voice discontent and clear mechanisms for getting things done in general removes the need for gossip to fill these roles. (Interestingly, elsewhere in this book economist Eli Berman recommends squishing terrorist organizations by increasing government social services, thus removing the population's need to turn to splinter groups for this help.)

Unfortunately, in the school Hallett studied, neither of these conditions was met and so gossip ran rampant. The task went from reducing its occurrence to "managing it informally by understanding how it works," says Hallett.

"First, the best thing to do is have lots of friends," he says. This seems obvious—if you're liked and respected, people are less likely to say bad things about you—but it also means that if gossip happens to turn against you, you're likely to have allies within earshot willing to deflect the damage. Assuming you or a friend is present, here's how to deflect the course of gossip.

In the early stages, Hallett found that gossipers were tentative, exploring the loyalties of the group in a way that allowed plausible deniability should a group member prove loyal to the monarchy. One way to do this is through sarcasm. "If the gossip gets back to the position of authority, sarcasm allows the gossiper to insist she was being literal, like 'I *said* you did a really good job!' "

Another obfuscation Hallett saw that attempted to infer bad things without saying them outright was something he called "praising the predecessor," as in a teacher describing conditions under the past administration as "so calm, and you could teach. There was no one constantly looking over your shoulder." What does this imply about the current administrator? This technique of praise as detraction works in any case of glaringly obvious comparison, as in a wife pointing out to her husband that her ex-boyfriend was such a good cook!

It's in this early evaluative stage that gossip can most easily be steered or diffused. To combat sarcasm or comparative praise, ask for clarification—force the gossiper to speak literally and thus take responsibility for the true meaning of the comments. Or try a preemptive positive evaluation—follow a loaded opening question (Did you see the boss's new shoes?) with abject praise (Yeah—Velcro's back, baby!). If all else fails, switch the gossip to an innocuous target (Dude, that was nothing—did you see the shoes on Steve from accounting?).

Nipping detrimental gossip adroitly in its early stages—before gossipers discover everyone's loyalties—can allow you to save the target of gossip without putting your head alongside his or hers on the chopping block of the resistance.

## In another study, Hallett found a positive

feedback loop for the spread of emotion through a workplace—if a person naturally or intentionally starts broadcasting an emotion, it not only spreads by interaction, but as it spreads the original emotion also amplifies. This, of course, causes more spreading and more amplification until the emotion, in Hallett's words, "blows up."

## Puzzle #10: The Gossip Web

Did you hear that Annabel and Mark told everybody they'd baked the cupcakes for the party, but actually bought them at the bakery in the next town over? Can you guide the important message through the social network on page 141? The message can only travel between touching boxes (no diagonals), and must be brought into any next box by someone in the first. For example, to get from the starting box to the one below it, you could go guy-with-glasses to guy-with-glasses. Then continuing down the column, you could go top-hat to top-hat.

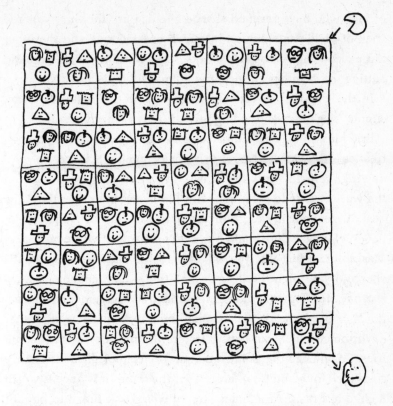

![Batman cake logo] **DO THE UTILITY SHUFFLE TO DIVIDE CAKE, CHORES, CARBON, AND THE BILL**

**Eric Maskin** ECONOMICS, INSTITUTE FOR ADVANCED STUDY

"Parents want both kids to be happy with the piece of cake they get," says Eric Maskin, economist at Princeton's Institute for Advanced Study. A parent can do his or her best to cut the cake evenly, but the problem is, "the kids themselves might not see this as an equal split," he says. In addition to the perception of size inequality, maybe only one piece has a sugar Batman, or maybe one is slightly more endowed with frosting. These things may matter more than you could possibly imagine— they may have different "utilities" to different kids. So parents of kids who have reached sharp-knife age use the time-honored trick of divide-and-choose, in which one kid cuts and the other kid picks. "The reason this works," says Maskin, "is that the kid cutting the cake has an incentive to make the pieces equal."

In the language of economists and game theorists this clean, simple, elegant cake-dividing procedure is a "mechanism."

Eric Maskin designs similar mechanisms for things like carbon treaties—he won the Nobel Prize in Economic Sciences for pioneering the field—only in the case of carbon cuts, no country in the world wants to get stuck with the bigger piece of cake. "The goal of mechanism design theory is to come up with the combination of concessions that gives everyone a positive payout," says Maskin. And just like the cake, this is possible because what's cheap to you might be dear to me—things like technological assistance, development aid, preferential trade agreements, international or domestic political capital, military assistance, a cleaner environment, etc., can have different utilities for different countries. Maybe giving some amount of technological assistance costs the United States 4 "chits," but the same assistance is worth 8 chits to Brazil. An efficient treaty would ask Brazil to pay for this assistance with 7.99 chits of carbon reductions, which might be worth more to the United States in political capital than the 4 chits of tech assistance it paid. Because both countries come out ahead, both would sign the treaty. And then we would all stand arm in arm atop a hill drinking Coca-Cola and singing.

This idea of personal, differing utility allows you to amiably divide many things. Think about splitting up household chores— maybe you'd do the dishes and the laundry if your spouse will set a mousetrap in the garage. Or imagine dividing a Sunday's worth of free time—is it worth six hours of strolling hand in hand on the beach for two hours of uninterrupted viewing of the Chelsea v. Manchester United game?

The variable utility of cutting cake and carbon also allows you to split the restaurant bill with a group of friends. It's not fair to split the bill evenly—you're not going to freeload lobster when all I got was a grilled cheese sandwich! (This is the venerable problem called "the diner's dilemma," but that's another long story.)

So imagine you're not splitting the bill evenly. Who should pay a bit more and who should be silently allowed to pay a bit less? Well, what's an extra $10.00 actually worth to you in terms of utility? Like cutting carbon, what somewhat intangible concessions might you get for paying extra? Might you gain the equivalent of $10.01 in goodwill? (The same amount of goodwill might only have $1.50 in utility to your cash-strapped high school buddy who still lives at home.) Does withholding $10.00 from the pot actually cost you $10.01 in the utility of reduced sex appeal due to looking like a cheapskate?

A good mechanism is efficient—everyone maximizes his or her personal utility by giving up what's cheap to gain what's dear, thus coming out ahead on aggregate. It might only take a little tricky utility shuffling to make a good deal all around. And at the very least, next time you get stuck paying the extra ten bucks on the tab, you'll be aware that you got something for it.

## Puzzle #11: Cake Cutting

For whatever reason, you've chosen DIY cake cutting over allowing your two kids to divide-and-choose. Now the problem is how to divide the cake evenly. Imagine the small pan is a perfect 10 × 8-inch rectangle, 2 inches deep. On one side sits an undividable sugar Batman, worth exactly 27 in$^3$ of cake to kid A and 8 in$^3$ to kid B. But it's kid B's birthday and so both see it as fair if kid B's piece is 1.5 times as big as kid A's. (What? Isn't this how it works in your family?) Who should get the sugar Batman, and how much cake should each kid get?

## MIGHT AS WELL FACE IT: ADDICTED TO LOVE

**Larry Young** NEUROSCIENCE, YERKES NATIONAL
PRIMATE RESEARCH CENTER

"Drugs hijack the circuitry that evolved for things like love," says
Larry Young, neuroscientist at Yerkes National Primate Research
Center. Most recreational drugs create dopamine release in the
brain—thus our drug-induced sense of exhilaration and euphoria.
And it's dopamine that's produced when you first fall in love. In
the brain, the early stages of a relationship are very much like
snorting cocaine.

And in many animals with one-and-done mating, that's where
the molecules of love end. It's pleasurable, it's exhilarating, then
it's done and the animal is croaking, dancing, or butting heads in
search of the next rush.

But not in prairie voles.

"In prairie voles, we see three molecules involved in mating,"
says Young. First, of course, is dopamine. But female voles add
oxytocin to the mix. "Mothers release it during labor and when
nursing," says Young, "and when a female vole is being mated by
a male, she releases oxytocin in the brain." Male voles release vasopressin, which is only a couple amino acids different from oxytocin, and in other species is involved with territorial behavior.

What does this overlay of oxytocin or vasopressin do? "We can
inject female brains with oxytocin or male brains with vasopressin and voles will bond without mating," says Young.

Does this imply that the human experience of love could be
chemical?

Young points to a Swedish study of one thousand couples that
charted which men were well endowed in something called the
microsatellite polymorphism in the brain's vasopressin receptors
(don't worry, you won't be tested on that), and asked the couples

questions about their relationships. Men who were biologically doomed to trap less vasopressin were twice as likely to report a crisis in their marriage in the past year, twice as likely to be unmarried but shacking up with a partner, and much more likely to report dissatisfaction with their relationship. In short, less vasopressin made males bond poorly.

Similarly, Young points to many studies that have confirmed the bonding properties of oxytocin, finding that it "increases eye-to-eye contact, increases ability to read emotions of other people, it increases empathy—also one study showed that if you gave oxytocin to a couple that was having a conflict, after the conflict they would have fewer bad emotions."

And so love is chemical.

But user beware: This neurochemical cocktail of love is addictive. "Love goes from lots of dopamine to a later phase which is basically togetherness to stop withdrawal symptoms," says Young. And once the dopamine is gone, there had better be enough vasopressin (men) or oxytocin (women) to make it in both partners' best interest to refrain from looking for a new source of dopamine outside the relationship.

So as new love gives way to the routine of sex every other Wednesday after *Dancing with the Stars*, dopamine cedes to vasopressin/oxytocin. But what happens when love is removed altogether? What happens when you split with a partner? "If a vole loses its partner, it shows symptoms of depression similar to withdrawal," Young says. "What does the animal do? It goes to seek a new partner."

This is the rodent equivalent of a rebound relationship. Rather than pushing through the depression of withdrawal that eventually allows your brain chemistry to return to prerelationship levels, it's much, much easier to find pleasure in a new drug, even when this new drug is a detrimental source of dopamine.

Instead of rebounding into whatever gives you a quick fix, give your brain chemistry a break. After an ending, take the time you need to reset your head before another beginning.

## The news flash in a study from Mount Sinai

School of Medicine is that both good and bad memories of Mom were strengthened with a dose of good old oxytocin. After a whiff, securely attached men remembered Mom more fondly, and insecurely attached men remembered Mom even less fondly. It may be that oxytocin doesn't simply increase attachment, but that it adds saliency to emotional memory of any sort.

## CREATE FALSE MEMORIES TO GET MORE PEACH SCHNAPPS

**Elizabeth Loftus** PSYCHOLOGY, UNIVERSITY OF CALIFORNIA–IRVINE

My earliest memory is of living in Bergen, Norway, when I was two. I vividly remember looking out at fjords from a ferryboat, and there's a picture of me standing next to a troll statue holding up two fingers and smiling. I've heard my parents talk fondly about Bergen. But the thing is, I recently found out my parents lived there before I was born. The picture in question was taken during a visit to the Tyrolean kitsch town of Leavenworth, Washington, and my vivid memory of fjords and ferries must be tangled with a trip to or from Bainbridge Island. It turns out that without meaning to, my parents planted within me a false memory.

Elizabeth Loftus knows how to do it on purpose.

First, she gathers information. "We learn about a subject's personality, about thoughts, about different foods, all to give what happens later some credibility," says Loftus, a psychologist at the University of California–Irvine and pioneer in the study of memory.

Then, (for example, in one series of studies) Loftus tells a subject that the research team fed the subject's information into a supercomputer that knows, based on this information, what happened to the subject as a child. The computer lists many of the subject's real experiences and intermixes one false experience—in the case of these studies, suggesting the "memory" of getting sick from dill pickles, hard-boiled eggs, or another food. Loftus then asks the subject to talk about these experiences. Eventually, many subjects will adopt the false memory, filling in details about the childhood food illness.

But how can you tell the subject has actually adopted the memory, rather than simply being agreeable by paying lip service to researchers' suggestions?

"After I seduce you into believing that you got sick from a food as a child, you'll avoid the food now," says Loftus, who watched subjects' food preferences after the memory insertion. Simply, the false memory of barfing pickles becomes embedded to the point that without further prompting, subjects avoid pickles in the postinterview buffet.

In addition to its implications for investigations, psychologists' couches, and courtrooms, the ease of false memory insertion should allow you to mind-punk your friends into giving up their share of the peach schnapps (my college friends will get this inside joke, which unfortunately requires no false memory). Start a week earlier with the story, "Dude, do you remember the time when . . ." and when your target denies it, counter with, "Well, of course you wouldn't remember it, but it was pretty gnarly. . . ." Once your target's accepted the truth of his past transgressions, you can safely pass around the schnapps, confident you'll get your fair share.

## SAVE THE WORLD IN YOUR SPARE TIME

**Luis von Ahn** COMPUTER SCIENCE, CARNEGIE MELLON UNIVERSITY

The idea is not a new one: All those people pedaling away in spinning class, going nowhere, burning calories to push against the adjustable friction of their back wheels. Shouldn't we, like, use that energy for something? Couldn't we power the lights in the gym, or heat the sauna, or digitize ancient manuscripts?

The good news is we're already doing the last one, thanks to Luis von Ahn. But the extra power he harnesses isn't calories from quadriceps, it's the computational power of millions of brains. It started with another of his projects, the Captcha. That's right, Luis von Ahn, MacArthur fellow and computer scientist at Carnegie Mellon University, is the guy (along with Manuel Blum) who developed the little text box gatekeepers that you squint at whenever you sign up for a new online service or post a link to a message board—it's the way computers can tell you're you, or at least human. "They're pretty annoying," says von Ahn, "and worldwide they waste about five hundred thousand hours a day." Von Ahn started wondering if, like powering the lights by pedal, he could put these half-million hours a day of cerebral busywork to better use.

And here's the thing about a Captcha: By design, it asks you to do something a computer can't, that is, translate a visual image of a distorted word into text. "Your brain is doing something amazing," says von Ahn.

Enter the Google Books Library Project. Ancient manuscripts are rotting, and before they go the way of *Tony Orlando and Dawn's Greatest Hits* (which died with the 8-track never to boogie again) Google hopes to digitize them. So there are people in libraries around the world scanning these decaying pages by hand. The scanned images are then fed into text recognition software, which translates the images into text files.

Trouble is, even the best OCR software isn't perfect, and in manuscripts more than one hundred years old OCR has an error rate more than 30 percent.

So instead of simply digitizing books as best they can and settling for Shakespeare's "To be ornut Tope, thatis the truncheon," the Google Books Library Project feeds each scan into two different text recognition softwares, and when the software disagrees on a word, they call in an impartial, third-party arbiter: you. The software snips the image of the word in question and places it in a Captcha box (now called reCaptcha), and you play the part of translator. Whenever you type the words you see in a reCaptcha box, you're translating a word from an ancient manuscript or from the *New York Times* archives or from any number of previously undigitizable text sources that would otherwise eventually fade into the great circular file of cultural forgetting.

This is why there are two words in a reCaptcha box—one against which the computer checks you, and one the computer doesn't know, that you translate. Your opinion is compared to other users' opinions until a word gets 2.5 consistent "votes" (humans are worth one vote, the OCR software is worth one-half), at which point it's considered solved. Easy words, on which all humans agree, are recycled to become the control words against which the computer measures your humanity.

"We're doing 70 million words a day," says von Ahn, "a couple million books a year; and there are 750 million distinct people who have digitized at least one word." That's one out of every nine people on earth who's helped turn decaying images of ink on paper into everlasting ones and zeros.

**"Humanity's greatest achievements—the**
pyramids of Egypt, the Great Wall of China, the Panama Canal—were
all done with, like, 100,000 people," says von Ahn. In his opinion, this
was due to the impossibility of coordinating more than this 100,000.
And so there was a cap on potential human achievement. "But now
with the Internet, we can coordinate 100 million. If 100,000 people
could put a man on the moon, what could we do with 100 million?"

**Researchers in the new field of "culturenomics"**
are mining the 5,195,769-and-growing volumes of the Google Books
Library Project for elements of cultural change. For example, you can
see the suppression of the Jewish artist Marc Chagall in Germany as
the difference in the frequency of his name in English and German
books. In English, Chagall continues to rise through the Nazi period,
whereas in Germany, there's a sharp drop-off in the printing of his
name. And, interestingly, Darwin took off during and just after his
lifetime, but it wasn't until the discovery of the structure of DNA that
his name exploded into the cultural lexicon.

## USE FACEBOOK TO PICK YOUR PARTY POSSE

**Robin Dunbar** ANTHROPOLOGY, OXFORD UNIVERSITY

Admit it: You'd love to—just once!—do a karaoke version of "Pinball Wizard" while standing on a bar in a sequined
cape, codpiece, and oversized sunglasses.

Or is that just me? Anyway. . . . you can't. That's because

it's no fun to party alone, and the 150 people you know would excommunicate you for the "Pinball" incident. In fact, Robin Dunbar, director of the Institute for Cognitive and Evolutionary Anthropology at Oxford University, has shown that people in societies around the world tend toward this magic number of 150 as what he calls "the cognitive limit to the number of individuals with whom any single person can maintain stable relationships." It's true in Tennessee, it's true in South Africa, and it's also true on Facebook. "Actually the average number of Facebook friends is between 120 and 130," says Dunbar, "perhaps because the other 20 or so people include Granny and the like, who aren't online."

So your goal is this: to act depraved while minimizing the damage to your 150-person network. The key is to pick just the right friends to party with. "In dense networks, people police the community," says Dunbar. You see this in the Amish or Hutterites. "If you do something offensive, you offend everyone in your community and become a social outcast." But Dunbar can show a developing trend toward more splintered networks. "Now, it may be that you're born in San Francisco, go to school in New York, and get a job in Florida," he says, meaning that your network is fragmented into perhaps five independent fingers of thirty people each. If you party with just the right, small splinter, the rest of your network need never know.

The trick is remaining hyperaware that whomever you party with will post pictures of you in a codpiece back to their own Facebook accounts, which will then be seen by all their friends. Are there people in your small, potential party splinter who are members of multiple lists? For example, is one of your college friends also on your list of current work buddies? If so, you may not be able to party with college friends for fear of your behavior leaking between groups and generally going viral through your 150-person network.

Rewrite your friends lists as a Venn diagram as shown below.

Now look for circles with the least (or no) overlap. If your friend circles are unusually dense, with unavoidable overlap—more Hutterite than modern American—look for the overlap with the shortest reach.

Now read this book's entry about identity economics to discover how much your depraved behavior is likely to cost you in any given splinter (acting contrary to your expected identity carries a cost in "personal utility"—and you may have different identities in different splinter groups). Imagine the identity cost in any group multiplied by the number of people in the group. How much does your desired brand of depravity cost you?

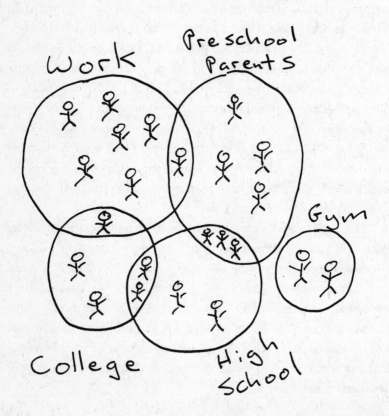

The splinter with the least cost, gentle reader, is the group with which you should sing "Pinball Wizard."

## Dunbar's recent work finds that people with

large social networks have distinctly looser emotional ties to most members. And so it's as if, instead of being bound by the number 150, the size of a social network is bound by a finite amount of emotional energy, which a person can choose to distribute as they see fit.

## Puzzle #12: Friends Add Up

You have friends from grade school, high school, summer camp, college, your first job, grad school, your kids' friends' parents, an online fantasy football league, and your current job. If friend groups can only be composed of 13, 15, 17, or 32 individuals and each subsequent friend group (in listed order) has equal to or greater than the number of friends as the previous group, how many friends does each group have in order for your total number of friends to be exactly 150?

**"There's this old question in sociology asking**
why your opinions and interests are similar to those of your friends,"
says MacArthur genius and Cornell computer scientist John Kleinberg.
"Do your friends influence you to become more like them, or do
you seek out like-minded friends?" Kleinberg answered this question
using Wikipedia, where you can quantifiably see that people who talk
have similar editing behavior. Great, you're like your friends. Only,
by downloading the multiterabyte file that holds all of Wikipedia's
history, Kleinberg was able to ask if "similarity in editing behavior
started before or after people started talking to each other." What
you see is this: "As people get closer to each other in the network,
their editing behaviors become much more similar," says Kleinberg,
"but after they meet, their editing becomes only marginally more
similar." So the answer to sociology's question is this: You seek out
like-minded friends.

## HOW TO GET AWAY WITH A CRIME IN BROAD DAYLIGHT

**Daniel Simons and Christopher Chabris** PSYCHOLOGY,
UNIVERSITY OF ILLINOIS–URBANA-CHAMPAIGN, UNION COLLEGE

In a recent fit of optimism, I joined a gym. And the day I signed
up, I noticed a police officer poking around the gym lobby. When
I asked the membership agent about it, he told me that the day
before, someone had stolen a spinning bike (like the life-sucking
machine in *The Princess Bride*). It had been there at the 5:30 p.m.
class, but was gone at the 7:00 p.m. class. There's only one exit
that doesn't set off a fire alarm, and the exit leads through a
crowded gym, down the stairs, and past the staffed front desk.

In other words, someone had walked out the door with a one-
hundred-pound bike in plain view of at least ten and likely fifty

people. Maybe it was under a huge tarp or something, but still . . . don't you think you would've noticed?

Maybe, maybe not. Check this out.

While both at Harvard, psychologists Dan Simons (now at the University of Illinois) and Christopher Chabris (Union College) filmed six people passing a basketball. Three wore white shirts and three wore black shirts. In the video they jump around while inexpertly bouncing and tossing the ball from one person to the next. Simons and Chabris showed subjects this film and asked them to count the number of passes by one or the other team. After the film they asked subjects if, just maybe, they noticed anything strange or unexpected during the film.

Half didn't.

This, despite the fact that a woman in a gorilla suit walks obviously into the center of the group, stops to look at the camera, and thumps her chest before continuing off screen.

Again, people failed to notice a lady in a fricking gorilla suit. You can find the video online by searching for "invisible gorilla," which is also the title of the duo's very well written, thoroughly researched, and entertaining book.

First, this is potentially the coolest experimental design ever. Second, again—Dude, a gorilla suit! Come on!

But the experiment isn't a one-hit wonder of coolness. Simons and another collaborator—Daniel Levin—ran a study that starts with a researcher stopping a stranger to ask directions. Great. Then two people carrying a large door walk through the middle of their conversation. And during the short time of obfuscation, the researcher grabs the door and one of the carriers takes his place. When the door passes, this new person picks up the conversation where it left off.

Imagine the mind trip: You're talking to someone who magically and immediately morphs into an entirely new person. It's enough to make you infarct something. That is, assuming you notice at all. Again, as you can see with a quick online video search, half of us don't.

Granted, these two studies are different—the first explores selective attention, and the second explores change blindness—but they both nicely demonstrate that people can be massively oblivious to even the patently obvious.

So it's very possible to carry a spinning bike through a crowded gym without anyone's noticing. Note this is very different from people's noticing and not intervening—that jumps into the realm of bystander apathy, with the decision to help or not help a victim depending on behavioral economic payoffs like risk, reward, and relatedness (see this book's entry on altruism). No, here we're dealing with another thing entirely: The bystanders are completely unaware of the crime.

So . . . how might you take advantage of this phenomenon?

In a nice twist on the original gorilla experiment (for which the good doctors received an Ig Noble Prize), Simons and Chabris asked subjects not only to count the number of passes on one team or the other, but to keep track of the number that were bounce passes or chest passes. "With a higher cognitive load, people notice the gorilla even less," says Chabris.

Simons explains, "We have a limited pool of attention. If you're paying a lot of attention to something, you have less attention available to spend on noticing other things. This helps us focus on important things while filtering out distractions. One consequence of filtering out distractions, though, is that we sometimes filter out things that we might want to see."

Like a lady in gorilla suit. Or the fact that your conversation partner has shape-shifted. Or someone lugging a spinning bike past the gym's front desk.

So if you're trying to do the lugging, do it among people whose brains are otherwise occupied. During the Final Jeopardy round is ideal. If not, the age-old technique of an accomplice creating a distraction is a good one—and it doesn't even need to pull attention away from your physical space as long as it takes up bystanders' mental space. Perhaps your accomplice can aggressively shout brain teasers?

Also, "if a bank robber has a gun, bystanders are less likely to remember his face," says Simons. Paying well-deserved attention to the gun detracts from the attention available for face recognition. This is similar to the theory of garish invisibility employed by Bill Murray in the underappreciated 1990 movie *Quick Change*, in which Murray flamboyantly navigates an airport in a clown suit while escaping after robbing a bank. While not exactly lab conditions, it's as if people see the clown suit and not the wearer.

As for the exercise bike, I'm sorry to report the mystery was never solved.

## Simons and Chabris also happen to be

freakishly good at chess. (Chabris has been a chess master since 1986, was editor of *Chess Horizons*, and founded the *American Chess Journal*.) Chess is a fertile ground for researchers because there are rankings—you know quantitatively how good people are. And Chabris and Simons used this data to find something cool: Players with lower rankings massively overestimated how good they were, while players with higher rankings were much closer in their estimations of their skill. (See this book's entry with David Dunning.)

# THE SHORTEST PATH BETWEEN ERRANDS

**William Cook**  MATHEMATICS, GEORGIA INSTITUTE OF TECHNOLOGY

OK, here's the situation: In the short time your kids are at preschool, you have to deposit a check, buy organic gummy vitamins with iron at the hippie grocery co-op, buy Drano at the nonhippie supermart (while avoiding eye contact with anyone you might've seen at the first), pick up dog food, drop off overdue books at the library, and get a bike tire repaired.

Six errands flung to the far corners of town, with a web of connecting roads and a ticking clock. Do you hear the *Mission Impossible* theme music? Go!

Oh, I forgot the added bonus: If you figure out how to find the shortest route, the Clay Mathematics Institute will give you a million dollars. That's because, to date, no one has provided a general solution (or proven a solution's impossible) to this type of problem—called "the traveling salesman"—in which you have to minimize total distance traveled among many points.

It has many applications: Imagine you're standing in the middle of a court littered with tennis balls. What's the shortest distance you can walk to pick them all up? Or how can you see all the major landmarks of Paris in an afternoon?

The problem is that, "as the number of stops grows toward infinity, so too does the number of possible routes," says William Cook, mathematician at Georgia Tech. At some point, the magnitude of possible choices simply overpowers computational resources. So Cook takes a novel approach. Instead of using brute force computation to search through the haystack of nearing-infinite routes for the best solution, Cook explores sufficing—how can you *nearly* find the shortest tour between errands, and once you have a candidate, how can you know how good or not good it is? Cook says, "If I give you a ten-mile tour, you might be unsatisfied, unless I can guarantee with some degree of certainty that there are no shorter tours."

This allows us to start our errands without having to wait the many generations the Deep Thought supercomputer might take to discover the optimal route of forty-two miles (and if you get this reference, I imagine you'll find many little chuckles throughout this book).

So how should you suffice? "If every time you go to the nearest place you haven't yet visited, it gets you within 25 percent of the shortest tour," says Cook. What errand is closest to you? Go there. And then look around again—now which one's closest? Continue until you've visited each stop, and you're mathematically certain to be within 25 percent of the shortest route. (Remember to think time and not distance when computing "nearest.")

Once you're cool with that, here's a nice refinement: Draw your tour, always going to the closest place not yet visited, and then look for places where the route intersects itself. Uncross any crosses. (This makes no sense until you draw it, like on the next page, and then it's obvious). This gets you within 10 percent of the optimal tour. If you can solve the tour completely, the Clay Institute has a million bucks for you.

# The traveling salesman problem is a clean

illustration of applied versus pure mathematics. Cook has solved optimal tours up to 33,810 stops and tours within 1 percent of optimal are available for millions of stops. But that's not a solution. To date, there exists no general procedure for finding the optimal route among X number of stops.

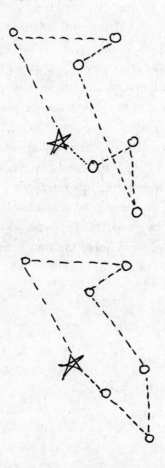

# Puzzle #13: **A Three-Hour Tour?**

Draw the shortest tour starting and ending at the house,
and touching all the points in the picture below.

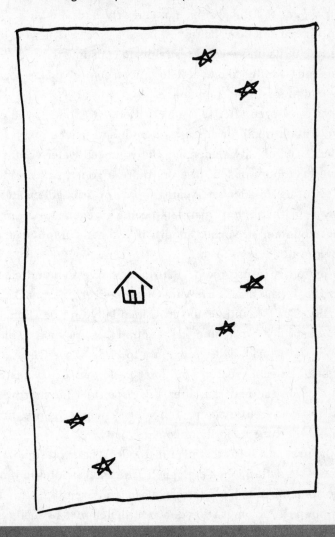

# HOW TO SURVIVE ARMAGEDDON

**Mira Olson** CIVIL ENGINEERING, DREXEL UNIVERSITY

Let's imagine Armageddon comes not in the form of a mighty asteroid that obliterates the planet, or as nuclear winter that blocks the sun and drives all life far underground for ten uranium half-lives, or as a Norwegian wolf that breaks free of its underworld restraints to consume the gods, but as something gentler like complete infrastructure collapse or an abrupt end to fossil fuel supplies.

In that case, even after the grocery stores are looted, you can survive without food for at least a month and maybe much longer (thank you, obesity epidemic!), but you need water within an absolute maximum of ten days or you're a goner. And in most areas, ensuring an adequate yearly supply of drinkable water is no easy feat (thank you, marmots peeing in even the clearest-looking mountain streams!). Simply, if you can't trap and treat your own water, you're toast.

One option is to use roofs. "Rainwater harvesting and catchment off roofs isn't new," says Mira Olson, civil engineer at Drexel University. The Byzantines did it residentially and the Romans did it industrially. First, tin or terra-cotta roofs are good, asphalt and shingles are bad, as is "proximity to birds," says Olson (the last due to the same reason you don't park your car beneath a roost). Also, in the first rain after a dry spell, let the first water run off the roof before connecting your system—this first flush will take with it the majority of contaminants.

But the neat part is in treatment methods. When you run out of chlorine tablets, throw in a crab shell. The shell's chitosan binds organic contaminants like bacteria, algae, and even that stray bit of marmot pee. As long as you don't eat the chunks of shell, you should be fine.

Or, "If you can filter water through a clear tube, the sunlight inactivates the bacteria for you," says Olson. Rather than killing bacteria, UV light fries bacterial DNA, making them unable to viably reproduce. You'll drink the few first bacteria, but they'll be unable to bloom in your gut. In fact, UV sterilization "pens" are available now for hiking and camping use, but forcing your harvested water to spend two to four hours percolating slowly through a clear tube in direct sunlight does the trick too.

The reward for this knowledge is the ultimate evolutionary prize: the right to repopulate the earth.

## Mira Olsen works with Engineers Without

Borders to design catchment and other water systems that can be used and maintained sustainably by third world populations. In its own way, third world engineering is very *Mad Max.*

### BE A TRENDSETTER
**Simon Levin**  EVOLUTIONARY BIOLOGY, PRINCETON UNIVERSITY

In 1972 Tony Alva jumped a fence to covertly skate a dry pool near California's Venice Beach neighborhood. Soon, a core group of Venice surfers-turned-skaters, including Stacy Peralta, made pool poaching a habit. When the police came, they ran. But now in the recessed pools of skate parks around the country, kids have made Alva's once innovative moves the norm. You know the story of *Dogtown and Z-Boys.* But how did Alva pull it off? How did this illegal, harebrained stunt become the social norm?

And how can you make your own harebrained ideas socially acceptable?

Simon Levin, evolutionary biologist at Princeton, explored the question from a slightly different angle: "In bird flocks and fish schools, you have a few individuals who think they know where they want to go, and the vast majority of individuals who are imitating," he says. Levin builds software models of these schools with his collaborator, Iain Couzin. Basically, he tags individuals as leaders or followers (or percentages thereof), connects them to others in the school, and then flips the switch on individual fish to see how the change propagates through the group. By tweaking the model until it acts like a natural school of fish, he discovers the mechanisms that allow change to flow through groups. It's like setting up a very detailed crowd of dominoes—when you knock one brick, how far and how fast does the ripple travel?

Or, that's what Levin used to do.

Now he applies the mathematics of fish changing directions to groups of people changing opinions.

"First, social change relies on distributed networks," says Levin. The opposite of "distributed" is a "well-mixed" network like that of a country with an authoritative central government, in which top-down control quickly suppresses novel opinions—nails that stick up are pounded down. "These systems are robust over short periods of time," says Levin. But when top-down control fails, the whole system is shot.

Now imagine Venice Beach in the 1970s. In this far-flung node of a distributed network, when Alva had the idea to skate a dry swimming pool, the sheriff wasn't able to kill it before it grew. These distributed networks, with pods of far-flung autonomy and an absence of top-down control, "have the capability for novel opinions and attitudes to spring up," says Levin.

So if you want to change cultural norms, you need to live in a place where the seed of your idea can take root without being summarily hit with Roundup by authority or the power of strong social norms. Perhaps innovating from a home base in Berkeley is easier than creating the same shift while based in Salt Lake City.

And the idea thus rooted can take over a population the same way a school of fish changes direction. "Individual fish or birds are attuned to the seven to ten fish or birds around them," says Levin, "thus the first to imitate a behavior are those most similar to the individual in which the behavior arises."

In the case of skating dry pools, these similar individuals were Alva's neighborhood friends, who coalesced into the Z-Boys, defining themselves based on this new skate culture. And just like closely following a leading fish's tight turn keeps following fish in the relatively safe center of the school, group members who quickly conformed to the new skateboard norms earned benefits. The Z-Boys had turf, they got girls, they were cool.

But in order for your innovation to spread beyond your posse, you need another important network feature: connectivity. The Z-Boys earned this connectivity at the 1975 Del Mar Nationals, where the pod of long-haired, Vans-wearing ne'er-do-wells rocked the socks off the clean-cut competition. The newly reformed *Skateboarding* magazine wrote a series of articles on Dogtown, and suddenly the Z-Boys had direct domino connection to kids across the country who wanted a piece of the action. The dominoes fell, and social norms changed course.

Levin points out the same progression of innovate-coalesce-connect in neckties, disallowing smoking in public places, tattoos, fingernail polish, gender equality, and recent rapid changes in the caste system of India. Today, you don't wear a tie because it's comfortable, but because it signals your membership in a group of professionals. What started as an affectation of Croatian mercenaries and earned fashion connectivity in Paris is now the social norm.

If you want to drive social norms, start by jumping a fence—any fence. Then push the idea on the seven to ten fish closest to you (see this book's entry with Eli Berman about creating a posse of obedient henchmen). Then connect your dominoes to the world at large.

## Puzzle #14: **Schooled by Fish**

Connections in a school of fish are shown below. Imagine each step of communication loses half its influence, so that direct communication is 50 percent influential, friend-of-a-friend communication is 25 percent influential, and thrice-removed communication is 12.5 percent influential. Which of these fish has the most influence?

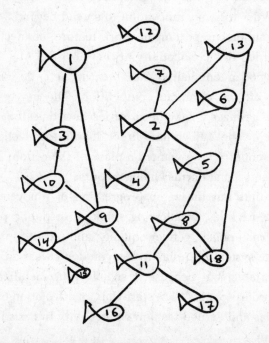

## Other things that pass through networks

include people through subway systems and soccer balls through World Cup teams. In 2009 Wall Street whiz kids Chris Solarz and Matt Ferresi used a cool math/computer science network analysis tool, graph theory, to discover the path of least resistance through the city's subway system, and then used their info to shave two hours off the existing record for visiting all 468 stations.

And after the 2010 World Cup, Hugo Touchette and Javier López Peña, applied mathematicians at Queen Mary, University of London, modeled teams' passing data as if a team were a network, players were nodes in the network, and the ball was the information passing through it. The resulting graphs showed team styles of play. "Mexico's passes are concentrated in the defense," says Peña, "and Spain's passes are mostly in the midfield." It also allowed them to calculate any given player's centrality—their importance to the network and thus how difficult it is for the network to adapt with the player removed. For example, in the early games of the 2010 World Cup, the Dutch player Arjen Robben had high centrality—ball movement went through him—and then in the final, he was nonexistent. Spain's aggressive marking of Arjen Robben pruned him from the system, thereby disrupting the entire flow of information through the network that was the team deemed the Clockwork Orange.

Spain was without a similar Achilles' heel: "Spain has a balanced centrality," says Touchette. In other words, it's a more flexible and thus a more robust network. If you cut off a head, the other ten heads on the pitch easily absorb the loss.

# TRAIN THE BRAIN OF THE ULTIMATE INVESTOR

**Antoine Bechara** NEUROLOGY,

UNIVERSITY OF SOUTHERN CALIFORNIA

A quick online video search returns hugely entertaining footage of four-year-olds presented with the choice of immediately eating a marshmallow sitting on a table in front of them, or waiting for twenty minutes, at which point if their initial marshmallow remains, they earn a second marshmallow. The question, Will they wait? quickly starts to look like the question, Can they possibly physically wait? Kids writhe, kids cover their eyes, one angelic girl hollows out and eats the marshmallow center before innocently·placing the gooey shell back on the table. Really, it's worth seeing.

But it's not just entertaining. The famous marshmallow test is highly predictive of success later in life. Kids who defer gratification get better SAT scores and have happier marriages.

Do you go to the dentist? Do you turn down an affair? Do you undergo surgery? Do you stay in school or reject a bribe or tie up money in investments that you could use immediately for a seven-day Caribbean cruise?

According to USC neurologist Antoine Bechara, this want/should is a teeter-totter between competing brain structures with the decision going to the weightier side (see this book's entry about oh-wow/oh-yikes shopping with Brian Knutson). "The immediate reward of a drug or a marshmallow or a bribe is processed by basic brain structures," says Bechara. The stronger the immediate reward, the more your lizard brain wants it. But then the ventral medial prefrontal cortex evaluates the consequences. "The prefrontal cortex signals that the bribe might put you in jail or the drug might take over your life," says Bechara.

That's easy: Your brain is a want/should teeter-totter.

But there are things that thumb this teeter-totter, and here's where the story gets especially interesting. For example, in 1848 the famous patient Phineas Gage blasted the "should" side of his teeter-totter clean off when the three-foot tamping rod he was using to pack blasting powder shot through his face, passed behind his left eye, and exited just above his forehead. Amazingly, not only did Gage survive, but he retained IQ and cognition. However, with the executive function portion of his brain aggressively pruned, he became impulsive to the point of dysfunction (see the tongue-in-cheek entry with Steve Schlozman on page 137 about frontal lobe degeneration and zombiism).

In addition to injury, lack of impulse control can be due to genetic abnormality. Or "traumatic early life experiences can cause dramatic rewiring of the brain in the prefrontal lobe and striatum, making a person perform much like someone with a lesion," says Bechara.

Among other shortcomings, these people are terrible investors, ruled completely by emotion without the check of logic. Bechara, along with the researchers Baba Shiv, George Loewenstein, and Hanna and Antonio Damasio, wondered how investors on the flip side of the emotion/logic teeter-totter would do—how would investors with lesions in the emotion centers of their brains perform?

The team engineered a study in which a participant is given $20.00 at the beginning of a twenty-round gambling game. In each round, the participant is given the choice to risk $1.00 on a coin flip to win $2.50. You can probably see that it's a good deal to bet every round—an expected value of $1.25 for playing versus $1.00 for declining. The result? On average, healthy subjects took home $22.80, while those with lesions to their emotion centers won $25.70.

Other researchers have shown similar is true on Wall Street. Traders who test as devoid of emotion earn more money. "Not everybody on Wall Street is a functional psychopath," says Bechara. "Instead you can learn to control your emotions. But many of the best investors do things that would be expected of functional psychopaths." So if Phineas Gage (and zombies) prioritize amygdala over frontal lobe, the brain of the ultimate investor does the opposite: pure rationality, without the influence of emotion.

And to bring this full circle, you can train this rational brain by practicing not eating the marshmallow. Delaying gratification prioritizes "should" over "want"—frontal lobe over amygdala—giving power to the rational rather than emotional areas of your brain. The more you do it, the better you'll get, not just at investing, but potentially at making decisions with the long run in mind—the delayed gratification that is so predictive of success.

But Phineas Gage's impulsivity ruined his life, and so too would living as the purely rational Spock ruin yours. In addition to training the brain of the ultimate investor, be sure you also practice leaving the functional psychopath at the office.

## Among other achievements, Bechara

developed the now überfamous Iowa Gambling Task, in which subjects choose a card from one of three facedown decks. In the IGT, each deck has a different payoff, and so over time, subjects learn to draw cards only from the richest deck. In fact, "learn" is a less precise word than "intuit" as it seems intuition is a quicker teacher than cognition in the IGT. More years of schooling and higher SAT scores both predict worse performance on the IGT, as these brainiacs are more likely to concoct and stick to theories of hot and cold decks, rather than listening to their hunches.

## Puzzle #15: **Time Discounting**

Psychologists and economists know that a future reward is worth less than a significantly smaller, immediate reward. Imagine you have the choice to eat a marshmallow now or delay this gratification to earn an additional four marshmallows at some point in the future. Also imagine that the value of a marshmallow reward decays like a radioactive material, losing a quarter of its value every three minutes. At how many minutes into the future would you have earned more "value" by simply eating the one initial marshmallow immediately?

### YOUR FUTURE SELF KNOWS BEST

**Katherine Milkman** BEHAVIORAL ECONOMICS, WHARTON SCHOOL, UNIVERSITY OF PENNSYLVANIA

It's early in the morning, everyone's asleep, and I just wandered into the kitchen to nuke a bowl of instant oatmeal. But here's the problem: Calling to me from atop the fridge are two buckets of Halloween candy. I just want the Snickers bars. Would the kids really even notice?

OK. I'm back upstairs. Those were delicious. And anyway, the microwave might've woken people up. But you know what? I'm feeling a little saccharine-saturated. My teeth are filmy and I think I hear the faint buzzing noise of excess sugar being burned in my brain like Lysol sprayed at a gas burner.

Ack! I should've had the oatmeal. What was I thinking?

The thing is, I know better. Truth be told, I did the same thing yesterday and felt the same filmy-toothed remorse. But in the face of sweet, sweet Snickers bars, something happens to me. Like Michael J. Fox in the pre–*Back to the Future* classic, I tend to wolf out a little bit.

And I'm not alone.

For example, Katherine Milkman, behavioral economist at the Wharton School, explored how people buy groceries online. Specifically, she looked at what people order when they buy for next-day delivery compared to what the same person buys when he/she orders for three days in advance. First, people spend much more when they buy for immediate consumption. And, "If you buy for rush, you buy junk," says Milkman, as shown by an increased percentage of your total haul.

Your current self buys Twinkies, while imagining what you'll need a couple days down the line puts your future self in charge and leads to the purchase of bulgur wheat and chard and other lovely things like that. (Damn, now I really want another Snickers bar.)

Milkman brought people into the lab to explore what other than time might influence splurging on junk food. After gathering folks, she explained that subjects would return tomorrow for a movie and a snack. Half the subjects were told what movie they'd be watching and half weren't. What snack did they want to accompany their movie? The uncertain half chose junk food.

Coupling these two experiments shows the power of a certain future self—it's more rational and more temperate than the self who's reading these words right now. (Admit it, you would've eaten the Snickers bars too—or maybe the Reese's cups. OK, I'm going back downstairs.)

The question is, how can you put that certain future self in charge?

First, the more certain the future is, the more power it has. So make lists, set agendas, and plan ahead to make tomorrow and the days after more definite. Second, Milkman recommends the use of a commitment device. If you want your future self to be in charge, you have to give it some leverage. For example, Milkman points to the work of Ian Ayres and Dean Karlan at Yale, who allow your future self to put out a contract on your current self. At stickK (www.stickk.com), you set a goal and bet money you'll achieve it. Then you get e-mail reminders monitoring your progress. If you fail, you lose the bet.

For you, a commitment device might be as contrived as putting your social reputation on the line (see this book's entry about behavior change with B. J. Fogg) or as simple as asking WWFSD? As you walk into the grocery store, think about your future self. Does it really want a rotisserie chicken and Ho Hos? What decisions would this future self make for you? If you can punk your psychology with this trick, great. Personally, my future self needs a little more oomph—I hereby give it the power to pilfer, burn, and then bury the ashes of all Halloween candy in the house.

## Milkman also explored how people spend an

unexpected $10 online grocery coupon. In classic economic theory, the mini-windfall shouldn't make a difference in your choices—you still need what you need and should spend what you spend—but as Milkman points out, "Psychologists think this should make you feel rich." And sure enough, people tend to spend this coupon on nontypical items like fresh seafood and fresh fruit. These windfall buys aren't necessarily unhealthy, but they are luxury. They're what you'd buy if you were rich.

## BIGGER, STRONGER, FASTER (WITHOUT EXERCISING)

**Ronald Evans** MOLECULAR BIOLOGY, SALK INSTITUTE

"The longstanding field of muscle physiology says that better performance is achieved only through training," says Ronald Evans, molecular biologist at the Salk Institute and Howard Hughes Medical Institute. In other words, "you may have the innate ability to be the fastest swimmer," says Evans, "but if you don't work hard, you'll be overtaken by the second-fastest swimmer."

Bummer. Down that line of reasoning lies long hours in the gym and self-denial in the face of Cherry Garcia.

But between exercise and muscle development is an important step. "The cell nucleus is the control system," says Evans. "Done right, you can make the nucleus undergo the changes it would experience during exercise, without exercise."

Booyah!

Unfortunately this cellular sleight of hand isn't as simple as visualizing running or watching *Sweating to the Oldies* while sucking an energy drink. Instead, the story starts with the body's chemical form of energy: ATP. When you exercise, your cells' mitochondria convert fat, carbs, or really whatever else is floating around your midsection into ATP, which you then break down to create energy and a by-product called AMP. More exercise equals more ATP use and thus more AMP by-product. So when the body detects AMP, it assumes it's exercising and burns more fat, carbs, and midsection to keep pace with its expected needs. Upon detecting AMP, your body also increases the rate of muscle building, which repairs the natural damage of exercise and beefs up muscle reserves in preparation for what it sees as likely future demands.

The drug AICAR mimics AMP.

When you inject it, your body thinks you've exercised. You burn more sugars and build more muscle, but, "Really only the signal of exercise has been given," says Evans. In the lab, mice on AICAR lost weight and increased endurance even when given a high-fat diet.

So simply get a prescription for AICAR and you'll qualify for the Boston Marathon while consuming all the Cherry Garcia and Krispy Kreme donuts your trans-fat-choked heart desires.

Only, there's a catch.

"There are two problems with this drug: It's [only] injectable, and it's old," says Evans. Simply, drugs aren't created to cure disease or increase health. They're created to make money. And the market doesn't want to inject. Also, with AICAR being old and off-patent, any drug company in the world can make it, and so any company that put $100 million into the R&D needed to push a human-ready drug through the FDA would face immediate market competition from generics.

So don't look for AICAR anytime soon.

But there's another pathway you can punk.

PPR-delta is a nuclear receptor—it hangs out on a nucleus's wall, waving like a sea anemone until it sees the molecule it wants, at which point it grabs it and relays the information of the catch inside the nucleus. What PPR-delta grabs is fat, and when it gets it, cells know that instead of conserving scarce resources, a glut is floating around your bloodstream and they can burn fat quickly. Evans and others have engineered synthetic molecules to mimic this effect—keep your eyes peeled for drug release in the next few years.

Until then, ditch saturated fats.

PPR-delta doesn't bind saturated fat, which goes straight into your body's storeroom without signaling your body to increase its burn rate. But the PPR-delta anemones love mono- and polyunsaturated fats—they grab them from your bloodstream and tell your body to get cranking. Foods high in omega-3s (fish) or resveratrol (red wine!) present PPR-delta only the fats it can grab and that thus fuel your body's fire, and not the saturated fat that quickly makes one unable to see one's toes. Dairy products consistently have the highest saturated fat percentage, and walnuts have one of the lowest. In oils, stay away from coconut and palm, and instead go for corn or flaxseed.

## Evans's work shows that stem cells

continually spit out new neurons in two areas of the brain: the olfactory bulb and the hippocampus. Once you're an adult, many of these new neurons are born and then immediately die, but some are woven into the architecture of the brain. New neurons in the olfactory bulb may allow you to smell better in later life (as it were), while tests with mice show that new neurons in the hippocampus may allow you continue coding new memories and learning new things. Evans found that both physical and mental exercise boost the rate at which neural stem cells spit out new neurons.

## Researchers at McMaster University showed

that lifting light weights to exhaustion builds as much muscle as lifting heavy weights. The key, they found, is muscle fatigue—and while lifting heavy weights might be a shortcut to this fatigue, the same addition of muscle was created by lifting lighter weights at higher reps.

## SEXY OF VOICE, SEXY OF BODY

**Gordon Gallup** EVOLUTIONARY PSYCHOLOGY,
UNIVERSITY OF ALBANY

Changing your body shape is time-consuming and effortful, requiring things like exercising and eating less (unless you read this book carefully). But adopting a sexy voice? With the help of University of Albany evolutionary psychologist Gordon Gallup, you can do it today.

Gallup had undergrads count to ten in a tape recorder and then played back these recordings to their peers. Even without flirtatious or smoldering content, there was strong agreement on which voices were sexy and which were not. And Gallup showed that these sexy voices were strong predictors of sexy bodies—sexy-voiced men had higher shoulder-to-hip ratios, and sexy-voiced women had lower waist-to-hip ratios. These sexy voices also predicted an earlier age of first sexual experience and higher total number of sex partners. In short, a sexy voice actually is a good predictor of sexiness.

So what were the characteristics of these sexy voices?

If you've seen any of the *Toy Story* movies, you know what makes a sexy male voice—Tim Allen as Buzz Lightyear is sexier than Tom Hanks as Woody. There's very clear and definite evidence that a low male voice is sexier, and Gallup points out that this low voice may be the product of the same hit of testosterone during puberty that creates desirable shoulder-to-hip ratios.

But the female sexy voice is trickier and independent of high or low pitch. Instead, the strongest factor in the sexy female voice is breathiness. We have two vocal cords, with a slight gap between them—women tend to have a bigger gap than men, and this is what creates breathiness. The bigger the gap, the more breathiness, and perhaps the more estrogen during puberty.

But here's the important part: Vocal attractiveness creates the perception of physical attractiveness. If a date hears your sexy voice, he or she expects a sexy person, and these expectations mean that when you meet, your date will, in fact, rate your physical attractiveness higher than if you'd had a mediocre voice. Why bother with a month's crash diet and agro iron-pumping when you can get a bump in beauty simply by talking sexy?

## "During a kiss there's a rich, complicated

exchange of information, that we think may activate hardwired systems to assess health, vitality, and thus genetic fitness of potential mates," says Gordon Gallup.

But if you're measuring success by number of progeny, men and women have very different goals—a man does best when he eats shoots and leaves (as it were), "whereas for women, having sex is just the start," says Gallup, "after which is weeks, months, and years of pregnancy, breastfeeding, and child care."

Gallup found that these different evolutionary goals lead to gender-specific uses of kissing. "Males are much more likely to attempt to initiate with an open mouth and much more likely to kiss with the tongue," says Gallup. This is sexual kissing and men use it as a tick on the preflight checklist. Whereas, "Females kiss not only during courtship and mate assessment, but to monitor the status of a committed relationship," says Gallup. For women, kissing is a way to get information that's otherwise hard to get.

## SPOTTING SINCERITY—A SLOW "YES" MEANS "NO"

**Colin Camerer** NEUROECONOMICS, CALIFORNIA INSTITUTE OF TECHNOLOGY

It's the end of what seemed like a good first date. You ask if he'll call and he says ". . . Yes!" But will he really?

"Slow means 'no,'" says Colin Camerer, economist and neuroscientist at Caltech. He explains that in consumer surveys, political polling, and many other situations in which the person questioned knows what the questioner wants to hear, people are likely to please during the conversation but fail to follow through. Would you buy this awesome product the nice person on the phone just spent two minutes explaining? [Pause] Yes. Would you vote for the political candidate the caller's stumping for? [Pause] Yes. Should you expect to hear from your date again soon? [Pause] Yes, of course!

This is known as the yes bias, and it's vexed pollsters from time immemorial.

But imagine we weren't dependent on the notoriously inaccurate words that come from people's mouths. Suppose, instead, we could look in consumers' or voters' or daters' brains for their opinions.

Camerer did just that. "What we found," he says, "is that hypothetical choices are a fifth of a second faster than real choices." People decide if they would (hypothetically) vote or buy or call very quickly. And so to a hypothetical question, a quick response is a true response. If there's a fifth of a second lag, it's likely due to the time it takes politeness the overrule the honest impulse— spackling the veneer that will please the questioner over the true answer that wouldn't. Lying takes longer.

But when making real decisions, an extra area of the brain is activated—the cingulate cortex. "It's like a second level of checking," says Camerer. For example, when you ask the very real question (with real consequences) of whether your date would like to kiss, it takes a fifth of a second to double-check the impulse. In real choices there should be a short delay, and you should trust the answer.

So spotting sincerity first requires recognizing the type of question you're asking—if it's a real question, you should expect a slight delay, followed by the true answer; but when you ask a yes/no question about any hypothetical future action—will he call?—the answer should be fast. Watch for a delay. If "yes" spits slowly, it may be politeness and the desire to please overriding the real answer: no.

In that fifth of a second, you can see the brain's true intent.

## YOU SUCK, SO I ROCK

**David Dunning** PSYCHOLOGY, CORNELL UNIVERSITY

Cornell psychologist David Dunning asked how many students would buy daffodils in an upcoming fund-raiser for the American Cancer Society. A full 80 percent of these saintly students said they would certainly purchase a flower, though they were less rosy in their predictions of peers' willingness to buy, opining that only 50 percent overall would pony up for the cause. You might have guessed the punch line: After the fund-raiser, only 43 percent of students actually bought flowers.

Similarly, he asked how many students would vote in the then upcoming November elections. Eighty-four percent said they'd vote, and they expected 67 percent of their peers to vote. The tale of the tape was 68 percent turnout.

"People are pretty accurate in their judgments of others," says Dunning. "But terrible in their judgments of themselves." This is why the vast majority of drivers and 94 percent of the college professors Dunning surveyed consider themselves "above average." It doesn't take a Fields Medal to see that's mathematically impossible.

And so across the board we overestimate our goodness while pretty much nailing predictions of others' actions.

But something cool happens when you go from concrete predictions of yes/no type behaviors to evaluations of others in which there's wiggle room. How intelligent or how good of a leader is someone? These evaluations are much more subjective than asking how many peers will buy a daffodil. To see if we're as accurate with subjective evaluations, Dunning brought college sophomores ("my species," he says) into the lab.

What he found is that we have very specific templates that we use to measure others. Simply, the template is the person doing the measuring. Is someone intelligent? Is someone a good leader? Well, if they're like us, then yes in both cases. And, "If you put someone's self-esteem under pressure by making them fail a task or something similar, then people even more strongly positively judge others who are like them," says Dunning. When you're down, you boost similar others as a way to get back your own lost sense of self. (Is this why blue-collar America cited the "just like me" quality when voting for Bush II?)

"If you step outside the lab, people show the same behaviors," says Dunning. For example, he asked nontenured professors how many published papers should be expected in order to gain tenure. It was a relatively low number compared to the number of papers that tenured professors thought should be required. Similarly, he asked college sophomores if others with certain math SAT scores were "mathematically gifted." Generally, students saw anyone who scored above their own SAT result as gifted.

We are the bar we set for others.

What's also cool is that the strength of this effect depends on how much we care about the topic. In the context of a test that's supposedly a gateway into a certain career, students who were premed, prelaw, or prebusiness set much more self-centered targets for others if the test was relevant to their specific career choice.

Reverse engineering this allows you to test how strongly a person feels about any topic. Are your friends quick to judge and likely to set the mark very close to their own behaviors when evaluating others' parenting? Or coolness? Or fashion sense? Or attention to detail? Or musical taste? Or . . . anything, really? By noticing these self-centered judgments, you can discover how strongly people care.

## The Dunning-Kruger effect describes people

who are blind to their own stupidity. Classically, people who scored in the lowest 12 percent in Dunning's tests of humor, logic, and grammar estimated they had scored in the top 62 percent. People who scored higher were much more accurate in their estimates.

## Other researchers at Cornell had students

come up with movie ideas and then pitch them to other students. In written form, narcissists' pitches were no more convincing than those of their peers. But when narcissists pitched their movie ideas in person, they were a full 50 percent more well received than their peers'. The conclusion is this: The narcissist in your group shouldn't be allowed to sculpt the product, but should be encouraged to present it.

## PROOF YOURSELF AGAINST SENSATIONALIZED STATS

**Keith Devlin** MATHEMATICS, STANFORD UNIVERSITY

WARNING: a long and somewhat involved path of (very cool) statistics lies ahead.

Keith Devlin is NPR's "Math Guy," a World Economic Forum fellow, and math professor at Stanford. And so he thinks about things differently than the world at large. For example, in his monthly column "Devlin's Angle," he quotes the following problem, originally designed by puzzle master Gary Foshee: "I tell you that I have two children, and that (at least) one of them is a boy born on Tuesday. What probability should you assign to the event that I have two boys?"

Does this sound like a bunch of confounding mumbo jumbo meant to obscure the obvious fact that the other kid has exactly 50/50 chance of being a boy and so if one kid's definitely a boy, the probability of them both being boys is one in two? Yes, yes it does.

But that's not the case.

Without the "Tuesday" part, this is a famous problem first published in *Scientific American* by the venerable mathematician and puzzler Martin Gardner. Imagine the possible genders and birth orders of two kids: B-B, B-G, G-B, G-G. Now, in Gardner's problem you know that at least one child is a boy, so you can nix only G-G as a possibility, leaving B-B, B-G, and G-B. In only one of these remaining three possibilities are both children boys, so instead of the knee-jerk one in two probability any sane person would expect, mathematicians like Devlin give only a one in three probability that, given one child is a boy, both kids are boys.

Yikes.

But the Tuesday bit can't possibly matter, can it?

"It depends if you ask a mathematician or a statistician," says

Devlin. The mathematician would simply extend the possibilities that were available in the original puzzle and then nix the possibilities that could be nixed. If we didn't know that one of the kids was born on a Tuesday, our possibilities would be all the possible crosses of: B-Mo, B-Tu, B-We, B-Th, B-Fr, B-Sa, B-Su, with G-Mo, G-Tu, G-We, G-Th, G-Fr, G-Sa, G-Su.

Cool so far?

Now, you know that either the first or the second child is a boy born on Tuesday, and here's how Devlin lays out the revised possibilities:

- First child B-Tu, second child: B-Mo, B-Tu, B-We, B-Th, B-Fr, B-Sa, B-Su, G-Mo, G-Tu, G-We, G-Th, G-Fr, G-Sa, G-Su.
- Second child B-Tu, first child: B-Mo, B-We, B-Th, B-Fr, B-Sa, B-Su, G-Mo, G-Tu, G-We, G-Th, G-Fr, G-Sa, G-Su.

Since "both boys born on Tuesday" is already listed in the first set, we don't need to list it again in the second, making 27 (instead of 28) possible combinations of gender and day of the week for two kids, if at least one is a boy born on Tuesday. And of these 27 possibilities, 13 of them include a second boy. So the answer is (instead of a one in two or one in three chance) a 13/27 chance that both will be boys.

D'you hear that crackling sound? That's the sound of your neurons trying to deal with the previous five hundred words. Don't say you weren't warned. But stick with it. It's worth it. You can do it.

Now, on to statisticians, who take another view entirely. To them it matters what else could have been said and the interpretations that can pop up when math is released into the real world. "For example," says Devlin, "we're taught that multiplication is commutative, that $3 \times 4$ is the same as $4 \times 3$; but in the real world three bags of four apples isn't the same as four bags of three apples." Similarly, he points out in his blog that if you're told that a quarter pound of ham costs $2 and then asked what three pounds will cost, a mathematician would tell you $24, but a statistician who's been to a supermarket knows there's not enough information to answer the question—of course, every supermarket discounts for bulk.

In the case of the Tuesday boy problem, imagine you're from a culture that requires you to speak about an elder child first, before mentioning the younger. That means it's the eldest child who's the boy, and you rule out both G-G (as before) but also G-B, leaving the possibilities BB and BG, and a one in two probability of both being boys.

So there are two broad interpretations of almost all real-world numbers problems—the stripped-down, mathematicians' approach and the interpretive statisticians' approach. And it's in this wiggle room of interpretation where pure math hits the real world that misleading statistics are born. For example, in 1993 the columnist George Will was mathematically correct when he wrote in the *Washington Post* that "the ten states with the lowest per-pupil spending included four—North Dakota, South Dakota, Tennessee, Utah—among the ten states with the top SAT scores. Only one of the ten states with the highest per-pupil expenditures—Wisconsin—was among the ten states with the highest SAT scores. New Jersey has the highest per-pupil expenditures, an astonishing $10,561 . . . New Jersey's rank regarding SAT scores? Thirty-ninth."

Take a minute and see if you can spot the moment at which pure math became a misleading statistic.

I found this quote in a 1999 article in the *Journal of Statistics Education* that points out one important fact: In New Jersey all college-bound students take the SAT, whereas in North Dakota, South Dakota, Tennessee, and Utah, only the kids applying to out-of-state schools take the SAT. And you can bet these students applying out of state are the cream of the crop. This is selection

. bias, and it pops up everywhere. Yes, it seems odd that nine out of ten dentists recommend Crass toothpaste, and nine out of ten also recommend Goldgate, but it's as easy as finding the right ten dentists to ask.

Or take the following headline (from WorldHealth.net), which demonstrates a trick central to a pop science writer's existence: SINCERE SMILING PROMOTES LONGEVITY. Sure enough, the data in the original study show that people who flash sincere smiles in photographs live longer—the original study title is SMILE INTENSITY IN PHOTOGRAPHS PREDICTS LONGEVITY.

Again, take a minute and see if you can spot the difference.

The trick is that the study demonstrates correlation, while the article implies causation. Does a Duchenne smile "predict" longevity? Yes. Does it "promote" longevity? Not necessarily. Mightn't it be more likely that these smilers are happy and that something in happiness and not the smile itself actually promotes longevity? Similarly, it's mathematically correct that gun owners have 2.7 times the chance of being murdered compared to non-gun owners. Does owning a gun cause the owner to be murdered, or might it be something in the character of people likely to own guns?

For another, take the 2010 claim by health reform director Nancy-Ann DeParle that due to the then recently passed health care bill, the average annual cost of insurance coverage would drop by one thousand dollars by 2019. Taken at face value, it's true. But the reason it's true is that nearly free health care would be extended to 32 million Americans who were currently without care, meaning that the cost to people who were already insured in 2010 would actually go up to cover the newly added.

This is an apples-to-oranges comparison, like decrying the increase in the average cost of a gallon of gas from $0.99/gal in February 1992 to $3.38/gal in February 2011 without adjusting for inflation. You can't compare the two, because the rules of comparison have changed. On the flip side of the political spectrum, conservative UK politician Chris Grayling cited a 35 percent increase in "violent" crime starting in 2002 as evidence of failed liberal law enforcement policies. But 2002 was the year civilians and not police were given the right to designate a crime "violent," and many chose to see violence where the police might not have. The "35 percent increase" was the difference between apples and oranges.

Finally, take data showing that the TSA misses 5 percent of people hired to test air security by trying to smuggle dangerous contraband. Yikes! One in twenty people sitting around you on the plane is packing a shoe bomb!

What's the error?

It's in sampling. Though some days it feels this way, not everyone is out to get you. In fact, imagine that even one of the two million passengers who try to fly over the United States every day is a deadly terrorist, and imagine the TSA misses 5 percent of them. This means that one in 40 million people flying is a deadly terrorist. Even on a Boeing 767 with a 300-person seating capacity, you'd have to fly more than 130,000 times to sit on a plane with a terrorist. (OK, that's misleading too: Statisticians would point out that a 1 in 130,000 chance means you could be on a plane with a terrorist at any point, it's just not ever very likely.) Compare that to a 1 in 100 lifetime chance of dying in a car crash. Actually, please do, because that's a mathematically correct, misleading statistic too—what if you don't drive, or drive cautiously, or are already over age twenty-five?

So the moral of this long and somewhat convoluted tale is that first there's math, then there's stats, and finally there are headlines. And like a game of telephone, it's easy to lose meaning along the way due to things like selection bias, correlation/causation, apples/oranges, and population error.

Mark Twain said there are lies, damned lies, and statistics.

Illuminating this, renowned business professor Aaron Levenstein said that statistics are like bikinis—what they reveal is suggestive but what they conceal is vital. But not for you. You now know how to reveal what is vital.

## Puzzle #16: October Boy

If I tell you that I have two children, both born in October, and at least one a boy born on a day whose date contains at least one "1," then what is the probability that both my children are boys?

## AVOID THE CARPLIKE STARE OF CHOICE PARALYSIS

**Jonah Berger** DECISION SCIENCE, WHARTON SCHOOL, UNIVERSITY OF PENNSYLVANIA

Next to the box of Cheerios on the grocery store's thirty-yard-long cereal shelf sits a box of store-brand Rolled O's. And there you stand, staring carplike at the two boxes, transfixed, slack-jawed—but tormented inside! You expected the choice to be easy and now for some reason it's . . . not. You've been mesmerized by choice paralysis and you aren't going anywhere soon.

Last night you did the same thing online with flight options. Last month you spent a combined twelve hours agonizing over what shade of white to paint your kitchen.

"Generally, important decisions take longer," says Jonah Berger of the Wharton School. Good, great, we expect them to, and so we're neither surprised nor frustrated when deciding between colleges or job offers or real estate options is a slow and difficult process.

But Berger found that something interesting happens when a trivial decision turns out to be difficult. "By the fact that it takes longer, we infer that it's important," says Berger, "and because it now seems important, we automatically give the decision more time."

Remember Niro Sivanathan's consumption quicksand, in which people in debt feel bad about themselves and so consume esteem goods on credit, putting them further in debt and thus making them feel even worse about themselves and more likely to consume esteem goods on credit? Well, this is a similar feedback loop: Once you've spent time on a trivial decision, you give it the veneer of an important decision, and you're trapped. The longer it takes, the longer it's going to take, and the more likely you are to find yourself drooling while staring cross-eyed at boxes of cereal.

Maybe you should read the nutrition panel one more time in hopes it will make the difference? Maybe you should ask other customers? Should you call your spouse?

Berger says the key in breaking choice paralysis is to stop it before it starts—or barring that, stop it in its infant stages before your mind becomes figgy pudding. If you can predict an upcoming decision of little consequence that—despite its unimportance—can provide closely matched and vexing options, set a time limit. In twenty minutes you will click BUY on the best airplane ticket you've found thus far. Or at the end of five minutes, you'll grab whatever Creative Commons image seems best to head your blog post. Or in thirty seconds, you'll be out of the cereal aisle.

Or imagine the initial surprise of a trivial/difficult decision that goes something like, Huh, I wonder if toothbrush bristles in square or circular designs remove the most plaque? Recognize trivial/difficult and counteract it quickly by setting a time limit. Act now, before it's too late.

# "Double Rainbow," the "Charlie Bit My

Finger!" kid, the surprised kitty, the Evian roller babies, the "Paparazzi" talent show kid, the "BP Spills Coffee" video, the "Bimbo Waka Waka" dancing baby—these are videos that "went viral" as the kids say these days, becoming massive cultural phenomena on the scale of the Declaration of Independence, the Constitution, and "Where's the beef?"

Jonah Berger knows how you can go viral too.

He explored the *New York Times* archives for factors that make articles highly shared. "Generally, we want to put people in good moods," says Berger, and so we share surprising and/or humorous positive content (that revelation may be neither surprising nor humorous). But Berger also found that certain negative emotions are highly shared, including vids and articles that create anxiety, anger, or outrage. It's arousal that predicts content sharing—both on the happy/surprised/humorous side and on the angry/outraged/incensed side. Simply, go big or doom your content to one-and-done. Or as *The Economist* described his finding, "It's better to be reviled than ignored."

## THE POWER OF A CONNECTED MINORITY

**Michael Kearns** COMPUTER SCIENCE,
UNIVERSITY OF PENNSYLVANIA

Generally, there are two ways to study networks. One is by creating mathematical models—like Simon Levin at Princeton, who we met in the entry about trendsetting and fish schools—and then poking and prodding these models in various ways. The other is to study existing networks, which allows you to see how behaviors or information flow in the real world (see, for instance, the book *Connected*, which details the ways behaviors like smoking and obesity flow through a social network in a

Massachusetts town). The first allows you to adjust the network design to see how tweaks affect its function. The second allows you to see real effects in real people.

But what if you could do both, at the same time?

Michael Kearns found a way to have his cake and eat it too. "About six years ago I started running these behavioral lab experiments in which I bring moderately large groups of people into the lab, impose various network structures, give them a game to play for real money, and study how they do," says Kearns, CS and information science guru at the University of Pennsylvania and the Wharton School. Thus he could design and tweak the network, while also seeing how real people act within it.

For example, in one of his games, subjects tried to coordinate colors. Kearns gathered thirty-six undergrads and stuck them in a room so that they could only see certain of their neighbors, then he started a one-minute timer. Everyone in the room could display red or blue, and if at any time in that one minute everyone coordinated on either color, the whole room got paid. If not, no payday for the undergrads. After the minute, Kearns switched the network structure, and they played again.

So there was high incentive for agreement. "We designed this just after the 2008 democratic primaries," says Kearns, in which you might remember Democrats had a high incentive for agreement—the sooner Dems could coordinate on Clinton or Obama, the sooner they could start hacking at the throats of Republicans instead of at one another. This proved challenging because, for one reason, while unanimity was good for all, people within the network tended to feel strongly that either Clinton or Obama was more good.

Similarly, Kearns threw into the mix of his lab games unequal payoffs—for some people, coordinating on red paid $1.50 while agreeing on blue paid only $0.50. For others, the reverse was true. So you'd really rather agree on your high-paying color, but barring that, the other's better than nothing. Did these networks still get paid, or did they devolve into infighting and general uncoordinated badness in which everyone suffered?

It depended on the network.

For example, in one experiment Kearns gave thirty players a blue preference and only six players an equal and opposite red preference. But he stuck the shorthanded red players in special spots in the network, with the largest number of neighbors. "We ran twenty-seven experiments like this," says Kearns, "and in twenty-four of these, the network was able to reach an agreement." Can you guess which color they agreed on? In every case, it was the preference of the highly connected minority—little, social red carried the day. "The minority opinion will dominate the outcome if the minority is sufficiently well connected," says Kearns. This might remind you of the effect of special-interest lobbyists.

You also might remember the earlier Simon Levin story, in which he showed mathematically that the behavior of a small, committed minority needed connectivity to flow through a population and change social norms. Well, you can see the mathematical model in human action in Kearns's lab.

But one interesting finding is that even within these scripted networks in which Kearns says he "tries to shoehorn human subjects into settings in which they perform like ants," personality continues to influence outcomes. One aspect of personality that's especially clear in coordination games is stubbornness—are you willing to switch your color in the face of a developing majority that disagrees with you? But the effect of stubbornness isn't necessarily all bad, as you might expect. Sure, if a network includes too much stubbornness, players end up entrenched in their little, opposing fiefdoms. But its opposite is equally detrimental—if everyone's too willing to flip-flop, the network does just that, oscillating wildly between colors without ever coming to full consensus on either.

This is like the group of indecisive friends trying to pick a restaurant. Maybe we should eat Thai! Sure. Or what about Mexican? Um, OK. Or Chinese? Sounds good. And you end up getting all muddled in overagreement. At some point the network needs some stubbornness.

In another game, Kearns gave humans a game that's classically hard for computers. In the map-coloring puzzle, you have four colors and must shade the countries on a map so that no two neighboring countries are the same color. If tiny Switzerland goes orange, it affects the color of China, and the rippling of this change quickly requires massive computational chutzpah.

But humans role-playing countries color themselves rather quickly. "One lesson I've learned that transcends all types of experiments," says Kearns, "is that I'm surprised how good people are at this stuff." He points to this as hope for more and more ambitious crowdsourcing.

Still, there are things that computers do better than humans, and things that one brain does better than many. "If a problem can be broken into a gazillion pieces, you can crowdsource," says Kearns. But if the pieces themselves require coordination, a problem may still best be solved by good old-fashioned expertise. I apologize in advance for the following sports simile (and not even a sport I play), but it's like golf: Sure you could crowdsource a hole, with hundreds of people teeing off and then playing only the best ball. But wouldn't this problem be more efficiently solved by pre-2009 Tiger Woods?

Imagine your problem. Any problem.

Is it "chunkable," like needing thirty recipes for lightning-fast dinners or the best Monty Python quotes or suggestions from your geeked-out friends for scientists to interview for a book you're writing? If so, you might throw it out to FB or Twitter or whatever social networking site seems most applicable (be sure to provide incentive, likely framing it as entertainment or offering some sort of credit to the solvers). If the problem requires backstory and foresight, consider looking up a leading expert or making yourself into one. Or is it simply a question of firepower? Likely, there's software and/or a bigger, badder box to help with that.

And then join Kearns in hoping that someday soon there will be a middle path that uses all three (see following coolness).

## "I have a research fantasy that we're far from

but that I like to think about sometimes," says Kearns. Today there exist "compilers" that take a computational problem and recruit components from a network of computers to solve it. This allows you to design a problem without worrying about memory management, or CPUs, or virtual versus physical memory, or any of the other computational limits of your solving system (within reason). "I like to imagine a crowdsourcing compiler," says Kearns. This compiler would break down a problem into its components and then recruit the optimal tool for solving each. Maybe one chunk requires expertise—the compiler would scroll through the Proceedings of the National Academy of Sciences publications until finding, recruiting, and motivating the top expert. One chunk could simply be computed, and the compiler would pull together the resources for it. And another component might best be crowdsourced, and the compiler would put out feelers into the human online world, creating an incentive like a game or a salary that gets a human network to solve the needed piece.

"We're moving into a new era," say Kearns, "in which human computing interfaces with computer computing." This isn't the old sci-fi scenario of übertech dominating humans, nor is it today's model of humans using tech as tool, but a completely new scenario in which humans and the machines we've created collaborate to solve problems in ways neither could possibly do on their own.

# Puzzle #17: **Map Problem**

Use only four colors to shade the following map so that no touching states share the same color.

## CREATE A KICK-ASS TRIBE, ANY TRIBE

**David Logan** ORGANIZATIONAL BEHAVIOR, UNIVERSITY OF SOUTHERN CALIFORNIA

If you've ever watched *Survivor*, you know that not all tribes are created equal. Some are rancorous and repressive, me-centered and backstabbing, while others are cooperative and inclusive, honest, and even idealistic. David Logan, expert in organizational communication at USC's Marshall School of Business, knows how to make your tribe the latter.

As you might imagine, Logan's studied these tribes mostly in the context of businesses, which he divides into five tribal stages.

The first he defines with the phrase "life sucks." "It's not that people in these organizations don't have individual core values but that the organizational culture says you have to undermine these values to survive," he says. You may be forced to cheat to get ahead in the company or encouraged to lie to customers. Thus the battle between core and company values and the overall sucking of life.

In the next tribal level, it's not that life sucks as a whole, only that each individual thinks "my life sucks." "Employees say 'I made suggestions but nobody listened,' or otherwise deflect accountability," says Logan.

Stage three includes 48 percent of the organizations Logan's documented in his eight-and-ongoing years of study. This stage is defined by the idea that "I'm great and you're not," he says. People might have positive individual relationships with many others in the tribe, but there's little coming together. You might solicit other group members to gain agreement for your ideas, but it creates little pods of stage two around the core group.

Leveraging the spirit born of shared values, 22 percent of tribes are able to make the leap from "I'm great" to "We're great." This is stage four—"the first stage at which the group becomes aware of its tribalness," says Logan. You can tell you're there when a two-person conversation that's interrupted absorbs and integrates the interrupter—if you're all truly in the same tribe, there's every reason to be inclusive and none to be exclusive.

So that's it—the four stages of tribal development. You can read more about it in Logan's book *Tribal Leadership* (with John King and Halee Fischer-Wright).

Only, that's not it. There's a fifth stage, "and these groups create amazing things," says Logan, "like reconciliation in South Africa or Apple famously asking the question, How can I create a computer so simple that even my mom could use it?" The theme of a stage-five tribe is "life is great," but the problem is that stage-five tribes can be idealistic to the point of being dreamy and not tied to the market, "like an Internet start-up that says 'We don't need cash, we've got clicks!'" says Logan. In his view, it's ideal to stay at stage four, while infrequently dipping into stage five to ask, How do we make history? or How do we shake up the industry? "Stage five is pure leadership," says Logan, pointing out that stage four is a nice mix of leadership and management, while stage three is pure management drowning out leadership, and below that not even management functions.

So that's great: five stages of tribal development. But more important than defining these stages is the ability to move up the food chain. How can you design a business with stage four in mind?

If you're starting from scratch, rather than hiring people at the start-up level who have the longest resumes, "first, find your own values," says Logan. "Then find people who share these values." Build around a value statement like Zappo's "We believe in doing more with less."

Once you grow past a small pod of naturally like-minded collaborators, "create initiatives that express these core values," says Logan. In addition to giving new employees a dinner-party answer to the question, What does your company do?, give them an answer to the question, What does your company believe in? Values give employees something to coalesce around, and this coming together creates a strong tribe.

## "If you look at the early Jedi, they became

inept and powerless by denying the Dark Side," says Logan, now speaking my language. "But at the end of *Return of the Jedi*, what you see is that Luke didn't defeat evil, but integrated it. As Luke rebuilds the Jedi, will they still be monklike and celibate? No, they'll balance the Light and Dark Sides."

To Logan, the same balance is true of good leaders. "My theory is that leaders have a larger dark side than most of us," he says. "They can tap into its power, but are always at risk of being destroyed by it." Jimmy Carter is a wonderful person, but was a terrible president, "partly because he never tapped into his dark side," says Logan. In fact, it's unclear that Carter even had one.

## There's a huge body of research on individual

intelligence, especially how to measure it, what predicts it, and how to train it. But researchers at Carnegie Mellon just recently provided the first direct evidence for a fixed collective intelligence in groups. Interestingly, factors you might assume made smart groups—including group cohesion, motivation, and satisfaction—had no effect. But there were three things that across many studies created smarter groups: (1) social sensitivity; (2) little variance in members' number of speaking turns—the conversation wasn't dominated by one voice; and (3) the proportion of members who were female—though this was due in part to social sensitivity.

# GOVERNMENT, GOD, OR SELF: WHERE DO YOU GET CONTROL?

**Aaron Kay** SOCIAL PSYCHOLOGY, DUKE UNIVERSITY

I like to believe both that the early bird catches the worm, and that he who mischief hatcheth, mischief catcheth. The root of this desire is surely the fact that I get up early and that for at least the last handful of years I've kept my mischief hatching to a minimum—and I like to think that my saintly actions will lead to reward. I also like to believe that if I drive well I will avoid accidents, that if I read to my kids and install the right preschool math applications on my smartphone they will go to Yale, and that if I eat well and exercise I can avoid unhealthy things like dying.

Duke social psychologist Aaron Kay points out that I'm not alone. "In the Western world, people like to believe in a high degree of personal control," says Kay, "that whatever happens, good or bad, is controlled by your actions." But sometimes it's a difficult belief to maintain—sometimes slackers win the lottery while saints are hit by falling pianos. "When we're reminded of randomness, it creates anxiety," says Kay, "and when we feel anxious we want to believe that even if we don't have control, something does."

By reminding people of this randomness in lab settings, he's shown that people with diminished personal control are more likely to turn to authoritarian gods or governments. If I wake up early and there are simply no worms, I want to believe that there's a reason for that lack of worms. God or the government must be to blame—certainly someone must be driving this funhouse ride, right?

Imagine a personal, internal teeter-totter that needs to stay level in order to make everything copacetic with the world (the angle of tilt is your level of anxiety). On one side is control, made up of personal control, governmental control, and religious control. And on the other side are the events of the world—sometimes a relatively orderly baseline and sometimes a wild jumble of chance.

Now imagine removing some weight from personal control. To keep your metaphysical teeter-totter in balance you need increased government or religious control (or both).

Now imagine plucking a weight from governmental control. Kay showed that in the period of governmental uncertainty before a major election, belief in God goes up (reduced governmental control balanced by increased religious control). Similarly, it seems in the United States as if high religious control is associated with the desire for low governmental control. And, "In countries with little personal or governmental control, you may find more belief channeled into the supernatural option," says Kay.

However, just as the teeter-totter tipping away from control creates anxiety that people heal by increasing government, religious, or personal control, when the teeter-totter tips toward too much control, people feel oppressed and try to get out from under its thumb. This is an authoritarian government's revolutionary proletariat or a controlling parent's teenage daughter.

So the key, as implied by the now overused simile of a teeter-totter, is that of balance. I'm sure you can imagine how to get rid of control in excess of what you need. But if you're feeling like Earth is tumbling toward the Sun, it can be trickier to take the control you want. Certainly, you can join a controlling church or political party (or even adopt a personal belief in an all-powerful god), but so too can you grab the bull by the horns and increase your personal control of life. Make the present more definite with a daily schedule, making sure to include time that you spend according to your own choosing (see this book's entry with Sheena Iyengar). And make the future definite with lists, agendas, and long-term life plans.

By taking control of the world around you, you can decrease the anxiety born of a topsy-turvy world.

## Aaron Kay and collaborators had Canadian

women read paragraphs about emigration, half of which implied that leaving the country would get easier in the next five years, and half of which implied it would get harder. Then they all read the same paragraph about gender inequality in Canada. How did these two groups view injustice? The group that felt trapped in Canada was less likely to blame inequality on a systemic flaw in their country. It seems that people trapped in a country—by policy or by poverty—are also likely to defend this same system that keeps them trapped.

## It's an old debate: Does perfectionism lead

to increased performance or does it sabotage the perfectionist? Researchers at the Canadian Dalhousie University found compelling evidence of the latter—psychology professors with perfectionist strivings had fewer journal articles, fewer citations, and were published in less prestigious journals than their messy-and-proud peers.

## HOW TO STOP A PENALTY KICK

**Gabriel Diaz** COGNITIVE SCIENCE, UNIVERSITY OF TEXAS-AUSTIN

The average Premier League goalkeeper makes about $1.5 million a year. Chelsea keeper Petr Čech makes $145,000 a week. With cognitive scientist Gabriel Diaz's help, you can too (or at least you can dominate your adult rec league . . .). Working in Brett Fajen's lab at Rensselaer Polytechnic Institute, Diaz covered kickers and the ball itself with enough sensors to make any Hollywood special effects modeler proud. His thought was this: If you can turn the movements that create left shots and right shots into numbers, you can mine these numbers to see which movements best predict right or left ball direction. If you can spot these movements, you can increase the success rate of preemptive dives. And if you can increase the success rate of your preemptive dives, you can yacht the Adriatic Sea and stuff your mattress with dollars (or, see above comment about your adult rec league).

"The point at which the foot contacts the ball is almost 100 percent predictive of left or right," says Diaz. You'd expect that—where a cue ball hits a colored ball creates the colored ball's direction. And he confirmed soccer players' long suspicions that things including plant foot, upper leg direction, hips, and shoulders are moderately predictive.

"But more important," Diaz continues, "is that we found three sources of distributed information throughout the body that were quite reliable." A penalty shooter can lie with a plant foot or with shoulders, and so it's not statistically beneficial to watch any single body part. But keepers would do well to recognize combinations of these body parts—and this remains true even if a kicker points her plant toe left and kicks right. "What this does," says Diaz, "is bring about changes that cascade through other parts of the body—the distributed information network continues to forecast ball direction." Perhaps if you deceptively turn your plant foot left, in order to kick the ball right without falling over, some combination of your shoulders, hips, head, and kicking-side hand have to compensate hard right.

To find out if the Force is strong enough with keepers to

recognize these distributed information networks, Diaz played video of the networks in action—they looked like very coordinated marionettes made of the light points that Diaz originally captured with his sensors. In the video, the point-light marionette approaches the ball, swings body and leg, and just as the "foot" hits the "ball" the screen goes blank and subjects have to punch a left or a right button to predict the ball's direction. Fifteen of thirty-one subjects couldn't do it. But even in novices, sixteen of the thirty-one were able to beat chance when predicting penalty kick direction based on a kicker's overall body language during the approach.

So the moral for a trained goalkeeper, especially at a skill level at which kicks are almost assured to go hard into the right- or left-side netting, is to trust the Force. Stretch out with your feelings and trust their evaluation of Diaz's distributed information networks. The more you trust, the more you'll beat chance.

## In their *Freakonomics* blog at the *New York*

*Times*, Stephen Dubner and Steven Levitt point out that penalty kicks are beholden to game theory. Because most goalies guess, the best scoring strategy for a kicker is to blast the ball directly at the goalie's head—which won't be there at the point of contact because it's already in motion trying to stop a ball into the right or left netting. But kickers don't do this because, "If he misses to the right or left, the moment will be remembered more for the keeper's competence than for the kicker's ignominy," write Dubner and Levitt. Penalty kicks have the game theory payout shown on page 204.

How will a penalty kick
be remembered?

|  | Open side | Keeper's side | Middle |
|---|---|---|---|
| Preemptive Dive | Nice shot | Stunning Save | Idiot keeper |
| Wait & React | ? | ? | Idiot shooter |

## "Keep your eye on the ball!" Even if you've

never played Little League, it's part of the cultural canon—do you hear it in your mind's ear when trying to finish a project, or swat a fly, or stay awake during a lecture? Well, Gabriel Diaz points to a study that suggests it may not be the best strategy after all. Michael Land and Peter McLeod tracked the eye movements of cricket batsmen and found that rather than keeping their eyes on the ball, the best batters picked up the ball only at specific points, and then made very quick and very accurate predictions about where to pick it up next. First they watched the release, then accurately ticked their eyes to where they knew the ball would bounce, then watched the bounce and the ball's trajectory about 100 to 200 ms after, then swung based on their prediction of time and position. The more ahead of the ball were their eyes—leaping from release to the predicted point of bounce—the better the batsman.

## WORLD-RECORD PAPER AIRPLANE

**Ken Blackburn** AERONAUTICAL ENGINEERING,
UNITED STATES AIR FORCE

Earning a world record allows paper plane designers to own football teams and date Russian oil heiresses. And according to aerospace engineer Ken Blackburn, current record holder and author of *The World Record Paper Airplane Book*, you need master only three things in your quest for paper plane glory: good folds, good throw, and good design.

Let's polish off the first two in a couple words: Good folds are extremely crisp, reducing the plane's profile and thus its drag. They also make the plane perfectly symmetrical. And a good throw means different things for different planes (we'll get into specs later), but for a world-record attempt, you use a baseball-style throw to launch the plane straight up, as high as possible—there's video of Blackburn's Georgia Dome launch and subsequent 27.6-second, world-record flight online at www.paperplane.org.

Now to design, wherein lies the true geekery of paper planes.

"Long, rectangular wings are for slow speeds and long glides, and short, swept-back wings are for high speeds and maneuverability," says Blackburn. You can see this in the difference between the condor and the swallow. The first is optimized for slow soaring, while the second—assuming an unladen European swallow—is optimized for quick dips and dives. You can also see these swept-back wings on the Space Shuttle, and because these high-speed wings have very little lift at low speeds, the Shuttle needs to keep an aggressive, nose-up angle of attack even when landing. A straight-winged Cessna can land almost flat to the runway.

These triangular wings certainly have a paper plane design purpose. "I make pointed airplanes myself," says Blackburn. "They certainly look cooler, and if you're just throwing a paper plane across the room, you might as well have something that looks cool."

But a world-record plane needs both the ability to act like a dart during launch, and like a glider after it levels off—a tricky balance. "People don't realize how desperately I would love to fold my plane the long way," says Blackburn, which would allow him to make wings from the 11-inch rather than 8.5-inch side of the paper. But so far he's been unable to find a design that has both long wings and the ability to withstand the force of the nearly 60 mph launching throw.

Wing shape defines other aspects of design too.

"For a rectangular, or nearly rectangular wing, the center of gravity should be a quarter of the distance from tip to tail," says Blackburn, "but for a plane with triangular wings, the center of gravity should be right at the midpoint." Basically, this is because the additional lift of a rectangular wing requires additional weight up front to keep the plane from pulling immediately nose-up and flipping instead of flying. "The further forward your center of gravity, the more your plane acts like a weather vane," says Blackburn. But you don't want to hang an anvil off the nose—that would negate the effect of lift. So optimal design is a balance between stability and lift.

Mathematically, it means that in a square-winged plane, you need exactly half the plane's weight right up front on the nose to make the full center of gravity rest a quarter of the way back. In the supersimple airplane below, it's easy to see that you want to fold exactly half the paper into the plane's leading edge.

Recreationally, you can adjust your paper plane's center of gravity with a paperclip. A cheater clip also helps ensure your plane's center of gravity remains below the wing, on the fuselage, making your plane stable right side up. But world-record rules disallow any additions to the paper and so creative folding is required.

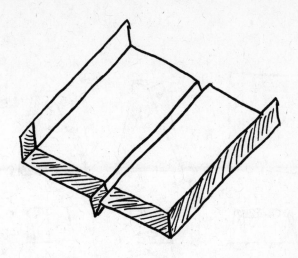

Instead of adding aerodynamically beneficial ballast, fold your wings slightly up, so that when you look directly at the plane's nose, the fuselage and wings form the letter "Y," not the letter "T" (horizontal wings) and certainly not like an upward-pointing arrow or three-line Christmas tree (downward angled wings).

Blackburn also gently folds up the wing's trailing edge to make his launchable dart a little more like a glider once it levels off. Flaps-up means that air pushes down on the trailing edge, slightly rotating the plane around its center of gravity and keeping the nose up. Like the Space Shuttle, which is forced to land with its nose high in the air, an increased angle of attack creates increased lift (as long as it doesn't make the plane flip).

Notice all these design features in the plans for Blackburn's world-record paper airplane, shown on the next page. But also notice that there might be room for improvement—can you lengthen the wings while still allowing a dartlike launch? If so, the paper plane world record and all its glory could be yours.

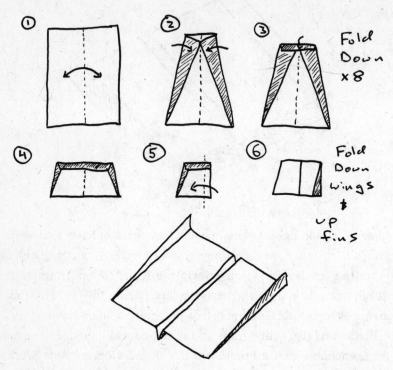

Fold Down x8

Fold Down wings & UP fins

\* From *The World Record Paper Airplane Book*, by Ken Blackburn

## SUCCEED, YOU SLACKER!

**Dolores Albarracin** SOCIAL PSYCHOLOGY,
UNIVERSITY OF ILLINOIS–URBANA-CHAMPAIGN

There are two kinds of people in this world: slack-ers and achievers. Achievers know how to spot slackers—they're the ones lounging by the lockers, collars turned up, sporting multiply pierced ears and asymmetrical smiles, listening to that new-fangled rock and roll music. And slackers know how to spot achievers—always on time and uptight, multiple sharpened pencils, taking notes as teachers blather on.

But do you know which one you are? Deceased Harvard researcher David McLelland saw the difference in tossers. He allowed subjects to choose the distance from which they tossed a ring at a post—people motivated by achievement picked a distance at which the task was tricky but not impossible, allowing them to succeed with effort and thus train their skills. People motivated by fun either chose close distances at which they could succeed every time, or impossibly far distances that required an entertaining, lucky throw to succeed. Do you push yourself at the gym (trying to lift ever heavier weights) or with your morning paper (you time the crossword)? If so, you're motivated by achievement rather than enjoyment.

OK, OK, social psychologist Dolores Albarracin of the University of Illinois points out that the difference isn't that stark—whether you're motivated by enjoyment or by achievement sits on a continuum, allowing you to hold both within you—maybe you have "6" motivation for fun and "8" motivation for achievement. But people sitting at different spots on that continuum are measurably different.

Albarracin showed this by testing fun/achievement motivation and then priming people with achievement words like *strive, attain, win, master,* and *compete*. Thus primed, achievers became even more motivated to achieve. But people naturally motivated by enjoyment rebelled against the priming and became even more motivated by fun.

In a follow-up, Albarracin showed that not only did this priming change attitudes, but it also changed behaviors. After again testing fun/achievement motivation and again priming subjects with achievement words, Albarracin plugged subjects into a word search task that she said was meant to measure verbal ability. Then the task was interrupted—blamed on computer problems—and after a couple minutes, subjects were given the choice to resume the word search task (achievement) or to switch to a cartoon rating task (fun). Primed achievers were more likely than unprimed achievers to go back to the word search. And fun-seekers primed with achievement words blew off the word search, defecting in droves to the cartoon task.

So making a fun-motivated person aware of an achievement context makes this person do even worse than he would naturally do. You can't push a slacker to succeed.

The reverse is true too: "If you frame a task as fun, achievers do worse," says Albarracin, "which is really depressing."

The implications are obvious: If you want fun-motivated students or workers (slackers!) to achieve, frame an activity as "so much fun!" rather than in the language of winning, losing, and striving. Likewise, if you know that you're one of these slackers and have a big project coming up, find a way to think of it as fun. If the task is simply horrible enough to preclude masking it with fun, Albarracin suggests using a "get your work done so you can play" mind-set. This allows fun to remain the goal, while ensuring slackers get their work done too.

Right now it's a beautiful, crisp fall day and I'd really like to wander downtown and pick up a used book and an ice-cream cone. Just five hundred more words and I'm out the door.

## Albarracin found that the more a person

believes they can defend an opinion from attack, the more likely the person is to change this same opinion in the face of contradictory evidence. Albarracin thinks it's likely that people with high "defensive confidence" have amassed these internal arguments as walls around a position they realize is weak.

## THE SCIENCE OF SMOOTH OPERATING

**Eastwick and Finkel** SOCIAL PSYCHOLOGY, TEXAS A&M, NORTHWESTERN

Remember Finkel and Eastwick and their recommendations for speed dating success? Well, now they're all up in the grill of smooth operating. What, specifically, makes an initial romantic encounter smooth and what makes it awkward?

To answer the question, they and their colleague Seema Saigal gathered four-minute tapes of (independently rated) smooth and awkward first conversations between romantically inclined Northwestern University undergrads and then coded the behaviors they saw. As you'd expect, dates who exuded warmth and who were more focused on their dates than they were on themselves tended to create smoother conversations.

Interestingly, though, what mattered most beyond these obvious tools was not how prospective Romeos and Juliets acted but how they reacted. How does Romeo respond when Juliet quips and vice versa? The best responses (in addition to being warm and other-focused) walked a tightrope between too passive and too active. On the too passive side, Romeo might accept and agree with whatever Juliet says, exerting as much direction on the conversation as the proverbial limp-wristed wet towel. On the too active side, Juliet might drop Romeo's ball (as it were) and restart the conversation in an entirely new direction of her own choosing. (Of course, the worst thing a conversant could do is drop the ball entirely—withdrawing or failing to respond.)

The trick, according to Finkel, Eastwick, and Saigal, is to avoid extremes in autonomy. Accept your date's pass, redirect it slightly, and then return the ball—all with warmth and genuine interest in his or her responses.

This acceptance and redirection is the push and pull that creates smoothness.

## The original smooth operating paper is

surprisingly accessible and worth a read. You can find it easily with a quick search for "Finkel, Eastwick, Saigal."

# There's a rich ecclesiastical, scientific, and

popular literature exploring how people have sex. To wit: the *Kama Sutra* describes sixty-four sex acts across ten chapters; we know from fMRI images what sexual arousal looks like in the brain; and at any point we're but an unrestricted video search away from an online cornucopia (pornucopia?) of sex in action. But "one day my colleague David Buss and I were chatting and I said to him, 'Nobody's ever looked at *why* people have sex!'" says Cindy Meston, psychologist at the University of Texas–Austin, and author of the book *Why Women Have Sex.*

She and Buss rectified that: 1,549 undergraduates settled on 237 reasons for sex. Women listed as their top ten reasons: (1) I was attracted to the person; (2) I wanted to experience the physical pleasure; (3) It feels good; (4) I wanted to show my affection for the person; (5) I wanted to express my love for the person; (6) I was sexually aroused and wanted the release; (7) It's fun; (8) I was horny; (9) I realized I was in love; and (10) I was in the heat of the moment.

Men had the same top three, with numbers 2 and 3 switched. Lower in the top ten, men mix in "I wanted to achieve orgasm" and "I wanted to please my partner."

"The stereotype that men have sex for pleasure and women have sex for love is unfounded," says Meston. But while the top ten show significant overlap, distinctions emerge lower in the list. "Women don't have sex because they're in love," says Meston, "but because they're protecting love, stealing love, trying to create love, or doing it out of duty."

One participant said, "My mother taught me to have sex with my man or someone else will." Another said, "I'd rather spend five minutes having sex with him than listen to him whine and complain about how horny he is for the next two days."

## WASH AWAY YOUR SINS

**Norbert Schwarz** SOCIAL PSYCHOLOGY,

UNIVERSITY OF MICHIGAN–ANN ARBOR

Have you ever tasted soap? It's not disgusting in the way you might imagine mashed worms or a yogurt cup of seagull guano could be. It's just sort of astringently chemical, olfactorily abrasive, and surprisingly long-lasting—the sensory equivalent of a spanking, which is how eating soap is commonly used. I know because in addition to chomping a bar of Dove for the purposes of this passage, I remember the taste well from my childhood.

Let's zoom out a click.

"Disgust is an evolutionary mechanism that ensures we don't touch corpses or feces, and if we do, we wash the affected body part afterward," says University of Michigan social psychologist Norbert Schwarz. And in Schwarz's opinion, morality co-opted this disgust pathway. Simply, immoral behavior provokes the same disgust as nastiness—Schwarz points to the vast majority of world religions that have rituals for washing away your sins. And so it stands to reason that if nastiness and immorality share a pathway, and if nastiness provokes the desire to wash, then so too should immorality provoke the same scrubophilia (now a word).

It's a nice story, but where's the evidence?

To find it, Schwarz designed a neat experiment. First, he asked subjects to imagine it's between them and another person for promotion in a law firm. The competitor has lost an important document and asks you to help her find it. Of course, there in your file cabinet you find the paper. What do you do now? In the ethical condition Schwarz had subjects call or e-mail the competitor and admit they'd found the doc. And in the unethical condition Schwarz had them lie (Sorry, haven't seen it!).

Subjects were told that was the end of the experiment. Oh, but with the extra time, would subjects mind filling out a quick product survey rating how likely they would be to purchase a range of products and how much they'd pay for them?

Subjects who lied in the law firm scenario said they were more likely to purchase Purell hand sanitizer and Scope mouthwash, and that they were willing to pay a higher price for those items. That's cool—immoral subjects wanted to wash—but it gets even cooler: Subjects who called the competitor and lied with their mouths wanted mouthwash, while subjects who e-mailed the competitor and lied with their fingers wanted hand sanitizer.

Not only does immorality provoke the same desire to wash as does nastiness, but it's just as body-part-specific.

Somewhere deep within your mother's evolutionary past, she knows that immorality of the mouth requires cleansing with soap. But sins are not the only things you can wash away with cleansers.

In another experiment, Schwarz explored the well-known phenomenon of postrationalization. Generally, if you rank your preferences for a list of ten things, in reality there's no distinction between numbers five and six—you could put either on top. But the act of choosing something over another—say, number five over number six—creates preference. In subsequent testing, you like number five much more than number six. In this way our brains create certainty from an uncertain world. Schwarz did something similar, but between the first preference ranking and the second test that shows the new, more distinct preferences, he had subjects either opine about antiseptic wipes or actually use the wipes. "Subjects who used the wipes literally wiped away their preferences," says Schwarz—it was as if they looked at the items anew, without ever having ranked them. Where there'd usually be a huge gap in preference between the object you previously chose and the object you previously spurned, after a quick swipe with an antiseptic wipe, subjects minds' were again open as the uncarved block.

Similarly, Schwarz had subjects gamble. Typically when people win a bet, they bet higher in the next round, and when they lose, they bet lower. (Thank you, irrational human psychology.) In his experiment, after the first round of betting, Schwarz gave half his subjects soap to smell and describe, and the other half actually used the soap to wash their hands. Just as with the antiseptic wipes, subjects who washed their hands with soap erased the effect of the previous win or loss—they didn't bet more or less the next round.

So not only is cleanliness next to godliness, but you can wash away the influence of your past, or "wash your hands of it." It's true of your past unsavory actions, irrelevant choices, and pointless experiences. If the past really isn't relevant to the future—or if you wish it weren't—a fresh start is only as far as your shower.

Out damn spot, indeed.

## In another experiment, Schwarz's subjects

passed an innocuous person in the hallway on the way to the study—half the time this innocuous plant sneezed, and half the time the plant just walked past. Perhaps it's not surprising that subjects who'd seen the sneezer estimated the risk of an average American catching a deadly disease as higher than subjects who hadn't recently been sneezed at. But what's cool is that their estimation of other risks increased as well—they thought it more likely to die of a heart attack or to be the victim of a violent crime. Schwarz called sneezing a "threat reminder," affecting perception of both relevant and irrelevant dangers.

## GET MORE PLEASURE FOR LESS PRICE

**Paul Bloom** PSYCHOLOGY, YALE UNIVERSITY

There's a complex relationship between money and pleasure. On one hand, money is the measure of how much we like something—the more people like an object, the higher the price (price balancing supply and demand, and all that). And on the other hand, money can help create pleasure—if you're told that one bottle of wine is more expensive than another, you're likely to think the supposedly expensive wine tastes better.

That's no surprise.

But what is it, exactly, about the pricey wine that makes us like it more? Paul Bloom, Yale psychologist and author of the book *How Pleasure Works*, believes the pleasure we take from something is due not only to the brick-and-mortar thing itself but also to "an object's history—who created it, who's been in touch with it, our knowledge about the object." This is the item's essence or the ineffable qualities a thing carries with it, and is the root of sentimental value or irrational attachment. It's why artwork that sells for millions of dollars can lose almost all its value if it's proved to be a forgery. Yes, the object remains the same, but its essence changes.

Darn art snobs. Darn wine snobs.

But is snobbery really the mechanism that makes art and wine lovers care about a product's provenance? To study the effect of essentialism, Bloom and coauthor Bruce Hood brought children into the lab. Half brought with them a treasured object—a blanket, stuffed animal, etc.—and half brought with them toys which held no sentimental value. Then Bloom and Hood put kids' objects into what they told kids was a "duplication machine" that would use nifty science to create an exact duplicate of their toy. After "duplication" the researchers let kids pick which toy they wanted to take home, the original or the copy. Kids who brought nonsentimental toys tended to choose the copy, which was now coolified by science. Kids who brought attachment objects almost universally stuck with the original. That is, if they let Bloom and Hood put their attachment objects in the machine at all.

Despite (supposed) identical duplication, sentimental value didn't transfer and so kids stuck with their beloved items, which retained the value-added of their essence.

"We see the same phenomenon in adults," says Bloom. "We have objects in our lives that are valuable not because of what they're made of, but because of our attachment to them." For me, it's the baseball cards I have boxed in the garage. A complete set of 1986 Topps goes for $24.95 on Amazon, but I remember sorting these cards on the basement Ping-Pong table as a ten-year-old, checking off each number on a dot-matrix printout that ran from one to 792. I knew stats and values. I didn't let myself buy singles, instead hoping that in each pack I'd plug the gaps. (This is why I have bad teeth.) And despite the $24.95 price tag, I think I'd probably sell for a minimum $9,500. Any buyers?

Back to wine. What creates the very subjective pleasure we get from such luxury objects, and how can you get more of it? According to Bloom, "the more you work to get something, the more you'll enjoy it. Music is going to sound different if you know about it. The taste of food depends critically on what you think you're eating. Sexual arousal depends on who you think you're looking at."

Not only is knowledge power, but it's pleasure, too.

So if you want more pleasure from something, increase your knowledge about it. Of course, one critically important piece of information about wine is its price—a high price reflects others' votes for the wine being good. But if you have other information, you don't need price. Maybe you like pinot and you know that 2006 was a good year for Santa Barbara wine country. In that case, you wouldn't need price to tell you that a 2006 Babcock Pinot is a good wine. You'd pick it off even the bottom shelf and enjoy it just as much as if you'd had to ask the store manager to get it out from behind glass and then paid for it through the nose.

The same is true of absolutely anything—information creates essence, and essence creates pleasure. Does your spouse have a hobby you find completely inane? Learn about it to increase your own pleasure. If you just can't care about the difference between a Dogfish Head microbrew and Bud Light, take a brewing class. If you want to increase the pleasure of your vacation, learn about a place's essence—its history and culture.

Using knowledge rather than price to add essence means you can get more pleasure for less money.

## Puzzle #18: Happiness at What Cost?

Jo makes $21.75/hr as a freelance medical transcriptionist. And let it be said that she also likes her wine. Every hour she spends learning about a bottle's origin (estate, winery, year, etc.) increases her enjoyment as much as buying a bottle half again the price of the first. How much must a bottle cost to make spending an hour learning about the wine a better buy than spending an hour working in order to buy a pricier bottle?

# PUZZLE ANSWERS

## 1. MATH IS TOO SEXY

Start with mat $=$ hematic

- Cancel "mat" leaving: 1 = heic
- Use $e = mc^2$ to get: $1 = H(mc^2)IC$
- Use $U = mgh$ to get: $1 = (u/mg)(mc^2)IC$
- Simplify: $mg = umc^2IC$
- Cancel "m" to get: $g = uc^2IC$
- Combine "c" to get $g = uc^3i$
- Write as: $G = uccci$

## 2. DR. STAT CRICKET PROP

In standard weather, the payout for a wager is the 1/46 chance of winning times the 46 payout, for exactly even money. Over time you break even. But in cold weather, Dr. Stat knows the chance of winning on each throw is $1/46 + 1/100 = 0.032$. This times the 46 payout is an expected value of 1.46 times his money with each bet. If he bets $1,000 on one throw, that's an expected $1,460, and more than one hundred throws, that's $146,000. Of that total, $1,000 is his original bankroll, so he should expect to win $145,000.

## 3. MULTITASKING MIX AND MATCH

| MIN | Task #1 | Task #2 |
|---|---|---|
| 1 | Get dressed | Check News |
| 2 | | |
| 3 | | |
| 4 | | Fret |
| 5 | | |
| 6 | Brush teeth | |
| 7 | | |
| 8 | Make B'Fast | Coffee |
| 9 | | |
| 10 | | |
| 11 | | |
| 12 | | Read 4 Work |
| 13 | Eat B'Fast | |
| 14 | | |
| 15 | | |
| 16 | | |
| 17 | | Clean |
| 18 | | |
| 19 | | |
| 20 | | |

## 4. MATCHMAKER

The power pair of Jake and Emma is a red herring. Their bliss would force enough unhappiness on others that it's not worth allowing this match made in heaven. Instead, the pairs that create the highest overall happiness are John/Ella, Jeremy/Eliza, Jake/Eva, and Justin with the (apparently) effervescent Emma for a total of 51 preference points.

## 5. TRAMP TROUBLE

The biggest quadrant of the garage is the lower left, which is shown below, with a hypothetical trampoline. The question is, is the dotted line longer than 6 feet? Well, the dotted diagonal is the hypotenuse of a right triangle with sides of 5 feet and 4 feet. So $5^2 + 4^2 = $ (Dotted line)$^2$ and the dotted line is 6.4 feet long. Yes! The tramp will fit! Now let's hope the door to the house is on the right and not the left side of the garage.

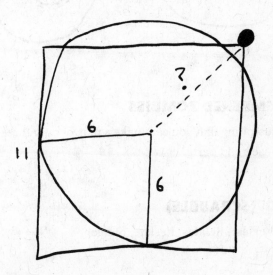

## 6. RACETRACK

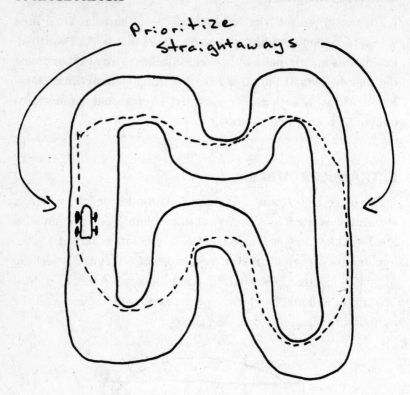

Prioritize Straightaways

## 7. DISMEMBERED ZOMBIES

Isn't it frustrating that you can make a max of only three zombies from all these good parts?

## 8. BINGO! (SCRABBLE)

Elaters, Realest, Relates, Reslate, Stealer

## 9. BOOMERANG V. ZOMBIE

This is mostly a problem of conversions. It takes the zombie 6.09 seconds to cover the span (including the 2-second delay). And it would take the boomerang 6.42 seconds to return. If our hero runs, he reaches safety in 6.63 seconds. This looks bad all around, until you realize that the zombie also has to cover the extra distance to the tree, which takes it an extra 1.09 seconds. If the hero runs for the tree, he'll avoid the unwilling donation of his gray matter. (If you really want to bend your mind, imagine what happens if the hero runs toward the returning boomerang. . . .)

## 10. THE GOSSIP WEB

Here is one answer. There might be more.

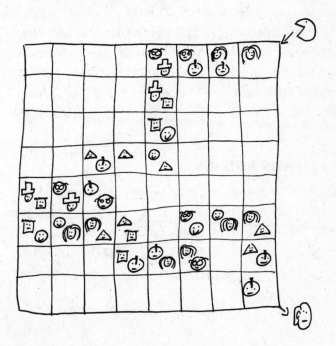

## 11. CAKE CUTTING

There are two fair ways to allocate the Batman. First imagine the cake as "points" combining volume with Batman—if B gets Batman, the cake is worth 168 total points, and if A gets Batman, the cake is worth 187 total points. And fair volume is B = 1.5A.

- So in the first case, A + 1.5A = 168. A gets 67.2 "points" of cake, and B gets 100.8 points of cake, of which 8 are due to Batman, so 92.8 in$^3$ of cake. Cutting the cake lengthwise, A gets a strip 3.36 inches wide, and B gets a strip 4.64 inches wide, including the Batman.

- In the second case, A + 1.5A = 187. A gets 74.8 points, of which 27 are due to Batman, so 47.8 in$^3$ of cake. B gets 112.2 points, all of which are due to cake. Cutting lengthwise, A gets a strip 2.29 inches wide including Batman, and B gets a strip 5.61 inches wide.

- But check this out: Giving A the Batman she so covets increases the overall value of the cake. And so to create maximum happiness, you should cut the cake so that she gets the Dark Knight, while compensating B with more cake.


## 12. FRIENDS ADD UP

Grade school = 13; high school = 13; summer camp = 13; college = 15; your first job = 15; grad school = 15; your kids' friends' parents = 17; an online fantasy football league = 17; and your current job = 32. 3(13) + 3(15) + 2(17) + 32 = 150.

# 13. A THREE-HOUR TOUR?

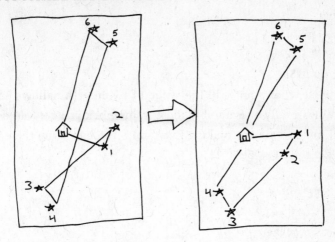

# 14. SCHOOLED BY FISH

Fish number 2 is a red herring (sorry . . .). Its personal connections are many but most of them are dead-end friends. Instead, fish numbers 9 and 11 are higher, with number 11's friends-of-friends-of-friends connections making it the winner, with a score of about 4.

# 15. TIME DISCOUNTING

The method is outed in the puzzle description—the "worth" of marshmallows at some point in the future is a problem of exponential decay, which uses the following equation:

(Remaining Amount) = (Starting Amount) e $^{(Decay\ Rate\ x\ Time)}$

Since marshmallows lose a quarter of their value every three minutes of wait time, 1 marshmallow will be worth only ¾ in

3 minutes. Plug these values into the equation for exponential decay to get this: ¾ = 1e$^{k3}$.

Solve:

- ¾ = e$^{3k}$
- ln4/3 = 3k
- k = 0.09589

Now, at what point will the value of five marshmallows equal the value of only one marshmallow (remember, you get four additional marshmallows, making five total)? You can write the equation like this: 1 = 5e$^{0.09589}$t.

Solve:

- 1 = 5e$^{0.09589}$t
- 1/5 = e$^{0.09589}$t
- ln5 = 0.09589t
- t = 16.78 minutes

So the value of eating your initial marshmallow immediately is exactly equal to the value of eating five marshmallows 16 minutes and 47 seconds in the future. If you have to wait 20 minutes for the reward, you'd be better off immediately scarfing your first marshmallow.

Bonus question: How long do you have to make your decision before you're better off waiting for the additional four marshmallows at 20 minutes?

## 16. OCTOBER BOY

This is another twist on Martin Gardner's famous gender problem. Again, combining birth order with gender means with two kids you could have B-B, B-G, G-G, or G-B. Now, imagine the number of distinct possibilities with the calendar:

- If you first have a boy on a day containing a "1," you could have a boy or a girl second, on any of the 31 days, for a total of 62 possibilities, 31 of which are two boys. Cool.

- And the same is true if you second have a boy on a "1": 62 possibilities, of which half are boys. Only, 13 of these "new" possibilities aren't distinct. You already included boy-boy on every day containing a one. So instead of adding 62 more distinct possibilities, this adds only 49 new possibilities, of which only 18 are two boys.
- So add up all the possibilities for two boys: 31 + 18 = 49. And add up all possibilities: 62 + 49 = 111. There's a 49/111 = 0.44 probability that both kids will be boys.

## 17. MAP PROBLEM

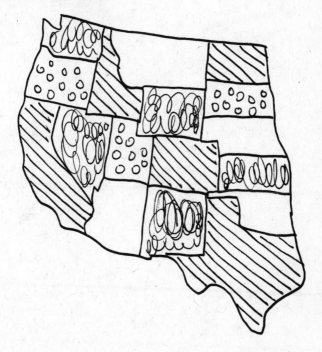

## 18. HAPPINESS AT WHAT COST?

A wine's "worth" is its cost multiplied by 1.5 times the hours Jo spends learning. That's not necessarily English. It's easier to write it as Worth = $1.5C_{ost}T_{ime}$. And if she spends the time working, the worth is the cost plus her pay, or Worth = $C_{ost} + 21.75T_{ime}$. Setting these equal (and working/studying for one hour) means $1.5C_{ost} = C_{ost} + 21.75$. Or $0.5C_{ost} = 21.75$. Or $C_{ost} = \$43.50$. For any bottle above that amount, Jo would be better off paying for increased worth by studying rather than working.

# ACKNOWLEDGMENTS

Thanks to Julian and Jen, my spectacular editor and agent respectively. You continue to ensure I keep writing and that what I write isn't total pap. And again, thanks to the scientists included in this book and the ones I chatted with, but whose work I couldn't find a way to bastardize into the framework of a short, usable tip. Any offbeat humor and gerrymandering for practicality herein is a testament to these scientists' willingness to both perform the world's greatest science and then allow it to be humanized in a way that makes it seem the stuff of offhand dinner-party conversation. Humor aside, I'm humbled by the opportunity to punch into your world, if however briefly. And my wife, two kids, and Labrador haven't yet thrown me out on my ear after hearing yet another totally fascinating conversation recapped over the breakfast table, and for that they deserve not only thanks but medals. And thank you, whoever bought this book! Because of you, I am right now basking on my yacht off the Croatian coast, eating salty caviar and sipping wine of a year whose digits sum to something other than three or four. Or I am at least in the backyard shed insulated with cardboard that is my office, watching in the early morning as hot-air balloons rise from Boulder and squirrels mate on the back fence, while planning my next book. Cheers.

# About the Author

**GARTH SUNDEM** is the bestselling author of *Geek Logik, The Geeks' Guide to World Domination,* and *Brain Candy.* You can find him at garthsundem.com, as the bimonthly puzzlemaster at *Wired's GeekDad* blog, at TED.com, and/or by using a searchlight to broadcast the periodic table of the elements into the night sky (or by baking berry pie). Garth and his wife live in Colorado with their two kids and a large Labrador.

# ALSO BY
# GARTH SUNDEM

Tastier than a Twizzlers yet more protein-packed than a spinach smoothie, *Brain Candy* is guaranteed to entertain your brain! These delicious and nutritious pages are packed with cutting-edge brain science, puzzles and paradoxes, and eye-opening perception tests and hacks.

**BRAIN CANDY**
$14.00 paper (Canada: $17.00)
978-0-307-58803-6

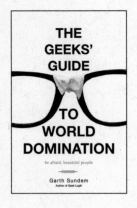

Sorry, beautiful people. These days, geeks rule the world. And here is the book no self-respecting geek can live without—a guide jam-packed with 314.1516 short entries exploring the essential joys of science, pop-culture trivia, paper airplanes, pure geekish nostalgia, and much, much more.

**THE GEEKS' GUIDE TO WORLD DOMINATION**
$13.95 paper (Canada: $15.95)
978-0-307-45034-0

 Available wherever books are sold